The Apocryphal Gospels

Ancient Texts and Translations

Series Editor
K. C. Hanson

Robert William Rogers
*Cuneiform Parallels to the
Old Testament*

D. Winton Thomas, editor
*Documents from
Old Testament Times*

Henry Frederick Lutz
*Early Babylonian Letters
from Larsa*

Albert T. Clay
Babylonian Epics, Hymns, Omens, and Other Texts

Daniel David Luckenbill
The Annals of Sennacherib

A. E. Cowley
*Aramaic Papyri of the
Fifth Century B.C.*

G. R. Driver
Aramaic Documents of the Fifth Century B.C., rev. ed.

Adolf Neubauer
The Book of Tobit

August Dillman
The Ethiopic Text of 1 Enoch

R. H. Charles
*The Apocrypha and Pseudepigrapha
of the Old Testament*

R. H. Charles
The Book of Enoch

R. H. Charles
The Book of Jubilees

R. H. Charles
*The Testaments of the
Twelve Patriarchs*

R. H. Charles
The Apocalypse of Baruch

Herbert Edward Ryle
& Montaque Rhodes James
*The Psalms of the Pharisees,
commonly called
The Psalms of Solomon*

B. Harris Cowper
The Apocryphal Gospels

H. B. Swete
The Gospel of Peter

Richard Adelbert Lipsius
& Max Bonnet
*Apocryphal Acts
of the Apostles (3 vols.)*

Bernard Pick
The Apocryphal Acts

The Apocryphal Gospels

And Other Documents Relating to the History of Christ, Translated from the Originals in Greek, Latin, Syriac, Etc., with Notes, Scriptural References, and Prolegomena

B. Harris Cowper

New Bibliography by K. C. Hanson

Wipf & Stock Publishers
Eugene, Oregon

THE APOCRYPHAL GOSPELS
And Other Documents Relating to the History of Christ, Translated from the Originals in Greek, Latin, Syriac, Etc., with Notes, Scriptural References, and Prolegomena

Ancient Texts and Translations

Copyright © 2006 Wipf & Stock Publishers. All rights reserved. Except for brief quotations in critical publications or reviews, no part of this book may be reproduced in any manner without prior written permission from the publisher. Write: Permissions, Wipf & Stock, 199 W. 8th Ave., Eugene, OR 97401.

ISBN: 1-59752-674-6

Cataloging-in-Publication data:

Bible. N.T. Apocryphal books. English. 1881. Cowper.
    The apocryphal gospels : and other documents relating to the history of Christ, translated from the originals in Greek, Latin, Syriac, etc., with notes, scriptural references, and prolegomena / B. Harris Cowper ; new bibliography by K. C. Hanson.

    ISBN: 1-59752-674-6
    lviii + 456 p. cm.

    Includes bibliographical references

    1. Apocryphal books (New Testament). 2. Apocryphal Gospels. 3. Christian literature, Early. 4. Jesus Christ—Words—Extra-canonical parallels. I. Cowper, B. Harris (Benjamin Harris). II. Hanson, K. C. (Kenneth C.). III. Title. IV. Series.

    BS2832 C7 2006

Manufactured in the U.S.A.

Series Foreword

The discoveries of documents from the ancient Near Eastern and Mediterranean worlds have altered our modern understanding of those worlds in both breadth and depth. Especially since the mid-nineteenth century, chance discoveries as well as archaeological excavations have brought to light thousands of clay tablets, stone inscriptions and stelae, leather scrolls, codices, papyri, seals, and ostraca.

The genres of these written documents are quite diverse: receipts, tax lists, inventories, letters, prophecies, blessings and curses, dowry documents, deeds, laws, instructions, collections of proverbs, philosophical treatises, state propaganda, myths and legends, hymns and prayers, liturgies and rituals, and many more. Some of them came to light in long-famous cities—such as Ur, Babylon, Nineveh, and Jerusalem—while others came from locations that were previously little-known or unknown—such as Ebla, Ugarit, Elephantine, Qumran, and Nag Hammadi.

But what good are these remnants from the distant past? Why should anyone bother with what are often fragmentary, obscure, or long-forgotten scraps of ancient cultures? Each person will answer those questions for herself or himself, depending upon interests and commitments. But the documents have influenced scholarly research in several areas.

It must first be said that the documents are of interest and importance in their own right, whatever their connections—or lack of them—to modern ethnic, religious, or ideological concerns. Many of them provide windows on how real people lived in the ancient world—what they grew and ate; how they related to their families, business associates, and states; how they were taxed; how and whom they worshiped; how they organized their communities; their hopes and fears; and how they understood and portrayed their own group's story.

They are of intense interest at the linguistic level. They provide us with previously unknown or undeciphered languages and dialects, broaden our range of vocabularies and meanings, assist us in mapping the relationships and developments of languages, and provide examples of loan-words and linguistic influences between languages. A monumental project such as *The Assyrian Dictionary,* produced by the Oriental Institute at the University of Chicago, would have been unthinkable without the broad range of Akkadian resources today.[1] And

---

[1] I. J. Gelb et al., editors, *The Assyrian Dictionary of the Oriental Institute of the University of Chicago* (Chicago: Univ. of Chicago Press, 1956–).

our study of Coptic and early gospels would be impoverished without the Nag Hammadi codices.[2]

The variety of genres also attracts our interest in terms of the history of literature. Such stories as Athra-hasis, Enumma Elish, and Gilgamesh have become important to the study of world literature. While modern readers may be most intrigued by something with obvious political or religious content, we often learn a great deal from a tax receipt or a dowry document. Hermann Gunkel influenced biblical studies not only because of his keen insights into the biblical books, but because he studied the biblical genres in the light of ancient Near Eastern texts. As he examined the genres in the Psalms, for example, he compared them to the poetic passages throughout the rest of the Bible, the Apocrypha, the Pseudepigrapha, Akkadian sources, and Egyptian sources.[3] While the Akkadian and Egyptian resources were much more limited in the 1920s and 1930s when he was working on the Psalms, his methodology and insights have had an on-going significance.

---

[2] James M. Robinson, editor, *The Nag Hammadi Library in English,* 4th ed. (Leiden: Brill, 1996).

[3] Hermann Gunkel, *Einleitung in die Psalmen: Die Gattungen der religiösen Lyrik Israels,* completed by Joachim Begrich, HAT (Göttingen: Vandenhoeck & Ruprecht, 1933). ET = *Introduction to the Psalms: The Genres of the Religious Lyric of Israel,* trans. James D. Nogalski, Mercer Library of Biblical Studies (Macon, Ga.: Mercer Univ. Press, 1998).

History is also a significant interest. Many of these texts mention kingdoms, ethnic and tribal groups, rulers, diplomats, generals, locations, or events that assist in establishing chronologies, give us different perspectives on previously known events, or fill in gaps in our knowledge. Historians can never have too many sources. The Amarna letters, for example, provide us with the names of local rulers in Canaan during the fourteenth century BCE, their relationship with the pharaoh, as well as the military issues of the period.[4]

Social analysis is another area of fertile research. A deed can reveal economic structures, production, land tenure, kinship relations, scribal conventions, calendars, and social hierarchies. Both the Elephantine papyri from Egypt (fifth century BCE) and the Babatha archive from the Judean desert (second century CE) include personal legal documents and letters relating to dowries, inheritance, and property transfers that provide glimpses of complex kinship relations, networking, and legal witnesses.[5] And the

---

[4] William L. Moran, *The Amarna Letters* (Baltimore: Johns Hopkins Univ. Press, 1992).

[5] Bezalel Porten et al., editors, *The Elephantine Papyri in English: Three Millennia of Cross-Cultural Continuity and Change,* Documenta et Monumenta Orientis Antiqui 22 (Leiden: Brill, 1996); Yigael Yadin et al., *The Finds from the Bar Kokhba Period in the Cave of Letters,* 3 vols., Judean Desert Studies (Jerusalem: Israel Exploration Society, 1963–2002) [NB: vols. 2 and 3 are titled *Documents* instead of *Finds*].

Elephantine documents also include letters to the high priest in Jerusalem from the priests of Elephantine regarding the rebuilding of the Elephantine temple.

Religion in the ancient world was usually embedded in either political or kinship structures. That is, it was normally a function of either the political group or kin-group to which one belonged. We are fortunate to have numerous texts of epic literature, liturgies, and rituals. These include such things as creation stories, purification rituals, and the interpretation of sheep livers for omens. The Dead Sea Scrolls, for example, provide us with biblical books, texts of biblical interpretation, community regulations, and liturgical texts from the second temple period.[6]

Another key element has been the study of law. A variety of legal principles, laws, and collections of regulations provide windows on social structures, economics, governance, property rights, and punishments. The stele of Hammurabi of Babylon (c. 1700 BCE) is certainly the most famous. But we have many more, for example: Ur-Nammu (c. 2100 BCE), Lipit-Ishtar (c. 1850 BCE), and the Middle Assyrian Laws (c. 1150 BCE).

The intention of Ancient Texts and Translations (ATT) is to make available a variety of ancient documents and document collections to a broad range

---

[6] Florentino Garcia Martinez, *The Dead Sea Scrolls Translated: The Qumran Texts in English,* 2d ed., trans. Wilfred G. E. Watson (Grand Rapids: Eerdmans, 1996).

of readers. The series will include reprints of long out-of-print volumes, revisions of earlier editions, and completely new volumes. The understanding of ancient societies depends upon our close reading of the documents, however fragmentary, that have survived.

—K. C. Hanson
Series Editor

Select Bibliography

Brown, Raymond E. "The Gospel of Peter and Canonical Gospel Priority." *New Testament Studies* 33 (1987) 321–43.

Cameron, Ron, editor. *The Other Gospels: Non-Canonical Gospel Texts.* Philadelphia: Westminster, 1982.

———, editor. *The Apocryphal Jesus and Christian Origins.* Semeia 49. Atlanta: Scholars, 1990.

Crossan, John Dominic. *In Fragments: The Aphorisms of Jesus.* San Francisco: Harper & Row, 1983.

———. *Four Other Gospels: Shadows on the Contours of Canon.* Minneapolis: Winston, 1985.

———. *The Cross that Spoke: The Origins of the Passion Narrative.* San Francisco: Harper & Row, 1988.

———. "Thoughts on Two Extracanonical Gospels." *Semeia* 49 (1990) 156–68.

Elliott, J. K. *The Apocryphal New Testament.* Oxford: Clarendon, 1993.

Kasser, Rudolphe, Marvin W. Meyer, and Gregor Wurst, editors. *The Gospel of Judas from Codex Tchacos.* Washington, DC: National Geographic,

2006.

Koester, Helmut. "Apocryphal and Canonical Gospels." *Harvard Theological Review* 73 (1980) 105–30.

———. *Ancient Christian Gospels: Their History and Development.* Philadelphia: Trinity, 1990.

Layton, Bentley. *The Gnostic Scriptures.* Garden City, NY: Doubleday, 1987.

Lührmann, Dieter. *Die apokryph gewordenen Evangelien: Studien zu neuen Texten und zu neuen Fragen.* Supplements to Novum Testamentum 112. Leiden: Brill, 2004.

Mack, Burton L. "All the Extra Jesuses: Christian Origins in the Light of Extra-Canonical Gospels." *Semeia* 49 (1990).

Meyer, Marvin W., translator and editor. *The Secret Teachings of Jesus: Four Gnostic Gospels.* San Francisco: HarperSanFrancisco, 1984.

———. *The Unknown Sayings of Jesus.* San Francisco: HarperSanFrancisco, 1998.

Miller, Robert L., editor. *The Complete Gospels: Annotated Scholars Version.* Rev. ed. Sonoma, CA: Polebridge, 1994.

Neirynck, Frans. "The Apocryphal Gospels and the Gospel of Mark." In *The New Testament in Early Christianity,* edited by Jean-Marie Sevrin, 123–75. Bibliotheca Ephemeridum theologicarum Lovaniensium 86. Leuven: Leuven Univ. Press, 1989.

Pagels, Elaine. *The Gnostic Gospels.* New York:

Random House, 1979.

Patterson, Stephen J. "Gospels, Apocryphal." In *Anchor Bible Dictionary*, edited by David Noel Freedman, 2:1079–81. New York: Doubleday, 1992.

Robinson, James M. "Jesus: From Easter to Valentinus (or to the Apostles' Creed)." *Journal of Biblical Literature* 101 (1982) 5–37.

———, editor. *The Nag Hammadi Library in English*. 4th ed. Leiden: Brill, 1996.

———. *The Secrets of Judas: The Story of the Misunderstood Disciple and His Lost Gospel*. New York: HarperSanFrancisco, 2006.

———, and Helmut Koester. *Trajectories through Early Christianity*. 1971. Reprinted, Eugene, OR: Wipf & Stock, 2006.

Swete, H. B. *The Gospel of Peter*. 1893. Reprinted, Ancient Texts and Translations. Eugene, OR: Wipf & Stock, 2005.

Wenham, David, editor. *Jesus Tradition Outside the Gospels*. Gospel Perspectives 5. Sheffield: JSOT Press, 1984.

PREFACE.

No one can wonder that men are curious to know something of a class of compositions dignified or branded with the name of Apocryphal Gospels. They hope to find in them at least some fragments of genuine history not contained in the Canonical Gospels. This hope must be disappointed; but a faithful version of the documents, with notes, and other accompaniments, will be found both useful and interesting. All who read them, with any attention, will see that they are fictions and not histories; not traditions even, so much as legends.

It would have been easy to add a great deal to what is here printed, by way of illustration and criticism; but I have not pretended to say everything. I have rather tried to say as little as I could, consistently with the subject and intention of the book.

For the first time the English reader will have anything that can honestly pretend to be a complete collection of the False Gospels, and other kindred documents, faithfully but not slavishly translated into the vernacular.

The remainder of the Christian Apocrypha will follow if circumstances permit.

I will only add that before I undertook this work I never realised, so completely as I do now, the impassable character of the gulf which separates the genuine Gospels from these. Trusting that others will obtain at least as much good from them, I send them forth into the world.

B. H. C.

THE THIRD EDITION.

This edition is issued at a lower price than its precursors, and has been revised throughout by the original texts.

B. H. C.

CONTENTS.

	Page
INTRODUCTION	ix
The Gospel of James (commonly called the Protevangelium)	1
The Gospel of Pseudo-Matthew, or of the Infancy of Mary and of Jesus	27
The Gospel of the Nativity of Mary	84
The History of Joseph the Carpenter	99
The Gospel of Thomas (I.)	128
,, ,, (II.)	144
,, ,, (III.)	152
The Arabic Gospel of the Infancy	170
The Letter of Abgar to Jesus	219
The Letter of Jesus to Abgar	220
The Letter of Lentulus	221
Prayer of Jesus, Son of Mary	222
The Story of Veronica	223
The Gospel of Nicodemus, or Acts of Pilate (I.)	227
,, ,, ,, ,, (II.)	267
,, ,, ,, ,, Second Part, or, Descent of Christ to the Underworld	299
The Latin Gospel of Nicodemus, Part I., or, Acts of Pilate	312

CONTENTS.

	Page
The Latin Gospel of Nicodemus, Part II., or, Descent of Christ to the Underworld	347
The Letter of Pilate to Tiberius	388
The Letters of Herod and Pilate	389
The Epistle of Pilate to Cæsar	398
The Report of Pilate the Governor (I.)	400
,, ,, ,, (II.)	405
The Trial and Condemnation of Pilate	410
The Death of Pilate	415
The Story of Joseph of Arimathea	420
The Revenging of the Saviour	432

APPENDIX.

The Syriac Gospel of the Boyhood of our Lord Jesus 448

INTRODUCTION.

I. GENERAL INTRODUCTION.—CHARACTER AND CLAIMS OF THE APOCRYPHAL GOSPELS.

MANY books are included under the name of Christian Apocrypha, or New Testament Apocrypha, as some call them. Several of these books are still extant in one language or another, but of the larger part we only possess fragments, or the mere titles. I would thus describe in a few words the character of the books in question: They are all spurious; they all relate to Christ and those who were associated with him in his earthly career, or to the apostles and their associates; they all seek to supplement or develope the writings of the New Testament; and all that we have are of more recent date than any of the canonical books. The series commenced in the second century at latest, and continued for many centuries. The materials are drawn partly from the New Testament, partly from traditions, and partly from the imagination of their authors. They are of no historical or doctrinal authority, and were never officially recognised in the Church. On many accounts they deserve nothing but reproach, and that has been liberally heaped upon them in all ages. It has been very truly observed of the false Gospels in particular, by Bishop Ellicott, in the "Cambridge Essays" for 1856, that,

"Their real demerits, their mendacities, their absurdities, their coarseness, the barbarities of their style, and the inconsequence of their narratives, have never been excused or condoned. It would be hard to find any competent writer, in any age of the Church, who has been beguiled into saying anything civil or commendatory." (p. 153.)

And again :—

"The torrent of abuse, condemnation, and invective, that issued from the fountains of early orthodoxy, and has never lacked an affluent in any generation since the days of Irenæus, has raged against these unhappy mythologies with an unabated vehemence, which, as far as the honour of the orthodox faith is concerned, must be pronounced both edifying and exemplary. The whole vocabulary of theological abhorrence, a vocabulary by no means limited in its extent, or culpably weak in its expressions, has been expended upon these unfortunate compositions, individually and collectively." (p. 154.)

Once more :—

"From all alike—from orthodox fathers, from early historians, from popes, from councils, from Romanist divines and Protestant commentators— the same amount of contempt and reprobation has been expended on the Apocryphal Gospels, and yet they live and thrive, and are, perhaps, now as much and as curiously read as ever." (p. 155.)

As I have in the present volume mainly to do with the spurious Gospels, and documents closely allied with them, I shall chiefly limit my remarks to them. It has been said then, in opposition to what Lardner, Jones, Ellicott, and others have affirmed, that the Churches once received these spurious Gospels. Writers who have been hostile to the four Canonical Gospels have been very anxious to prove that either fewer or more than four were originally accepted, and they have not been over anxious which of these they proved. For popular purposes much use has been made of, this argument, on the faith of an idle story quoted by Pappus

(16th century) from an obscure Greek work, of perhaps the 10th century, to the effect that certain books were rejected at the council of Nice in A.D. 325, as the result of a miracle. They pretend to believe the occurrence, although they deny the miracle; but it would be more becoming to find some passage in some author of credit who lived near the date alleged, and to show that the tale has at least real antiquity on its side. This they neither have done nor can do. Not one ancient writer intimates that the council of Nice entertained the question of the Canon at all. The use that is frequently made of Jerome's casual remark is simply disgraceful. It amounts to this,—that some people said the book of Judith was quoted as an authority at the council of Nice. Such, and no more, is the meaning of Jerome's few words. Yet out of them one party has concocted the fiction that the council determined the Canon of the Scriptures, and authorised the Old Testament Apocrypha; and another party has foisted in the idea of a miraculous rejection of the false Gospels, and other Christian Apocrypha. Why, even the old Greek does not say one word as to the books which were, according to his fable, rejected, except that they were 'spurious.' Now since an honest man will acquaint himself with facts, I do not see how any honest man, or any but the impudent and malicious, can ascribe an atom of value to the fable which Pappus raked out of obscurity. It is well known, moreover, that most of the Christian Apocrypha were still unwritten when the Nicene council was held.

I have elsewhere written as follows: Any statement made now, that the spurious Gospels were ever regarded in the Church as inspired and true, must arise from ignorance or malicious misrepresentation, and must be condemned as false and deceitful. It is of course probable that individuals who knew no better may have been imposed upon by the forged fables we have in view, and it is certain that some of the wilder sects of heresy appear to have accepted one or two of the false Gospels, but neither of these facts is opposed to our assertion. At the present day the Mormons receive the absurd Book of Mormon as an inspired document, but it would be an insult to tell us that this volume is accepted by the Christian Church. The case of the one or two false Gospels, which some heretics received, is exactly parallel, because the heretics in question, and their Gospels, were repudiated by the Church. We could mention heretics who rejected a part or the whole of some of our

Gospels, but this would not prevent us from repeating as true what we have already said, that our four Gospels have always and alone been received as inspired and authentic by the Universal Church of Christ.

It will be said, perhaps, that some of the forged Gospels are quoted by recognised and orthodox writers. This is true, but fitted to mislead: the false Gospels are *often* quoted and referred to by writers who disbelieved and expressly rejected them; in *a few cases*, alleged quotations from them are doubtful; and here and there we find them quoted as containing true statements. Only these last quotations concern us, and we say in reference to them, that there are some true statements in the forged Gospels; that whether true or false, they contain statements which some men believed to be true; and that no mere quotation from a book proves it to have been inspired in the opinion of him that quotes it. But, even supposing that one, or two, or three of the early Fathers quoted false Gospels as inspired, we could only infer from the circumstance that they were mistaken, and stood almost alone.

There have always been, as there are now, weak-minded, credulous, and superstitious persons, who are easily imposed upon. In the Romish Church, books professedly inspired have repeatedly been published and accepted by many. For example, two hundred years since, a Spanish nun, a dreamy fanatic, professed to write, by divine revelation, a history of Christ, of Mary, and of the Apostles. This book was voluminous, and gathered from various sources, including the disordered imagination of the writer. Many received it as from God, and to this day, at least French and Italian abridgements of it are widely circulated and devoutly believed in. Yet would anybody affirm that the Church of Rome has added this book to the canon of Holy Scripture? Certainly not.

"But," say those who wish to discredit the true Gospels by giving prominence to the false, "How is it that councils and bishops have forbidden and rejected the Apocryphal Gospels?" The facts already adduced supply a sufficient answer: but I will be a little more precise. For the information and security of weak and erring Christians, and for the instruction of unbelievers, it was found needful to publish lists of the inspired books of Scripture. Appended to these lists we naturally find sometimes mention of other books, which were very popular, or really believed by certain persons to be divine; but they are mentioned only by way of warning and caution. The most remarkable example of the kind, perhaps, is the list which commonly passes under the name of Gelasius, who was bishop of Rome in A.D. 492 to 496. A synod is said to have been held at Rome, in which seventy bishops agreed to certain catalogues of books. The first catalogue comprises the books of the Old and New Testament. The second catalogue is of books not to be regarded as canonical or of Divine authority. Among these are some which still exist. The genuineness of this remarkable document has been denied, but, whether genuine or a forgery, it may fairly claim to represent the character and position of the writings enumerated towards the year 500 after Christ.

Some modern writers have, like Archbishop Wake, greatly overvalued some books which never even pretended to form part of Holy Scripture. The learned, but illogical, Whiston also would have admitted into the New Testament some of the most notorious forgeries.

Towards the close of the seventeenth century some unguarded expressions of Toland, in his life of Milton, were laid hold of by Dr. Blackhall as the ground of a charge of having used apocryphal books to discredit those that were genuine. Toland replied in his 'Amyntor,' denying the accusation, especially as it applied to the New Testament. Notwithstanding his denial, the charge was repeated, as will be seen by the quotation below,[1] and it has continued to be repeated down to our own day. Certainly he does not state the case in such a manner as to favour the common belief, but he says, "Several of these books (apocryphal and spurious) whereof I now treat, are quoted to prove important points of the Christian religion, by the most celebrated Fathers, as of equal authority with those we now receive; and the testimony of those Fathers was the principal reason of establishing these in our present canon, and is still alleged to that purpose, by all that write in defence of the Scriptures."[2] I regard this as a most inaccurate statement, but I cannot here occupy space with its refutation. Perhaps, however, it may be as

---

[1] Toland affirms in his "Amyntor" (p. 52) that several spurious pieces have been quoted by the Fathers as of *equal authority* with those which we receive; even by those Fathers upon whose testimony the present canon is established. From thence it is evident, he would infer that those spurious and our canonical books ought to go together, and either be equally admitted or equally rejected, since they are founded upon the same testimonies. Richardson on the Canon. London, 1700. p. 2.

[2] Amyntor, p. 52.

xviii INTRODUCTION.

well to note that the books which Toland instances, as quoted in the way he describes, are those which bear the names of Barnabas, Hermas, Polycarp, Clement (to the Corinthians), and Ignatius (seven epistles). We now call these the Apostolical Fathers, and, whether spurious or genuine, nobody classes them with the Apocrypha.

It is very curious, that while the views of Wake and Whiston, and the opinions ascribed to Toland, were repudiated by the vast majority of sober-minded people, they had their followers among the prejudiced, the credulous, and the ignorant. Toland's alleged opinions were eagerly reproduced upon the continent.[1] But earnest men arose to investigate the whole matter. The English Dissenter, Jeremiah Jones, was the first to publish in his own language, and side by side with the originals, all that he could find of the false Gospels. His book on the Canon is still of real value, although, as a whole, not fitted for the present age. A more conscientious and painstaking editor never took pen in hand. As the result of his investigations he maintains,—" That, for the most part, the Apocry-

---

[1] See for example, *Histoire Critique de Jesus-Christ, ou Analyse Raisonnée des Evangiles.* (*circa* 1770). 8vo. Amsterdam, M.M. Rey.

phal books are expressly, and in so many words, rejected by those who have mentioned them, as the forgeries of heretics, and so, as spurious and apocryphal." Moreover, he says that "When any such book is cited, and not expressly rejected, there are other evidences to prove the author did not receive it as canonical; for instance, Origen quotes once or twice a false gospel, which he *elsewhere* rejects as heretical, and, besides, declares that the Church receives four Gospels only." I will add another of his remarks:—
" Sometimes the Fathers made use of the apocryphal books to show their learning, or, that the heretics might not charge them with partiality and ignorance, as being acquainted only with their own books."

I must not overlook Dr. Lardner, whose materials and conclusions are to be found in his great work on the Credibility of the Gospel History. Both he and Jones owed not a little to Fabricius, but their opinions are their own. Lardner maintains that the false Gospels are quoted by none of the apostolical Fathers, nor by many other early Christian writers; that several of the Fathers expressly condemn them; that there is no evidence of their reception by the Church; that those we know anything about were written later than our four Gospels, which they often copy, and sometimes alter and contradict; that they are inconsistent with themselves, and with one another, with reason, and with sound doctrine; and that they have no claim upon our belief, and, as literary productions, are quite contemptible.

I think both Jones and Lardner have overlooked some probable traces of the Apocryphal Gospels, but I am quite ready to receive their judgment as to the real character and claims of these productions.

In the compilation of the present volume, I have necessarily come into contact with a great many books, but I do not propose to fill pages with lists of titles which the learned may find elsewhere, and which the unlearned could not use if they found them here. I only mention that the first great collector of Christian Apocrypha was John Albert Fabricius, early in the last century; that a second was J. C. Thilo, whose book came out in 1832; and that the third and chief is Dr. Tischendorf, of whom more will be found in the following pages. It is, in fact, his edition of the Apocryphal Gospels which I have translated, though with additions from other sources, and a few variations from his texts.

There are two or three other books that I should, perhaps, not omit. The first is the " Codex Apocryphus N.T.," or, "Uncanonical Gospels and other writings," brought out by Dr. Giles, in 1852, but the editor had the misfortune to know nothing about the books he published.

Considerably lower is the "Apocryphal New Testament: being all the Gospels, Epistles, and other pieces now extant, attributed, in the first four centuries, to Jesus Christ, His Apostles, and their companions, and not included in the New Testament by its compilers;" by William Hone, London, 1820. This mean affair has had an immense run, and is constantly reprinted with the original date and swarms of blunders. Hone much regretted publishing this book when he came to a better mind, but it was beyond his power to recall it, or it would have been suppressed. What he did in preparing it, was to select some of the translations of Jones, and attach to them the version of the Apostolic Fathers by Wake; all these he cut up into chapters and verses, prefixing headings to his chapters, to make them look like ordinary editions of the New Testament. His introductions and notes are borrowed (without acknowledgment in great part) from the same sources as his text, and hashed up to suit his purpose. It is a standing reproach to our literature that this heterogeneous jumble should have remained alone, and no effort made to give the people the means of correcting its misrepresentations. Only think of the Apostolical Fathers figuring in an *Apocryphal* New Testament!

I am not quite correct in saying Hone's book has remained alone, for a mangled edition of it has appeared in a still more repulsive form. The new book is a reprint of Hone, with two or three fresh notes, and some old ones omitted, some inversion of order, misprints uncorrected, and new ones introduced. The preface is partly new, and partly reduced from that of Hone. A so-called "Poem," by the editor, has been appended, and a new title has been prefixed. The new title indicates the miserable character and spirit of this outrageous affair: "The suppressed Gospels and Epistles of the Original New Testament of Jesus Christ, and other portions of the ancient Holy Scriptures, now extant, attributed to His Apostles and their Disciples, and venerated by the primitive Christian Churches during the first four centuries; but since, after violent disputations, forbidden by the bishops of the Nicene Council, in the reign of the Emperor Constantine; and omitted from the Catholic and Protestant editions of the New Testament, by its compilers. Translated from the Original tongues, with historical references to their authenticity, by Archbishop Wake, and other learned divines. London, 1863." This imposture, for it is nothing less, has been reproduced with a new and still more flagrant title, which is too ridiculous to deceive any but the most ignorant.

I cannot conclude this part of the subject without naming two respectable French publications. "Les Evangiles Apocryphes" is a French version of several of the apocryphal books, with notes by Gustave Brunet (Second edition, Paris, 1863). "Etudes sur les Evangiles Apocryphes" is a portly volume by Michel Nicolas (Paris, 1866). This last is an elaborate discussion of the subject, conducted with learning and ability, but I can by no means accept all the conclusions of the author. This I do accept: *"In reality they are all, without exception, infinitely beneath the Canonical Gospels in all respects."* Pref. p. xxiii.

II. THE ORIGIN AND INTENTION OF THE FALSE GOSPELS.

The principal causes which originated the writings commonly known as Apocryphal Gospels, may be soon stated. Men were curious to know more than the Canonical Gospels contained. Fragmentary stories or traditions were abroad, relating to Joseph and Mary and their families, to the birth and infancy, the trial and crucifixion of Jesus, to Pilate, Joseph of Arimathea, Nicodemus, and so on. How pleasant if all these fragments could be rendered complete, and especially if the silence of the four Gospels could be supplemented! The wish was not a barren one, and from time to time writings appeared professing to supply the information which was wanted. Some of these writings may be considered introductory to the Evangelical narratives, others as appendices, but all as supplementary in one way or another. Joseph and Mary were no longer the obscure individuals the Gospels had left them; the incarnation, birth, and early life of Jesus no more remained imperfectly recorded; the last days of Christ's earthly life were set forth with wondrous minuteness of detail; the space between the death and resurrection of the Saviour was filled up with particulars of what happened in the unseen world, as well as at Jerusalem and elsewhere; Pilate was pursued into every nook and corner, all he did and said was noted down, and the steps of the Nemesis which haunted him beyond the very grave, were diligently traced; the results of the imprecation of the Jews, "His blood be upon us, and upon our children," were in like manner chronicled. Ancient invention and industry went even further, and produced sundry scraps about Herod, Veronica, Lentulus, and Abgar, wrote epistles for Christ and his mother, and I know not how much besides. No difficulty stood in the way; ancient documents could easily be appealed to without necessarily existing; spirits could be summoned from the other world by a stroke of the pen, and be made to say anything; sacred names could be written and made a passport to fictions, and so on *ad libitum*.

We find among the most powerful impulses to which men yield, that which prompts them to the production of legends in connection with their religion. Illustrations are abundant, but I only mention Mahomedanism and Judaism, particularly the latter. The Jews have a form of literature called Agada, or Hagadah, which has been defined as a historical or theological essay on some Scripture character or fact, in a pleasant and an attractive form. The narration in the Hagadah may be fictitious; hence Rabbi Azariah is quoted as saying in *Meor Ennaim,* "The Hagadoth are historical pieces like those which poets sometimes feign and frame." After reading some of the Jewish pieces I have arrived at the conclusion that the Christian Apocrypha are often simply *Christian Hagadoth*, and so I would call them, as a far more appropriate name than the one which usage has attached to them. The Hagadah is written for instruction and not amusement merely, and so the Christian compositions generally have a didactic element underlying the narrative, or intercalated with it.

I will here exhibit in a summary form the details which in my opinion account for the origin, and indicate the intention of the apocryphal Gospels, and most of the other Christian Apocrypha.

I. The Evangelical narratives were simple and meagre in their mode of describing what (1) preceded, (2) attended, and (3) followed, the facts with which they are mainly concerned. This applies to

(1) The family of Christ,
(2) His Infancy,
(3) His Inauguration,
(4) His Trial and Crucifixion,
(5) His Visit to the Underworld,
(6) His Resurrection and Ascension,
(7) His Mother and the Apostles afterwards.

II. The Evangelical narratives were almost or wholly silent on various points, *e.g.*,

(1) Doctrines to be believed, but requiring explanation,

(2) Certain matters connected with the unseen and spiritual world,

(3) The organization and discipline of the Church.

III. Sundry sects, heresies, and parties wanted support from Apostolical and Divine Authorities.

IV. Men took pleasure in producing religious novels, fictions, Hagadoth, or whatever we may call them; and they knew such things were popular.

Of course the putting of the names of Christ, Mary, the Apostles, etc., to these writings was a trick intended to give weight to what would otherwise perhaps have attracted no attention.

I hardly think any of the false Gospels can be ascribed to the simple intention to weave into one consecutive narrative the traditions which were actually known to the writers. Such traditions were introduced freely enough, but subject to the restraints which the author or compiler imposed on himself. We have in fact no such collection; because no false Gospel extends over the entire period of the Evangelical history.[1] The nearest approach to such a compilation as I refer to, may have been that of Papias, but it is almost wholly lost, and therefore we cannot say positively that it had the character in question. Of the lost Apocryphal Gospels which we read of, some were mainly compilations from those in the Canon, and are not included in the plan of the present work.

The learned reader who desires to study more closely this matter should have recourse to the Essay of Dr. Tischendorf " De Evangeliorum Apocryphorum Origine et Usu," 1851. He may also study the work of M. Nicolas, who mentions other authorities; but I repeat my dissent from many of his opinions.

III. USES WHICH HAVE BEEN MADE OF THE APOCRYPHAL GOSPELS.

AFTER what has been said of the intention of these documents, it may seem needless to speak of their uses, but a moment's reflection will show that the two things are different. It is quite true that some of the uses to which they have been applied

---

[1] This remark is only meant to refer to ancient documents. The " Historia Christi " written in Persian by the Jesuit Jerome Xavier appeared early in the 17th century. The edition and Latin version of De Dieu was published at Leyden in 1639.

are involved in the preceding inquiry, but I now proceed to notice various unconnected facts, which illustrate historically the purposes for which they have been employed, apart from the intention of their writers. The facts I allude to are equally apart from attempts to refute and throw discredit upon them.

We already know that Justin, Irenæus, Clement of Alexandria, and other early Christian authors, mention circumstances which appear to have been derived from the Apocryphal Gospels. Baronius quotes Nicephorus as saying that Hippolytus is one who mentions such circumstances, but I cannot discover any such passage in his extant remains. Origen certainly has allusions, but they appear to be for controversial purposes. Gregory of Nyssa and Epiphanius, and the writer of a discourse ascribed to Eusebius, make use of statements contained in the Apocryphal Gospels. But after all, very few genuine passages from Christian writers of the first four centuries can be confidently appealed to. At the same time, I am of opinion that a careful examination of the Fathers would very likely bring to light other passages corresponding in a remarkable manner with what we read in the false Gospels. Thus Athanasius, in his treatise on the "Incarnation of the Word," refers to the downfall of idols in Egypt, when Christ went thither: "Who, among righteous men or kings, went down into Egypt, and at his coming the idols of Egypt fell?" etc. In his fourth oration against the Arians, also, he mentions the fear of the keepers of Hades when Christ descended to the underworld. Elsewhere he mentions that Christ arose from the dead at midnight. He may not really have read any of our extant false Gospels, but he knew some of the traditions contained in them. It is when we come to later writers that we find the apocryphal traditions set forth as verities. John of Damascus, Nicephorus, and a host of others might be mentioned in this connection. Hence it has come to pass that, short of a place among the books of the New Testament, many apocryphal writings have been elevated to the highest possible dignity. If some of the false Gospels and revelations have not been formally adopted, stories from them, as told by John of Damascus and others, have been transferred to the Roman Breviary. It is well known that the *Legenda Aurea*[1] drew largely from several of the spu-

---

[1] "Jacobi a Voragine Legenda Aurea, vulgo Historia Lombardica dicta. Ed. Dr. Th. Graesse. Lipsiæ, 1850." I venture to strongly

rious Gospels. The histories of Joachim, Anna, Joseph, and Mary, as contained in the service books of the Romish Church, and in other authoritative works, are mainly founded on the Christian Apocrypha. Such facts show the importance of these documents, and the desirableness of an acquaintance with them. Books of this kind cannot become truly obsolete so long as they lie at the basis of the faith and practice of millions. The work of Maria d'Agreda even, owes no little of its actual vitality in Italy, France, etc., to the free use made in it of the more ancient Apocrypha. The absence of this element may explain the disappearance of such visions as those of Hildegard, Elizabeth, and Matilda, if not those of Huguetinus and Friar Robert, all of which have been printed for the benefit of the faithful. It must be owned with reference to the five last, that we find in them some of the most terrible exposures and denunciations of the crimes of popes, cardinals, bishops, priests, friars, and nuns, and that they would naturally be unpalatable on that account. Hildegard in particular is often simply disgusting, and we should find it hard to believe that a holy woman

recommend this edition to such as wish to know more of mediæval mythological trash.

could know, much less write, what she did, if we were unaware of the frightful iniquity of her times.[1]

In the middle ages and onward the Apocryphal books were very popular; were read with avidity, were reproduced in poetry, and were literally translated into a variety of languages. In one form or another we encounter them in Egypt, Syria, Persia, and India, in Greece and Italy, in Germany, Spain, and France, in Britain, and as far north as Iceland. To begin with the last, I find in a recent collection of Icelandic Legends, a version of the well known story of Christ and the birds, adapted, of course, to the latitude of Iceland. Here it is:—

THE SAVIOUR AND THE GOLDEN PLOVERS.

"Once on a Sabbath, Christ, in company with other Jewish children, amused himself in fashioning birds out of clay.

After that the children had amused themselves awhile herewith, one of the Sadducees chanced to come up to them. He was old and very zealous, and he rebuked the children for spending their Sabbath in so profane an employment. And he let it not

[1] She was born in 1098 and died in 1180; and was admitted as a Saint in the Roman Calendar at September 17th, the day of her death. See "Nouvelle Biographie Generale," Tom. 24, pp. 673–675.

rest at chidings alone; but went to the clay birds and broke them all, to the great grief of the children.

Now, when Christ saw this, he waved his hands over all the birds he had fashioned, and they became forthwith alive, and soared up into the heavens.

And these birds are the golden plovers, whose note 'deerrin' sounds like to the Iceland word 'dýrdhin,' namely, 'glory;' for these birds sing praise to their Lord, for in that he mercifully saved them from the merciless hand of the Sadducee."

I find the following curious stories in the "Sermones Dominicales" of Hugo de Prato, who is said to have died in 1322. The copy I quote from was printed in 1476 or 1483, and its pages are not numbered. The passage is in the ninth sermon,—On the Nativity of Christ:—

"All his creatures bore witness to his coming. For 1. The angels bore witness unto Him, for they, as soon as he was born, appeared to men, saying, Unto you is born this day a Saviour; 2. The sun, moon, and stars bore witness to Him; for on this day, in the East, three suns appeared, and were immediately joined into one to signify that the three, *i.e.* divinity, soul, and flesh, are combined in Christ: the new, *i.e.* the soul newly created, and the old, *i.e.* the flesh, descending from Adam, and the eternal, *i.e.* the deity, are conjoined together, and are made one sun, one man Jesus Christ. Also, on this day there appeared at Rome, a golden circle round the sun, in which circle was a most beautiful maiden, in whose lap was a child. And it was told the emperor that that child was greater than he. Now when the Romans wished to adore Octavianus Cæsar as a god, because he presided over the whole world in peace, the emperor refused, saying, I wish to know first whether anybody greater than I shall ever be born. And he called the Sibyl, who, while he was occupied with prophecies on the natal day of Christ in the chamber of the emperor, saw the aforesaid circle and the maiden nursing the child in her lap; all which things the Sibyl showed to the emperor, saying, This child is greater than thou. And straightway a voice was heard in the chamber of the emperor in the capitol, Here is the altar of heaven.

Wherefore until this day the aforesaid chamber, which is now a church, is called St. Mary altar of heaven (*Sancta Maria Ara Celi*). Now the emperor immediately put off his diadem and worshipped that child, and thenceforth refused to be worshipped by men.

On this night when the Lord was born there appeared in the East a star in which was a child having a cross on his forehead, and he spake to the Magi, saying, that they were to go into Judea to worship Him that was born King of the Jews.

3. All the elements bore witness unto Him; for

on this night the darkness of the air was changed as into the light of day; and at Rome a fountain of oil gushed out and flowed into the Tiber, in token that the Fountain of piety and mercy was born, and would confer grace and mercy upon all. And the Temple of Peace fell down. Now the Romans, having enjoyed continual peace for twelve years, built the Temple of Peace, wherein they set the image of Romulus, and they inquired of Apollo how long it would last. And they received as answer, "Until a virgin should bring forth, and remain a virgin." And thinking it impossible that a virgin should bring forth, they put up this inscription, "The Eternal Temple of Peace" (*Templum Pacis Eternum*). But on this night the said temple fell. On this night also the vineyards of Engaddi flowered and produced balsam, in token that He was born who should preserve all things, by the virtue of the stream of his blood.

4. The animals bare witness to Him. For when the virgin laid him in the manger, the animals which were there, *i.e.* the ox and the ass, bowed their knees to him. And many unhappy Christians to-day bend not their knees to Christ. Isai. i.: The ox knoweth his owner, and the ass his master's manger, but Israel knoweth me not, and my people doth not understand," etc.[1]

From an old catalogue of the Bibliotheca Uffen-

---

[1] Most or all of these stories are contained in the "Legenda Aurea," compiled by Jacobus à Voragine near the close of the 13th century.

bachiana, I copy this fragment of a German Gospel of the Infancy in metre :—

> Hie hebet sich an Marien leben.
> Uns leret dis buch furbass me
> Das in dem lande zu Galilee
> In einer Stat die was genant
> Nazareth und was wol bekant
> Da was eyn riche Man gesessen
> Zu Togenden was er wol vormessen.
> Er was geheissen Joachim,
> Nach Gotes Dinste stunt sin Synne
> Er was geborn von eyme geslechte,
> Konig Davides mit allem rechte.[1]

The table of contents shows that the poem extended from the exclusion of Joachim out of the temple to the reception of Mary in heaven after the assumption; it therefore includes the Gospel narrative, as well as several apocryphal stories.

M. Brunet extracts from the "Lexique Roman" of M. Raynouard, part of a Gospel of the Infancy in the dialect current in the south of France in the 13th century.

The old traveller, Sir John Maundeville, a great collector of legends, brought home a version of the legend of Seth, which we find in the second part of the Gospel of Nicodemus. Doubtless there are

[1] Bibl, Uffenb. Part IV, p. 41.

some who will be amused by it, and therefore, as well as because it has been reproduced in a book ascribed to Dr. J. M. Neale,[1] I insert a copy of it here:—

"The Cristene Men, that dwellen bezond the See, in Grece, seyn that the Tree of the Cros, that we callen cypresse, was of that Tree, that Adam ete the Appulle of: and that fynde thei writen. And thei seyn also, that here Scripture seythe, that Adam was seek, and seyde to his Sone Sethe, that he scholde go to the Aungelle, that kepte Paradys, that he wolde senden hym Oyle of Mercy, for to anoynte with his Membres, that he myghte have hele. And Sethe wente. But the Aungelle wolde not late him come in, but seyd to him, that he myghte not have of the Oyle of Mercy. But he toke him three Greynes of the same Tree, that his Fadre eet the Appelle offe; and bad him, als sone as his Fadre was ded, that he scholde putte theise three Greynes undre his Tonge, and grave him so: and he dide. And of theise three Greynes sprong a Tree as the Aungelle seyde, that it scholde, and bere a Fruyt, thorghe the whiche Fruyt Adam scholde be saved. And whan Sethe cam azen he fonde his Fadre nere ded. And whan he was ded, he did with the Greynes, as the Aungelle bad him; of the whiche sprongen three Trees, of the whiche the Cros was made, that bare gode Fruyt and

---

[1] Communications from the Unseen World. London. 1847. p. 26.

blessed, oure Lord Jesu Crist; thorghe whom, Adam and alle that comen of him, scholde be saved and delyvered from drede of Dethe withouten ende, but it be here own defaute."

Many pages might be filled from all sorts of writers in illustration of the present topic, but possibly my readers will be better pleased with examples from the popular literature of our own country and time. Moralities, miracle plays, mysteries, and carols drew largely from apocryphal materials, and were all the more popular in consequence. Confining myself to Carols, I select three from a chap-book printed in or about 1843 at Birmingham. The resemblance between these and some of our Apocryphal Gospels will not be called in question.

THE CHERRY TREE.

When Joseph was an old man, an old man was he,
And he married Mary the Queen of Galilee;
When Joseph he had his cousin Mary got,
Mary proved with child, by whom Joseph knew not.

As Joseph and Mary walked the garden gay,
Where cherries were growing upon every spray;
O then bespoke Mary with words so meek and mild,
"Gather me some cherries, for I am with child:

---

[1] *The Voiage and Travaile of Sir John Maundeville, Kt., which treateth of the way to Hierusalem; and of Marvayles of Inde, with other Ilands and Countryes.* London, 1725. Reprinted 1839. (Cap. II. Of the Crosse and the Croune of oure Lord Jesu Crist.)

Gather me some cherries, they run so in my mind."
Then bespoke Joseph with wordes so unkind,
"I will not gather cherries." Then said Mary, "You shall see,
By what will happen, these cherries were for me."

Then bespoke Jesus all in his mother's womb,
" Go to the tree, Mary, and it shall bow down,
And the highest branch shall bow to Mary's knee,
And she shall gather cherries by one, two, and three."

As Joseph was a walking he heard an angel sing,
"This night shall be born our Heavenly King ;
He neither shall be clothed in purple nor in pall,
But in fine linen, as were babies all.

"He never did require white wine and bread,[1]
But cold spring-water with which we were christened ;
He shall neither be rocked in silver and gold,
But in a wooden cradle that rocks on the mould."

Then Mary took her young Son and sat him on her knee,
" Come tell me dear child, how this world shall be."
" This world shall be like the stones in the street,
For the sun and the moon shall bow down at my feet."

THE HOLY WELL.

As it fell out one May morning,
   And on a bright holiday,
Sweet Jesus asked of his dear mother,
   If he might go and play.

" To play, to play sweet Jesus shall go,
   And to play now get you gone ;
And let me hear of no complaint
   At night when you come home."

---

[1] I suppose this line ought to be written,
   ' He never shall require white wine and red.'

Sweet Jesus went down to yonder town,
  As far as the Holy Well,
And there did see as fine children
  As any tongue can tell.

He said, "God bless you everyone;
  May Christ your portion be!
Little children shall I play with you,
  And you shall play with me?"

But they jointly answered, "No;"
  They were lords' and ladies' sons,
And he the meanest of them all,
  Was born in an ox's stall.

Sweet Jesus turned him around,
  And he neither laughed nor smiled;
But tears came trickling from his eyes
  Like water from the skies.

Sweet Jesus turned him about,
  To his mother's dear home went he,
And said, "I have been in yonder town,
  As far as you can see.

"I have been down to yonder town,
  As far as the Holy Well;
There did I meet as fine children
  As any tongue can tell.

"I bid God bless them every one,
  And their bodies Christ save and see;
Little children, shall I play with you,
  And you shall play with me?

But they answered me, 'No,'
  They were lords' and ladies' sons,
And I the meanest of them all,
  Was born in an ox's stall."

"Though you are but a maiden's child,
  Born in an ox's stall,
Thou art the Christ, the King of Heaven,
  And the Saviour of them all.

"Sweet Jesus, go down to yonder town,
  As far as the Holy Well,
And take away those sinful souls,
  And dip them deep in Hell."

"Nay, nay," sweet Jesus mildly said,
  "Nay, nay, that must not be;
For there are too many sinful souls,
  Crying out for the help of me."

O then bespoke th' angel Gabriel,
  Upon one good St. Stephen,[1]
"Although you are but a maiden's child,
  You are the King of Heaven."

An old ballad or carol called "Carnal and Crane," seems to embody some curious reminiscences of passages in the Apocryphal Gospels, mixing up with them other legends. The piece consists of thirty verses of four lines each, and is therefore too long to be quoted entire, but I cannot refrain from giving some portions of it.

Ver. 8. There was a star in the west land,
  Which shed a cheerful ray,
Into King Herod's chamber,
  And where King Herod lay.

---

[1] That is, St. Stephen's-day, Dec. 26.

The wise men soon espied it,
   And told the king on high,—
A princely babe was born that night,
   No king should e'er destroy.

"If this be true," King Herod said,
   "As thou tellest unto me,
This roasted cock that lies in the dish,
   Shall crow full fences three."

The cock soon freshly feathered was,
   By the work of God's own hand;
And then three fences crowed he
   In the dish where he did stand.

"Rise up, rise up, you merry men all,
   See that you ready be;
All children under two years old,
   Now shall destroyed be."

Then Jesus, ah! and Joseph,
   And Mary that was so pure,
They travelled into Egypt;
   As you shall find it sure.

And when they came to Egypt's land,
   Amongst those fierce wild beasts,
Mary, she being weary,
   Must needs sit down to rest.

"Come, sit thee down," says Jesus,
   "Come sit thee down by me;
And thou shalt see how these wild beasts
   Do come and worship me."

First came the lovely lion,
   Which Jesu's grace did spring;
And of the wild beasts of the field,
   The lion shall be king.

[We'll choose our virtuous princes,
　Of birth and high degree,
In every sundry nation,
　Where'er we come and see.]

Then Jesus, ah! and Joseph,
　And Mary that was unknown,
They travelled by a husbandman,
　Just while his seed was sown.

"God speed thee, man," says Jesus,
　"Go fetch thy ox and wain,
And carry home thy corn again
　Which thou this day hast sown."

The husbandman fell on his knees,
　Even before his face;—
"Long time hast thou been looked for,
　But now thou'rt come at last.

　　*　　*　　*　　*

Ver. 25. "If any one should come this way,
　And enquire for me alone;
Tell them that Jesus passed by,
　As thou thy seed didst sow."

After that came King Herod,
　With his train so furiously,
Enquiring of the husbandman
　Whether Jesus passed by.

"Why the truth it must be spoken,
　And the truth it must be known,
For Jesus passed by this way,
　When I my seed had sown.

"But now I have it reapen,
　And some laid on my wain,
Ready to fetch and carry,
　Into my barn again."

"Turn back," says the captain,
 "Your labour and mine's in vain:
"It's full three-quarters of a year,
 Since he has his seed sown."

So Herod was deceived,
 By the work of God's own hand,
And further he proceeded,
 Into the Holy Land.

Dr. Tischendorf's Essay, "on the Origin and Use of the Apocryphal Gospels," may now be mentioned. The author, among other things, shows the use made of them in supporting various doctrines and opinions concerning Christ, Mary, Joseph, the parents of Mary, the descent of Christ into the Underworld, and so forth. But inasmuch as they were written for such uses, I say no more of them here. He next proceeds to indicate the many evidences of their general and special influence in the Catholic Church, which condemned and yet adopted them. He then mentions the well known fact that Mohammed and other Arabic writers drew largely from the Christian Apocrypha. After this he resumes his illustrations from Church writers, who have accepted as facts what they have taken from the Apocryphal Gospels. His examples demonstrate that the fabric of ecclesiastical tradition is built up very much of fictions and founded upon the same. The picture is very humiliating, but the contrivance has been remarkably successful, and old falsehoods have been preferred to older truths. I do not think any sane man would raise any of these books to the dignity of real history; and yet the unreasoning adoption, by men of repute, of things borrowed from them, has been turned to good account. John of Damascus hashes up the stories which he finds in these books, and his hash is dished up in the Breviary; while the books he took his material from are condemned by popes and councils. In like manner numerous localities are accounted particularly sacred in consequence of incidents, the sole record of which is in the Christian Apocrypha. They pretend to show, at Rome and other places, at least one relic, the preservation of which is recorded in an apocryphal book (Arabic Gospel, chap. v. pp. 174, 175). Events and persons mentioned only in the false Gospels are solemnly commemorated; among the latter I will only mention Joachim and Anna, and among the former the feast of the immaculate conception of Mary. Joachim and Anna are purely apocryphal names, and yet the latter is one of the principal saints, and the following paragraph from a newspaper, published in September

1866, will show that the former is not without his honour:—

"CHEAP AND INFALLIBLE REMEDY FOR THE CHOLERA.—The *Chiesa Cattolica*, a clerical paper published at Naples, gives the following as a cheap and infallible remedy for the cholera: 'Apply to the abdomen a picture of St. Joachim, the glorious father of the Holy Virgin. This remedy is unfailing. The malady rarely attacks a person so protected; if it does, it is immediately cured. God sends us the cholera to punish us for our sins; but St. Joachim drives it away! One trial only solicited!'"

Dr. Tischendorf observes that certain recognised religious rites are also derived from apocryphal sources. Still more numerous are the uses to which apocryphal books have been put by painters, sculptors, etc. The well known ox and ass in representations of the nativity have no other origin. But it would be weary work to enumerate all the examples which could be adduced, and therefore I add no more: I only mention these because the subject requires it.

Looking more generally at the influence which the Apocryphal Gospels have exercised and still exercise, we are naturally led to ask how it is to be explained. Why is it that what has been condemned for so many ages, and been abused to such low ends, continues to occupy so prominent a place? Bishop Ellicott, in his Essay, supplies an answer, which, so far as it goes, is admirable, and after the disgust we must have felt at some previous details, is positively refreshing. It shows that after all there is a reason for the phenomena. The Bishop says:—

"Our vital interest in Him of whom they pretend to tell us more than the Canonical Scriptures have recorded, is the real, though it may be, hidden reason why these poor figments are read with interest even while they are despised." (p. 156.)

And again:—

"We know before we read them that they are weak, silly, and profitless—that they are despicable monuments even of religious fiction,—yet still the secret conviction buoys us up, that perchance they may contain a few traces of time-honoured traditions—some faint, feeble glimpse of that blessed childhood, that pensive and secluded youth, over which, in passive moments, we muse with such irrepressible longing to know more—such deep, deep desideration." (p. 157.)

After showing that the interest in the Apocryphal Gospels has revived since the mythical theory of the true Gospels was started, he makes the following remarks :—

"If they do not deserve to be known for their own sakes, they still involve several singular and interesting questions; they illustrate some curious phases of early Christian thought, and feeling; they throw some light on ancient traditions, and certainly have not been without influence on ancient and medieval art." (p. 158.)

IV. SPECIAL NOTICES OF SEPARATE BOOKS.

1. *The Gospel of James, or Protevangelium.*

THIS document is neither genuine nor authentic, but a compilation of such early traditions and facts as the writer found it expedient to throw into a narrative form. That it might look like a contemporary history by an eyewitness of great authority, it was ascribed to James, who was traditionally one of the sons of Joseph the carpenter. The reason for giving it this name is found in the nature of the story which deals with incidents such as James, of all the apostles of Jesus, was most likely to know, if not to record. The concluding chapter seems to refer the composition to the period which immediately followed the death of Herod, and consequently about the date of the return of Jesus from Egypt,—a circumstance which is not recorded in the book. All this is fraudulent; the book was in no case written before the second century; and in its actual form it belongs to a later century.

The author made use of the Gospels of Matthew and Luke, of certain portions of the Old Testament, both Canonical and Apocryphal, and of popular traditions, as well Jewish as Christian. This is probably the oldest existing writing which professes to give the names of the parents of the mother of Jesus. Elsewhere, I cannot find them until Epiphanius, who died in A.D. 403. The names and story of Joachim and Anna must not be regarded as an original creation, but rather as a remodelling of pre-existing materials. The character of Joachim is a combination of Elkanah, the father of Samuel (1 Sam. i.), with Joachim, the husband of Susanna (Apocryphal Daniel xiii.), and Manoah, the father of Samson (Judg. xiii.). Similarly, Anna is made up of Hannah the mother of Samuel, Susanna, and the wife of Manoah; possibly also the Anna of Luke (ii. 36–38) has not been overlooked. The angelic visions, promises, etc., made to Joachim and Anna, come especially from Judg. xiii. and 1 Sam. i. The nourishment of Mary in the temple is rather based upon a known custom in Egypt; but not without a reference to the history of Samuel (i.–iii.). The congealing of the blood of Zacharias (chap. xxiv.) is a Jewish tradition.

The book abounds in mistakes and inconsistencies. The twelve tribes of Israel are spoken of as though still united. Reuben, the high priest, and his successors, Zacharias and Samuel, are fictitious; Joachim's fasting forty days and forty nights in the wilderness is a parody of the fasting of Christ; the oracular plate on the forehead of the high priest had long been unknown; the allotment of Mary to Joseph is a fiction, based on Num. xvii.; the account of the angelic annunciation to Mary is contradicted by her subsequent swearing that she knew not the cause of her pregnancy; Joseph and Mary both prevaricate before the priest; the water of jealousy was not administered to men; Joseph is looking for a midwife, and sees one approaching at the very time when he sees the catalepsy of all things; the Magi were warned not to go into Judea when they were already there; the escape of John the Baptist is a mere fable, a counterpart to which

INTRODUCTION. li

is now found in the Hindoo mythology; Zacharias is wrongly identified with the one mentioned in Matt. xxiii. 35; Simeon was not a high priest. This long list will show the unhistorical character of the book.

With regard to the birth of Christ in a cave, Justin mentions the same thing (Trypho, 78), but with significant differences, as that Joseph could not find a lodging in the village, whereas the Pseudo-James represents the nativity as occurring before they went to the village at all. Justin refers to Isaiah xxxiii. 16, as a prediction of the birth in a cave, relying on the Septuagint version, whereas the Pseudo-James says nothing of the alleged prophecy, which may, for all that, have originated the tradition. This tradition is referred to by Origen (c. Celsum, i. 51), and by later writers. Justin says the wise men came from Arabia, but the Protevangelium says no such thing. On these accounts I doubt whether Justin ever saw the book.

Clement of Alexandria mentions the notion that Mary remained a virgin after the birth of Christ, but refers to no document as recording the circumstance. The food of angels (chap. viii.) is said by Athanasius to be fasting (de Virg.); the same writer calls Gabriel an archangel, as here, chap. xii. (c. Hæres.); and he has a phrase resembling that in chap. xix., "A virgin hath brought forth," etc. (de Divin. Christi). It is very likely that when Athanasius wrote, this false Gospel was well known. Much earlier Origen mentions a Gospel of Peter or Book of James as containing the assertion that Joseph already had sons when he was espoused to Mary (chap. ix.; Origen on Matthew). Tertullian mentions the congealing of the blood of Zacharias, but as this was a Jewish tradition, I cannot attach much importance to what he says on the subject.

After examining all the genuine passages in ancient writers, which seem to bear upon the Protevangelium, I cannot find one which unmistakeably proves its existence before the fourth century. Part of an ancient Syriac version of it has been published by Dr. W. Wright, of the British Museum.[1]

The Protevangel was used by the compilers of the Pseudo-Matthew, the Nativity of Mary, the History of Joseph the Carpenter, and the Arabic Gospel of the Infancy.

The author aimed to produce a consecutive narra-

[1] Contributions to the Apocryphal Literature of the New Testament. 8vo. London, 1865.

tive of events not fully recorded in the Gospels, and mainly introductory to them. When he wrote, men in the church had begun to love the marvellous, and were partial to traditions. It is curious, however, that the author mentions only one or two of the infant miracles of Jesus, which afterwards became so popular.

The manuscript copies abound in various readings of an extraordinary character, showing that the scribes took whatever liberties they chose with the text. It was originally written in Greek, and probably by a Jewish convert to Christianity. Dr. Tischendorf's edition, which is here followed, is from a MS. of the tenth or eleventh century, collated with many other MSS. and editions.

I am not at all sure that the author had any doctrinal or ecclesiastical motive in writing the book. The prodigies he relates in connection with Mary, may indicate that in his time special attention and honour had begun to be paid her; but there is nothing to indicate that extravagant personal worship which gradually came to be rendered to her. Whatever the writer says in honour of Mary and her parents, is designed to add lustre to Jesus, by showing how wonderfully God provided for His holy incarnation and advent, and watched over His infancy.

2. *The Gospel of Pseudo-Matthew: or of the Birth of Mary and the Infancy of the Saviour.*

THIS is not so ancient as the Pseudo-James, having probably not been written before the 5th century. It is not in any proper sense an original composition, but a compilation, apparently from three other documents, with incidental additions, and rhetorical developments. It may be divided into three portions according to its chief sources: (1) Chapters i.-xvii., from the Protevangelium; (2) chapters xviii.-xxv., from same unknown document; (3) chapters xxvi.-xlii., principally from the Pseudo-Thomas. The author or compiler may have written in Greek, as he sometimes follows the Septuagint version, but this is not decisive, as he may have translated what he found in his Greek authorities. No Greek copy has been found, and the Latin of chapters i.-xxiv. was first published by Thilo. The inscription which says it was written in Hebrew by Matthew, and translated into Latin by Jerome, is spurious.

Tischendorf prefixes a pretended correspondence between Jerome and two bishops, Chromatius and Heliodorus, but both the letters are a forgery. There is a third epistle, professedly written by Jerome on the subject, but this also is fictitious. The name of Jerome was already great when the correspondence alluded to was concocted.

I agree, generally, with Bishop Ellicott when he says of the Pseudo-Matthew: "It is scarcely necessary to say that nothing can be made out of such an agglomeration of folly and fraud. The Gospel is built up out of the Protevangel, certain oriental traditions which we afterwards find in the Arabic Gospel of the Infancy, and the Gospel of Thomas. The additions and embellishments are probably pure fiction, and for the most part do not seem referable to any ancient traditions."[1]

In the first chapter of this book we find Achar as the name of Anna's father, and I do not remember to have seen it elsewhere. It represents Abiathar as high priest when Mary was espoused to Joseph, whereas the Protevangelium calls him Zacharias. Sundry other details of the first portion differ from those of the Protevangelium, and the whole document may be fairly viewed as preparing the way for the Arabic Gospel of the Infancy.

Thilo prints the following prologue, which appears in some copies: "I James the Son of Joseph, having

[1] "On the Apocryphal Gospels." In the Cambridge Essays for 1856.

my conversation in the fear of God, have written all which with my own eyes I saw happen at the time of the nativity of St. Mary or of the Saviour; giving thanks to God, who gave me wisdom in the histories of his advent, showing the fulfilment unto the twelve tribes of Israel." The writer of this supposed he might as well refer the book to James as to any one else. Others have preferred to prefix to it the name of Matthew.

A book which contains so few incidents not to be found in other and more independent documents of its class, supplies little matter for comment. It resembles the Protevangelium in a feature which I have not referred to in the introduction to that book: I mean the sudden and total disappearance of the parents of Mary on her presentation in the temple. In the Protevangelium this occurs in chap. viii., and in Pseudo-Matthew in chap. v. Herein they both differ in a remarkable manner from the Gospel of the Nativity of Mary, which says she went to the house of her parents in Galilee after her espousal to Joseph (Nativ. viii.). Mary's going up the fifteen steps at the temple is omitted by Pseudo-James, but is found in the Nativity (Pseudo-Matt. iv., Nativ. vi.). The names of the high-priests differ from those in the Protevangel, but are equally fictitious. Joseph is said to have had not only children, but grand-children older than Mary (chap. viii.). In general the author was either very careless in copying the documents from which he took his materials, or those documents were widely different from such as we now have. Probably both occurred. He uses Scripture rather more freely than several others who preceded him. A good number of his incidents were reproduced in a modified form in the legends and literature of the Middle Ages in Europe; but the older Christian writers appear to say very little that bears on topics peculiar to him. This is precisely what we should expect. In Pseudo-Matth. xiv. we read that the infant Jesus was adored by the ox and ass, in fulfilment of Is. i. 3. It is easy to see that the popular notion of the ox and ass at the nativity comes from this passage, and quite as easy to see that the legend is nothing but a misapplication of Isaiah's words. Similar inventions are not infrequent, and I mention another from this same book. In chap. iii. the angel who appears to Joachim forbids him to call himself his servant, almost in the words of Rev. xx. 9. A reference of this sort is valuable as showing that angel-worship had not become fully developed when the book was written.

The compiler resembles the author of the Protevangelium in his ignorance concerning Jewish rites, and Jewish matters in general; he even represents the high priest as going into the holy of holies and burning sacrifice there (chap. viii.). This incident, however, is not found in Pseudo-James, but is probably one of those rhetorical embellishments which the compiler himself devised in order to add completeness to his story. His purpose is not to be wondered at, for Pseudo-James overlooks much that he might have recorded,—the circumcision for instance, and the purification. The events just named are duly introduced in the false Matthew, but with unaccountable confusion of language (chap. xv.). He properly places the circumcision on the eighth day, and then mentions the purification and the appointed offering; but he seems to regard the offering as made at the time of circumcision, and on account of it. The reason of the blunder is obvious. He read in Luke ii. 27, that the parents came to do for Jesus "according to the custom of the law," and supposed it meant either the circumcision or an offering because of it, whereas, it was the offering for the first-born (Exod. xiii. 2). The words which I have rendered "and when the infant had received *peritome*, (*peritome*, that is, circumcision,") are in the Latin, " Cumque accepisset parhithomum infans—parhithomus id est circumcisio," and look like a lame translation out of Greek, with an explanatory gloss. The barbarous *parhithomus* for περιτόμη (*peritomé*) may, however, not be chargeable upon the translator. The age of 112 assigned to Simeon is a fiction, and not much better is the assertion that Anna "had been a widow now for 84 years;" and I may say the same of the intimation that the wise men came to Jerusalem after two years (chap. xvi.), and that Joseph was warned to flee into Egypt, *one* day before the murder of the infants.

The second portion of the book introduces us into the true region of the marvellous, and we encounter prodigies at every step. Where did these fables come from? I suppose the Christian Hagadists fancied they might make a pretty story out of any Old Testament text they chose. The Psalmist says " Praise the Lord from the earth, ye dragons," so dragons come out of a cave and worship Jesus. The prophet speaks of wolves feeding with lambs, and of lions eating chaff with oxen, so lions and leopards and all sorts of wild beasts, form a sort of body guard for the Holy Family in the desert. The bride in Solomon's Song says, "I will go up to the palm tree, I will take hold of its boughs," so the palm tree bows down to Mary for her to have its fruit. The Israelites sang, "Spring up, O well!" and the prophet said, "waters shall break out in the wilderness," so a fountain gushes forth in the desert. The prophet said, "the idols of Egypt shall be moved at his presence," so the idols of Egypt fall, and are shattered when Jesus comes thither. Such are the prodigies of the second part, and such their genesis, which, in most instances, the writer himself really indicates. I remark in passing that an amusing story is told by Philostratus, about a lion which was brought to Apollonius of Tyana, when in Egypt, and which Apollonius said inherited the soul of king Amasis (Life, v. 42). I repeat, also, that Athanasius speaks of the downfall of the idols in Egypt (de Incarn. Verbi; and, de Divin. Christi).

The third part of the Pseudo-Matthew was not published by Thilo. It is chiefly borrowed from Pseudo-Thomas, and therefore very little need be said of it here. The variations from the prototype are in this part similar to those which were observed in the first part. Some of the fables or legends almost seem to have been written from memory.

Among them we find examples which are not now to be found in Pseudo-Thomas. This raises the question, whether Pseudo-Thomas itself is in its original form. I think not; but at present can only say so much, and that the Pseudo-Matthew account of the infant miracles of Jesus is not so exclusively malevolent as the other. The fiction in chap. xxxv-xxxvi. is really an excellent parable, or might be easily converted into one; and of course is not in the false Thomas.

The epilogue (chap. xlii.) is a pretty family picture, and may be original.

3. *The Gospel of the Nativity of Mary.*

THE writer of the Protevangel has embodied in his story the greater portion of the incidents contained in this Gospel of Mary's nativity; but the position of Mary is there only secondary after all, and she is not the *subject* of the book. In course of time, however, Mary began to be regarded as worthy of honour on her own account, and the comparatively independent position she took suggested corresponding literary modifications. Somebody, therefore, drew up the document before us. To give it authority, recourse was had to one of the most common of "pious" frauds, and it was fathered upon Jerome. The letters, mentioned as heading the Pseudo-Matthew, were also emblazoned at the head of this. Its association with the name of Jerome, and its comparatively modest style secured it popularity and authority, and during the Middle Ages it was accepted by the multitudes as so much Gospel. Copies of it were multiplied everywhere in Europe, and the incidents of it were reproduced in every possible form. The greater part of it was quietly slipped into the 'Legenda Aurea,' and its statements were in some cases declared infallible truth, to be denied only on pain of heresy here, and perdition hereafter.

The compiler may have wished to exhibit the current biography of Mary in the most modest form. His work is based on older apocrypha, but it sometimes differs in important details. For example, Issachar and not Reuben, is here the high-priest who rebuked Joachim. It summarises and paraphrases other narratives, and says as much at the end of chap. ix. No sign of originality appears in it, and it was probably drawn up by a Latin writer late in the fifth century, or within a hundred years after. We should observe that the compiler says Jesus was born at Bethlehem, when Joseph and Mary were there, in which he follows the true Gospels rather than apocryphal stories. Again, Jesus is called the first-born son of Mary, which is also a return to the simple and unsuspecting style of the Evangelists: thus in Chap. ix. Jesus is said to be "alone conceived and born without sin," p. 96. The use made of the Latin Vulgate is satisfactory evidence that the book appeared considerably later than the time of Jerome.

4. *The History of Joseph, the Carpenter.*

THIS is altogether of oriental origin, and comes to us through the Arabic. The introduction which I have thrown into a note, may be the work of the Arabic translator. It is supposed to have been first written in Coptic, in which language it is in great part, if not entirely, extant, both in the Sahidic and in the Memphitic dialects. Portions of the Coptic have been published by Zoega and Dulaurier. The date is uncertain. It has been referred to the fourth century, but may not be so ancient, as it is well known that what are viewed as early opinions existed longer in some places than in others. The author, whoever he was, wrote in an age of superstition, and when an exaggerated importance was attached to the observance of the days set apart for the commemoration of Saints.[1]

Some of the older traditions are incorporated by the author, but he drew largely upon his imagination, both for his plan and many of the details. The writer pretends that the substance of the book was verbally spoken by Christ to his disciples on the mount of Olives, where *they* were all assembled when He addressed *them*. But, forgetting this reference to the disciples in the *third* person, towards the close of the book he introduces them in the second person: 'Now *we* apostles, when we heard,' etc. (chap. xxx. and similarly in chap. xxxii). The sojourn of the Holy Family in Egypt is limited to one year, whereas three years are assigned to it in the Arabic Gospel of the Infancy, and at least as many are required by Pseudo-Matthew. Such facts show that the tradi-

---

[1] The legend has been turned to account by some modern writers; as by the author of "Reflections on the prerogatives, power, and protection of St. Joseph, etc. London, 1825." At the same time the doleful account it gives of Joseph's death does not appear to be a popular one if we may judge from the following lines:—

> "Thrice happy Saint of God, whose dying breath
> Was poured forth in the fond encircling arms
> Of Jesus and of Mary, glorious death,
> That knew no fears, no terrors, or alarms!"

("Hymn to St. Joseph," translated by D. French, Esq.)

tions of the Infancy varied considerably in some of their details, and that those who wrote them took no pains to harmonise them.

The Arabic introduction says, "the holy Apostles kept this discourse, and left it in writing in the library at Jerusalem." The Coptic introduction, which tells the same story, may be given entire; it is to this effect: "The 26th day of Epep. This is the departure from the body of our father Joseph the Carpenter, the father of Christ according to the flesh, who was 111 years of age. Our Saviour narrated all his life to his Apostles on Mount Olivet, and the Apostles wrote it and deposited it in the library which is at Jerusalem. Also the day on which the holy old man laid down his body was the 26th of the month Epep. In the peace of God, Amen." Both introductions make the Apostles the writers, according to the plain intention of the later chapters of the book. It would be a waste of time to refute so palpable a fiction.

Bishop Ellicott remarks very correctly that 'the writing " seems to have been drawn up in its present form to be read at the festival of Joseph, who was held in peculiar reverence by the early Christians in Africa, whether semi-heretical or Catholic. The object of the book is very clear: it was intended to give to Joseph some small share of the glorification, which had been already so liberally bestowed on Mary." While I agree with this in general, I cannot see any reason for suggesting some connection between Joseph's History and Nestorianism. The author is unguarded in some of his statements, as in calling Joseph a priest, but I doubt whether he was identified with any avowed heresy. His notions of death and the unseen world, of merit, and of some other matters, are strange enough, but such as we might expect in the benighted age to which I should assign this document. Whatever that age may be, Mary was already in high honour, and Joseph had an annual commemoration.

It must be noticed that the Arabic text sufficiently differs from the Coptic, for Dulaurier to say the former is an abridged translation: "En comparant les récits de l'écrivain Arabe avec ceux de l'auteur Copte, on se convaincra que l'ouvrage du premier n'est qu'une traduction abrégée de l'original égyptien."

After the note at p. 113 was printed, I met with the Hebrew confession quoted by Thilo, in the "Book of Life, a manual for the sick and mourners, by Rev. B. H. Ascher," (Second edition, London: 1861)

As the volume is not much known among Christians, I copy here the translation of Mr. Ascher: "My God, and the God of my ancestors! O deign that my prayers may come before Thee, and hide not Thyself from my supplications; efface all my sins which I have sinned against Thee all my life long unto this day, for I have acted foolishly; I am ashamed and confused; my evil inclinations enticed me to rebellion. O may my trouble and affliction be my atonement, and blot out the deeds of my backsliding; for against Thee only have I sinned. Alas! I have trespassed, I have been treacherous, I have stolen, I have spoken slander, I have committed iniquity, and acted wickedly, I have sinned designedly, and I have committed violence, I have framed falsehood, I have given evil counsel, I have uttered lies; I have blasphemed and revolted, I have been rebellious, I have acted perversely; I have been stiffnecked, I have acted wickedly and corrupted myself; I have done abominably, I have gone astray, and caused others to err; I have also turned aside from Thy excellent precepts and institutions, and which hath not profited me: but Thou art just concerning all that is come upon us, for Thou hast dealt most truly, and I have done most wickedly." (p. 119.)

In the Hebrew of this confession the sins are arranged in alphabetical order, from the first letter to the last. There are other forms in use among the Jews to which attention might also be directed. The reference to the 'fiery sea' in chap. xxvi. may remind us of Rev. xix. 20; xx. 14, or of purgatory in a modified form, but it also recalls the Jewish opinion thus stated by a certain Rabbi Leo, "The souls of the wicked are tortured with fire and other punishments, which some of the condemned suffer with no hope of redemption, but others for a certain time." The author from whom I take this extract, says the deliverance of those who are freed, is expected at the end of twelve months.[1] After all, the passage p. 121, may not mean an intermediate state, but the judgment itself, as, St. Paul, in 1 Cor. iii. 15.

5, 6, 7. *The Gospel of Thomas, or Gospel of the Infancy of Jesus.*

IN carrying out my purpose to translate the whole of the false Gospels published by Dr. Tischendorf, I have translated all three of the recensions of Thomas which he has printed. That nothing might

[1] J. à Lent, Mod. Theol. Jud. p. 683. Herbornæ, 1694.

be wanting, I have added, by way of supplement to this work, a version of the very ancient Syriac History of the "Boyhood of our Lord Jesus," which is but another form of the Thomas.

This book vies in antiquity with the Protevangelium, and claims to have originally appeared about the middle of the second century, if not before. We seem not to possess it in an unmutilated form, but what we have is very curious. It was the offspring of heresy for which heterodoxy is too mild a term, and after all the expurgation it has undergone, the evidence of its paternity remains upon its face. The author, or compiler, as in similar cases, wished to produce a sort of preliminary Gospel, and as he imagined the infant Jesus was wayward and captious, mischievous and arbitrary, he made him so in the fables he wrote.

Justin Martyr speaks of Jesus doing carpenter's work (Trypho 88), in almost the same words as Pseudo-Thomas speaks of Joseph (1 Thomas xiii.). Irenæus also, when speaking of Marcus, the founder of the Marcosians, mentions the mysteries he found in the alphabet (Bk. i. 10–17). Special reference is made by Irenæus to "an unspeakable multitude of apocryphal and spurious writings," which these heretics forged, and from one of them he extracts the story about Jesus and the man who went to teach him letters, much as we have it in some copies of Thomas. Origen mentions a Gospel of Thomas, but does not help us to identify it with ours. Hippolytus also, writing of the sect of the Naasenes, quotes from their Gospel of Thomas, but the passage is not in the book as we have it. Eusebius, too, mentions a Gospel of Thomas, and he is followed by others in the same century. Cyril of Jerusalem says, a Gospel of Thomas was written by one of the three disciples of Manes, but this cannot be true of the false Gospel mentioned by Origen and Hippolytus, unless he means to say simply that the Manichæans re-modelled it.

Whoever the writer was, he believed Jesus to be the Messiah, and the peculiar institutions of Judaism to be abolished. He disliked the Jews, but he made Jesus petulant and revengeful. Joseph is made more prominent than Mary; but Jesus is not really viewed as his natural son, so much as a mysterious Being manifested in a human form, and yet Joseph is called his "father." The author's favourite Evangelist was St. John, and perhaps he was one of the Docetæ, in whose interests he wrote.

INTRODUCTION. lxxi

Tischendorf supposes the book was written by some Gnostic, that it was adopted by the Naasenes, that it became popular among the Manichæans, and at last found favour with the orthodox (notwithstanding its condemnation by high authority, including the second Nicene Council in A.D. 787).

After all that has been said about the authorship of this book, I am strongly tempted to ask whether it may not be the so-called Gospel of Basilides, or a part of it? As the discussion of this question would extend to some considerable length, I must be content with recording it.

The Pseudo-Thomas was substantially incorporated with other documents in the third part of Pseudo-Matthew, and the Arabic Gospel of the Infancy. It covers a definite period, reaching from Christ's fifth year to his twelfth, and its intention is precisely stated in the introduction—to record "the infant acts" of Jesus. I am also inclined to think that the unknown document from which Pseudo-Matthew drew the second part of his book, may represent one of the lost portions of Pseudo-Thomas.[1]

---

[1] In illustration of the ideas thrown out about the connection of Thomas with Basilides, and of the second part of Pseudo-Matthew with Thomas, I append a note. Pseudo-Matthew, xxii. records the

Bishop Ellicott observes in his excellent essay, that in this story "we can scarcely recognize more than two elements, pious fraud and disguised heresy: the third element in these productions, ancient traditions and a credulity that reproduces or embellishes them, finds here but little place." And again, "the miracle-mongering is so gross, and the dogmatical propensions of the writer are so obvious, that it may be reasonably doubted, whether, even at the time it appeared, it was regarded as a regular historical compilation at all." It is tolerably certain that the orthodox would not believe it; but if it was written in the interests of a sect it was meant to be accepted as a true portrait of the character and mode of life of the child Jesus.

Bishop Ellicott says again: "The language is unusually barbarous, the style hopelessly bad, and the narrative itself unconnected and incoherent." All this is true; but what the original language was I am not prepared to say. The book itself was circulated in the West and in the East; we have it in

fall of the 355 (one copy has 365) idols of Egypt. In the book "de Hæresibus," ascribed to Augustine, we read that Basilides said there were 365 heavens, according to the number of days in a year. Hence his so-called holy name ABRASAX, the letters of which in Greek amount to 365. The 365 of Basilides is mentioned also by Philastrius, Epiphanius, and Damascenus.

Greek, Latin, and Syriac, and it seems to exist also in Armenian.

I must now say a few words upon each of the four texts of Pseudo-Thomas contained in this volume.

I regard all the copies as more or less altered in the interests of Catholic doctrine.

That which stands first is from the Greek, as it commonly appears in printed books.

The second, also from the Greek, was extracted by Dr. Tischendorf from a MS. found by him among the monks of Mount Sinai. The writer or editor seems to have modified a larger document by striking out some incidents, altering others, adding occasionally, and changing the order of some of the sections. In general the result has been to render the narrative less heterodox. The expression "Joseph his father," which is so often found in the Syriac recension, occurs only once in the longer Greek, and not at all in the shorter book. This last also has at the close the orthodox formula, "glorifying Him, with the Father, and the Holy Spirit."

The Latin Gospel of Thomas is remarkable on several accounts. It commences with the rehearsal of an incident similar to one which we find at the close of the Protevangel. But while Pseudo-James refers to a tumult at the death of Herod, Pseudo-Thomas mentions the commotion caused by Herod's search after the infant Jesus. The whole of the first three chapters of Pseudo-Thomas in the Latin are wanting in the other texts, and look like an independent composition: they may, however, embody another fragment of the book in its original form. The fourth chapter consists of an introduction like that which appears in the two Greek texts, but is not in the Syriac. The editor treated his original with a good deal of freedom, paraphrasing and altering the phraseology. As in the case of the two Greek texts, the document appears to have received a certain tinge of orthodoxy. I imagine that it is less ancient than the first Greek copy, (probably less ancient than the second,) and that it is not earlier than the end of the seventh century (very likely not quite so early).

This Latin Thomas has a special conclusion, which pretends to be a declaration made by Thomas the Israelite, and is meant to have a practical tendency. It can hardly be accepted as representing anything contained in the original writing, but is, most likely, the afterthought of the Latin editor.

It would be useless to speculate who "Thomas the

Israelite" was, or "Thomas the Ishmaelite," as some copies call him.

Dr. Tischendorf has found some fragments of another Latin text considerably more ancient than the one here printed. These fragments are in a Palimpsest MS. at Vienna and are thought to be of the fifth or sixth century. As we should expect, they approach nearer to the first Greek text, and nearer still to the Syriac in some respects. Some of the readings differ from all the other texts, but may be partly traced in Pseudo-Matthew, which made free use of Pseudo-Thomas.

The Syriac recension altogether omits the name of Thomas, and is simply called "The Boyhood of our Lord Jesus." Dr. Wright's copy is of the sixth century, and exhibits a more ancient text than any other now extant complete. It has been less subject to expurgation on the one hand and to additions on the other. Manipulation it has most likely undergone, but much of its primitive heretical aspect remains. The great antiquity of the copy, and the interest and importance which attach to it, justify my giving it a place in this volume.

8. *The Arabic Gospel of the Infancy.*

I HAVE intimated in the note prefixed to my translation of this false Gospel, that it has been drawn from three principal sources, the first and third of which generally correspond to the Protevangel and the Pseudo-Thomas. As for the second source, it has not been clearly determined. As a compilation it has been ascribed to the fifth or sixth century, but I regard this as too early, for which I shall mention some reasons. The book is apparently an Egyptian production, whatever the language in which it first appeared. We only possess the Arabic text, for I feel justified in believing that the Syriac copies of a Gospel of the Infancy said to exist at Rome and Paris, will prove to be a Syriac recension of Pseudo-Thomas. No trace of it has been found in Coptic or any other ancient language.

The compiler put into a connected form the legends and traditions which he had at his disposal, but he executed his task without skill and judgment. His object was to glorify the infant Jesus and his mother. He pretends to have borrowed from a book by Joseph or Caiaphas the high priest, but it is uncertain whether this applies to anything more than the first chapter. The Syrian Jacobites believed that Caiaphas became a Christian, and other traces of Syrian traditions may be pointed out in this book. But if we remember the close connection which subsisted between the Syrian Christians and Egypt, we shall see that an Egyptian writer would be very likely to know their traditions. It is even possible that the book was originally written in Arabic by a Syrian Christian, just as other books were, and this would account for the traces of Syriac words found in it.

Mohammed was acquainted with some of the incidents here put down, as that Jesus talked in his cradle (Koran, Suras 3, 5, 19). This fact, however, is no proof that our document was compiled at that early period. The position taken by Mary is tolerable evidence that the book is not of very high antiquity, and renders it very difficult for me to believe that the compiler was a Nestorian, as some have thought. Whoever he was, he softened down the malevolent aspect of the portions which he derived from the Pseudo-Thomas.

Repeated perusal of the book has convinced me that it is by no means so ancient as has been thought. The whole tone and texture of the composition betrays a degenerate age. The actual Arabic text cannot well claim a great antiquity for several reasons, and if the Arabic was the original we must cease to refer it to the fifth or sixth century. The rise of Arabic literature was very little earlier than Mohammed, and this book was written when the language was the familiar vehicle for literary composition. In chapter xxiv. the name Matarea is twice mentioned; but this name is Arabic and therefore the present text was not produced until the place had received that appellation from the Mohammedans. When this was I cannot say, but I have failed to discover any certain occurrence of Matarea before the time of Abulfeda (died 1331) in his description of Egypt, and even there the copies appear to differ. The Nubian Geographer, who wrote about A.D. 1150, mentions Ain Shems and the balsam which grew near it, but has no allusion to the name of Matarea.

The Arabic Gospel gives the name of Matarea to the sycamore tree. Sozomen seems to place this tree in the Thebaid (Eccles. Hist. v. 21), at a great distance from Matarea. I suppose it was afterwards found convenient to shift the locality of the legendary tree, and if so, the Arabic Gospel was not written till much later than Sozomen (A.D. 440). No ancient copy of the book has been discovered, and the first allusion to it which seems to be identified is that of Solomon of Bassora (A.D. 1222).

Chapters l.–lii. deserve special consideration in connection with the date of this compilation. Other traces of modern origin might be thought referrible to transcribers, but these chapters indicate a development of Arabic science which is utterly inconsistent with an early date. Could the chapters in question have been produced prior to the ninth or tenth century? The ninth century is the era to which the rise of scientific studies among the Arabs is assigned; and here we have a formidable array of scientific terms and topics. In default of evidence to the contrary I must conclude that what I may call the science of the book forbids us to ascribe it to a period earlier than that which I have mentioned for the rise of scientific studies among the Arabs.

Even if the idea of a Syriac origin be still pleaded for, we shall not be able to go back beyond the eighth century, when the scientific writings of the Greeks were studied and translated by Syrians.[1]

[1] Sergius of Rhesaina belongs to the sixth century, but he failed to popularise the Greek philosophy and science. A chief agent in this

It is needless to carry this discussion further; but I must say a word about the order of events in the book. There is some confusion arising from the misplacing of certain transactions. This defect of arrangement may arise from the compiler having copied different documents without observing that the sequence of events was incomplete. Chapter i. really does not stand first in order of time. Chapter xxvi. seems to have been a transition to another document, but is inconsistent with chapter xxvii., because Joseph is told to go to Nazareth, and the story is resumed at Bethlehem. This parenthesis continues to chapter xxxvi. where the thread of the narrative is taken up again. Very likely what we usually regard as the second part of the book comes from two distinct sources at least. Of the puerilities and absurdities of the book I shall say nothing. As the Arabic Gospel is the largest of all the Gospels of the Infancy, so it is the most marked by credulity, superstition, and folly. The long array of miracles effected by the water in which Christ was washed, or the linen he had worn, will speak for themselves. Ignorance, folly, and mendacity, are here at least as conspicuous as piety.

work was Honain Ben Isaac who wrote in Syriac and Arabic what he derived from the Greek. He died about A.D. 873 (Assemani B. O. ii. 272).

INTRODUCTION. lxxxi

9. *Correspondence between Abgar and Jesus, etc.*

UNDER this head I have inserted in the text a few small items not included by Dr. Tischendorf in his volume. Very little need be said about them after the remarks prefixed to them (pp. 217, 218).

(1.) *Letter of Abgar to Jesus.*—This Abgar, was Abgar Uchomo, or Uchama,[1] king of Edessa, who began to reign in A.D. 2, and reigned nearly forty years. There is a long account of him in Bayer's "Historia Osrhoena et Edessena," and a number of references in ancient writers, who record the tradition with which this letter is connected. The tradition appears with considerable variety of detail, but its general purport is that Abgar was afflicted with a disease which his physicians could not cure, and that having heard of the miracles of Christ, he sent him the letter to ask him to come and heal him. According to one version of the story our Lord not only sent back the reply ascribed to him, but His own portrait, imprinted upon a towel or cloth. Subsequently, they say, Thaddæus or Addi, one of our Saviour's disciples, went to Edessa, cured Abgar, preached the Gospel to him, and baptized him.

[2] *i.e.* Niger, or the Black.

lxxxii   INTRODUCTION.

Eusebius, who first mentions the correspondence, says nothing of the miraculous portrait. I have no doubt the letters are spurious, but they are sufficiently ancient to deserve a place in this collection. They were incorporated in an account of the introduction of the Gospel to Edessa, part of which is preserved by Eusebius, and a further portion exists in a Syriac MS. in the British Museum. This MS. is probably of the sixth century, and among other things contains a letter which Abgar is said to have written to Tiberius, and the alleged reply of Tiberius. The document was published by Canon Cureton,[1] and contains valuable historical matter, mixed up with fables.

(2.) *The Letter of Jesus to Abgar.*—This is inseparably connected with the preceding, and was probably, like it, first written in Syriac by some Edessene Christian in the third century. There is some variation in the copies of these letters, which exist in Syriac, Greek, Arabic, etc.[2]

---

[1] "Ancient Syriac Documents relative to the Earliest Establishment of Christianity in Edessa, and the neighbouring Countries, from the Year after Our Lord's Ascension, to the beginning of the Fourth Century. Discovered, Edited, Translated, and Annotated by W. Cureton, D.D., Canon of Westminster." 4to. London, 1864.

[2] De Dieu supplies an Arabic copy of the Letter of Christ to Abgar, differing exceedingly from those in ordinary circulation, but I have not

(3.) *The Epistle of Lentulus.*—This epistle is avowedly addressed to the Roman people and Senate, but is a late mediæval forgery. No such person as Lentulus, or Publius Lentulus, was "president of the people of Jerusalem;" no ancient writer ever mentions the epistle, which is only extant in Latin copies exhibiting all sorts of differences. It may have been intended to authenticate one of the many alleged portraits of Christ, which were manufactured in the Middle Ages.

(4.) *The Prayer of Jesus, the Son of Mary.*—I derive this from Jones on the Canon; but I have not exactly followed his translation. He took it from the Commentary of Selden upon Eutychius's Arabic Annals of Alexandria. Selden found it among certain Arabic forms of prayer, and published it in Arabic, with a Latin version. The document speaks for itself, and I need only say, with Jones: "I suppose no one at all acquainted with Christianity can believe this prayer genuine, and composed by our blessed Saviour." (Jones on the Canon, vol. ii. p. 25. Oxford edition, 1827).

---

thought it worth while to print a translation of it. The curious may see it, with a Latin version, in the notes to Xavier's " Historia Christi Persice conscripta," pp. 611, 612. (Lugduni Batavorum, 1639).

(5.) *The Story of Veronica.*—At p. 218, I have said all that is requisite about this. Malela says, and truly, no doubt, that he took it from a book in the possession of a Christian Jew named Bassus, but he gives no clue to the date of its production. It does not profess to be a contemporary document, and it probably grew out of the circumstances reported by Eusebius. The name of Veronica, or Berenice, figures in a number of legends, more or less ancient, the most popular being that which represents her as lending the Saviour a cloth to wipe his face, on the way to crucifixion, and receiving the cloth back from Him, with His likeness upon it. The petition of Veronica, preserved by Malela, is an undoubted forgery. It may be noted that Eusebius (Hist. Eccles. vii. 17, 18) does not mention the name of Veronica; neither does Sozomen (Hist. Eccles. v. 20). Malela simply speaks of a monument or *stele*, without indicating its form. The original records of the cure of the woman (Matt. ix. 20-22; Mark v. 5, 25; Luke viii. 43) show that it did not take place at Paneas. They still pretend to show a house of Veronica at Jerusalem.[1]

---

[1] Cotovicus, Itiner. Hierosol. 1619, p. 254.

10. *The Gospel of Nicodemus, or Acts of Pilate.*

Under this general title I include no fewer than six documents printed by Dr. Tischendorf, and representing two compositions which are often combined.

(1.) The Gospel of Nicodemus, Part I., which I put first, records the trial, crucifixion, burial, resurrection, and ascension of Jesus, and involves a variety of incidents connected with those events. The writer draws largely from the evangelical narratives, all of which were before him, including the closing section of Mark. But while he uses the Gospels, he introduces a great many fictitious details of a purely mythical, or rather prodigious character. Some of the foreign elements were perhaps traditions, but the way in which they are worked up, shows that the writer was a genuine Hagadist, and consequently we must treat his story as a romance rather than as a history. The title adopted by Dr. Tischendorf, "Acts of our Lord Jesus Christ, wrought in the time of Pontius Pilate," differs considerably from several other forms of it. In one copy it is said the book was written in Hebrew by Nicodemus; and in another, that Pilate sent it to Augustus Cæsar. These titles are not worth much.

The prologue represents one Ananias as saying that he found the Acts in Hebrew and translated them into Greek, in the time of Theodosius and Valentinian. This may be taken as pretty good evidence that our Greek text did not appear before A.D. 440.

A second introduction professes to give the date of the events recorded, and refers the original composition to Nicodemus, who is said to have written in Hebrew.

If the first prologue has any value, it teaches us that the book was really unknown till the date mentioned, because Ananias claims to have been the discoverer as well as the translator.

Dr. Tischendorf, however, believes the book appeared as early as the second century. If so, the prologue is a forgery, and all that the supposed Ananias could have done was to modify a document already widely circulated. Tertullian, some two centuries and a quarter earlier, had appealed to certain Acts of Pilate, and Justin Martyr long before that had done the same. If they meant this book, it existed in Africa (in Latin), and in Europe (probably in Greek). I cannot see the force of the arguments for the early origin of the book, but the style in which it is written compels me to refer our present Greek text to the fifth century. From beginning to end, prologue included, we have the degraded and corrupt Greek of the fifth and following centuries. As for the chronological note at the beginning, the writer could have found the materials for that very easily. Meanwhile these introductions are not contained in all the copies, and as I have said, those which have them do not by any means agree. The reader has only to turn to the examples contained in this volume to see what I mean. I even venture to doubt whether we ought to call this book in any of its forms "The Acts of Pilate," although Dr. Tischendorf has thus entitled his first Latin text on the authority of Gregory of Tours, and not from any manuscript of the document itself. "Acts of Pilate," and "Gospel of Nicodemus," are convenient popular designations, and nothing more, for they do not appear to have originally belonged to the book. "Acts of Pilate" is no doubt adopted because it is supposed that Justin Martyr, Tertullian, and Epiphanius quoted substantially the same work as we now have; but it is a misnomer, as there is nothing about it resembling the official report to which the two first-named Fathers allude.

Having mentioned Gregory of Tours, I add that he is the first writer who, in my opinion, unquestionably cites our present Acts of Pilate. He is placed by Cave at A.D. 573. I have found no traces of it in Syriac, but it partly exists in Latin in a MS. of possibly the fifth century, and in a Coptic MS. of about the same date. Later on it became immensely popular in Europe and was translated into Anglo-Saxon and other languages.

Not to prolong this discussion about the date of the book, let us ask who wrote it? and in what language it was written? I answer briefly, it was written in Greek, by a converted Jew, who was acquainted with Hebrew. The Greek is, as I have said, very corrupt, and is tinged by Latin influences on the one hand, and by Hebrew influences on the other. Greek forms of Latin words are frequent, and sundry Hebrew words and phrases also appear in Greek characters. There are also a number of places where the idiom is Hebrew rather than Greek. The writer had at least the Old Testament in Hebrew. That he was a Jew is tolerably clear from the occurrence of details of a purely Jewish character, except so far as they have been modified to suit the convenience of the author. At the same time the book was written by one who had never been in Judæa, and who was ill informed in regard to its topography especially; he was not even careful to follow the hints supplied him by the New Testament. I will now point out a few details which seem to require a particular remark.

The accusation of the Jews that Jesus wrought miracles by magical and diabolical agency is, it is true, in accordance with what we read in the Gospels, but then we do not find them recorded in connection with His trial. Pilate's assertion that unclean spirits could only be cast out by Esculapius is also open to question, as I find no trace of such an opinion among the Romans. Esculapius was simply the god of healing: but how about *demoniacal* possession, and his province in relation to it?

The prodigies connected with the summoning of Jesus before Pilate are fictions which appear to be peculiar to this story. The calumny that Jesus was illegitimate finds no place in the account of the trial as recorded in the four Gospels. The assertion of the Jews that they had a law forbidding them to take an oath is a fiction. The series of witnesses, who bare testimony of Jesus, is an invention founded on incidents scattered over the Gospels. Pilate is represented as well acquainted with Jewish history, which is inconsistent with the general tone of the narrative (chapter ix.). The two malefactors crucified with Christ are called Dysmas and Gestas, which names are mere inventions. The Jews are represented as taking the law into their own hands in arresting and imprisoning Joseph of Arimathea. The guards of the tomb are represented as having been still there when the angel announced the resurrection to the women—a misunderstanding of Matth. xxviii. 11, which shows that the soldiers had left before the women arrived.

It is apparent that some time must be allowed to have elapsed between the events of chapters xiii. and xiv., because in the fourteenth chapter the ascension is recorded by men who had come out of Galilee. But the ascension took place near Bethany and not in Galilee. Mount Mamilk or Melek was thought to be in Galilee, and was confounded with Olivet, the traditional scene of the ascension. The writer who here quotes from Mark xvi. thus proves his ignorance of Jewish topography. Mount Melek was not in Galilee and was not Olivet, but was the hilly range south of Jerusalem, as is shown by Jewish authorities. Still, the reference to Mount Melek is one of the evidences that the book was written by a converted Jew. The sending out of men to search for Jesus, in chapter xv., is a mere imitation of the account of Elijah. The story which Joseph tells of his miraculous deliverance from prison is a fiction which seems to be peculiar to this book. The name of Longinus, given to the soldier who pierced the Saviour's side, may be regarded as traditional, though it is clearly made out of the Greek word λόγχη, a "lance" or "spear," and means "a spearman." The wonderful change which comes over the Jewish leaders is a fable, and quite inconsistent with the statements in the early chapters of the Acts of the Apostles.

(2.) The second version of Nicodemus is mainly a loose copy of the former. The inscription and title have been materially altered. Before, Ananias was the translator and Nicodemus the author, but here Nicodemus is the translator and Æneas the compiler. I cannot account for the entire change, but I think it probable that Æneas was substituted for Ananias when the account of the journey to the Underworld was added. The name of Æneas was very likely a conscious or unconscious imitation due to the story of Virgil of the descent of Æneas to the Underworld, as found in the Æneid. Again, in the first translation the reader will see that Ananias renders the Hebrew into Greek in the time of Theodosius and Valentinian, but here it is said that the book was translated into Greek as soon as it was written in Hebrew. The copy now under notice is a later revision of the first, and frequently omits expressions to be found in the older document, among which may be mentioned the Hebrew quotations. The Greek is less barbarous, but is still corrupt. A few of the defects of the former book are remedied, but most of them remain, and therefore, for example, they both omit our Lord's appearance before the high priest, the denial of Peter, and other incidents. In the later copy the woman healed by Christ is duly called Berenice or Veronica, which the older book omits. The earlier book says he was to be crucified in the garden where he was taken, but the later drops the statement in stricter harmony with tradition, places the crucifixion at Calvary and introduces a number of additional details.

I suppose this recension of the book to be not older than the sixth century, and to be the work of one who regarded the former as not giving sufficient prominence to Mary. I recommend such as would see how such books were subject to condensation, alteration, and development, carefully to compare the two translations from the Greek of Nicodemus.

(3.) The Gospel of Nicodemus, Part II., or Descent of Christ to the Underworld. The most ancient copies of Nicodemus known are in Latin and Coptic, and neither of them seems to have contained Part II., which is nevertheless frequently found in Greek and Latin MSS. as a continuation of Part I. Dr. Tischendorf's first text of the Descent to the Underworld is in Greek, and is closely connected with the second text of Nicodemus, Part I.; indeed the copies do not mark any division. The first part closes with the demonstration of the resurrection and ascension, and the second opens with a statement that Jesus not only raised himself but others, some of whom soon come upon the stage and record what happened when He went to the Underworld. This pretended revelation is ascribed to two sons of Simeon, who were brought before the chief Jews, and wrote what is here written. Before writing, the two visitants make the sign of the cross on their faces! When they have written they suddenly vanish, leaving their narratives behind them. It is very apparent that this second part was appended as a sort of Odyssey to follow the Iliad. I omit to say more of this fable at present, except that the names of the sons of Simeon are not given in the Greek text which Dr. Tischendorf has followed.

(4.) The Latin Gospel of Nicodemus, or Acts of Pilate, Part I., has a prologue similar to that of the first Greek text, but with some differences; as that Æneas is put for Ananias as translator. The second introduction is also given, and with certain variations. Nicodemus is said to have been the author. These prefaces vary considerably in the copies, some of which in fact either omit them altogether, or place the second at the end of the book. The edition printed in the "Orthodoxographa," in 1555, has no introduction, but at the end is a subscription which says that Theodosius the emperor found the book at Jerusalem in the prætorium of Pilate, and that it had been written in Hebrew by Nicodemus. The Latin text differs in sundry particulars from those in Greek, with which it will be interesting to compare it.

(5.) The second part of the Latin Nicodemus exhibits still further variations from the Greek, and in particular calls the sons of Simeon, Karinus and Leucius. New materials are introduced into it, and especially at the end, where Pilate is said to have written an account of the transactions and placed it among the archives of his prætorium; various calculations are added; and the whole concludes with a pretended letter from Pilate to Claudius. The letter is not found in all copies,[1] nor are the whole of the foregoing calculations. To point out all the discrepancies between the copies would be endless.

(6.) The second text of the Latin Gospel of Nicodemus, Part II., materially deviates from the preceding, and is a more modern recension. The editor in the commencement speaks of the *Abbats* (*i.e.* Fathers) raised from the dead at the resurrection of Christ, he was therefore probably a monk. The last chapter was almost wholly re-written by the editor, who seems to have thought the older books represented Pilate and the Jews in too favourable a light.

Treating both parts of the book before us as one, why is it called by the name of Nicodemus?

Nicodemus was a man of eminence, and had come

[1] This letter appears in Greek in the Acts of Peter and Paul, sec. 40. See Tischendorf's "Acta Apostolorum Apocrypha," p. 16.

to Christ by night to consult him, had ventured to speak for him in a moment of peril, and had taken part in his burial.[1] Hence he is made a prominent character in the book. The Jewish author may have had another motive also, for the name of Nicodemus was borne by a personage famous in Jewish legends.

Why is it called the Acts of Pilate?

Pilate was believed to have written an account of the trial and sufferings of Jesus, which he sent to Rome. Justin and Tertullian confidently appeal to such a document, whether they had seen it or not. The immense value of a composition of the sort would also be evident. Hence the Nicodemus came to be called the Acts of Pilate, as representing similar transactions. That the composition we now have is the original of Pilate, none but a madman could believe. To me it is matter of simple amazement that any one should think our Acts of Pilate are in any sense derived from the materials of Pilate's report; and the more I study them the more I am convinced they are nothing but a forgery of the fifth and sixth centuries. Some of the materials are older, but some are not so ancient, although they sub-

[1] John iii., 1; vii. 50; xix, 39.

stantially belong to the period I mention. The original official Acts perished; the first forged Acts, which continued to exist in the fourth century perished; the Acts forged by order of Maximin also perished; and those now in existence were practically a new composition, so new that they had to be launched as a discovery made in the reign of Theodosius, if not by Theodosius himself.

Dr. Tischendorf thinks that "the Acts of Pilate which have come down to us are not different in the main from those which Justin shows already existed in the second century, save that they are to be regarded as having been gradually and in many ways changed and interpolated." He supposes the great alteration to have taken place about A.D. 424. (De Evangeliorum Apocryphorum Origine et Usu, 1851. pp. 67 et seqq.)

M. Alfred Maury has written an erudite dissertation on this book (Revue de Philologie, etc. tom. ii. no. 5), and concludes that, as we have it, it was written early in the fifth century, perhaps by a converted Jew who made use of an older apocryph or older legends; and that it was indirectly aimed against Apollinarius, who denied the descent into hell.

M. Nicolas discusses the question, but cannot accept the conclusion of Dr. Tischendorf. He says, "What seems to me most decisive against Tischendorf is, that Justin Martyr and Tertullian appeal, or believe they appeal, to *an official document;* without this their arguments have no meaning. Now of the two writings, the Report of Pilate to Tiberius alone affects this form." M. Nicolas is right. The Acts of Pilate, or Gospel of Nicodemus, cannot be what Justin and Tertullian appeal to, because it is not an official document in any sense.

M. Maury considers the first and second parts of Nicodemus to be the work of one author; but Bishop Ellicott believes they are the work of two, and I agree with him. As to the former part of Nicodemus, the bishop follows the opinion of Dr. Tischendorf.

It is not needful for me to carry this enquiry further. I repeat then, that in my opinion the first part of the book was not written earlier than Maury says, and the second part somewhat later. Although the composition of two persons, they were early combined, and probably in the West. Their popularity is shown by the number of versions and MSS., and by the numerous quotations from them found in ancient authors.

One of the stories told in the second part of Nicodemus has been so amazingly popular that it really deserves a separate note. I refer to the legend of Seth, in which we read of the tree of life and the oil of mercy. I have already illustrated this to some extent, but I wish now to add the following observations. The story to which allusion is made may be safely said to be of Jewish origin, or to rest upon a Jewish foundation, and, if the documents were extant, would be traced to the legends and traditions of the Jews in the first ages after Christ. There is tolerably clear indication that the writer of the second part of Nicodemus copied it bodily from some book with which he was acquainted. We read in the first Latin text of the story that Michael told Seth that the Son of God should come after 5500 years (chapter iii. (xix.)). In chapter xii. Pilate speaks to the Jews of a certain great book (*Bibliotheca*) which they have; and soon after the high priests tell Pilate that they have found in the first book of the Septuagint the place where Michael told Seth of the coming of Christ in 5500 years. They add, among other things, that having taken the sum of the successive generations they find the 5500 years which the book says Michael spoke of to Seth. It is easy to believe that the writer had overlooked his first statement, which represents the story as told by Seth in the Underworld. Whether he forgot it or not, he eventually mentions that *the same thing was already written in a book which the Jews had.* I am inclined to believe that the last assertion is perfectly correct.

If I am asked what the writer means by "the first book of the Septuagint," I must own my ignorance. The expression naturally signifies the book of Genesis, but it never contained what is quoted about Michael and Seth; and therefore I conclude the title is either intentionally or accidentally misstated. One thing is certain, however, and it is that Seth cut a great figure in the legends and literary forgeries of the first few centuries of our era. One of the early Christian sects was named after him. All sorts of visions, inventions, etc., were ascribed to him. He was taught by angels, and carried away to heaven for forty days: was the father of the prophets and the inventor of letters, gave names to the stars and observed the motion of the heavens, divided time by months, weeks, etc., wrote a book about the star which should appear at the nativity of Christ, and was the author of many other books. He was also famous amongst the Mohammedans, Sabeans, Samaritans, Ethiopians, Syrians (see Fabricius, "Codex Pseudepigr. Vet. Test." i. 139-157). The journey of Seth to Paradise is then, I suppose, a Jewish Hagadah or pleasant fiction. A curious recension of it is contained in the Greek "Apocalypse of Moses," published by Dr. Tischendorf ("Apocalypses Apocryphæ"). The story is also found in the book called "The Repentance of Adam" (A. Maury, "Croyances et Legendes," p. 294). This last I have not read, but the "Apocalypse of Moses" is a Christian production, and possibly the author of the Appendix to Nicodemus drew this part of his materials from it; whether or no, its existence in these different works makes one doubt the right of any of them to its origination.

An interesting account of the history of the legend of the Oil of Mercy will be found in an article entitled "The Tree of Life," translated from the German of Dr. Piper, in the Journal of Sacred Literature (Oct. 1864). I do not agree with Dr. Piper in referring our document to the second century, but I have pleasure in referring to his curious narration, which first appeared in the "Evangelischer Kalender," for 1863.

The reader who wishes to see more on the subject may consult the notes to Dr. Piper's essay; Dr. Barlow's "Essays on Symbolism" ("The Tree of Life," and "Sacred Trees," first printed in the Journal of Sacred Literature, 1862); Didron's "Iconography," (Bohn's edition, p. 367, et seq.), and the authorities referred to by the different writers.

11. *Letters ascribed to Pilate, etc.*

It was very natural, perhaps, that men should be curious to know what sort of a report of the trial and condemnation of Jesus was sent by Pilate to head quarters. That Pilate did write to Rome on the subject I am quite ready to believe, for not only have we the reiterated assertions of Justin and Tertullian and others to that effect, but we have examples to show what sort of a letter he may have written. The letters of the second Pliny are still extant, and among them are some arising out of his official position and addressed to his masters. Now his famous letter to Trajan about the Christians in Bithynia, affecting the life or death of multitudes, would only occupy about three pages of this volume while Trajan's reply would only take up a few lines.

Have we Pilate's official letter? Certainly not. The so-called Acts of Pilate cannot be distorted into any resemblance to such a thing, and the consciousness of this has led to sundry fictions as to their origin, and even to the supplementing of them with letters said to have been written by Pilate. One such letter will be found translated in this volume at the end of the first Latin version of the Descent to the Underworld. Other similar documents are contained in this collection, as well as one avowedly addressed to Herod, whose so-called letter is also given. Of these I shall now proceed very briefly to speak.

(1.) The letter which Pilate is said to have sent to Cæsar is from a copy found in a Persian "History of Christ," written by a Jesuit named Jerome Xavier in 1602. This book is full of lying legends and fables, and was translated into Latin by De Dieu in 1639. The letter occurs at p. 388 of the translation. De Dieu thinks its author was more likely Xavier than Pilate, and, as I have found it nowhere else, I am inclined to think so too; but since it is fathered upon Pilate I have included it in this collection. The hint for it was probably taken from Josephus, Antiq. xviii. 3, 3. My version is from the Latin, but as the copy I use has been carefully read by the celebrated Oriental scholar Schultens, I think it may be depended upon.

(2.) The Letter of Herod to Pilate.—This is from the Syriac, and may have been forged in the fourth century. Dr. Tischendorf says he has the same in Greek with considerable variations, but it is unpublished.

(3.) The Letter of Pilate to Herod, in reply to the preceding, is from the same source, and equally fictitious. Three extracts are appended to it, but form no portion of it, although joined with it in the manuscript.

(*a.*) The writer called Justinus is not identified, unless, as I think, he is Justus of Tiberias whose history is lost. But if he be meant, the quotation may be false, as Photius says he wrote nothing about Christ.

(*b.*) By Theodorus, no doubt Tiberius is intended. The emperor is represented as asking Pilate a reason for his conduct in reference to Christ. The answer of Pilate to this request is also given. The passage seems to come from an apocryphal book, similar to the so-called "Paradosis" of Pilate, which contains much the same matter.

(*c.*) The extract referred to Josephus is not literally quoted either from him or from the corresponding passage in Eusebius, but it is certain that the version of Eusebius was used. (Josephus, Antiq. xix. 8; Euseb. Hist. Eccles. ii. 10).

(4.) Pilate's Letter to the Roman Emperor.—This is addressed to Tiberius, and is as much intended to excuse Pilate for condemning Jesus, as to speak to the injustice of the Jews in demanding His condemnation. The writer was a Latin, and probably had before him the account which Tacitus gives of the persecution of the Christians by Nero (Annals, xv. 44). He mentions the Sibyls in the same breath with the prophets, speaks of Christ's disciples as still flourishing, and appeals to the Scriptures as proving that the Jews caused the suffering of Christ to their own destruction. The idea of Pilate's quoting the prophets and the Scriptures!

12. *The Report of Pilate.*

Under this head we have a document which pretends to be official, and addressed by Pilate to "Augustus Cæsar in Rome." Some copies represent it as addressed to "Tiberius Augustus." It was first printed by Fabricius. The text as usual varies considerably, and on this account Tischendorf has published it in two forms, both of which I have translated. The first copy is from a MS. of about the twelfth century. The second is also from a MS. of about the same date. No great antiquity has been assigned to the fiction, which seems to have had a Greek origin. Whatever its source, it is based upon the ancient opinion that Pilate sent to Rome a report concerning Christ. I am not able to suggest a date for the production, but the variations in the ancient copies show that it must have been often transcribed. Abraham, Isaac, Jacob, Moses, and Job, are all spoken of as being dead 3500 years. If this may be construed as indicating the date of this composition, it will not allow us to go back beyond the ninth century, which is probably not far wrong.

13. *The Paradosis or Trial and Condemnation of Pilate.*

The Greek *Paradosis* denotes the handing over of something, and may therefore mean Pilate's being delivered into the hands of justice. It contains an account of Pilate's trial before Cæsar at Rome, of his conversion, and of his death by beheading. The writer adds that Procla, Pilate's wife, died of very joy at the time of her husband's death, and that she was buried along with him. The glorification of Pilate was never carried further than here, where a voice from heaven tells him, "All generations and families of nations shall call thee blessed, etc."

14. *The Death of Pilate.*

This treats of the coming of Volusian and Veronica to Rome, and of Tiberius's recovery from disease by means of an image of Christ—the well-known Veronica. Pilate is brought to Rome, where he is perfectly safe for a time, because he has on him the seamless coat of Jesus! After he lays aside this coat he is condemned to death, but kills himself with his own dagger. The body is thrown into the Tiber, but the devils raise such a commotion about it that it is taken up and cast into the Rhone, where similar results follow. Thence it was removed to Losania, (*i.e.* Lucerne) and finally to a pit among the mountains, where it remained, but did not rest at peace.

The bitter animosity to Pilate here exhibited suggests a late date for the composition. I suppose it to be a mediæval Latin production, and as such it was largely used by the editor of the "Legenda Aurea." It was very likely written in France.

15. *The Story of Joseph.*

This is probably not so modern as the "Death of Pilate." The writer seems to have had his eye upon the Nicodemus, but he borrowed from his own fancy and other sources. No particular interest attaches to the details, which are palpably fictitious. Thus Pilate is said to have had a daughter, but she is also said to have had the *Hebrew* name of Sarah. The author's dispositions and tendencies have given an apocalyptic turn to certain parts of the composition. The principal favorite of the author was Saint Good-thief (Sanctus Bonus Latro), as he is called in the proper office for his day (April 24th), and who is here called Demas—a modification of the earlier Dysmas. Tischendorf very properly added this to the pieces which he regards as supplementary to the Acts of Pilate. Some of the notions are decidedly original, such as Christ's writing a letter to the Cherubim and giving it to the deceased robber.

16. *The Saviour's Revenge.*

An old anti-Jewish fiction of Latin origin, and the work of some one who was as ignorant as he was prejudiced. The details are absurd in the extreme, and have some connection with the piece called The Death of Pilate. Like that, it probably is of Gallic origin. A recension of it exists in an Anglo-Saxon book of about the eleventh century (see Anglo-Saxon Legends of Andrew and Veronica. C. W. Goodwin. Cambridge, 1851). Other forms of the story are met with, and most of them indicated by Tischendorf in his prolegomena to the Apocryphal Gospels, pp. 81–83. It shows what rubbish contented the popular taste a thousand years ago. The notion of baptizing Tiberius, and instructing him " in all the articles of the faith," is almost as amusing as connecting the circumstance with the capture of Jerusalem by Titus and Vespasian. The historic accomplishments of the author further appear in his making King Archelaus abdicate and commit suicide on the approach of the Romans (who went simply to avenge the death of Christ! a real holy war! the first crusade!). As a fact, Archelaus was deposed about A.D. 6, and Jerusalem taken sixty-four years later. That Pilate still continued in office at Jerusalem is only what we should expect to be told, but that the author should merely shut him in prison at Damascus, and be content to leave him there, is a favour, or an oversight, which no one would have looked for.

17. *Syriac Gospel of the Boyhood of Jesus.*

By way of supplement to the present volume I have introduced a translation of this which I regard as the oldest form in which the Gospel of Thomas is now known, but not so full as the original. The reader will observe that it is not called the Gospel of Thomas at all, and will, not without reason, infer that, like other books of its class, it changed its title to suit the convenience of its copyists or editors.

ADDITIONAL NOTE.

Besides the documents contained in this volume, there are in existence various titles and fragments of others of the same class, the following list of which is given from Herzog's *Realencyklopädie*, vol. xii. pp. 328-331 :—

1. The Gospel according to the Egyptians.
2. The Eternal Gospel.
3. The Gospel of Andrew.
4. The Gospel of Apelles.
5. The Gospel of the Twelve Apostles.
6. The Gospel of Barnabas.
7. The Gospel of Bartholomew.
8. The Gospel of Basilides.
9. The Gospel of Cerinthus.
10. The Gospel of the Ebionites.
11. The Gospel according to the Hebrews.
12. The Gospel of Eve.
13. The Gospel of James the Less.
14. The Descent from the Cross, by John.
15. The Gospel of Judas Iscariot.
16. The Gospel of Leucius.
17. The Gospels of Lucianus.
18. The Gospels of the Manichæans.
19. The Gospel of Marcion.
20. The Questions of Mary.
21. The Gospel of Matthias.
22. The Legal Priesthood of Christ.
23. The Gospel of Perfection.
24. The Gospel of Peter.
25. The Gospel of Philip.
26. The Gospel of the Simonites.
27. The Gospel according to the Syrians.

28. The Gospel of Tatian.
29. The Gospel of Thaddæus.
30. The Gospel of Valentinus.

Some of these are the same book under various names, and others are not Gospels at all, in any proper sense; as, for instance, No. 29, which is clearly the Acts of Addi, quoted by Eusebius, and for the most part extant in Syriac.[1]

Various extra-evangelical sayings ascribed to Christ have been collected, and some of them may be genuine, but others are very Apocryphal.

Modern forgeries and fictitious narratives are, almost without exception, unworthy of mention, because they are mainly founded upon more ancient documents of the Apocryphal class, and worked up with patristic and more recent fancies. I must, however, observe that extracts from a so-called Gospel of Barnabas have been printed as important. The whole was seen and described by Sale (*Koran*, To the Reader), but the book is called "a most barefaced forgery." It seems to have been extant in Italian and Spanish, the former being apparently the original. Where it now is I do not know. [See Jones on the Canon, Pt. 2, chap. 8.]

---

[1] Cureton's "Ancient Syriac Documents," edited by Dr. W. Wright, contains an English version of this along with the Syriac text.

APOCRYPHAL GOSPELS.

I.

THE GOSPEL OF JAMES.

(COMMONLY CALLED THE PROTEVANGELIUM.)

THE Apocryphal Gospel to which we have given the first place, is extant in several Greek manuscripts, the oldest of which may belong to the eleventh century. It is also found in Arabic, and part of it in Coptic. Its date and authorship are unknown. Dr. Tischendorf thinks it may belong to the middle of the second century. Some have thought it was known to Justin Martyr (Trypho, Ch. 78), to Clement of Alexandria (Stromata, Bk. vii.), and Origen (on Matth.), and perhaps Tertullian (de Scorpiaco, sec. 8), but we cannot be certain. Gregory of Nyssa and Epiphanius, however, either had it, or a closely similar book. Later authors often allude to it.

The title varies in the copies. It is often ascribed to James, though what James is not always stated.

The name Protevangelium was given to it by Postel, who brought it to Europe, soon after which it was printed in Latin (1552, 1555, etc.), and in Greek (1564). Jeremiah Jones translated it into English (1722)

The book contains an account of Joachim and Anna the parents of Mary, and of the wonderful circumstances attending her birth (chaps. i.–v.). Mary is said to have been presented to the Lord at three years old, and brought up in the temple. Here, as in imagining the mother's name, and the birth of the child in answer to prayer, the ideas were probably taken from the history of Samuel. When twelve years old, Mary is placed under the protection of Joseph (chaps. vi.–x.). The annunciation and conception, the jealousy of Joseph and his troubles in consequence of her condition, and the nativity, are narrated at length (chaps. xi.–xxi.). The visit of the Magi, the flight into Egypt, the slaughter of the children by Herod, the escape of John, and the murder of his father, occupy the rest of the book, which closes with a subscription professing to tell the author and occasion of the work (chaps. xxii.–xxv.)

THE GOSPEL OF JAMES; COMMONLY CALLED THE PROTEVANGELIUM OF JAMES.

The Birth of Mary, the Holy Mother of God and Very Glorious Mother of Jesus Christ.

CHAPTER I.

IN the histories[1] of the twelve tribes of Israel there was one Joachim,[2] who was very rich, and he offered his gifts two-fold, saying, There shall be of my substance for all the people, and for my forgiveness with the Lord as a propitiation for me. And the great day of the Lord drew nigh, and the children of Israel offered their gifts. And Reuben the high priest resisted him, saying, It is not lawful for thee to offer thy gifts first, because thou hast not produced seed in Israel. And

---

[1] The author might have more properly said 'genealogies' or 'records,' as his object is simply to intimate the purely Israelitish descent of Mary's parents.

[2] Some think that Mary's father was called Heli, understanding Luke iii. 23, to mean as much. Jerome supposed he was called Cleophas; but we have no evidence that the name Joachim was given him before the appearance of this document. In like manner the name Anna is quite without authority, although both it and Joseph have been adopted by the Greek and Roman churches. Reuben also, as the name of the high priest, is supported by no authority.

Joachim was very grieved, and went to the genealogy of the twelve tribes of the people, saying, I will see the genealogy of the twelve tribes of Israel, whether I alone have not produced seed in Israel. And he sought and found that all the righteous had raised up seed in Israel; and he remembered the patriarch Abraham, that at the last day God gave him his son Isaac. And Joachim was very grieved, and did not show himself to his wife, but betook himself into the wilderness, and there pitched his tent, and fasted forty days and forty nights,[1] saying in himself, I will not go down either for meat or for drink, until the Lord my God shall visit me; and prayer shall be my meat and drink.

CHAPTER II.

Now his wife Anna grieved with double grief, and lamented with a double lamentation, saying, I will bewail my widowhood, and I will bewail my childless condition. And the great day of the Lord drew nigh, and Judith her maiden said, How long dost thou humble thy soul? Behold the great day of the Lord is at hand, and it is not lawful for thee to mourn; but take this headband, which the lady who made it gave to me, and it is not proper

[1] Comp. Matt. iii. 1.

for me to put it on, because I am a servant, and it hath a royal character. And Anna said, Leave me, and, I would not do thus, and, The Lord hath greatly humbled me. Perhaps some crafty person gave thee this, and thou hast come to make me partaker in thy sin. And Judith said, Why shall I curse thee, because the Lord hath closed thy womb, so as not to give thee fruit in Israel? And Anna was very grieved, and took off her mourning garments, and anointed her head, and put on her wedding garments, and about the ninth hour went down into her garden to walk, and she saw a laurel tree, and sat under it, and supplicated the Lord, saying, O God of our fathers, bless me, and hearken to my prayer, as thou didst bless the womb of Sarah, and gavest her a son, Isaac.[1]

CHAPTER III.

AND as she looked towards heaven she saw a nest of sparrows in the laurel tree, and she made a lamentation in herself, saying, Woe is me; who begat me? and what womb bare me? For I have become a curse before the children of Israel, and I am reproached, and they revile me from the temple of the Lord. Woe is me; what am I like unto? I am not like the fowls of heaven, for even the fowls of

[1] Comp. 1 Sam. i. 9-18.

heaven are fruitful before thee, O Lord. Woe is me; what am I like unto? I am not like the beasts of the earth, for even the beasts of the earth are fruitful before thee, O Lord. Woe is me; what am I like unto? I am not like these waters, for even these waters are fruitful before thee, O Lord. Woe is me; what am I like unto? I am not like this earth, for even the earth produceth its fruits in due season, and blesseth thee, O Lord.

CHAPTER IV.

AND, behold, an angel of the Lord stood by, saying unto her, Anna, Anna, the Lord hath heard thy prayer, and thou shalt conceive and bring forth, and thy seed shall be spoken of in all the world. And Anna said, As the Lord my God liveth, if I bring forth either male or female, I will bring it as a gift to the Lord my God, and it shall minister to him all the days of its life. And behold, there came two angels, saying unto her, Behold, Joachim thy husband is coming with his flocks. For an angel of the Lord went down to him, saying, Joachim, Joachim, the Lord God hath heard thy prayer; go down hence: for, behold, thy wife Anna shall conceive. And Joachim went down, and called his shepherds, saying, Bring me hither ten she-lambs without spot and blemish, and they shall be for the Lord my God. And bring me twelve tender calves, and they shall be for the priests and the elders; also a hundred goats for all the people. And behold, Joachim came with his flocks, and Anna stood at the gate, and saw Joachim coming, and she ran and hung upon his neck, saying, Now I know that the Lord God hath blessed me greatly; for behold, the widow is no more a widow, and I that am childless shall conceive. And Joachim rested the first day in his house.

CHAPTER V.

Now on the morrow he offered his gifts, saying in himself, If the Lord God be propitious to me, he will make the plate on the priest's forehead manifest to me. And Joachim offered his gifts, and observed the plate on the priest's forehead, as he went up to the altar of the Lord, and he saw no sin in himself, and Joachim said, Now I know that the Lord is propitious to me, and hath pardoned all my sins.[1] And he went down from the temple of the Lord justified, and departed to his own house.

And her months were accomplished, and in the ninth month Anna bare a child. And she said to the midwife, What have I borne? And she said, A girl. And Anna said, This day my soul is magnified; and she laid it down. And when the days were accomplished, Anna purified herself, and gave the child the breast, and called its name Mary.

[1] Comp. Ex. xxviii. 36-38.

CHAPTER VI.

AND the child increased in strength from day to day, and when she was six months old her mother set her on the ground, to try if she could stand; and having walked seven steps she came to her lap. And she caught her up, saying, As the Lord my God liveth, thou shalt not walk upon this earth, until I bring thee to the temple of the Lord. And she made a sanctuary in her chamber, and suffered nothing common and unclean to pass by her, and called the undefiled daughters of the Hebrews, and they led her about. And the child's first birthday came, and Joachim made a great feast, and called the priests and scribes, and elders, and all the people of Israel. And Joachim brought the child to the priests, and they blessed her, saying, O God of our fathers, bless this child, and give her a name eternally to be named in all generations! And all the people said, So be it, so be it, Amen. And he brought her to the high priests, and they blessed her, saying, O God most High, look upon this child, and bless her with a last blessing which hath none to follow it. And her mother took her up to the sanctuary of her chamber and gave her the breast. And Anna made a song to the Lord God, saying, I will sing a song to the Lord my God, for he hath visited me, and hath removed from me the reproach of my enemies; and the Lord hath given me the fruit of his righteousness, [fruit which is] peculiar and very rich before him. Who shall tell to the children of Reuben that Anna giveth suck? Hearken, hearken, ye twelve tribes of Israel, for Anna giveth suck. And she laid it to rest in the chamber of her sanctuary, and went out and served them. And when the supper was ended they went down rejoicing, and glorifying the God of Israel.

CHAPTER VII.

AND months were added to the child; and the child became two years old, and Joachim said, Let us conduct her to the temple of the Lord, that we may render the vow which we vowed, lest perchance the Lord refuse us, and our gift become unacceptable. And Anna said, Let us wait till the third year, that the child may not require its father or mother. And Joachim said, Let us wait. And the child became three years old, and Joachim said, Call the undefiled daughters of the Hebrews, and let them take a lamp apiece, and let these be burning, that the child may not turn back, and its heart be taken captive from the temple of the Lord. And they did thus until they came up into the temple of the Lord. And the priest received her, and kissed and blessed her, and said, The Lord hath magnified his name in all generations: with thee at the end of days, the Lord will manifest his redemption to the children of Israel. And he set her upon the third step of the altar, and the Lord God bestowed grace upon her, and she danced about on her feet, and all the house of Israel loved her.

CHAPTER VIII.

AND her parents went down wondering, and praising the Lord God, because the child did not turn back. And Mary was like a dove brought up in the temple of the Lord, and received food from the hand of an angel. And when she became twelve years old, there was held a council of the priests, who said, Behold, Mary is become twelve years old in the temple of the Lord. What then shall we do with her, lest perchance the sanctuary of the Lord be defiled? And they said to the high priest, Thou hast stood at the altar of the Lord; go in, and pray for her, and whatever the Lord shall manifest to thee, that also will we do. And the high priest entered, taking the breastplate into the holy of holies, and prayed for her. And behold the angel of the Lord stood by, saying unto him, Zacharias, Zacharias,[1] go forth and summon the widowers of the

---

[1] According to this, Zacharias was the high priest; but the copies differ, and some do not represent him as such.

people, and let them take a rod apiece, and she shall be the wife of him to whom the Lord shall show a sign. And the criers went out through all the region of Judea round about, and the trumpet of the Lord sounded, and all ran together

CHAPTER IX.

Now Joseph cast down his axe and went out to meet them. And having assembled, they went away to the high priest, taking the rods; and he received the rods of all, and entered the holy place and prayed; and when he had finished praying, he took the rods, and went out and delivered them to them; and there was no sign among them. But Joseph received the last rod, and, behold, a dove went out of the rod, and flew upon the head of Joseph. And the priest said to Joseph, Thou hast been allotted to receive the virgin of the Lord to keep with thyself. And Joseph refused, saying, I have sons, and I am old, and she is a girl. Let me not become ridiculous to the children of Israel. And the priest said to Joseph, Fear the Lord thy God; and remember what God did to Dathan, and Abiram, and Korah, how the earth opened, and they were swallowed up because of their gainsaying. And now, fear, Joseph, lest this should come to pass in thy house. And Joseph feared, and took her to keep with himself.

And Joseph said unto Mary, Behold, I have received thee from the temple of the Lord, and now I leave thee in my house, and go to build my buildings, and will come to thee. The Lord will protect thee.

CHAPTER X.

AND there was a council of the priests, who said, Let us make a curtain for the temple of the Lord. And the priest said, Call me undefiled virgins of the house of David. And the servants went and sought and found seven virgins. And the priest recollected the girl Mary, that she was of the tribe of David, and was uncorrupt before God. And the servants went and brought her. And they led them into the temple of the Lord; and the priest said, Cast me lots, who shall spin the gold, and green, and fine linen, and silk, and blue, and scarlet, and true purple. And the true purple and the scarlet fell to the lot of Mary, and she took it and went away to her home. And at that time Zacharias became speechless, and Samuel was in his stead, until Zacharias spake. And Mary took the scarlet and spun it.

CHAPTER XI.

AND she took the waterpot and went out to draw water; and behold a voice, saying, Hail, thou favoured one,[1] the Lord is with thee, blessed art thou among women. And she looked about right and left, to see whence this voice came. And becoming afraid, she went away to her home, and set down the waterpot; and taking the purple she sat on her seat and spun it. And, behold, an angel of the Lord stood before her, saying, Fear not, Mary, for thou hast found favour before the Lord of all, and thou shalt conceive from his word. And when she heard she disputed in herself, saying, Shall I conceive from the Lord, the living God, and bear as every woman beareth? And the angel of the Lord said, Not so, Mary; for the power of the Lord will overshadow thee; wherefore also that holy thing which is born of thee shall be called the son of the Most High; and thou shalt call his name Jesus; for he shall save his people from their sins. And Mary said, Behold, the servant of the Lord is before him; be it unto me according to thy word.

CHAPTER XII.

And she wrought the purple and the scarlet, and took it to the priest. And the priest blessed her, and said, Mary, the Lord God hath magnified thy name, and thou shalt be blessed in all the generations of the earth. And Mary was glad, and went

---

[1] The Greek has κεχαριτωμένη.—Luke i. 28-38.

away to Elizabeth, her kinswoman;[1] and she knocked at the door; and when Elizabeth heard, she threw down the scarlet, and ran to the door and opened it; and seeing Mary, she blessed her, and said, Whence is this to me, that the mother of my Lord should come to me? for, behold, that which is within me, leaped and blessed thee. And Mary was unaware of the mysteries which Gabriel the Archangel[2] told her, and she looked up to heaven, and said, Who am I, Lord, that all the generations of the earth shall bless me? And she spent three months with Elizabeth. And day by day her condition became more manifest; and being afraid, Mary went to her house, and hid herself from the children of Israel. Now she was sixteen[3] years old when these strange things happened.

CHAPTER XIII.

AND her sixth month came, and, behold, Joseph came from his housebuilding; and entering his house he found her pregnant. And he smote his face, and threw himself upon the ground on sackcloth, and wept bitterly, saying, With what face shall I look at the Lord my God? and what shall I

---

[1] Luke i. 39-56.
[2] In Luke i. 26, Gabriel is simply called an 'angel,' and so some read here.
[3] The copies vary, reading 14, 15, 17, and even 18, as well as 16.

entreat concerning this damsel? for I received her a virgin from the temple of the Lord, and have not kept her. Who hath circumvented me? Who hath done this evil in my house, and defiled the virgin? Is not the history of Adam repeated in me? for just as Adam was at the hour of his thanksgiving, and the Serpent came and found Eve alone, and deceived her, so also hath it befallen me. And Joseph arose from his sackcloth, and called Mary, and said to her, Thou that hast been cared for of God, why hast thou done this, and hast forgotten the Lord thy God? why hast thou humbled thy soul, thou that wast brought up in the holy of holies, and didst receive food at the hand of an angel? And she wept bitterly, saying, I am pure and know no man. And Joseph said to her, Whence then is it that thou art pregnant? and she said, As the Lord my God liveth, I know not whence it is come to me.

CHAPTER XIV.

AND Joseph was greatly afraid, and separated from her, and reasoned what he should do with her. And Joseph said, If I hide her fault, I find myself fighting with the law of the Lord; and if I expose her to the children of Israel, I fear lest that which is in her is angelic,[1] and I shall be found betraying innocent blood to the sentence of death. What,

---

[1] For 'angelic' another reading is 'holy.'

then, shall I do with her? I will secretly divorce her from me. And night overtook him; and, behold, an angel of the Lord appeared to him in a dream, saying, Be not afraid about this damsel; for that which she hath conceived is of the Holy Spirit; and she shall bear a son, and thou shalt call his name Jesus; for he shall save his people from their sins. And Joseph arose from sleep, and glorified the God of Israel, who had granted him this favour, and he kept her.[1]

CHAPTER XV.

And Annas, the scribe, came to him, and said to him, Why didst thou not appear in our council? And Joseph said to him, Because I was wearied with the journey, and rested the first day. And he turned and saw Mary pregnant. And he went running to the priest, and said to him, Joseph, whom thou hast attested, hath greatly transgressed. And the priest said, What is this? And he said, The virgin which he received from the temple of the Lord, her he hath defiled, and hath hidden his marriage, and not made it known to the children of Israel. And the priest answered and said, Hath Joseph done this? And Annas the scribe said, Send servants, and thou shalt find the virgin pregnant. And the servants de-

[1] Matt. i. 18–21.

parted, and found as he said; and they brought her away along with Joseph to the place of judgment. And the priest said, Mary, why hast thou done this? and wherefore hast thou humbled thy soul, and hast been forgetful of the Lord thy God? thou that wast brought up in the holy of holies, and didst receive food at the hand of an angel, and didst hear hymns, and didst dance before him; why hast thou done this? And she wept bitterly, saying, As the Lord my God liveth, I am pure before him, and I know not a man. And the priest said to Joseph, What is this that thou hast done? And Joseph said, As the Lord liveth, I am pure in regard to her. And the priest said, Bear not false witness, but say the truth. Thou hast hidden her marriage, and not made it known to the children of Israel, and hast not bowed thine head under the strong hand, that thy seed might be blessed. And Joseph was silent.

CHAPTER XVI.

AND the priest said, Restore the virgin which thou receivedst from the temple of the Lord. And Joseph wept very much. And the priest said, I will cause you to drink the water of the Lord's reproof, and it shall manifest your sins before your eyes.[1] And the priest took and gave it to Joseph to

[1] Num. v. 17.

drink, and sent him into the hill country; and he returned quite sound. And he also gave it to Mary to drink, and sent her into the hill country; and she returned quite sound. And all the people wondered that sin was not seen in them. And the priest said, If the Lord God hath not manifested your sins, neither do I judge you; and he dismissed them. And Joseph took Mary, and went to his house rejoicing, and glorifying the God of Israel.

CHAPTER XVII.

AND there was a command from Augustus the king, that all who were in Bethlehem of Judea should be enrolled.[1] And Joseph said, I will enrol my children, but what shall I do with this damsel? How shall I enrol her? As my wife? I am ashamed to do it. As my daughter? But all the children of Israel know that she is not my daughter. The day of the Lord will itself bring it about as the Lord willeth it. And he saddled the ass, and set her upon it, and his son led it, and Joseph followed. And they came within three miles. And Joseph turned and saw her sad, and he said in himself, Perhaps her burden troubleth her. And Joseph turned again, and saw her laughing; and he said to her, Mary, what aileth thee, because I see thy face at

[1] Luke ii. 1.

one time laughing, and at another time sad? And Mary said to Joseph, I see two peoples with my eyes, one weeping and lamenting, and one rejoicing and exulting. And they came in the midst of the road, and Mary said to him, Take me down from the ass, for my burden urgeth me to be delivered. And he took her down from the ass, and said to her, Whither shall I take thee, and hide thy shame? for the place is desolate.

CHAPTER XVIII.

AND he found a cave there,[1] and took her in, and set his sons by her, and he went out and sought a midwife in the country of Bethlehem. And I Joseph walked, and I walked not;[2] and I looked up into the air, and saw the air violently agitated; and I looked up at the pole of heaven, and saw it stationary, and the fowls of heaven still; and I looked at the earth and saw a vessel lying, and workmen reclining by it, and their hands in the vessel, and those who handled did not handle it, and those who took did not lift, and those who presented it to their mouth did not present it, but the faces of all were looking up; and I saw the sheep scattered, and the sheep stood, and the shepherd lifted up his hand to strike

[1] This cave is mentioned by Justin Martyr.—(*Trypho*,
[2] Here Joseph himself is introduced as the narrator.

them, and his hand remained up; and I looked at the stream of the river, and I saw that the mouths of the kids were down, and not drinking; and everything which was being impelled forward was intercepted in its course.

CHAPTER XIX.

AND I saw a woman coming down from the hill country, and she said to me, O man, whither art thou going? and I said, I am seeking a Hebrew midwife. And she answered and said to me, Art thou of Israel? And I said to her, Yea. And she said, And who is it that bringeth forth in the cave? And I said, She that is espoused to me. And she said to me, Is she not thy wife? And I said to her, It is Mary who was brought up in the temple of the Lord, and she was allotted to me to wife, and she is not my wife, but hath conceived by the Holy Spirit. And the midwife said to him, Is this true? And Joseph said to her, Come and see. And the midwife went with him. And they stood in the place where the cave was, and behold a bright cloud overshadowed the cave. And the midwife said, My soul is magnified to-day, because my eyes have seen strange things; for salvation is born to Israel. And suddenly the cloud withdrew from the cave, and there appeared a great light in the cave, so that their eyes could not bear it. And gradually that light withdrew until the babe was seen, and it came and took the breast from its mother Mary. And the midwife cried out and said, To day is a great day to me, for I have seen this novel sight. And the midwife went out of the cave, and Salome met her; and she said to her, Salome, Salome, I have a novel sight to tell thee: A virgin hath brought forth, which is not in accordance with the course of nature.[1] And Salome said, As the Lord my God liveth, except I put out my hand and examine her, I will not believe that a virgin hath brought forth.

CHAPTER XX.

AND the midwife went in, and said to Mary, Arrange thyself; for there is no small contest about thee. And Salome stretched out her hand to her, and she shrieked, and said, Woe to my wickedness and unbelief, for I have tempted the living God; and lo, my hand is on fire, and falls away from me. And she bowed her knees to the Lord, saying, O God of my fathers, remember me that I am of the seed of Abraham, and Isaac, and Jacob. Make me not an example to the children of Israel, but restore me to the poor; for thou knowest, O Lord, that in

---

[1] Latin, "quem non capit natura ipsius, et virgo manet virgo." The Greek is "What her nature doth not contain." I give the probable sense.

thy name I performed my cures, and received my reward from thee. And, behold, an angel of the Lord stood by, saying to her, Salome, Salome, the Lord hath heard thee: present thy hand to the child, and lift it, and there shall be to thee salvation and joy. And Salome came near, and lifted him up, saying, I will worship him, for a great king is born to Israel; and lo, Salome was straightway healed, and went out of the cave justified. And, behold, a voice, saying, Tell not the strange things thou hast seen until the child shall enter into Jerusalem.

CHAPTER XXI.

AND behold Joseph made ready to go into Judea. And there was a great tumult in Bethlehem of Judea; for Magi came, saying, Where is he that is born king of the Jews? for we have seen his star in the East, and are come to worship him.[1] And when Herod heard, he was troubled; and sent his servants to the Magi, and sent for the high priests, and examined them, saying, How is it written concerning the Christ? Where is he born? They say to him, In Bethlehem of Judea; for so it is written. And he dismissed them. And he examined the Magi saying unto them, What sign did ye see of the king that is born? And the Magi said, We saw a very

[1] Matt. ii. 1-12; Mic. v. 2.

great star shining among these stars and dimming them, so that the stars were not seen. And thus we knew that a king was born unto Israel, and came to worship him. And Herod said, Go and search; and if ye find him, tell it me, that I too may come and worship him. And the Magi departed. And behold, the star which they saw in the East, led them until they came to the cave, and it stood at the entrance of the cave. And the Magi saw the child with his mother Mary, and they took out of their scrip, gold, and frankincense, and myrrh. And being warned by the angel not to go into Judea, they went to their country by another way.

CHAPTER XXII.

AND when Herod knew that he was deluded by the Magi, he was angry and sent assassins, saying unto them, Slay the infants from two years old and under.[1] And when Mary heard that they slew the infants, she was afraid and took the child and swathed it and put it in a crib for oxen. And Elizabeth, hearing that John was sought for, took him and went up into the hill country, and looked for somewhere to hide him; and there was no place of concealment.[2] And Elizabeth groaned

[1] Matt. ii. 16–18.
[2] No such story is traceable in the New Testament.

and said with a loud voice, Mount of God, receive a mother with her child. And suddenly the mountain was divided and received her. And light shone through to them; for the angel of the Lord was with them, preserving them.

CHAPTER XXIII.

AND Herod sought after John, and sent his servants to Zacharias, saying, Where hast thou hidden thy son? And he answered and said to them, I am the minister of God, and I am busied with the temple of the Lord, I know not where my son is. And the servants went away and reported to Herod all these things, and Herod was angry and said, His son is going to be king of Israel. And he sent to him again, saying, Tell the truth; where is thy son? for thou knowest that thy blood is under my hand. And Zacharias said, I am a witness for God, if thou dost shed my blood; for the Lord will receive my spirit, for thou sheddest innocent blood in the porch of the Lord's temple. And about daybreak Zacharias was slain; and the children of Israel knew not that he was slain.

CHAPTER XXIV.

BUT at the hour of greeting the priests went, and the blessing of Zacharias did not meet them according to custom. And the priests stood waiting for Zacharias, to greet him with prayer, and to glorify the Most High. And when he tarried they were all afraid; but one of them ventured and went in and perceived near the altar, blood congealed, and a voice saying, Zacharias is murdered, and his blood shall not be wiped out until his avenger cometh.[1] And when he heard the word he was afraid, and went out and told the priests; and they ventured and went in and saw what had occurred. And the wainscotings of the temple shrieked out, and were cleft from top to bottom. And they found not his body, but found his blood turned into stone. And they were afraid and went out, and told the people that Zacharias was murdered. And all the tribes of the people heard, and mourned for him, and lamented three days and three nights. And after the three days the priests took counsel whom they should appoint instead of him. And the lot fell upon Simeon;[2] for he it was who was admonished by the Holy Spirit, that he should not see death, until he saw the Christ in the flesh.

CHAPTER XXV.

Now I, James, who wrote this history in Jeru-

[1] The idea that the blood of a murdered man cannot be washed out is very ancient; it frequently appears in the writings of early Christian travellers, and still prevails to some extent even in England.

[2] The New Testament leads to the conclusion that Simeon was not a priest.—Luke ii. 25-32.

salem, because a tumult arose when Herod died, withdrew myself into the wilderness, until the tumult ceased in Jerusalem, glorifying the Lord God who gave me the gift and the wisdom to write this history. And grace shall be with those who fear our Lord Jesus Christ, to whom be glory for ever and ever, Amen.

II.

THE GOSPEL OF PSEUDO-MATTHEW,

OR OF THE INFANCY OF MARY AND OF JESUS.

This composition is extant in Latin in different forms. Thilo published a recension of it containing chaps. i.–xxv., and ending with the return of Joseph, Mary, and Jesus from Egypt; but the text followed by Tischendorf, and here translated, includes a narration of subsequent occurrences. Two letters relating to some such document are by Tischendorf prefixed to this, and probably he is right, but it has not been deemed necessary to give them here. The first letter pretends to be addressed to Jerome by two bishops, Chromatius and Heliodorus, requesting him to translate it out of Hebrew. The second letter, in the name of Jerome, refers to the fulfilment of the request, and ascribes the book to a certain Leucius, a Manichæan. Both letters must be rejected as spurious, but the work itself may belong to the fifth century. The Scripture texts quoted do not always accord with the version of Jerome, but some of them are directly rendered from the Greek of the LXX. The original may have been in Greek; certainly there is good reason for believing it not to have been in Hebrew. No one translating from Hebrew into Latin would be likely to go to the LXX. for his rendering of texts of Scripture

The writer repeats with many variations from the Protevangelium, the story of Mary's parents, birth, and infancy (chaps. i.–viii.). He then narrates the Annunciation and the events which followed till the birth of Jesus (chaps. ix.–xiii.). After these he gives us accounts of the Circumcision, the visit of the Magi, the slaughter of the infants, and the flight into Egypt (chaps. xiv.–xvii.). The journey to Egypt and sojourn there (chaps. xviii.–xxv.) are followed by a series of miraculous deeds which Jesus is said to have performed in his childhood (chaps. xxvi.–xlii.). The miraculous element is puerile and ridiculous, and shows clearly that the author or authors ill understood the true spirit of Christ.

THE GOSPEL OF PSEUDO-MATTHEW.

The Book of the Birth of the Blessed Mary and of the Infancy of the Saviour. Written in Hebrew by the Blessed Evangelist Matthew, and translated into Latin by the Blessed Presbyter Jerome.

CHAPTER I.

IN those days there was a man in Jerusalem by name Joachim, of the tribe of Judah. He was the shepherd of his sheep, fearing the Lord in his simplicity and goodness. He had no care but that of his flocks, with the produce whereof he nourished all who feared God, and offered double presents in the fear of God to the labourers in doctrine[1] who ministered to him. Therefore, whether of lambs, or sheep, or wool, or any of his goods, of whatever he saw that he possessed, he made three portions: one part he bestowed upon the orphans, widows, and strangers, and poor; a second part he gave to them that worshipped God; the third part he reserved for himself and all his house. Now while he did these things, the Lord

---

[1] Comp. 1 Tim. v. 17. Here and elsewhere the readings of the copies vary to an almost incredible degree.

so multiplied his flocks that there was no man like him among the people of Israel. This then he began to do when he was fifteen years of age. When he was twenty years old, he took Anna, the daughter of Achar,[1] to wife, of his own tribe, that is, of the tribe of Judah of the stock of David. And when they had remained together twenty years, he had no sons nor daughters by her.

CHAPTER II.

Now it came to pass that on the feast days Joachim stood among those who offered incense to the Lord, preparing his gifts in the presence of the Lord. And the priest, Reuben by name, came to him and said, It is not lawful for thee to stand among those who perform the sacrifices of God, because God hath not blessed thee to give thee a branch in Israel. Therefore being put to shame in the sight of the people, he retired weeping from the temple of the Lord, and did not return home, but went away to his sheep, taking with him the shepherds to the mountains in a far off land, so that Anna his wife could hear no message from him for five months. She meanwhile wept in her prayer, and said, O Lord God of Israel, most mighty, seeing that thou hast not yet given me sons, why hast thou also taken my husband from

---

[1] There is no historical foundation for this name. The author imitates, alters, and adds to the Protevangelium according to his fancy.

me? Behold, for five months already, I have not seen my husband. And I know not where he tarrieth: if I only knew that he was dead, I would perform his funeral ceremonies. And as she wept exceedingly, she went into the garden of her house, prostrating herself in prayer, and poured out her petitions before the Lord. After this she rose from prayer, and as she lifted up her eyes to God, she saw a nest of sparrows in a laurel tree, and uttered her voice to the Lord with groaning and said, O Lord God Almighty, who hast given offspring to every creature, to beasts and cattle, to serpents and fowls and fish, and all rejoice in their offspring,—me alone dost thou exclude from the gift of thy bounty. For thou, God, knowest my heart, that from the beginning of my marriage, I confess to have made this vow, that if thou, O God, shouldst give me son or daughter I would offer them to thee in thy holy temple. And, while she said these things, suddenly the angel of the Lord appeared before her face, saying, Fear not, Anna, for thy offspring is in the purpose of God; for that which shall be born of thee shall be in admiration to all ages unto the end. And when he had said this, he vanished from her sight. But she, fearing and trembling because she had seen such a vision and heard such a saying, at length entered her chamber, and threw herself on her bed, as if she were dead. And all day and night she continued in excessive trembling and in prayer. But after this she called her maidservant to her, and said to her, Thou seest me in widowhood deceived, and brought into tribulation, and wast thou unwilling to come in to me? Then she, with a little complaining, answered thus, saying, If God hath closed thy womb, and taken thy husband from thee, what am I to do for thee? When Anna heard this, she cried with a loud voice and wept.

CHAPTER III.

At the same time there appeared a certain young man unto Joachim on the mountains where he fed his flocks, and said to him, Wherefore dost thou not return to thy wife? And Joachim said, For twenty years, I have had her, and God would not give me children by her. I therefore, when reproached, went forth with shame from the temple of the Lord. Why should I return to her, when I have been once degraded and greatly despised? Here then will I be with my sheep. And so long as the God of this world will grant me light, I will willingly, by the hands of my servants, bestow their portions upon the poor and orphans and them that worship God. And when he had said this the young man answered him, I am the angel of God, and have appeared to-day to thy wife, who was weeping and praying, and I have comforted her. Thou shouldst know she hath conceived a daughter by thee, and thou not knowing hast left her. She shall be in the temple of God, and the Holy Spirit shall rest on her; and her blessedness shall be beyond that of all holy women, so that none can say that any hath been like her before her, or shall be after her in this world. Therefore go down from the mountains and return to thy wife, whom thou shalt find pregnant; for God hath raised seed by her, for which give thanks to God, and her seed shall be blessed, and she shall be blessed, and shall be constituted mother of eternal benediction. Then Joachim, adoring the angel, said to him, If I have found favour before thee, sit a little in my tent and bless thy servant. And the angel said to him, Do not call thyself servant, but fellow-servant, for we are servants of one Lord. Besides, my food is invisible, and my drink can be seen by no mortal. Therefore thou oughtest not to ask me to enter thy tent; but if thou wast about to give me anything, offer it for a burnt offering to the Lord. Then Joachim took an unspotted lamb, and said to the angel, I should not have dared to offer a burnt offering to the Lord, unless thy command had given me priestly authority to offer it. And the angel said to him, I should not ask thee to offer unless I knew the Lord's will. Now when Joachim offered the sacrifice to God, the angel and the perfume of the sacrifice went up to heaven together with the smoke.

Then Joachim cast himself down upon his face, and lay in prayer from the sixth hour of the day until the evening. Now when his servants and hirelings saw, and knew not for what cause he lay there, they thought him to be dead, and, coming to him, almost raised him from the ground. But when he had told them the vision of the angel, smitten with exceeding fear and wonder, they urged him that without delay, he should carry out the vision of the angel, and speedily return to his wife. And when Joachim turned the matter over in his mind, and thought whether he should return or not, it came to pass that he was overcome with sleep, and behold, the angel which had already appeared to him while awake, appeared to him in sleep, saying, I am an angel and am given thee by God as a guardian; go down in confidence, and return to Anna, because the kind acts which thou and thy wife Anna have done are rehearsed in the presence of the Most High; and God will give you such fruit as neither the prophets nor any saint ever had from the beginning, nor shall have. Now when Joachim had awaked from sleep, he called all his herdsmen to him, and told them the dream. And they adored the Lord, and said to him, Take heed not to contemn the sayings of the angel any further. But arise, let us go hence, and let us return at a slow pace, feeding our flocks.

When they had tarried the space of thirty days on their return, and were now nigh,[1] behold, the angel of the Lord appeared to Anna as she stood and prayed, saying to her, Go to the gate which is called the Golden Gate,[2] and meet thy husband in the way, for to-day he will return to thee. She therefore went out in haste to meet him, with her maidens, and, praying to the Lord, she stood in the gate a long time waiting for him. When she was growing faint with very long expectation, she raised her eyes and saw Joachim afar off coming with his flocks; and she met him, and hung upon his neck, giving thanks to God, and saying, I was a widow, and lo, I am not one now; I was barren, and, behold, I have already conceived. So then, having worshipped the Lord, they entered the house. When this was heard, great joy was caused to all his neighbours and acquaintances, so that the whole land of Israel was gladdened by this report.

CHAPTER IV.

Now when nine months were completed after

[1] The thirty days of slow travelling here can hardly be reconciled with the five months mentioned in chap. ii.
[2] The Golden Gate is not regarded by modern writers as a gate of the city of Jerusalem, but of the temple. In the Protevangelium, chap. iv., the gate of Joachim's residence alone is intended, and in some copies distinctly affirmed.

this, Anna brought forth a daughter, and called her Mary. When she had weaned her in her third year, Joachim and Anna his wife, went together to the temple of the Lord, to offer sacrifices to God, and placed the babe that was named Mary in the apartment of virgins, wherein virgins continued day and night in the praises of God.[1] When she had been set before the gates of the temple, she went up the fifteen steps[2] at such a rapid pace, that she did not at all look back, nor ask for her parents as is usual with infancy. Her parents, therefore, being anxious, and each of them asking for the infant, were both alike astonished, till they found her in the temple, so that even the very priests of the temple marvelled.

CHAPTER V.

THEN Anna was filled with the Holy Spirit in the sight of all, and said, The Lord Almighty God of

[1] This tradition of young virgins being kept in the temple rests on no historical foundation, though it has been strongly defended by later writers.

[2] The 'fifteen steps (quindecim gradus) correspond with the fifteen Psalms of *degrees* (Psalms 120-134). Some believe that there were fifteen steps leading from the court of women up to that of the priests. Other explanations have been offered, but no reliance can be placed upon the author, whom one reading makes to say, after mentioning the steps: "For there were about the temple—according to the fifteen Psalms of degrees—fifteen steps to ascend: the temple was on a mount, and there was constructed there the altar of burnt offering, which could not be reached from without except by steps." Comp. the Gosp. of the Nativity of Mary, chap. vi. This last statement about the steps around the altar is perhaps correct.

hosts, being mindful of his word, hath visited his people with a good and holy visitation, to humble the hearts of the nations who rose up against us, and to convert them to himself. He hath opened his ears to our prayers, he hath banished from us the exultations of all our enemies. She that was barren is made a mother, and hath borne exultation and joy to Israel. Behold, I was set to offer gifts to my Lord, and my enemies could not prevent me. But God hath turned their heart towards me, and he hath given me eternal joy.

CHAPTER VI.

Now Mary was in admiration with all the people of Israel. When she was three years old, she walked with so firm a step, spoke so perfectly, and was so assiduous in the praises of God, that all were astonished at her, and marvelled; and she was not regarded as a little child, but as an adult of about thirty years, she was so earnest in prayer. And her face was beautiful and splendid, to such a degree that scarcely any one could look upon her countenance. Now she applied herself to wool-work, so that whatever the elder women could not do, she accomplished when set to it in her tender age. And she adopted this rule for herself, that she would continue in prayer from morning until the third hour; from the third to the ninth she would occupy herself at her weaving and from the ninth again she would apply herself to prayer. Nor did she retire from prayer until an angel of God appeared to her, from whose hand she received food; and so she advanced more and better in the work of God. Further, when the elder virgins left off the praises of God, she did not leave off, so that in God's praises and vigils no one was found before her, nor any more skilled in the wisdom of God's law, more humble in humility, more beautiful in singing, or more perfect in all virtue. Indeed, she was constant, immoveable, unalterable, and daily advanced to better things. None saw her angry, or heard her reviling. For all her speech was so full of grace, that God might be known to be in her tongue. She was ever diligent in prayer and in searching of the law, and was anxious not to sin by any word against her companions. Moreover, she feared to make any mistake in laughter or by the sound of her lovely voice, or lest any insult or pride should show itself against her equals. She blessed the Lord without intermission; and lest perchance even in her salutations she should cease from God's praise, if any one saluted her, she answered by way of salutation, Thank God! From her it first originated that men, when they would salute each other, replied, Thank God! With the food which she daily received from the hand of the angel she refreshed herself alone; but she distributed to the poor the food which she received from the priests. The angels of God were frequently seen to talk with her, and they most diligently obeyed her. If any one that was sick touched her, that same hour he returned home whole.

CHAPTER VII.

THEN Abiathar the priest[1] offered infinite gifts to the high priests, that he might receive her for a wife for his son. But Mary forbad them, saying, It cannot be that I should know man, or man know me. Now the high priests and all her kindred said to her, God is honoured in children, and is adored in posterity, as it ever was among the children of Israel. But Mary answered and said to them, God is honoured in chastity, so that it is approved before all things; for before Abel there was none just among men, and he pleased God by offerings, and he was mercilessly slain by him who displeased God. Therefore he received the two crowns of offering and of virginity, because he admitted no pollution in his flesh. Elijah, too, when he was in the flesh, was taken up in the flesh because he preserved his flesh

[1] Abiathar is called the high priest in the next chapter; but nothing is known of him.

in its virginity. Now, from my infancy I have learned in the temple of God that virginity could be sufficiently dear to God; and therefore, because I can offer what is dear to God, I have decreed to him in my heart that I would not at all know man.

CHAPTER VIII.

Now it came to pass, that when she was fourteen years of age, and this gave occasion to the Pharisees to say that according to custom a woman of that age could not remain in the temple of God, a decision of this kind was come to, that a crier should be sent among all the tribes of Israel, (saying) that all should meet on the third day, at the temple of the Lord. Now when all the people had met, Abiathar, the high priest, arose, and ascended to the upper step, so that he could be heard and seen by all the people; and when great silence was made, he said, Hear me, O children of Israel, and receive my words in your ears. Since this temple was built by Solomon, there have been therein virgins, the daughters of kings, and the daughters of prophets, and of high priests, and of priests, and they have been great and admirable. But when they have come to a lawful age, they have been given in marriage to husbands, and have followed the course of their precursors, and have pleased God. But by

Mary alone a new order of life has been invented, and she promiseth God that she will remain a virgin. Wherefore it seems to me, that by our inquiry and the answer of God, we should seek to know to whom she ought to be committed to be kept. Then his saying pleased all the synagogue. And the lot was cast by the priests for the twelve tribes, and the lot fell upon the tribe of Judah. And the priest said, On the next day, let whoever is without a wife come and bring a rod in his hand. Wherefore it came to pass, that Joseph brought a rod along with the younger men. And when they had delivered their rods to the high priest, he offered sacrifice to the Lord God, and asked of the Lord; and the Lord said to him, Put the rods of all in God's holy of holies, and there let the rods remain, and bid them come to thee in the morning to receive their rods, and to him from the top of whose rod a dove shall come forth and fly to heaven, and in whose hand the rod, when returned, shall give this sign, Mary shall be delivered to be kept.

Now on the next day, when they all came early, and an offering of incense had been made, the high priest went into the holy of holies and brought out the rods. And when he had given a rod to each, and a dove had not gone forth from any, the chief priest arrayed himself with twelve bells and a priestly robe and went into the holy of holies and burned sacrifice and poured out prayer there. And an angel of God appeared, saying, There is here a very short rod which thou hast counted for nothing, and hast placed it with the rest, but hast not taken it out with the rest: when thou hast taken that out and given to him to whom it belongs, there shall appear in it the sign which I have spoken to thee of. It was the rod of Joseph, and because he was old he was as it were discarded, as though he could not receive it; but neither would he himself ask for his rod. And when he stood, humble and the last, the chief-priest with a loud voice cried to him, saying, Come Joseph, and receive thy rod, because thou art waited for. And Joseph came fearing, because the high priest called him with so very loud a voice. But straightway as he stretched out his hand to receive his rod, immediately a dove went forth from its top, whiter than snow and most beautiful, and fluttering a long time among the pinnacles of the temple, at last it flew towards the heavens. Then all the people congratulated the old man, saying, Thou art become blessed in thy old age, father Joseph, in that God hath shown thee fit to receive Mary. And when the priests had said to him, Take her, for out of all the tribe of Judah thou alone art elected by God, Joseph began to worship them with modesty, saying, I am old and have sons, and why do ye deliver to me this little child, whose age is less even than that of my grandchildren? Then Abiathar the chief priest said to him, Remember, Joseph, how Dathan and Abiram and Korah perished, because they contemned the will of God. So will it happen to thee if thou contemnest what is commanded thee by God. Joseph answered him, I do not contemn the will of God, indeed, but I will be her keeper until I know this by the will of God,—which of my sons can have her to wife. Let there be given her certain virgins of her companions for a solace, with whom she may meanwhile abide. Abiathar the chief priest answered, saying, Five[1] virgins shall be given, indeed, for her solace, until the day appointed cometh in which thou shalt take her, for she cannot be joined to another in matrimony.

Then Joseph took Mary with five other virgins, who were to be with her in the house of Joseph. Now these virgins were Rebecca, Zipporah, Susanna, Abigea, and Cael, to whom there was given by the chief priest, silk and blue, and fine linen, and scarlet, and purple, and flax. And they cast lots among themselves what each virgin should do; and it fell out that Mary received the purple for the veil of the temple of the Lord. When she had received it, the virgins said, Since thou art the last, and humble, and less than all, thou hast deserved to receive and obtain the purple. And saying this, as though in a vexa-

[1] Seven virgins are assigned in the Protevangelium, chap. x.

tious speech, they began to call her the queen of virgins. Therefore, while they did thus among themselves, an angel of the Lord appeared among them saying unto them, That saying shall not be uttered for vexing, but prophesied for a most true prophecy. Therefore, being terrified at the presence of the angel and at his words, they asked her to pardon them and pray for them.

CHAPTER IX.

Now on the second day, while Mary stood near the fountain to fill her pitcher, the angel of the Lord appeared unto her, saying, Blessed art thou Mary, for in thy womb thou hast prepared a habitation for the Lord. Behold, light from heaven shall come and dwell in thee, and through thee shall shine in all the world.

Again on the third day, while she wrought the purple with her fingers, there came in to her a young man whose beauty could not be told. When Mary saw him she feared and trembled. And he said to her, Hail Mary! full of grace, the Lord is with thee; blessed art thou among women, and blessed is the fruit of thy womb.[1] When she heard this she trembled and feared. Then the angel of the Lord

[1] The author of the Protevangelium represents this salutation as uttered at the fountain. The words are, however, here introduced more in harmony with Luke i. 28.

added, Fear not Mary, thou hast found favour with God; behold, thou shalt conceive in thy womb and shalt bear the king who filleth not only earth but heaven, and reigneth for ever and ever.

CHAPTER X.

WHILE these things were doing, Joseph was busy at work in making tabernacles in the maritime regions; for he was a carpenter. But after nine months he returned to his house and found Mary with child. Wherefore being in a great strait, he trembled, and cried, saying, Lord God, receive my spirit; for it is better for me to die than to live longer. The virgins who were with Mary said to him, What sayest thou, master Joseph? We know that man hath not touched her: we are witnesses that virginity and integrity remain in her. We have kept ward over her: she hath ever continued in prayer with us; the angels of God daily talk with her; daily hath she received food from the hand of the Lord.[1] We know not how it can be that any sin should be in her. For if thou wishest us to reveal to thee our surmise, no one hath made her pregnant but the angel of the Lord. Joseph said, Why do you mislead me to believe you, that an angel of the Lord

[1] *Cf.* 1 Kings, xix. 5. In the Protevangelium, chap. viii., it is said that Mary received her food from the hand of an angel. See also chap. xii., below.

hath made her pregnant? For it may be that some one hath feigned himself an angel of the Lord and deceived her. And saying these things he wept and said, With what face shall I look to the temple of the Lord, or with what face shall I see the priests of God? What am I to do? And saying this, he thought he would flee and send her away.

CHAPTER XI.

And while he thought to rise and hide himself, and to dwell in secret, behold the same night an angel of the Lord appeared to him in sleep, saying, Joseph, son of David, fear not; take Mary thy wife, for that which is in her womb, is of the Holy Spirit. Now she shall bear a son, and his name shall be called Jesus, for he shall save his people from their sins.[1] And Joseph, rising from sleep, gave thanks to God, and spoke to Mary and the virgins who were with her, and told his vision. And he was comforted concerning Mary, saying, I have sinned, in that I had some suspicion of thee.

CHAPTER XII.

After this there arose a great rumour that Mary was with child. And Joseph was laid hold of and led by the ministers of the temple, with Mary, to the

[1] *Cf.* Matt. i. 20-24, in the Latin Vulgate.

chief priest, who together with the priests began to reproach him and to say, Why hast thou wronged her who is such and so eminent a virgin, whom as a dove the angels of God nourished in the temple, who would never see nor have a husband, and who had the best learning in the law of God? If thou hadst not done violence to her, she had still remained in her virginity. And Joseph took a solemn oath that he had never touched her at all. The chief priest Abiathar answered him, As God liveth, I will now cause thee to drink the water of the Lord's drinking,[1] and forthwith thy sin will appear.

Then there gathered together a multitude of people which could not be numbered, and Mary was brought to the temple. Now the priests, and her relatives and her parents, weeping said to Mary, Confess to the priests thy sin, thou who wast as a dove in the temple of God, and used to receive food from the hand of an angel.

Joseph again was called to the altar and there was given to him the water of the Lord's drinking, which when anybody who told a lie had tasted he went round the altar seven times, and God gave a certain sign in his face. When therefore Joseph had drunk it without fear, and had gone round the altar seven times, no sign of sin appeared in him. Then

---

[1] A Hebraism; for the water which the Lord commanded to be drunk.

all the priests and attendants and people justified him, saying, Thou art become blessed, because no guilt is found in thee.

And they called Mary and said to her, And what excuse canst thou have? or what greater sign will appear in thee than this, that thy pregnancy betrayeth thee? This only we ask of thee, since Joseph is pure concerning thee, that thou shouldst confess who it is that deceived thee. For it is better that thy confession should expose thee, than that the anger of God should make thee manifest among the people by giving a sign in thy face. Then Mary confidently and intrepidly said, O Lord God, the King of all, who art conscious of secret things, if there is any pollution in me, or any sin, or any lust or immodesty, reveal me in the sight of all peoples, that I may be an example for the correction of all. Having said this she approached the altar of the Lord with confidence, and drank the water for drinking, and went round the altar seven times, and there was found no spot in her.[1]

And when all the people were beside themselves with amazement, seeing her pregnancy and that no sign appeared in her face, the people began, with varied talk together, to be troubled. Some said she was holy and spotless, but others that she was bad and defiled. Then Mary, seeing she was held in

[1] Lev. v. 14, etc.

suspicion of the people, and did not seem to them to be entirely cleared, said with a loud voice in the hearing of all, As the Lord Adonai liveth, the Lord of hosts in whose presence I stand, I have never known man; but I am known by Him to whom from my infancy I have devoted my mind. And I made this vow to my God from my infancy, that with him who created me I would abide in integrity, wherein I trust to live to him alone, and serve him alone: and as long as I live in him I shall abide without defilement. Then they all began to kiss her feet, and to embrace her knees, praying her to pardon their evil suspicions. And the people and priests and all the virgins led her with exultation and great joy to her house, crying out and saying, The name of the Lord be blessed for ever, for he hath manifested thy holiness to all his people Israel.

CHAPTER XIII.

Now it came to pass after some little time, that a registration took place, according to the edict of Augustus Cæsar, that all the world was to be registered every man in his own native place. This registration was made by Cyrinus, the president of Syria.[1] It was needful, therefore, that Joseph should be registered with the blessed Mary in Bethlehem,

[1] Luke ii. 1, etc.

because thence came Joseph and Mary, of the tribe of Judah, and of the house and family of David. When, therefore, Joseph and the blessed Mary were going by the way which leads to Bethlehem, Mary said to Joseph, I see two peoples before me, the one weeping, and the other rejoicing. And Joseph answered her, Sit on thy beast, and do not speak superfluous words. Then there appeared before them a certain beautiful youth, clothed in white array, and he said to Joseph, Why didst thou call superfluous the words concerning the two peoples of whom Mary hath spoken? For she saw the people of the Jews weeping, who have departed from their God, —and the people of the Gentiles rejoicing, who have now approached and are made nigh to the Lord, as he promised our fathers Abraham, Isaac, and Jacob; for the time is come that in the seed of Abraham a blessing should be bestowed on all nations.[1]

And when he had said thus, the angel commanded the beast to stop, for her time to bear had come; and he directed the blessed Mary to come down from the animal, and to enter a cave below a cavern, in which there was never any light, but always darkness, because it could not receive the light of day. And when the blessed Mary had entered it, it began to become all light with brightness, as if it had been

[1] Gen. xii. 3.

the sixth hour of the day; divine light so illumined the cave, that light did not fail there by day or night, as long as the blessed Mary was there. And there she brought forth a male child, whom angels instantly surrounded at his birth, and whom, when born and standing at once upon his feet, they adored, saying, Glory to God on high, and on earth peace to men of good will.[1] For the nativity of the Lord had already come, and Joseph was gone to seek midwives. When he had found them, he returned to the cave, and found Mary with the infant she had borne. And Joseph said to the blessed Mary, I have brought thee Zelomi and Salome the midwives, who stand without before the door of the cave, not daring to enter here for the too great splendour. And the blessed Mary smiled at hearing this. And Joseph said to her, Do not smile, but be cautious, that they may visit thee, lest perchance thou shouldest require medicine. Then she bade them enter unto her. And when Zelomi had come in, Salome not having come in, Zelomi said to Mary, Allow me to touch thee. And when she had suffered herself to be examined, the midwife cried with a loud voice, and said, O Lord, great Lord, have mercy! Never hath it been heard, or suspected, that the breasts of any woman should be full of milk, and the child born show its mother to be a virgin. But as there

[1] Luke ii. 14; Justin, *Trypho*, sect. 78.

is no defilement of blood on the child, there is no pain in the mother. A virgin hath conceived, a virgin hath borne, and a virgin she hath continued.[1] And when Salome heard this word, she said, Suffer me to touch thee, and to prove whether Zelomi hath said the truth. And when the blessed Mary had consented to be touched by her, Salome put out her hand. But when she withdrew her hand from touching her, her hand dried up, and through excessive pain she began to weep violently and to be distressed, crying and saying, Lord God, Thou knowest that I have always feared thee, and have healed all the poor without reward, of the widow and orphan I have taken nothing, and I have not permitted the needy to go from me empty. And lo, I am made wretched because of my unbelief, for without cause I wished to test thy virgin.

When she said this, there appeared near her a certain youth, who was very splendid, saying to her, Approach the infant and adore him, and touch him with thy hand, and he shall deliver thee; for he is the Saviour of the world and of all who hope in him. And she straightway approached the infant, and adoring him, touched the border of the cloths in which the infant was wrapped, and immediately her hand was healed. And going forth she began to

---

[1] The perpetual virginity of Mary is referred to by Clemens Alexandrinus as a prevalent opinion in his day. *Stromata*, lib. vii.

cry out, saying what great things she had seen and suffered, and how she had been healed, so that through her preaching many believed.

For the shepherds of sheep also declared that they had seen angels at midnight, singing a hymn, praising and blessing the God of heaven, and saying that the Saviour of all was born, which is Christ the Lord, by whom the salvation of Israel will be restored.[1]

Moreover, from evening until morning, a great star shone above the cave, and one so great had never been seen from the beginning of the world. And prophets who were in Jerusalem said that this star indicated the nativity of Christ, who should restore the promise, not only to Israel, but to all nations.

CHAPTER XIV.

Now on the third day after the nativity of our Lord Jesus Christ, the most blessed Mary went out of the cave, and, entering a stable, put her child in a manger,[2] and the ox and ass adored him. Then was fulfilled that which was spoken by Isaiah the prophet, who said, The ox doth know his owner, and the ass his master's crib.[3] The very animals, therefore, ox and ass, having him between them, incessantly adored

[1] Luke ii. 8, etc.   [2] Luke ii. 7.   [3] Isaiah i. 3.

him. Then was fulfilled that which was spoken by Habakkuk the prophet, who said, Between two animals thou art made known.[1] In the same place Joseph tarried with Mary three days.

CHAPTER XV.

Now on the sixth day they entered Bethlehem, where they spent the seventh day. But on the eighth day they circumcised the child, and his name was called Jesus, as he was called by the angel before he was conceived in the womb.[2] Now after the days of the purification of Mary were fulfilled according to the law of Moses, then Joseph took the infant to the temple of the Lord; and, when the infant had received *peritome* (*peritome*, that is circumcision), they offered for him a pair of turtles, or two young pigeons.

Now there was in the temple a certain man of God, perfect and just, whose name was Simeon, a hundred and twelve years old.[3] This man had received an answer from the Lord that he should not taste death unless he saw Christ the Son of God living in the flesh. When he saw the infant he cried out with a

---

[1] Hab. iii. 2, in the Greek. The Latin Vulgate is, "In medio annorum notum facies,"—In the midst of the years thou shalt make it known.
[2] Luke ii. 21-24.
[3] This age for Simeon seems quite imaginary. Luke ii. 25-38.

loud voice, saying, God hath visited his people, and the Lord hath fulfilled his promise. And he made haste and adored him. And after this he took him into his cloak, and kissing his feet, said, Now Lord, thou sendest away thy servant in peace, according to thy word, because mine eyes have seen thy salvation, which thou hast prepared before the face of all peoples; a light for the revelation of the Gentiles and the glory of thy people Israel.

There was also in the temple of the Lord, Anna a prophetess, daughter of Phanuel, of the tribe of Asher, who had lived with her husband seven years from her virginity; and she had been a widow now for eighty-four years, and had never departed from the temple of the Lord, spending her time in fastings and prayers. She also likewise adored the infant, saying, In him is the redemption of the world.

CHAPTER XVI.

Now when the second year was past, Magi came from the East to Jerusalem, bringing large gifts. And they earnestly asked the Jews, saying, Where is the King who is born to you? for we have seen his star in the East, and have come to adore him.[1] And this report came to King Herod, and so terrified him

---

[1] Matt. ii. 1, etc.

that he assembled the Scribes and Pharisees and Doctors of the people, inquiring of them where the prophets had foretold that Christ should be born. And they said to him, In Bethlehem of Judah. For it is written, And thou Bethlehem, the land of Judah, art not the least among the princes of Judah, for out of thee shall come forth the ruler who shall rule my people Israel.[1] Then Herod the king called the Magi to himself, and diligently inquired of them when the star appeared to them. Then sending them to Bethlehem, he said, Go and ask diligently about the child, and when you have found him, report it to me, that I too may come and adore him.

Now as the Magi went on their way, the star appeared to them, and was, as it were, their guide, going before them until they came where the child was. And when they saw the star the Magi rejoiced with great joy, and entered into the house and found the infant Jesus sitting in the lap of his mother. Then they opened their treasures and bestowed large presents upon the blessed Mary and Joseph; but to the infant himself each offered a single piece of gold; in like manner one (offered) gold, another frankincense, and a third myrrh. But when they would have returned to King Herod, they were warned by an angel in a dream not to return to Herod; and they returned to their own country by another road.

[2] Mic. v. 2.

CHAPTER XVII.

Now when Herod saw that he was mocked by the Magi, his heart was puffed up, and he sent all ways, wishing to catch and kill them. But when he found them not at all, he sent anew to Bethlehem and all its borders, and slew all the male children whom he found, from two years old and under, according to the time which he had enquired of the Magi.[1]

But one day before this happened, Joseph was warned in a dream by an angel of the Lord, which said to him, Take up Mary and the infant, and go into Egypt by way of the desert. And Joseph went according to the saying of the angel.[2]

CHAPTER XVIII.

AND when they had come to a certain cave and wished to rest in it, the blessed Mary came down from the beast, and sat and held the child Jesus in her lap. Now there were with Joseph three youths, and with Mary a certain damsel, who went on their way at the same time; and behold there suddenly came out of the cave many dragons, seeing which the youths cried out through excessive fear. Then Jesus, descending from his mother's lap, stood on his feet before the dragons, and they adored Jesus

[1] Matt. ii. 16.   [2] Matt. ii. 14.

and then departed from them. Then was fulfilled that which was spoken by David the prophet, saying, Praise the Lord from the earth, ye dragons, ye dragons and all deeps.[1] And the little infant Jesus, walking before them, commanded them to hurt no man. But Mary and Joseph feared greatly lest perchance the little infant should be injured by the dragons. And Jesus said to them, Fear not, nor consider me because I am a little infant, for I was, and am ever perfect; it must needs be that all the wild beasts of the woods should grow tame before me.

CHAPTER XIX.

IN like manner lions and leopards adored him, and kept company with them in the desert; whithersoever Joseph and blessed Mary went, they went before them, showing the way and bowing their heads; and showing subjection by wagging their tails, they adored him with great reverence. Now when Mary saw lions and leopards and various kinds of wild beasts coming round them, she was at first exceedingly afraid; and Jesus with a glad countenance, looking into her face, said, Fear not, mother; because they come not for thy hurt, but they hasten to come for thy service and mine. By these sayings he removed fear from her heart. Now the lions walked

[1] Ps. cxlviii. 7.

along with them, and with the oxen and asses, and the beasts of burden which carried necessaries for them, and hurt no one although they remained with them; but they were tame among the sheep and rams which they had brought with them from Judea, and had with them. They walked among wolves and feared nothing, and no one was hurt by another. Then was fulfilled that which was spoken by the prophet: Wolves shall feed with lambs; lion and ox shall eat chaff together.[1] There were two oxen also with them, and a cart, wherein they carried necessaries; and the lions directed them in their way.

CHAPTER XX.

Now it came to pass on the third day from their departure, as they went along, the blessed Mary was wearied by the too great heat of the sun in the desert; and seeing a palm tree she said to Joseph, Let me rest a little under the shadow of this tree. Joseph hastened therefore, and led her to the palm, and caused her to descend from the beast. And when the blessed Mary had sat down there, she looked at the foliage of the palm and saw it full of fruit, and she said to Joseph, I desire that I may be able to partake of the fruit of this palm. And Joseph saith to her, I wonder thou sayest this, when thou

[1] Is. xi. 6-9; lxv. 25.

seest what a height the palm is, and that thou thinkest to eat of the fruit of the palm. I think more of scarcity of water, which is already failing us in the bottles, and we have not wherewith we may refresh ourselves and the beasts. Then the little child Jesus, sitting with a glad countenance in his mother's lap, saith to the palm, O tree, bend down thy branches, and with thy fruit refresh my mother. And straightway at this word, the palm bowed down its top to the feet of the blessed Mary, and they gathered from it fruit wherewith all were refreshed. Now after they had gathered all its fruit, it remained bowed down, waiting to rise at his command at whose command it had bowed down. Then Jesus said to it, Raise thee, O palm, and be strong, and be a partner with my trees which are in the paradise of my Father. And open from thy roots a spring of water which is hidden in the earth; and let waters flow forth from it to our satisfying. And immediately it arose, and there began to flow forth at its root a most pure fount of waters, very cool, and exceedingly clear. Now when they saw the fount of water they rejoiced with great joy; and they, and all the beasts and cattle were satisfied; wherefore they gave thanks to God.

CHAPTER XXI.

On the next day when they were departing thence,

and at the hour wherein they began to pursue their journey, Jesus, turning to the palm tree, said, This privilege I grant thee, O palm, that one of thy branches should be taken by my angels, and planted in the paradise of my Father. And this blessing I will confer upon thee, that unto all who have conquered in any contest, it may be said, Ye have attained the palm of victory.[1] As he said these things, behold, an angel of the Lord appeared, standing above the palm-tree; and taking away one of its branches, he flew to heaven having the branch in his hand. When they saw this they fell on their faces and became as dead. And Jesus spake unto them, saying, Why doth fear possess your hearts? Know ye not that this palm, which I have caused to be removed to paradise, will be prepared for all the saints in the place of delight, as it was prepared for us in this place of solitude? And they were filled with joy, and being strengthened, all arose.

CHAPTER XXII.

AFTER these things, as they pursued their journey, Joseph said to Jesus, Lord, this heat broils us; if it please thee, let us hold our course near the sea, that we may rest in the towns on the coast. Jesus said to

---

[1] This account of the palm as a symbol of victory is of course an anachronism. Readers of Cicero, for example, will remember that he frequently employs the figure.

him, Fear not, Joseph, I will shorten the way for you, so that what you were to go in the space of thirty days, you shall accomplish in this one day. While they said these things, behold, they looked forward, and began to see the Egyptian mountains and cities.

And they came, rejoicing and exulting, into the borders of Hermopolis,[1] and entered into a certain city of Egypt, which is called Sotinen; and because there was no one known in it from whom they could have requested hospitality, they went into a temple, which was called the capitol of Egypt, in which temple three hundred and fifty-five[2] idols were placed, to which, on separate days, the honour of deity was rendered in sacrilegious rites. Now the Egyptians of that city entered the capitol, in which the priests admonished them how many sacrifices they should offer on each day according to the honour of their deity.

---

[1] There were in Egypt two or three cities with this name. The Church historian, Sozomen, who tells some of the stories current in his time, mentions the tree above referred to as having miraculous virtues; and he also mentions the story of the text. He says the tree was at Hermopolis in the Thebaid, near to which city its miraculous bowing down took place. He knows nothing of the marvellous journey reported in the first paragraph of this chapter. See Sozomen's Ecclesiastical History, book v. 20. Sotinen is in the text of Thilo the only name given, whence we may infer that it was regarded as the Egyptian name for Hermopolis. It is rather unfortunate for the story that the Thebaid was the upper province of Egypt.

[2] Evidently a mistake for three hundred and sixty-five; one for every day in the year.

CHAPTER XXIII.

Now it came to pass that when the most blessed Mary, with her little Infant, had entered the temple, all the idols were prostrate on the earth, so that they all lay upon their faces wholly shattered and broken, and so they showed evidently that they were nothing. Then was fulfilled what was spoken by the prophet Isaiah : Behold the Lord shall come upon a light cloud, and shall enter Egypt, and all the handiworks of the Egyptians shall be moved at his presence.[1]

CHAPTER XXIV.

Then when it had been told to Aphrodosius the ruler of that city, he came with all his army to the temple. But when the priests of the temple saw that Aphrodosius, with all his army, came to the temple, they thought that he hastened only to see his revenge on those because of whom the gods had fallen. But he, having entered the temple, when he saw all the idols lie prostrate on their faces, drew nigh to the blessed Mary, who bore the Lord in her lap, and adoring him, said to all his army, and to all his friends, If this were not the God of our gods, our gods would by no means have fallen on their faces before him, neither would they lie prostrate in his sight; wherefore, they silently avow him to be

[1] Is. xix. 1.

their Lord. We then, if we do not very carefully what we see our gods do, may incur the peril of his indignation, and may all come to destruction, as befel Pharoah, king of the Egyptians; who, not believing such great miracles, was drowned with all his army in the sea.[1] Then all the people of that city believed in the Lord God through Jesus Christ.

CHAPTER XXV.

Not much time after, an angel said to Joseph, Return to the land of Judah, for they are dead who sought the child's life.[2]

CHAPTER XXVI.

And it came to pass, that after the return of Jesus from Egypt, when he was in Galilee, and now entered on the fourth year of his age, one Sabbath day he played with the children by the bed of the Jordan. When, therefore, he had sat down, Jesus made himself seven pools with mud, to each of which he made little channels, through which, at his command he brought water from the stream into a pool, and sent it back again. Then one of those children, a son of the devil, with envious mind shut up the channels which supplied water to the pools, and overthrew what Jesus had

---

[1] Ps. cxxxvi. 15. Ex. xv. 4.
[2] Matt. ii. 26. The book ends here in the text followed by Thilo.

made. Then said Jesus unto him, Woe unto thee, son of death, son of Satan. Dost thou destroy the works which I have wrought? And straightway he who had done this, died. Then, with a quarrelsome voice, the parents of the dead cried against Mary and Joseph, saying to them, Your son hath cursed our son, and he is dead. When Joseph and Mary heard, they came at once to Jesus, on account of the complaint of the parents of the boy, and the crowd of Jews. But Joseph secretly said to Mary, I dare not speak to him; but do thou admonish him, and say, Why hast thou raised against us the enmity of the people, and why do we bear the painful enmity of men? And when his mother had come to him, she asked him, saying, My Lord, what hath he done that he should die? But he said, He was worthy of death, because he destroyed the works which I had wrought. Therefore his mother besought him, saying, Do not, my Lord, because they all rise against us. And he, not willing that his mother should be grieved, spurned the body of the dead with his right foot, and said to him, Arise, O son of iniquity; for thou art not worthy to enter into the rest of my Father, because thou hast destroyed the works which I have wrought. Then he who was dead arose and departed. But Jesus, at his own command, brought the water into the pools through the water-channels.

CHAPTER XXVII.

AND it came to pass after these things, that in the sight of all, Jesus took mud from the pools which he had made, and made twelve sparrows out of it. Now it was the Sabbath when Jesus did this, and there were many children with him. When therefore, one of the Jews had seen him do this, he said to Joseph, Joseph, seest thou not that the child Jesus worketh on the Sabbath, which it is not lawful for him to do? for he hath made twelve sparrows of mud. When he heard this, Joseph reproved him, saying, Why doest thou, on the Sabbath, such things as it is not lawful for us to do? And Jesus, hearing Joseph, and clapping his hands together, said to the sparows, Fly! and at the voice of his command they began to fly. And as all who stood there saw and heard, he said to the birds, Go and fly through the globe and all the world, and live! Now when they who were there saw such signs, they were filled with great amazement. Some praised him and admired him; but others blamed him. And some went away to the chief priests, and to the chiefs of the Pharisees, and told them that Jesus the son of Joseph had done great signs and miracles in sight of all the people of Israel. And this was published among the twelve tribes of Israel.[1]

---

[1] The constant assumption of the continued integrity of the twelve

CHAPTER XXVIII.

Now again, the son of Annas the priest of the temple, who had come with Joseph, holding a stick in his hand, while all beheld, with excessive rage broke open the pools which Jesus had made with his hands, and spilled out of them the water which he had gathered in them from the stream. For he stopped the water-channel by which the water entered, and then destroyed it. When Jesus saw this, he said to the boy who had destroyed his pools, O, most base seed of iniquity! O, son of death! workman of Satan! truly the fruit of thy seed shall be without vigour, and thy roots without moisture, and thy branches dry and not bearing fruit. And, at once, as all beheld, the boy withered and died.

CHAPTER XXIX.

Then Joseph trembled, and took hold of Jesus, and went with him to his house, and his mother with him. And behold, suddenly from the opposite side, a certain boy, himself also a worker of iniquity, ran and thrust himself against the shoulder of Jesus,

---

tribes of Israel in these Apocrypha is worth noting, as an additional proof that their writers were ill informed on some very important points. The malevolent character of the early miracles ascribed to Jesus, is good evidence that the early Christian fabulists were as ignorant of the true spirit of Christ as of some other matters.

meaning to insult him or to hurt him if he could. But Jesus said to him, Thou shalt not return whole from the way in which thou goest. And immediately he fell down and died. And the parents of the dead, who had seen what was done, cried out, saying, Whence is this child born? It is manifest that every word which he saith is true; and it is often accomplished before he speaketh. And the parents of the dead boy came to Joseph, and said to him, Take away that Jesus of thine from this place, for he cannot dwell with us in this town. Or, indeed, teach him to bless, and not to curse. And Joseph came to Jesus and admonished him, saying, Wherefore doest thou such things? Already many are grieved against thee, and because of thee, hold us in dislike, and we bear the reproaches of men on thy account. Jesus answered and said to Joseph, No son is wise save he whom his father hath taught according to the knowledge of this time; and the curse of his father hurteth none but evil doers. Then they assembled against Jesus, and accused him to Joseph. When Joseph saw this he was exceedingly terrified, fearing the violence and tumult of the people of Israel. The same hour Jesus took the dead child by the ear, and held him up from the ground in the sight of all; and they saw Jesus talking with him as a father with his son. And his spirit returned into him, and he lived again. And they all marvelled.

CHAPTER XXX.

Now a certain teacher, a Jew, by name Zaccheus,[1] heard Jesus saying such words, and seeing that there was insuperable knowledge of virtue in him, became angry, and began without restraint, and foolishly, and without fear, to speak against Joseph. And he said, Dost thou not wish to give thy son to be instructed in human wisdom and respect? But I see that thou and Mary will rather love your son than what the elders of the people say in opposition. For he ought more to honour us, the elders of the whole church of Israel, and to have mutual love with children, and to be instructed among us in Jewish doctrine. On the other hand, Joseph said to him, And is there anyone who can restrain and teach this child? But if thou art able to restrain and teach him, we by no means forbid him to be taught by thee what is learned by all. When Jesus heard what Zaccheus said, he answered him and said, The precepts of the law which thou didst mention a little while ago, and all that thou hast named, ought to be kept by those who are taught by the rules of men: but I am an alien to your courts, because I have no carnal parent. Thou who readest the law, and art instructed so, remainest in the law: but I was before the law.

---

[1] In Tischendorf's text this name is always written Zachyas. Here, however, as in many other like cases, I have adopted a more usual form of spelling.

But while thou thinkest thou hast no equal in learning, thou shalt be instructed by me, for no other can teach aught but the things which thou hast named. For he is able who is worthy. But I, when I have been exalted in the earth, will cause all mention of your genealogy to cease. Thou knowest not when thou wast born; but I alone know when ye were born, and how long your life is in the earth. Then all who heard these words uttered were astonished, and cried out, saying, O! O! O! this marvellously great, and admirable mystery! Never did we hear in this wise! Never was it heard by any other; neither by prophets, nor by Pharisees, nor by Scribes, was it ever said or heard. We know him whence he was born, and he is scarcely five years old; and whence doth he say these words? The Pharisees answered, We never heard such words spoken by another child at such a childish age. And Jesus answering, said to them, Wonder ye at this that such things are spoken by a child? Why then do ye not believe me in the things which I have spoken to you? And because I said to you that I know when ye were born, ye all marvel. I will say more to you, that ye may marvel more. I have seen Abraham, whom ye call your father, and talked with him, and he hath seen me.[1] And when they heard this, they were silent, nor did any of them dare to speak. And Jesus

[1] *Cf.* John viii. 56-58.

said to them, I was among you with children, and ye knew me not. I have talked with you as with wise men, and ye have not understood my voice, because ye are inferior to me, and of little faith.

CHAPTER XXXI.

THE teacher Zaccheus, a doctor of the law, again said to Joseph and Mary, Give me the boy, and I will hand him over to the teacher Levi, to teach him letters, and to instruct him. Then Joseph and Mary coaxing Jesus, led him to the school, that he might be taught his letters by the old man Levi. When he entered he was silent; and the master, Levi, told one letter to Jesus, and beginning at the first letter, Aleph, said to him, Answer. But Jesus was silent and answered nothing. Wherefore, the preceptor, Levi, being angry, took a rod of a storax-tree,[1] and smote him on the head. And Jesus said to the teacher Levi, Why dost thou smite me? Know in truth, that he who is smitten rather teacheth him who smiteth him, than is taught by him. For

[1] Or, "a storax-tree stick," for such is no doubt the meaning of "virgam storatinam." The storax is never mentioned in the canonical works, but its odoriferous product is named in Ecclesiasticus xxiv. 15 (Anglican version), or xxiv. 21 (Latin Vulgate). Jerome's version also introduces it in Gen. xliii. 11, but with no apparent authority. It should be observed that the storax-tree is still found in Palestine. Mr. Tristram, for instance, speaks of it as abundant in Carmel ("Land of Israel," p. 492). The adjective *storatina* is of course put for *storacina*, from *storax* or *styrax*.

I am able to teach thee what is said by thyself. But these are all blind, who say and hear, like sounding brass or a tinkling cymbal in which there is no consciousness of things which are understood by their sound.[1] And Jesus added, and said to Zaccheus, Every letter from Aleph to Tau[2] is known by its order; thou, therefore, first say what is Tau, and I will tell thee what Aleph is. And Jesus said again to them, They who know not Aleph, how can they say Tau, ye hypocrites? First say what Aleph is, and I shall then believe you when you say Beth. And Jesus began to ask the names of the separate letters, and said, Let the teacher of the law say what the first letter is, or why it hath many triangles, scalene,[3] acute-angled, equiangular, unequal-sided, with unequal angles, rectangular, rectilinear, and curvilinear.

Now when Levi heard this, he was amazed at such an arrangement of the names of the letters. Then

---

[1] *Cf.* 1 Cor. xiii. 1; xiv. 7.

[2] Instead of Tau, the Latin text reads Thet in each case: it is possible that the writer meant to give the name of Teth, but since the last letter of the Hebrew alphabet is required by the context, Tau has been employed in the translation.

[3] The words in the original are *gradatos, subacutos, mediatos, obductos, productos, erectos, stratos, curvistratos*. We are by no means confident that the terms we have given are the equivalents of these, or all correct; indeed it seems impossible to make sense of the passage as it stands. It is very well known that Christians as well as Jews have speculated, or rather, let their fancies run wild on the subject of the mystic properties of letters, as indicated by their names, forms, powers, positions in certain words, etc. The author of Pseudo-Matthew evidently wished to supply high authority for such laborious trifling.

began he, in the hearing of all, to cry out, and say, Ought he to live upon earth? Verily he deserves to be hung on a great cross. For he can extinguish fire, and mock at other torments. I think he was before the flood,—born before the deluge. What womb bore him? or what mother conceived him? or what breasts gave him suck? I flee before him; for I cannot endure the word of his mouth, but my heart is astounded at hearing such words. For I think no man can attain to his word, except God hath been with him. Now wretched I, have yielded myself to him for derision. For when I thought I had a scholar, I found my master, not knowing him. What shall I say? I cannot endure the words of this boy: I will now flee from this town, for I cannot understand these things. An old man, I am conquered by a child; for I can find neither beginning nor end to what he affirmeth; for it is difficult to find a beginning from one's self. I tell you truly, I lie not, that to my eyes, the conduct of this boy, the beginning of his speech, and the end of his meaning, seem to have nothing in common with men. Therefore, I know not whether he is a magician or a God; certainly an angel of God speaketh in him. I know not whence he is, or where he cometh from, or who he will become.

Then Jesus, with a pleasant countenance, smiling at him, said with command, as all the children of

Israel stood by and heard: Let the unfruitful be fruitful, and the blind see, and the lame walk well, and the poor enjoy good things, and the dead live again, that in a restored condition, every one may return and abide in Him who is the root of life, and of perpetual sweetness. And when the child Jesus had said this, forthwith all were restored who had fallen under painful infirmities. And they dared not say anything to him, or hear anything from him further.

CHAPTER XXXII.

AFTER these things Joseph and Mary departed thence with Jesus to the city of Nazareth, and he was there with his parents. And when he was there, on the first day of the week,[1] while Jesus was playing with the children on the top of a certain house, it happened that one of the children pushed another off the roof on to the ground, and he died. And although the parents of the deceased had not seen it, they cried out against Joseph and Mary, saying, Your son hath thrust our son to the ground and he is dead. But Jesus was silent and answered them nothing. Now Joseph and Mary came in haste to Jesus, and his mother asked him saying, My Lord, tell me if thou didst thrust him to the ground. And immediately

---

[1] The Latin is *una sabbati*.

Jesus came down from the roof to the ground, and called the boy by his name Zeno, and he answered him, Lord. And Jesus, said to him, Did I throw thee down from the roof to the ground? And he said, No, Lord. And the parents of the child who had been dead, marvelled, and honoured Jesus for the miracle that was done. And Joseph and Mary departed thence with Jesus to Jericho.

CHAPTER XXXIII.

Now Jesus was six years old, and his mother sent him with a pitcher to the fountain to draw water with the children. And it came to pass after he drew the water, that one of the children thrust against him and shattered the pitcher and broke it. But Jesus spread out the cloak which he wore, and took in his cloak as much water as there was in the pitcher, and carried it to his mother. And she marvelled when she saw it, and thought within herself, and laid up all these things in her heart.

CHAPTER XXXIV.

AGAIN on a certain day, he went out into the field, and took a little wheat from his mother's barn and sowed it. And it sprang up and grew and multiplied exceedingly. And it came to pass at length that he reaped it, and gathered from it three quarters of corn, and gave it to many.[1]

CHAPTER XXXV.

THERE is a road which leads out of Jericho and goes to the river Jordan where the children of Israel went over. There the ark of the covenant is said to have rested. And Jesus was eight years old, and he went out from Jericho and went to the Jordan. And there was by the way side near the bank of the Jordan, a cavern where a lioness brought up her whelps; and no one could go along the road in safety. Now as Jesus came from Jericho, knowing that in that cavern the lioness had brought forth her young, he entered it in the sight of all.[2] But when the lions saw Jesus they ran to meet him and adored him. And Jesus sat in the cavern, and the lions' whelps ran about his feet, fawning and playing with him. But the older lions stood at a distance with lowered head, and adored him; and fawning, wagged their tails before him. Then the people, who stood at a distance, not seeing Jesus, said, Unless he or his parents had done very grievous sins,

---

[1] The Latin is *et collegit fructus ex eo tres choros, et donavit multiplicibus suis.*

[2] There are no lions in Palestine now; but Reland quotes a passage from John Phocas, in the twelfth century, affirming that they were then to be found among the reeds on the banks of the Jordan (*Palæstina*, p. 274).

he would not have willingly exposed himself to the lions. And while the people thought thus within themselves, and were overcome by excessive sorrow, behold, suddenly, in the sight of the people, Jesus came out of the cavern, and the lions went before him, and the lions' whelps played together before his feet. But the parents of Jesus stood afar off with their heads hanging down, and watched; the people too, in like manner, stood afar off because of the lions; for they dared not come up to them. Then Jesus began to say to the people, How much better than you are the beasts, which recognise and glorify their Lord; and ye men, who are made in the image and likeness of God, know him not. Beasts acknowledge me, and grow gentle; men see me, and know me not.

CHAPTER XXXVI.

AFTER this Jesus crossed the Jordan with the lions, in the sight of all; and the water of the Jordan was divided to the right hand and the left. Then he said to the lions, so that all heard, Go in peace, and hurt nobody; neither let any man hurt you, until ye return whence ye set out. And they, bidding him farewell, not only with their voice but with bodily gesture, went away to their places. But Jesus returned to his mother.

CHAPTER XXXVII.

And Joseph was a carpenter, and made of wood nothing except yokes for oxen, and ploughs, and implements for turning up the soil and suited for agriculture, and made wooden bedsteads. And it happened that a certain youth desired him to make a couch six cubits long. And Joseph ordered his boy to cut the wood with an iron saw, according to the measure which he had sent. But he did not keep to the dimensions given him, and made one board shorter than another. And Joseph in anger, began to think what he must do in the case. And when Jesus saw him thus angrily thinking, and not able to remedy what had been done, he addressed him with a consoling voice, saying, Come, let us take hold of the ends of each piece of wood, and lay them together end to end, and let us put them level and pull them to us, for we shall be able to make them equal. Then Joseph obeyed his command, for he knew that he could do what he would, and Joseph took the ends of the boards and put them against the wall and even together, and Jesus held the other ends of the wood, and pulled the shorter piece towards himself, and made it equal to the longer piece. And he said to Joseph, Go on with thy work, and do what thou hast promised to do. And Joseph did what he had promised.

Joseph that, by their blandishments, they would take him to another master to learn. And Joseph and Mary, fearing the people, and the insolence of the princes, and the threats of the priests, took him again to school, knowing that from man he could learn nothing, who from God alone had perfect knowledge. Now when Jesus had entered the school, being led by the Holy Spirit, he took the book from the hand of the tutor teaching the law, and in the sight and hearing of all the people, began to read; not indeed what was written in their book, but he spoke by the Spirit of the living God, as if a stream of water went forth from a living spring, and the spring ever remained full. And in such power did he teach the people the great things of the living God, that the very master even fell upon the ground and adored him. But the heart of the people who sat and heard him saying such things, was filled with astonishment. When Joseph had heard this, he came running to Jesus, fearing lest the master should die. Seeing him, the master said to him, Thou hast not given me a pupil, but a master; and who can endure his words? Then was fulfilled that which was spoken by the Psalmist, The river of God is full of water. Thou has prepared their food, for such is its preparation.[1]

---

[1] Ps. lxv. 9. As in the *Vulgate*, 64, 10.

CHAPTER XXXVIII.

And it came to pass a second time that Joseph and Mary were asked by the people, that Jesus might be taught his letters in the school; which, also, they did not refuse to do; and, according to the precepts of the elders, took him to a master to be taught human science by him. And then the master began imperiously to teach him, saying, Say Alpha.[1] But Jesus said to him, Do thou first tell me what Beta is, and I will tell thee what Alpha is. And for this, the master, being angry, smote Jesus; and soon after he smote him he died.

And Jesus returned home to his mother. But Joseph being afraid, called Mary to him, and said to her, Know truly that my soul is sad unto death, on account of that boy. For it might happen sometime, that somebody should smite the boy in malice, and he should die. But Mary answered and said, Man of God, do not believe that this can be. Nay, surely believe that He who sent him to be born among men, will keep him from all malice; and in His own name, preserve him from evil.

CHAPTER XXXIX.

Again, a third time, the Jews asked Mary and

[1] In chapter xxxi. the names of the letters are Hebrew, whereas here they are Greek. We may suppose that this is a later addition to the book.

CHAPTER XL.

AFTER these things Joseph removed thence with Mary and Jesus, in order to come to Capernaum on the coast, because of the malice of the men who were hostile to them. And when Jesus dwelt in Capernaum, there was in the city a certain man by name Joseph, very rich. But sinking under his illness, he died, and was lying dead upon a bed. But when Jesus had heard them in the city lamenting and weeping and wailing over the dead, he said to Joseph, Wherefore, since he is called by thy name, dost thou not vouchsafe the benefit of thy favour to him? Joseph answered him, What power or faculty have I of vouchsafing benefit to him? Jesus replied, Take the kerchief that is upon thy head, and go and put it on the face of the dead, and say to him, Christ save thee! and forthwith he will be saved, and the dead shall rise from his bed. When he heard this, Joseph departed, running at once at the command of Jesus, and entered the house of the dead man; and he put the kerchief which he had upon his head, on the face of him that lay on the bed, and said, Jesus save thee! And the dead man forthwith arose from his bed, and asked who Jesus was.

CHAPTER XLI.

AND they departed from Capernaum into a city

which is called Bethlehem; and Joseph was with Mary in his house and Jesus along with them. And on a certain day Joseph called his first-born son James to him and sent him into the kitchen-garden to gather herbs to make pottage. And Jesus followed his brother James into the garden, and Joseph and Mary knew it not. And while James gathered herbs there suddenly came a viper out of a hole and wounded the hand of James, and he began to cry out through excessive pain. And when already fainting he said with a bitter cry, Oh! Oh! a very bad viper has wounded my hand. And Jesus, who stood opposite, at that bitter cry ran to James and took hold of his hand, and did no more than merely breathe upon the hand of James, and soothed it. And immediately James was healed, and the serpent died. And Joseph and Mary knew not what had happened; but at the cry of James, and at the bidding of Jesus they ran into the garden, and found the serpent already dead and James quite healed.

CHAPTER XLII.

Now when Joseph came to a feast with his sons, James, Joseph, and Judah, and Simeon, and his two daughters, Jesus and Mary his mother met them, together with her sister Mary the daughter of Cleophas, whom the Lord God gave to Cleophas her father and Anna her mother because they had offered to the Lord Mary the mother of Jesus.[1] And this Mary was called by the like name of Mary for the comfort of her parents. And when they assembled Jesus sanctified and blessed them, and began himself first to eat and drink; for none of them dared eat or drink, nor sit at table or break bread, till he had sanctified them and first done this. And if he by chance was absent they waited till he did this. And when he would not come to the repast, neither did Joseph and Mary and his brethren the sons of Joseph come. These brethren, indeed, having his life before their eyes as a light, regarded and feared him. And when Jesus slept, whether by day or by night, the brightness of God shone on him. To him be all praise for ever and ever. Amen. Amen.[2]

[1] According to the MS. which Tischendorf calls B, the reading is: "And when Joseph, being worn out with old age, was dead and buried with his parents, the blessed Mary was with her nephews or with the children of her sisters. For Anna and Emerina were sisters. Of Emerina was born Elisabeth the mother of John the Baptist. Now because Anna the mother of the Blessed Mary was very lovely, when Joachim died, she married Cleophas, by whom she had a second daughter, whom she called Mary, and gave her to Alphæus to wife, and of her came James the son of Alphæus, and Philip his brother. When her second husband was dead, Anna was married to a third husband, named Salome, by whom she had a third daughter, whom she likewise called Mary, and gave her to Zebedee to wife; of her was born James the son of Zebedee, and John the Evangelist." Another account is prefixed to this false Gospel in a copy used by Tischendorf, who quotes the passage (Evang. Apocr., p. 104).

[2] The MS. called B concludes in a rather different manner, and has the following appended: "The holy apostle and evangelist John with his own hand wrote this book set forth in Hebrew letters which the learned doctor Jerome translated out of Hebrew into Latin." The title and one of the letters prefixed to the book just as plainly ascribe the writing to the evangelist Matthew, and just as truly.

III.

THE GOSPEL OF THE NATIVITY OF MARY.

As Bishop Ellicott has said, "This Gospel is usually found among the works of Jerome, and has been edited separately by Fabricius, Thilo, and after them by Tischendorf. It has gained no little celebrity from having been admitted nearly entire into the *Aurea Legenda*." Judging from the style, it would seem to be less a translation than a Latin recension of the popular story respecting the birth and childhood of Mary. The writer uses the Latin Vulgate, and therefore wrote after that was published. It is far less extravagant, and in a better style, than some other compilations of its class, both earlier and later. Mary is represented as being fourteen years of age before she was espoused to Joseph, who afterwards went into Galilee to take her as his wife. The birth of Jesus is simply said to have occurred at Bethlehem, 'as the holy evangelists have taught,' and the book concludes with a doxology to the Holy Trinity.

THE GOSPEL OF THE NATIVITY OF MARY.

CHAPTER I.

THE blessed and glorious Mary ever virgin, sprung of the royal stock and family of David, and born in the city of Nazareth, was brought up at Jerusalem in the temple of the Lord. Her father was called Joachim and her mother Anna. Her father's house was of Galilee and the city of Nazareth, and her mother's race was of Bethlehem. Their life was simple and upright before the Lord, and pious and blameless before men. For they divided all their substance into three parts; one part they gave to the temple and the servants of the temple, another they devoted to strangers and the poor, the third they reserved for the use of their family and for themselves. Thus these persons, dear to God, and good to men, passed about twenty years in chaste matrimony at home without producing children. But they vowed, that if God perchance should give them offspring they would yield it to the service of the Lord; for which cause they were wont to frequent the temple of the Lord at every festival in the year.

CHAPTER II.

Now it came to pass that the feast of the dedication drew on; wherefore Joachim also with some of his kindred went up to Jerusalem. Now at that time Issachar was chief priest there. And when among his other fellow townsmen he also saw Joachim with his offering, he despised him and spurned his gifts, asking why he who was childless should presume to stand among those who had children; saying that his gifts could not at all seem worthy to God, seeing that He had judged him unworthy of offspring, when the scripture saith, that every one is accursed who hath not begotten male or female in Israel.[1] He said therefore that he must first be released from this curse by having offspring, and then at length he was to come before the Lord with his offerings. Joachim being covered with much shame by this reproach cast upon him, withdrew to the shepherds who were with the flocks in their pastures; for he would not return home, lest he should be stigmatised with the same reproach by his kinsmen, who were also present and heard this from the priest.

CHAPTER III.

But when he had been there some time, on a cer-

[1] I find no text in which any such statement is made.

tain day when he was alone, the angel of the Lord stood by him with a very great light. He being troubled at the sight of him, the angel who appeared to him allayed his fear, saying, Fear not, Joachim, nor be troubled at the sight of me; for I am an angel of the Lord, sent by Him to thee to tell thee that thy prayers are heard, and that thy alms have come up in His sight. For He hath truly seen thy shame and heard the reproach of barrenness not rightly cast upon thee. For God is the avenger of sin, not of nature, and therefore when He maketh any childless, He doth it for this cause, that He may the more wonderfully afford relief, and that that which is born may be known not to be of concupiscence but of the divine gift. For was not Sarah the first mother of your race unfruitful till her eightieth year? and yet in the last period of old age she bore Isaac, to whom was promised the blessing of all nations.[1] Rachel also, so pleasant to the Lord and so loved by holy Jacob, was long barren, and yet bore Joseph, not only lord of Egypt, but the deliverer of many nations who were about to perish of hunger. Who among the princes was stronger than Samson, or holier than Samuel? and yet both of them had barren mothers. If then reason persuadeth thee not by my words, believe in fact, that conceptions long delayed and barren births are wont

[1] Gen. xvii. 17. Sarah was ninety years old at the time referred to.

to be more wonderful. Therefore Anna thy wife shall bear thee a daughter, and thou shalt call her name Mary; she shall be, as you have vowed, consecrated to the Lord from her infancy, and shall be filled with the Holy Spirit even from her mother's womb.[1] She shall neither eat nor drink anything impure, nor shall her conversation be among public crowds out of doors, but in the temple of the Lord, that nothing evil may be said or so much as suspected of her. Therefore with advancing age, as she shall be marvellously born of one barren, so she who is incomparably a virgin shall conceive the son of the Most High who shall be called Jesus, and according to the etymology of his name shall be the Saviour of all nations. And this shall be to thee a sign of what I announce: when thou comest to the Golden Gate at Jerusalem,[2] thou shalt have there to meet thee Anna thy wife, who now being anxious through the delay of thy return, will then rejoice in seeing thee. This said, the angel departed from him.

CHAPTER IV.

THEN he appeared to Anna his wife, saying, Fear not, Anna, nor think it is a fantasm which thou

---

[1] This promise is a mere paraphrase of Luke i. 11-15, which relates to the birth of John the Baptist.

[2] As already observed, the Golden-Gate was not a gate of the city, but of the Temple.

seest. For I am that angel which hath offered your prayers and alms in the sight of God, and am now sent to you to announce that a daughter shall be born to you, who shall be called Mary and be blessed above all women. She, being full of the grace of the Lord from her very birth, shall remain in the house of her parents the three years of her suckling :[1] afterwards being given up to the service of the Lord, she shall not leave the temple till her years of understanding; there in fine, serving God night and day in fastings and prayers, she shall abstain from everything unclean, she shall never know man, but alone, without example, without spot, without corruption, without intercourse with man, as a virgin shall conceive a son, and as a handmaid (shall conceive) the Lord who by grace and name and work shall be the Saviour of the world. Therefore arise, go up to Jerusalem, and when thou comest to the gate, which is called Golden, because it is gilded, there for a sign shalt thou meet thy husband for whose safety and welfare thou art anxious. Therefore when these things fall out thus, know that what I tell thee will be without doubt accomplished.[2]

CHAPTER V.

THEREFORE according to the precept of the angel,

[1] Literally, *weaning*.
[2] This annunciation to Anna seems invented as a counterpart to the one recorded of Mary in the Gospels.

both of them leaving the places in which they were, went up to Jerusalem; and when they had come to the place indicated by the angelic prediction, there they met together. Then rejoicing at the sight of one another, and certainly sure of the promised offspring, they gave due thanks to the Lord the exalter of the humble. Therefore, having adored the Lord, they returned home sure of the divine promise; and they cheerfully waited. Therefore Anna conceived and bore a daughter, and according to the angel's bidding, her parents called her name Mary.

CHAPTER VI.

AND when the course of three years had rolled round, and the time for weaning was accomplished, they brought the virgin to the temple of the Lord with their offerings. Now there were around the temple, according to the fifteen psalms of degrees, fifteen steps to go up: for since the temple was set upon a mount, the altar of burnt offering, which was outside, could not be approached except by steps. Upon one of these, therefore, her parents set the blessed little Virgin Mary. And while they took off the garments which they had worn on the journey, and arrayed themselves, according to custom, in vesture more gay and clean, the virgin of the Lord went up all the steps in order, without the hand of anyone to lead and lift her; so that, in this case, you might suppose she came nothing short of perfect age. Already then, the Lord wrought something great in the infancy of his virgin, and showed beforehand, by the indication of this miracle, how great she should be. Therefore, when the sacrifice was accomplished, according to the custom of the law, and their vow performed, they left the virgin with other virgins within the precincts of the temple to be brought up there; but they themselves returned home.[1]

CHAPTER VII.

Now the virgin of the Lord, with advancing age, also made progress in virtue; and, according to the Psalmist, Father and mother had left her, but the Lord took her up.[2] For she was daily attended by angels, and daily she enjoyed the divine vision, which kept her from all evil, and caused her to abound in all good. She came, therefore, to her fourteenth year, and not only could they devise against her no evil, nor anything worthy of blame, but all good men who knew her judged her life and conversation worthy of admiration. Then the chief priest publicly announced that the virgins who were publicly placed in the temple, and had arrived at this time of life,

[1] Comp. Pseudo-Matthew, iv., *notes*. [2] Ps. xxvii. 10.

should return home and seek to be married, according to the custom of the nation, and the maturity of their age. But when the others had promptly obeyed this command, Mary alone, the virgin of the Lord, answered that she could not do this, saying that her parents had given her up to the service of the Lord; and that moreover she had herself vowed her virginity to the Lord, and would never violate it by any carnal association with man. Now the chief priest, being perplexed in mind, because he did not think the vow should be broken against the Scripture, which saith, Vow and pay;[1] neither dared he introduce a custom unusual with the nation: so he gave order that, at the impending festival all the chief men of Jerusalem and the neighbouring places should attend, with whose counsel he might know what was to be done in so doubtful a matter. When this took place, it pleased them all alike, that the Lord should be consulted in this affair. And while they all bowed down in prayer, the chief priest went to consult God, according to custom: nor was there any delay, for in the hearing of all, there came a voice from the oracle and the place of the mercy-seat, that, according to the prophecy of Isaiah, inquiry must be made, to whom that virgin ought to be commended and espoused. For it is clear that Isaiah saith, A rod shall go forth from the root of Jesse,

[1] Deut. xxiii. 21; Ps. xxvi. 4; Eccles. v. 4.

THE GOSPEL OF THE NATIVITY OF MARY. 93

and a flower shall arise from his root, and the Spirit of the Lord shall rest upon him, a Spirit of wisdom and understanding, a Spirit of counsel and might, a Spirit of knowledge and piety, and the Spirit of the fear of the Lord shall fill him.[1] According to this prophecy therefore, he foretold that all of the house and family of David who were fit to be married but not married, should bring their rods to, the altar ; and he whose rod, after it was brought should produce a flower, while on its top the Spirit of the Lord sat in the form of a dove, he it was to whom the virgin ought to be commended and espoused.[2]

CHAPTER VIII.

Now among others was Joseph, an aged man of the house and family of David; but when all of them brought their rods in order, he alone withdrew his. Therefore, when nothing appeared agreeable to the divine voice, the chief priest thought that God should be consulted again ; and He answered that of those who were designated, he alone to whom He must espouse the virgin had not brought his rod. Joseph therefore was betrayed ; for when he brought his rod, and a dove came from heaven and sat on the top of it, it was plainly apparent to

[1] Is. xi. 1-2.   [2] Comp. Pseudo-Matthew, vi.-viii.

all that the virgin was to be espoused to him. When, therefore, the betrothal had been celebrated in the wonted manner, he retired to the city of Bethlehem to set his house in order, and to procure what was required by his marriage. But Mary, the virgin of the Lord, with seven other virgins of like age, and brought up with her, whom she had received from the priest, returned to the house of her parents in Galilee.[1]

CHAPTER IX.

Now in those days, namely, at the time when she first came into Galilee, the angel Gabriel was sent to her from God, to make known to her the Lord's conception, and to explain to her the method or order of the conception. At length, having entered unto her, he filled the chamber where she abode with an immense light, and saluting her most courteously, he said, Hail, Mary! most acceptable virgin of the Lord! Virgin, full of grace, the Lord be with thee; blessed art thou before all women; blessed art thou before all men hitherto born.[2] But the virgin, who already well knew the countenances of angels, and was not unused to heavenly light, was neither terrified by the angelic vision, nor stupefied by the greatness of the light, but was troubled at his word alone; and

[1] *Cf.* Pseudo-Matthew, viii.　　[2] Luke i. 26-38.

began to think what that salutation, so unwonted, could be, or what it portended, or what end it would have. But the angel, divinely inspired, counteracting this thought, said, Fear not, Mary, as though I meant something contrary to thy chastity by this salutation; for thou hast found grace with the Lord, because thou hast chosen chastity; therefore, thou, as a virgin, shalt conceive without sin, and shalt bear a son. He shall be great, for he shall rule from sea to sea, and from the river to the ends of the world; and he shall be called the Son of the Most High, for he who is born humble on earth, reigneth exalted in heaven: and the Lord God shall give to him the seat of his father David, and he shall reign in the house of Jacob for ever, and of his kingdom shall be no end; since he is himself King of kings, and Lord of Lords, and his throne for ever and ever.[1]

The virgin, not incredulous at these words of the angel, but wishing to know the mode of their accomplishment, answered, How can this be? For since according to my vow I never knew man, how can I bring forth without human seed? To this the angel replied, Think not, Mary, that thou wilt conceive in human manner, for without intercourse with man, as a virgin thou shalt conceive, as a virgin thou shalt bring forth, as a virgin thou shalt nourish: for the Holy Spirit shall come upon thee, and the power of

[1] Ps. lxxii. 8; Luke i. 33.

the Most High shall overshadow thee contrary to all fire of concupiscence; therefore, what is born of thee will be alone holy, because alone conceived and born without sin, and shall be called the Son of God. Then Mary, with outspread hands and eyes lifted up to heaven, said, Behold the handmaid of the Lord, for I am unworthy of the name of lady; let it be unto me according to thy word.

It would perhaps be long and tedious to some, if we wished to insert, in this little work, all that we read preceded or followed the Lord's nativity; wherefore, omitting those things which are more fully written in the Gospel, let us come to the narration of those things which are less detailed.[1]

CHAPTER X.

JOSEPH, therefore, having come from Judea into Galilee, intended to take as wife the virgin who was espoused to him; for three months had now elapsed, and the fourth approached from the time when she had been espoused to him. Meanwhile her pregnancy began gradually to show itself, and it could not be hidden from Joseph; for entering freely to the virgin in the manner of a spouse, and talking

[1] This last paragraph reads like an addition, but is not such of necessity. Comp. Pseudo-Matthew ix.

familiarly with her, he perceived her to be with child. Therefore, he began to be disturbed and troubled in mind, because he knew not what it was best for him to do; for he neither wished to expose her, because he was a just man, nor to defame her by a suspicion of unchastity, because he was a good man. Therefore, he thought to dissolve his marriage privately, and to put her away secretly. But while he thought thus, behold the angel of the Lord appeared to him in a dream, saying, Joseph, son of David, fear not: that is, cherish no suspicion of unchastity against the virgin, nor think anything bad, nor fear to take her to wife; for that which she hath conceived and now vexeth thy mind, is not the work of man, but of the Holy Spirit. For she alone, of all, as a virgin, shall bear the Son of God; and thou shalt call his name Jesus, that is, a Saviour; for he shall save his people from their sins. Therefore, Joseph, according to the command of the angel, took the virgin to wife, yet knew her not, but kept her carefully under his protection in chastity.[1] And now the ninth month from her conception drew near, when Joseph, having taking his wife, with what else was necessary, went to the city of Bethlehem, whence he was. And it came to pass while they were there, her days were accomplished that she should bring forth, and, as the holy Evangelists have taught, she

[1] Matt. 1. 11–24.

brought forth her first born Son, our Lord Jesus Christ, who, with the Father and the Son and the Holy Spirit, liveth and reigneth God for ever and ever.[1]

[1] Matt. i. 25; ii. 1; Luke ii. 4–7. The concluding doxology looks as if taken from some liturgical formula. Compare Pseudo-Matthew x.

IV.

THE HISTORY OF JOSEPH THE CARPENTER.

THIS very singular production comes to us through the Arabic; but part of it, at least, is extant in Coptic, in which language it is supposed to have been originally written. It was first published by Wallin, with a Latin version in 1722. Thilo also gives the Arabic with a revised translation, but Tischendorf only prints the Latin. It has been thought to have originated in the fourth century, but it is very doubtful whether it is so ancient in its actual form, which manifests a development of superstitious notions hardly consistent with so early a date. The intention of the writer was no doubt to exalt Joseph in the eyes of a people who had wandered far from the simplicity of the Gospel. The references to the feast of a thousand years have a millenarian tinge, but are not conclusive as to the high antiquity of the book, which may, however, belong to the fifth or to the sixth century.

The writer represents our Saviour as seated with his disciples on the Mount of Olives, and repeating to them the story which is here told. Christ, then, is almost throughout, the only speaker. After a sort of introduction, we have a brief account of Joseph, who is represented as a priest, married, and having six children. After the death of his wife, he is espoused to Mary. The history then proceeds to narrate the incarnation and birth of Christ, and other details. A long account of Joseph's last days, his terrors at the approach of death, his eventual decease and burial, follows. This book is characterised by features by no means devoid of interest, although most improbable, unreasonable, and in the worst possible taste. The marvellous and the supernatural abound, and the writer is not always careful to be consistent even with himself; his audacity in ascribing the narration to our Lord, and in claiming the same authority for the observance of the annual commemoration of Joseph, will be apparent to every reader. Although it embodies some older traditions, it does not always accurately reproduce them, and contains independent fictions, for which its author alone must be held responsible.

HISTORY OF JOSEPH THE CARPENTER.[1]

CHAPTER I.

It happened, one day, when our Saviour, Master, God and Saviour, Jesus Christ, sat with his disciples, and they were all assembled on the Mount of Olives, that he said to them, O, my brethren and friends, sons of my Father, who hath chosen you out of all men! you know that I have often told you I must be crucified, and die for the salvation of Adam and his descendants, and that I shall rise from the dead. Now I shall commit to you the doctrine of the Holy Gospel (before) announced (to you), that you may proclaim it through all the world; and I will clothe you with power from above, and will fill you with

---

[1] The Arabic text has an introduction to the following effect:—
In the name of God, one in His essence and threefold in His Persons.
The history of the death of our father, the holy old man, Joseph the carpenter.
His blessings and prayers preserve us all, O brethren! Amen.
His whole life was a hundred and eleven years, and his departure from this world fell on the 26th of the month Abib, which answers to the month Ab. His prayer preserve us, Amen. And, indeed, it was our Lord Jesus Christ himself who rehearsed this to his holy disciples on Mount Olivet, and all his (Joseph's) labour, and the completion of his days. Now the holy Apostles kept this discourse and left it in writing in the library at Jerusalem. Their prayer preserve us, Amen.

the Holy Spirit.[1] And ye shall announce to all nations repentance and remission of sins.[2] For a single cup of water, if a man shall obtain it in the world to come, is better and greater than all the riches of the whole of this world. And a place no greater than one foot can fill, in the house of my Father, is greater and more excellent than all the wealth of earth. Nay, a single hour in the glad abode of the pious, is more happy and precious than a thousand years among sinners; for their weeping and wailing will not end, and their tears will not cease, nor will they find solace or rest to themselves at any time whatever. And now, O, my honoured members! go and preach to all nations; declare and say to them, Surely the Saviour seeketh diligently for his due heritage, and is the administrator of justice. And the angels shall put to flight the enemies, and fight for them in the day of conflict. And God shall try every idle and foolish word which men speak, and they shall give account for it.[3] For as no one shall be exempt from death, so also, the works of every man will be manifest in the day of judgment, whether they be good or bad.[4] Declare also this word which I have said to you to-day: let not the strong man glory in his strength, nor the rich man in his riches, let him that will glory, glory in the Lord.[5]

---

[1] Luke xxiv. 49; Acts i. 8. [2] Luke xxiv. 47.
[3] Matt. xii. 36. [4] 2 Cor. v. 10; 1 Cor. iii. 15.
[5] Jer. ix. 23-24.

CHAPTER II.

THERE was a man whose name was Joseph, sprung of a family of Bethlehem, a city of Judah, and the city of David the King. The same being well instructed in knowledge and doctrine, was made a priest in the temple of the Lord. Moreover, he understood the carpenter's trade, and like all men, married a wife. He also begat sons and daughters, that is to say, four sons and two daughters; and these are their names,—Judas, Justus, James, and Simon; the names of the two daughters were Assia and Lydia. At length the wife of Joseph the Just deceased, intent upon divine glory in all her works. Now Joseph, that just man, my father according to the flesh, and the spouse of Mary my mother, went with his sons to his calling, following the trade of a carpenter.

CHAPTER III.

Now when Joseph the Just became a widower, Mary my mother, blessed, holy, and pure, had already accomplished twelve years. Her parents offered her in the temple at three years old, and she remained nine years in the temple of the Lord. Then, when the priests saw that the holy virgin, who feared the Lord, was grown up, they talked together, saying: Let us seek for a just and pious man to whom Mary may be committed till the time of marriage, lest, by remaining in the temple, there should happen to her what often happens to women, and we sin on that account, and God be angry with us.

CHAPTER IV.

THEREFORE, having forthwith sent out messengers, they called together twelve aged men of the tribe of Judah, and they wrote the names of the twelve tribes of Israel. Now the lot fell upon the pious old man, Joseph the Just. Then the priests answered and said to my blessed mother,—Go with Joseph and be with him until the time of marriage. Therefore Joseph the Just received my mother and took her to his home. And Mary found James the Less in the house of his father, broken in mind and sad because of his bereavement of his mother, and she brought him up. Hence she is called Mary the Mother of James. After this Joseph left her in his house and went to his workshop, where his calling of carpenter was carried on. But after the holy virgin had spent two years in his house, her age became exactly fourteen years, including the time from which Joseph received her.

CHAPTER V.

I LOVED her with a peculiar affection, with the

good pleasure of my Father, and the counsel of the Holy Spirit; and I was incarnate of her, by a mystery surpassing the capacity of the reason of creatures. But when three months had passed since the conception, the just man Joseph returned from the place where he followed his trade, and when he found the virgin my mother pregnant, he was troubled in mind, and thought of dismissing her secretly.[1] For fear also, and the sorrow and anguish of his heart, he could not bear either to eat or drink that day.

CHAPTER VI.

Now about the middle of the day, holy Gabriel, the prince of the angels, appeared to him in a dream, being supplied with a command from my Father; and he said to him, Joseph, son of David, fear not to take Mary thy spouse; for she hath conceived by the Holy Spirit, and shall bear a son, whose name shall be called Jesus. He it is who shall govern all nations with an iron sceptre.[2] When he had said this the angel departed from him. But Joseph arose out of his sleep, and did as the angel of the Lord said to him; and Mary continued with him.[3]

[1] Matt. i. 19. [2] Ps. ii. 9; Rev. ii. 27; xii. 5.
[3] Matt. i. 20-24.

CHAPTER VII.

AFTER the lapse of some time, a command went forth from Augustus Cæsar, the king, that all the habitable globe should be enrolled, every one in his own city. Therefore the just old man Joseph arose, and took with him Mary the virgin, and they came to Bethlehem, because her time to be delivered drew nigh. Now Joseph inscribed his name on the register: for Joseph the son of David, whose spouse was Mary, was of the tribe of Judah. And Mary, my mother, brought me forth at Bethlehem in a cave, very nigh to the sepulchre of Rachel, the wife of Jacob the patriarch, and mother of Joseph and Benjamin.

CHAPTER VIII.

BUT Satan went and reported this to Herod the Great, the father of Archelaus. It was this same Herod who commanded John my friend and kinsman to be beheaded.[1] Therefore he diligently sought after me, supposing my kingdom would be of this world.[2] But Joseph, the pious old man, was admonished of this matter by a dream. He therefore arose and took Mary my mother: and I lay in her bosom. Salome also added herself to them as the

---

[1] John the Baptist was put to death by order of Herod Antipas; there is therefore an error in the text, whether the writer means Herod the Great, or Archelaus.

[2] John xviii. 36.

companion of their journey. Therefore, leaving home, he retired into Egypt, and remained there the space of one whole year, until Herod's jealousy passed away.

CHAPTER IX.

Now Herod died the worst kind of death, suffering punishment for the shed blood of the children, whom he iniquitously destroyed when there was no sin in them.[1] And when that impious tyrant Herod was dead, the parents of Jesus returned with him to the land of Israel, and dwelt in a city of Galilee which is called Nazareth. Now Joseph, resuming his carpenter's trade, supported life by the work of his hands; for he did not seek his food for nought by the labour of another; as the law of Moses had commanded.[2]

CHAPTER X.

At length, his years increasing, the old man arrived at an advanced age. Yet he laboured under no infirmity of body, his sight failed not, and no tooth in his mouth decayed, nor was he ever insane in mind in all his life; but, like a youth, he always displayed juvenile vigour in his affairs, and his members remained whole and free from all pain. His whole

---

[1] Josephus, Antiquities, xvii. 6, 8.　　[2] Gen. iii. 19; 2 Thess. iii. 10.

life consisted of a hundred and eleven years; his age having been prolonged to the utmost limit.

CHAPTER XI.

JUSTUS and Simeon the elder sons of Joseph, having married wives, went away to their families. Both the daughters likewise married, and went to their houses. But Judas and James the Less, and the virgin my mother, remained in the house of Joseph. I also continued along with them, not otherwise than if I had been one of his sons. I passed all my time without fault. I called Mary my mother, and Joseph father, and in all they said I was obedient to them; nor did I ever resist them, but submitted to them, just as other men whom earth produceth are wont to do; nor did I provoke their anger any day, nor return any harsh word or answer to them; on the contrary, I cherished them with immense love, as the apple of my eye.

CHAPTER XII.

IT happened after this that the death of the pious old man Joseph and his departure from this world approached, just as with other men who owe their origin to this earth. And when his body was inclining towards its decease, an angel of the Lord made known to him that the hour of death now drew nigh. Therefore fear and great trouble of mind came over him. But he arose and went to Jerusalem, and having entered the temple of the Lord and poured out his prayers there before the sanctuary, he said:—

CHAPTER XIII.

O God, who art the author of all comfort, the God of all mercy, and Lord of the whole human race, the God (I say) of my soul, spirit, and body: I suppliantly venerate thee, O my Lord and God, if now my days are finished, and the time is at hand in which I must go out of this world, send me, I pray, the great Michael, prince of thy holy angels, and let him abide with me, that my wretched soul may depart from this miserable body without distress, without terror and impatience. For immense fear and vehement sorrow seizeth all bodies on the day of their death, whether male or female, whether cattle or wild beast, whatever either creepeth upon the ground or flieth in the air; in sum, all creatures which are under heaven, and in which vital spirit is, are stricken with horror, with great fear, and immense faintness, when their souls depart from their bodies. Now, therefore, O my Lord and God, let thy holy angel, with his aid, attend upon my soul and body, until they are separated from each other. Nor let the face of the angel appointed for my keeping from the day when I was made, be turned away from me; but let him offer himself to me as the companion of my journey, until he hath brought me to thee; let his countenance be sweet and cheerful to me, and let him accompany me in peace. But suffer not that demons terrible in aspect should come to me in the way wherein I am to go, until I come happily to thee. Nor let the door-keepers prevent my soul at the entrance of Paradise. Nor by unfolding my sins expose me to rebuke before thy terrible tribunal. Nor let the lions rush upon me. Nor let the waves of the fiery sea submerge my soul —for every soul must pass through this—before I behold the glory of thy divinity. O, God! judge most just, who wilt judge mortals in justice and equity, and repay to every one according to his works, O my Lord and God! let thy mercy be with me, and enlighten thou my way that I may attain to thee: for thou art a fount abounding in all good and glory for ever. Amen![1]

---

[1] The reader will observe the remarkable development of the author's eschatology in the prayer assigned to Joseph; and he will see that the whole spirit and attitude of Joseph ill accords with that of the earlier ages of the Church. As we proceed we shall find abundant confirmation of the points hinted at in this note. It is needless to say that we have, neither in the New Testament nor in any other authentic record, a single hint concerning the last days and death of Joseph.

CHAPTER XIV.

AFTER this it came to pass, when he returned home to the city of Nazareth, that he fell sick and kept his bed. And this was the time in which he died, as it is appointed unto all men. Now he was grievously afflicted by this sickness, nor had he ever been so ill as at present, from the time he was born. And thus truly it pleased Christ to arrange the affairs of Joseph the Just.[1] Forty years he lived before he entered the married state; his wife remained under his protection forty-nine years, and died when they were gone. One year after her death, my mother, the blessed Mary, was committed to Joseph by the priests, that he might keep her until the time for marriage. Two years she spent in his house, with nothing remarkable occurring, but in the third year of her sojourn with Joseph, and the fifteenth of her age, she bore me in the earth, by a mystery which no creature can penetrate or apprehend, save myself and my Father, and the Holy Spirit, constituting one essence with me.[2]

CHAPTER XV.

THEREFORE, the whole age of my father, the just

---

[1] The mention of Christ here in the third person, seems to be due to momentary forgetfulness on the part of the author.

[2] This theological definition savours of no very early date. A similar expression is pointed out by Thilo in a Syriac liturgy.

old man, made up one hundred and eleven years, for so my heavenly Father decreed. And the day on which his soul departed from his body, was the twenty-sixth of the month Abib. For now the fine gold began to lose its brightness, and the silver to be worn with use, I mean his intellect and understanding. Moreover, he loathed his food and drink, and his skill in the carpenter's trade failed him, nor did he any longer have regard to it. It came to pass, therefore, at daybreak on the twenty-sixth day of the month of Abib, that the soul of the old man, Joseph the Just, was rendered unquiet as he lay in his bed. Wherefore, he opened his mouth and sighed, and smote his hands together, and cried out, with a loud voice, saying after this manner :—

CHAPTER XVI.

WOE to the day on which I was born into the world! woe to the womb which bore me! woe to the body which received me! woe to the breasts which gave me suck! woe to the knees on which I sat and rested! woe to the hands which carried and led me till I grew up! For I was conceived in iniquity, and in sin my mother longed for me![1] Woe to my

---

[1] For 'concepit,' which the Latin versions of Ps. li. 5 correctly have, the Arabic here has what is equivalent to 'concupivit.' It is well to note this, because 'longed for' might be suspected to be an oversight for 'conceived.'

tongue and lips, which have uttered and spoken vanity, reproach, falsehood, folly, ridicule, fiction, craft, and hypocrisy! Woe to my eyes, which have looked upon offence! Woe to my ears, which have taken pleasure in the talk of calumniators! Woe to my hands, which have seized what did not lawfully pertain to them! Woe to my stomach, which has longed for food which it was forbidden it to eat! Woe to my throat, which, like a fire, consumed all things, whatever it took hold of? Woe to my feet, which have too often walked in ways displeasing to God! Woe to my body, and woe to my unhappy soul, which is now averse from God its maker! What shall I do when I come to the place where I must stand before the most just Judge, and he shall rebuke me for the works which I have multiplied in my youth? Woe to every man who dieth in his sins! Certainly that same terrible hour which overtook my father Jacob when his soul took flight from his body, behold to me is now imminent. O, how miserable I am to-day, and worthy of lamentation! But God alone is the director of my soul and body; he also will do with them according to his pleasure.[1]

CHAPTER XVII.

THIS is what Joseph, that just old man, said. Now

[1] The lamentation and confession of Joseph finds its counterpart in a Jewish confession quoted by Thilo from Buxtorf's *Synodus Judaica*.

when I went in to him, I perceived his soul to be greatly troubled; for he was in great anguish. And I said to him, Hail, my father Joseph, thou just man; how art thou? And he answered me, The best of greetings, O, my beloved little son! Verily, the pain and fear of death already surrounded me; but as soon as I heard thy voice, my soul found rest. O, Jesus the Nazarene! Jesus my Saviour! Jesus the Deliverer of my soul! Jesus my protector! Jesus, O, sweetest name in the mouth of me, and of all who love it! Eye which seest, and ear which hearest, hearken to me![1] I, thy servant, to-day most humbly venerate thee, and pour out my tears before thee. Thou art altogether my God, thou art my Lord, as the angel very often told me; but chiefly on that day when my soul was tossed about by perverse thoughts on account of the pure and blessed Mary, who was with child, and whom I thought to put away secretly. But while I meditated these things, behold there appeared unto me in my sleep, angels of the Lord, in a wondrous mystery, saying unto me, O, Joseph, son of David, fear not to take Mary thy spouse, neither be sad, nor say unseemly words of her conception, for she is with child of the Holy Spirit, and shall bear a son, whose name shall be called Jesus; for he shall save his people from their sins. Bear me no ill will on this account, O, Lord;

[1] Thilo compares a similar phrase in the Hebrew *Pirke Aboth*, ii. 2.

for I knew not the mystery of thy nativity. I remember, also, my Lord, that day when the boy was killed by the bite of a serpent. Now his relations wished to deliver thee to Herod, saying thou hadst killed him: but thou didst restore him to them raised from the dead. Then I came and took thee by the hand, and said, My son, take care for thyself. But thou answeredst me, Art thou not my father according to the flesh? I will teach thee who I am. Now, therefore, O, my Lord and God, be not angry with me, nor condemn me because of that hour. I am thy servant, and the son of thy handmaid;[1] but thou art my Lord, my God and Saviour; most certainly the Son of God.

CHAPTER XVIII.

WHEN my father Joseph had said this, he could weep no more, and I saw death already prevailing over him. But my mother, the unsullied virgin, rising and coming to me, said, O, my beloved son, this pious old man Joseph is already dying. And I replied, O, my mother, most loving, surely upon all creatures, which are born in this world, lieth the same necessity of dying: for death hath dominion over all the human race. Thou, also, O, my virgin mother, must expect the same end of life with all

[1] Ps. cxvi. 16. This chapter contains allusions to the Evangelists, and also to other Apocryphal Gospels.

other mortals. Nevertheless, thy death, as also the death of this pious man, is not death, but perennial life for ever. But it behoveth me too to die, as respects the body which I received from thee. But arise, O, my venerable mother, go and enter to Joseph, the blessed old man, that thou mayest see what happeneth when his soul goeth up from his body.

CHAPTER XIX

THEREFORE, Mary, my pure mother, went and entered the place where Joseph was, and I sat at his feet looking at him; but the signs of death now appeared in his face. And that blessed old man, with head raised, and fixed eyes, looked into my face: yet he possessed no power to address me, because of the pain of death, which held him enclosed round; but he drew many sighs. And I held his hand for the space of one whole hour: and he, with his face turned towards me, signified that I should not leave him. Afterwards, placing my hand upon his breast, I perceived his soul already near his throat, preparing to depart from its receptacle.

CHAPTER XX.

Now when my virgin mother saw me touching his body, she also touched his feet; and finding them already half-dead, and without heat, she said to me, O, my beloved son, clearly his feet now begin to grow cold, and are like the coldness of snow. Then when his sons and daughters had been called, she said to them, 'Come, all of you, and approach your father: for certainly he is now come to his end. Assia, the daughter of Joseph, answered, saying, Woe, unto me, O, my brethren, surely this is the same disease as was that of my beloved mother. And she wailed and wept, and all the other children of Joseph lamented with her. I also, and Mary my mother, wept with them.

CHAPTER XXI.

AND turning my eyes to the south side, I saw Death now coming, and all Gehenna with it, crowded with its host and attendants; and their garments, faces, and mouths cast out fire. When my father Joseph saw these come straight to him, his eyes were bathed in tears; and the same moment he groaned in a wonderful manner. Therefore, seeing the violence of his sighs, I repulsed Death, and all the host of followers which attended him. And I called upon my good Father, saying:

CHAPTER XXII.

O FATHER of all mercy, Eye which seest, and

Ear which hearest, hearken to my supplication and prayers for the old man Joseph; and send Michael, the prince of thy angels, and Gabriel, the herald of light, and all the light of thy angels; and let their whole order journey with the soul of my father Joseph, until they have brought it to thee. This is the hour wherein my father hath need of mercy. Now I say to you, that all saints, nay, all men that are born in the world, whether they be just or wicked, must needs taste death.

CHAPTER XXIII.

THEREFORE, Michael and Gabriel came to the soul of my father Joseph; and, having received it, wrapped it in a bright wrapper.[1] So he committed his spirit into the hands of my good Father, who bestowed upon him peace. And none of his children yet knew that he had fallen asleep. But the angels preserved his soul from the demons of darkness, which were in the way; and they praised God, until they brought it to the habitation of the pious.

CHAPTER XXIV.

BUT his body lay prostrate and lifeless; where-

---

[1] The wrapping up of Joseph's soul is an anomaly. It might seem as if the body were meant. The Hebrew *Nephesh* sometimes means a dead body. What follows, however, compels us to retain the word 'soul.'

fore, putting my hands to his eyes, I arranged them, and I closed his mouth. And I said to Mary the virgin, O, my mother, where is his trade, which he professed all the time he lived in this world? Behold it is now perished, and is as if it had never existed. When his children heard me speaking thus with my pure virgin mother, they knew that he had now expired; and, mingling their tears, they wailed. But I said to them, Surely the death of your father is not death, but life eternal; for he is delivered from the sorrows of this world, and hath passed away to rest which is perpetual and will endure for ever. When they heard this, they rent their garments, weeping.

CHAPTER XXV.

AND the inhabitants of the city of Nazareth and of Galilee, when they knew of their mourning, flocked unto them, and wept from the third hour till the ninth. And at the ninth hour, they all went together to the bed of Joseph. And they took up his body after they had anointed it with excellent ointments. But I prayed to my Father with the prayer of the heavenly ones: it was the same which I wrote with my hand before. I was borne in the womb of Mary, my virgin mother. Now as soon as I had finished it, and uttered Amen, an immense multitude of angels came; and I commanded two of them to spread out a bright vestment, and wrap in it the body of the blessed old man Joseph.[1]

CHAPTER XXVI.

AND addressing Joseph, I said, The odour or stink of death shall not prevail in thee, nor shall worm ever proceed from thy body. Not a single limb of it shall be broken, nor shall any hair in thy head be changed, nor shall any of thy body perish, O, my father Joseph; but it shall remain entire and uncorrupted, until the banquet of a thousand years.[2] And whatever mortal is mindful of the oblation on the day of thy memorial, him will I bless and reward in the congregation of virgins. And whoever giveth food to the wretched, and poor, and widows, and orphans, of the work of his hands on the day when thy memory is celebrated, and in thy name, he shall not be without good all the days of his life. Whoever, also, shall offer to drink a cup of water or of wine to the widow or orphan in thy name, I will give him to thee, that thou mayest go in with him to the banquet of a thousand years. And every man that shall

[1] See the preceding note, p. 118.
[2] This millenarian idea does not of necessity imply a very early date for the book, but may be due to certain texts in the Apocalypse, as Rev. xx. 4, or to Jewish notions. What follows about the annual commemoration of Joseph, can certainly lay no claim to high antiquity.

attend to the oblation on the day of thy commemoration, I will bless him, and give him a recompense in the church of virgins: I will return him (I say) thirty, sixty, and one hundred for one. And whoever writeth the history of thy life, thy labour, and thy departure from this world, and this discourse delivered by my mouth, I will commit him to thy guardianship while he shall remain in this life. And when his soul departeth from his body, and when he must leave this world, I will burn the book of his sins, nor will I torment him with any punishment in the day of judgment; but he shall cross the fiery sea, and shall traverse it without difficulty and pain. This is incumbent upon every needy man who cannot do any of the things which I have mentioned,— that if a son is born to him, he shall call his name Joseph. So neither poverty nor sudden death shall have place in that house for ever.

CHAPTER XXVII.

THEN came the chief men of the city to the place where the body of the blessed old man Joseph was laid; and they brought with them mourning garments, and wished to wrap it in them, according to the manner in which the Jews are wont to arrange dead bodies. But they perceived that he held his shroud as if it were fastened; for so did it adhere to his body that, when they desired to take it off, it was found like iron—immoveable and inseparable. Nor could they find any edges in the shroud, which thing filled them with the greatest astonishment. At length they bore him away to a place where there was a cave, and they opened the door to deposit his body among the bodies of his fathers. Then came into my mind the day on which he journeyed with me into Egypt, and that great trouble which he endured on my account. Then I wept for his death a long time, and bowing over his body, I said:—

CHAPTER XXVIII.

O Death! who renderest all human knowledge vain, and callest forth so many tears and lamentations, certainly it is God my Father who hath allowed thee this power. For through the transgression of Adam and his wife, Eve, men die, and death spareth not even one.[1] Yet nothing happeneth or befalleth any one without the commandment of my Father. Men have existed, indeed, who have prolonged their life to as much as nine hundred years; but they have died.[2] Nay, though some of them may have lived longer, they nevertheless succumbed to the same fate, nor did any of them ever say, I have not tasted death. But the Lord never inflicteth

[1] Gen. iii. 6; Rom. v. 12; 1 Cor. xv. 21, 22.   [2] Gen. v. 5.

the same penalty more than once, when it hath pleased my Father to send it upon a man.[1] In the same moment when it cometh forth it seeth the command descending to it out of heaven, and it saith, I will go forth against that man to cause him great trouble. Then without delay an assault is made upon the soul, and death ruleth over it, doing with it as it will. For because Adam did not the will of my Father, but transgressed his commandment, my Father, being provoked to anger against him, devoted him to death, and for this cause death entered the world.[2] But if Adam had kept the precept of my Father, death would never have befallen him. Think ye that I can seek from my good Father that he would send me a fiery chariot,[3] to receive the body of my father Joseph, and remove it to a place of rest, to dwell with spiritual beings? But for the prevarication of Adam, this affliction and violence of death descended upon the whole human race; and this is the reason why it behoveth me to die according to the flesh, namely, for my work, or men whom I created, that they may obtain favour.

CHAPTER XXIX.

HAVING said thus I embraced the body of my father Joseph, and wept over it; but the others

[1] Heb. ix. 27.   [2] Gen. iii. xix.   [3] 2 Kings, ii. 11.

opened the door of the sepulchre and laid his body in it beside the body of his father Jacob. Now when he fell asleep he had completed one hundred and eleven years. Never did any tooth ache in his mouth, nor did the sight of his eyes grow dim, nor did his form bend, nor his strength fail; but he applied himself to his carpenter's trade, even to the last day of his life, and that day was the 26th of the month Abib.

CHAPTER XXX.

Now we apostles, when we heard this from our Saviour, joyfully arose, and with prostrate body rendered honour to him, saying, O our Saviour, display to us thy grace; for now we have heard the word of life. Yet we wonder, O our Saviour, at the fate of Enoch and Elijah, that they were not exposed to any death. For they dwell in the place of the just, unto the present day, and their bodies have not seen corruption. But that old man Joseph, the carpenter, was still thy father after the flesh. Now thou hast commanded that we should go through all the world and preach the holy Gospel, and thou hast said, Tell them also the death of my father Joseph, and celebrate a festal and sacred day to him in an annual solemnity.[1] But whoever shall diminish aught from

[1] The importance attached to the commemoration of Joseph savours of no early date. The day mentioned, Abib 26th, is said in the

this word, or add anything to it, he sinneth. Now we are surprised that Joseph, from the day when thou wast born at Bethlehem, called thee his son according to the flesh. Why, then, hast thou not made him immortal as Enoch and Elijah are? and thou sayest he was just and elect.

CHAPTER XXXI.

AND our Saviour answered and said, Now indeed is the prophecy of my Father fulfilled concerning Adam for his disobedience. And all things are disposed according to the nod and will of my Father. If a man setteth aside the command of God, and followeth the works of the devil by committing sin, his age is prolonged: thus, indeed, is he preserved alive that, perchance, he may repent, and consider that he must be delivered into the hand of death. And if anyone hath been zealous of good works, also his time of life is prolonged, that as the fame of his old age increaseth good men may imitate him. But when ye see a man whose soul is hasty to wrath, his days are surely shortened; for it is these who are taken away in the flower of their age. Therefore every prophecy, which my Father hath uttered

---

Arabic preface to answer to Ab, which was the Syriac name of the month falling in July and August. The Ethiopic and Coptic churches still observe the death of Joseph about the same time. The Church of Rome places Joseph at March 19th.

concerning the sons of men, must in all respects be fulfilled. But as to Enoch and Elijah, that they continue alive to this day, retaining the same bodies with which they were born, and as to my father Joseph to whom continuance in his body is not allotted as to them; verily, even if a man lives many myriads of years in the world, he is nevertheless compelled at some time to exchange life for death. And I tell you, O my brethren, that these same men (Enoch and Elijah), must return into the world at the end of time, and depart this life, namely in the day of commotion, terror, anguish, and affliction.[1] For Antichrist will slay four bodies, and will shed their blood like water, for the reproach to which they will expose him, and the ignominy wherewith, when they have detected his impiety, while they live they will brand him.

CHAPTER XXXII.

AND we said, O our Lord, our God and Saviour, who are those four that thou saidst Antichrist would put out of the way because of their rebuke? The Saviour answered, They are Enoch, Elijah, Shila, and Tabitha.[2] When we heard this word from our Saviour, we rejoiced and were glad, and offered all

[1] It was an old notion that the two witnesses to be slain by Antichrist were Enoch and Elijah (Rev. xi. 3-12).
[2] For Tabitha see Acts ix. 36. Shila I am unable to identify.

glory and thanksgiving to the Lord God and our Saviour Jesus Christ. He it is to whom is due glory, honour, dignity, dominion, power, and praise, as well as to the good Father with him, and to the Holy life-giving Spirit henceforth and at all time for ever and ever. Amen.[1]

[1] Thilo observes that some of the epithets of this doxology occur in some of the Syrian, Coptic, and Greek liturgies.

V.

THE GOSPEL OF THOMAS. (I.)

TISCHENDORF gives us two Greek texts of this apocryphal book, and a Latin translation. It is of unquestionably early origin; indeed it is thought to have been known to Irenæus before the end of the second century. Judging from its character, it has been regarded as written originally with the intention of favouring Docetism, though M. Nicolas finds in it traces of Judaising Christianity as well as of Docetism. Whatever its origin, it is a document in many ways remarkable. The style of the Greek is often obscure and always rude and inferior, and its tone and temper betray a singular misapprehension of the true spirit and character of Christ. Possibly it was drawn up in Syria, and a Syriac text has been found in the British Museum and published by Dr. W. Wright. The Syriac text, of which a translation is given in the present volume, differs in various details from those of Tischendorf. The true authorship is of course unknown. It may be viewed as a collection of foolish traditions, or fables invented to supply an account of that period in our Lord's history, respecting which the genuine Gospels are almost silent. These fables were probably varied and multiplied by the writer. The most noticeable features of the book are its grossly fictitious character, and its anti-evangelical representations; or, as Bishop Ellicott says, "pious fraud and disguised heresy." It is of course utterly worthless, except as illustrating the recklessness of many professed followers of Christ at an early period. The miracles which it narrates are mostly either puerile, or malevolent and cruel. Some of its details are to be found in other Apocryphal Gospels, but next to the Protevangelium its plan is most specific; indeed, so far as Christ's infancy is concerned it is the most specific document of its class. The time over which it extends is supposed to be seven years. The stories of which it is made up are arranged chronologically, but it appears needless to exhibit a summary of them. There is good reason for believing that the Gospel of Thomas has not only at different times borne different names, but has varied much in its extent.

THE GOSPEL OF THOMAS.

Sayings of Thomas, the Israelite Philosopher, on the Infant Acts of the Lord.

CHAPTER I.

I THOMAS the Israelite declare to all of you, who are brethren of the Gentiles, that I make known the infant acts and great deeds of our Lord Jesus Christ, which he did when he had been born in our country: the beginning whereof is in this wise:

CHAPTER II.

THIS child Jesus, being five years old, was playing at the crossing of a stream, and he collected the running waters into pools, and immediately made them pure; and by his word alone he commanded them. And having made some soft clay he fashioned out of it twelve sparrows; and it was the Sabbath when he did these things. And there were also many other children playing with him. And a certain Jew seeing what Jesus did, playing on the Sabbath, went immediately and said to Joseph his father: Behold thy child is at the watercourse, and hath taken clay and formed twelve birds, and hath profaned the Sabbath. And Joseph came to the place, and when he saw him he cried unto him saying, Why art thou doing these things on the Sabbath, which it is not lawful to do? And Jesus clapped his hands and cried unto the sparrows, and said to them, Go away: and the sparrows flew up, and departed, making a noise. And when the Jews saw it they were astonished, and went and told their leaders what they had seen Jesus do.[1]

CHAPTER III.

Now the son of Annas the Scribe was standing there with Joseph, and took a branch of a willow and spilled the water which Jesus had collected. And when Jesus saw what was done he was angry and said to him, Wicked, impious, and foolish one, wherein have the pools and the water wronged thee? Behold, now thou also shalt wither as a tree, and shalt not produce either leaves, or root, or fruit. And suddenly the boy withered altogether. And Jesus departed and went away to the house of Joseph. And the parents of him that was withered

[1] Comp. Pseudo-Matth. xxvi., etc.

carried him, bemoaning his youth, and brought him to Joseph, and accused him (saying), Such a son hast thou as doeth such things.

CHAPTER IV.

THEN again he went through the village, and a boy ran and thrust against his shoulder; and Jesus being vexed, said to him, Thou shalt not finish thy journey. And immediately he fell down and died. And some who saw what was done, said, Whence was this boy born? for every word of his becometh at once a deed. And the parents of him that was dead came to Joseph and made complaint, saying, Thou who hast such a child, canst not dwell with us in the village; teach him to bless and not to curse; for he killeth our children.

CHAPTER V.

AND Joseph called the boy to him privately and admonished him, saying, Why dost thou perpetrate such things, and (why do) these suffer, and hate and persecute us? And Jesus said, I know that these thy words are not thine; nevertheless I will be silent because of thee; but they shall bear their punishment. And immediately they who accused him became blind. And they who saw it were greatly afraid and perplexed, and said concerning him, that every word he spake, whether good or bad, was a deed, and became a wonder. And when they saw that Jesus did thus, Joseph arose and took him by the ear and pulled it violently. And the child was angry and said to him, It is enough for thee to seek and not to find, and thou hast done very unwisely. Knowest thou not that I am thine? grieve me not.[1]

CHAPTER VI.

AND a certain teacher named Zacchæus stood in a certain place and heard Jesus saying these things to his father; and he wondered greatly that being a child he said such things. And after a few days he came to Joseph and said to him, Thou hast an intelligent child, and he hath understanding; come, give him to me, that he may learn letters, and I will teach him with his letters all science, and how to address all his elders, and to honour them as ancestors and fathers, and to love those of his own age. And he told him all the letters from Alpha to Omega with much distinctness and clearly. And looking at the teacher Zacchæus he saith to him, Thou that knowest not Alpha naturally, how dost thou teach Beta to others? Hypocrite; if thou knowest, first teach Alpha, and then we shall believe thee con-

[1] Pseudo-Matth. xxix.

cerning Beta. Then he began to puzzle the teacher about the first letter, and he could not answer him. And in the hearing of many, the child said to Zacchæus, Hear, teacher, the arrangement of the first letter, and notice here how it hath lines and a middle stroke which thou seest crossing those that are common, connected, with top projecting and again contracting, (thou seest) they are triform of the same kind, chief and subordinate, equal in length. Thou hast the lines of the Alpha.[1]

CHAPTER VII.

AND when the teacher Zacchæus heard the boy speak such and so great allegories of the first letter, he was perplexed by his great vindication and teaching, and said to those who were present, Alas, unhappy me! I am at a loss, I have brought shame upon myself by taking charge of this child. Take him away then, I entreat thee, brother Joseph, I cannot bear the severity of his gaze; I cannot explain the matter at all. This child is not of earthly parents, he is able to subdue even fire. Perhaps he was begotten before the world was made. What womb bore him, and what lap nursed him I know not. Alas, my friend, he surpasseth me, I shall not attain to his understanding. I have deceived my-

[1] Pseudo-Matth. xxx., xxxi.

self, O most wretched me! I desired to obtain a pupil, and found I had a tutor. My friends, I am filled with shame, that I who am an old man am defeated by a child. I suffer affliction and death through this child; for this very hour I cannot look into his face. And when all say I was overcome by a little child, what can I say? or what can I tell of the lines of the first letter, which he told me of? I know not, O friends; for I know not its beginning and end. Wherefore I beseech thee, brother Joseph, take him away to thy house. Whatever great thing He is, whether God or Angel, or what to say, I know not.

CHAPTER VIII.

AND when the Jews encouraged Zacchæus, the child laughed greatly, and said: Now let thy works be fruitful, and let the blind in heart see. I come from above that I may curse them, and call to things on high, as He who sent me ordained for your sakes. And as the child paused in his speech, straightway all who had fallen under his curse were delivered. And thenceforward no one dared provoke him, lest he should curse him and he become blind.

CHAPTER IX.

AND after some days Jesus was playing in a certain house in an upper room, and one of the children who were playing with him fell down from the house and died. And when the other children saw it, they fled, and Jesus remained alone. And the parents of him that was dead came and accused him. . . . . . [saying, verily thou causedst him to fall. But Jesus said, I did not cause him to fall.] . . . . and they threatened him.[1] Jesus leaped down from the roof and stood by the dead body of the child and cried with a loud voice, and said,—Zeno! (for so his name was called), rise and tell me; did I cast thee down? And immediately he rose and said,— Nay, Lord, thou hast not cast me down, but raised me up. And seeing this they were amazed. And the parents of the boy glorified God for the miracle which had been done, and worshipped Jesus.[2]

CHAPTER X.

AFTER a few days, a certain young man was cleaving wood in the corner, and the axe fell and cut asunder the sole of his foot; and losing all his blood, he died. And there was a clamour and a crowd, and the child Jesus ran thither, and by force he passed through the throng, and took hold of the young man that was wounded in the foot, and straightway he was healed. And he said to the young man,—Rise now,

[1] The text is here corrupt or defective.   [2] Pseudo-Matt. xxxii.

cleave the wood, and remember me. And the crowd who saw what was done, worshipped the Child, saying,—Truly the Spirit of God dwelleth in this Child.

CHAPTER XI.

AND when he was six years old, his mother sent him to draw water and bring it home, having given him a water-pot. And being thronged by the crowd, the water-pot was broken. But Jesus spreading out the garment with which he was clothed, filled it with water, and carried it to his mother. And when his mother saw the miracle which was done, she kissed him, and kept to herself the wonders which she saw him do.[1]

CHAPTER XII.

AND again, at the time for sowing, the Child went out with his father to sow corn in their field, and when his father sowed, the child Jesus also sowed one grain of corn. And having reaped and threshed it, he made a hundred quarters of it. And having called all the poor of the village to the threshing floor, he bestowed the corn on them; and Joseph took away what was left of the corn. Now Jesus was eight years old when he wrought this miracle.[2]

[1] Pseudo-Matt. xxxiii. [2] Pseudo-Matt. xxxiv.

CHAPTER XIII.

Now his father was a carpenter, and made at that time ploughs and yokes; and a couch was ordered of him by a certain rich man, to make it for him; and one of the pieces known as a side piece, being too short, they knew not what to do, wherefore the child Jesus said to his father Joseph,—Lay down the two pieces of wood, and let the centre of one be upon the centre of the other. And Joseph did as the child said to him; and Jesus stood at the other end, and took hold of the wood which was too short, and stretched it and made it equal to the other. And his father Joseph saw and marvelled, and embracing the child he kissed him, saying: Happy am I, because God hath given this child to me.[1]

CHAPTER XIV.

AND Joseph seeing the understanding of the child and his growth, that he was becoming a youth, considered again that he should not remain unacquainted with letters, and he took him and handed him over to another teacher: and the teacher said to Joseph, I will first instruct him in Greek, and then in Hebrew, for the teacher knew the cleverness of the child, and was afraid of him. Nevertheless he wrote the alpha-

[1] Pseudo-Matth. xxxvii.

bet and repeated it to him for a long time; and he did not answer him; and Jesus said to him, If thou art indeed a teacher, and if thou knowest the letters well, tell me the power of Alpha, and I will tell thee that of Beta ; and the teacher, being annoyed, struck him on the head; and the child was vexed and cursed him, and immediately he became senseless, and fell upon his face on the ground; and the child returned to the house of Joseph. And Joseph was grieved, and charged his mother, (saying,) thou shalt not send him outside the door, for they die who provoke him to anger.[1]

CHAPTER XV.

AND after some time again another instructor, who was a near friend of Joseph, said to him, Bring me the child to school, perhaps I may be able with coaxing to teach him letters. And Joseph said, If thou art bold enough, brother, take him with thee; and he took him with him with fear and much inward conflict; but the child went cheerfully; and boldly entering the school, he found a book lying upon the desk, and he took it up but did not read the letters in it, but opened his mouth and spake by the Holy Spirit, and taught the law to those who stood around. And a great crowd assembled and stood by listening to him, and they wondered at the beauty of his

[1] Pseudo-Matth. xxxviii.

teaching, and the fluency of his words, because, although a child, he spake such things. Now when Joseph heard it, he was afraid, and ran into the school, thinking whether this teacher was unskilful. But the teacher said to Joseph, Thou must know, brother, that I received the child as a pupil, but he is full of much grace and wisdom; and now I beseech thee, brother, take him to thy house. And when the child heard this, he straightway laughed at him and said, Because thou hast rightly spoken and rightly testified, for thy sake he also that was smitten shall be healed. And forthwith the other teacher was healed. And Joseph took the child and went to his home.[1]

CHAPTER XVI.

AND Joseph sent his son James to tie up wood and carry it into his house; and the child Jesus also followed him; and as James was gathering sticks, a viper bit the hand of James; and when he was tortured and near dying, Jesus approached and blew on the bite; and the pain at once ceased; and the beast was rent, and immediately James remained well.[2]

CHAPTER XVII.

AND after these things, a certain child among the

[1] Pseudo-Matth. xxxix.   [2] Pseudo-Matth. xli.

neighbours of Joseph, fell sick and died, and his mother wept for him exceedingly; and Jesus heard that great grief and trouble prevailed, and ran in haste, and found the child dead; and he touched him on the breast and said to him, I say unto thee, babe, do not die, but live, and be with thy mother. And immediately he looked up and smiled. And he said to the woman, Take him and give him milk, and remember me. And the crowd that stood by wondered and said, Verily this Child was either God or an angel of God, for every word of his is at once a deed. And Jesus went out thence to play with other children.[1]

CHAPTER XVIII.

AND after some time, there was a house building, and a great clamour, and Jesus arose and went thither, and seeing a man lying dead, he took him by his hand and said, I say unto thee, man, arise, and do thy work; and he straightway arose and worshipped him. And the crowd which saw, wondered and said, This is a heavenly child; for he hath saved many souls from death, and hath to save them all his life.

[1] Comp. Pseudo-Matth. xl.

CHAPTER XIX.

AND when he was twelve years old, his parents went, according to custom, to Jerusalem to the feast of the passover with their companions, and after the passover, they were returning to their homes, and as they returned, the child Jesus went up to Jerusalem; but his parents thought he was in the company. And when they had journeyed one day, they sought him among their kinsfolk, and not finding him they were sorrowful, and went back to the city seeking him; and after the third day they found him in the temple sitting among the doctors, and hearing the law and questioning them. And all gave heed and marvelled how he, being a child, puzzled the elders and doctors of the people, resolving the chapters of the law and the parables of the prophets. And his mother, Mary, came to him and said, Child, why hast thou done this to us? Behold, we have sought thee sorrowing. And Jesus said to them, Why seek ye me? Know ye not that I must be about my Father's business? And the scribes and Pharisees said, Art thou the mother of this child? And she said, I am. And they said to her, Blessed art thou among women, for God hath blessed the fruit of thy womb; for such glory and such virtue and wisdom, we never either saw or heard. And Jesus arose and followed his mother.

and was subject to his parents. And his mother observed all that happened. And Jesus advanced in wisdom, and stature, and grace.[1] To him be glory for ever and ever. Amen.

[1] Luke ii. 41-52.

VI.

THE GOSPEL OF THOMAS. (II.)

AFTER the remarks prefixed to the former recension of the Gospel of Thomas, little remains to be said. This is a briefer collection of the same stories, commencing when Jesus was five years old and ending when he was eight. The details, however, are not always the same in the two books. If the longer text of this false Gospel contains less than some ancient copies, it is to be supposed that, for one reason or another, transcribers and editors only appropriated so much of it as suited their purpose. This shorter copy is inserted here to show how little importance was really attached to documents of this kind. That it was so is manifest from the extraordinary freedom which was taken with them, altering, abridging, omitting, or adding to them at pleasure. To such an extent was this carried that probably the restoration of a single original text of this class is beyond all hope of attainment. The shorter Thomas was first published by Tischendorf.

BOOK OF THE HOLY APOSTLE THOMAS,

CONCERNING THE CONDUCT OF THE LORD WHEN A CHILD.

CHAPTER I.

I THOMAS the Israelite have thought it necessary to make known to all the brethren of my nation the infantine marvels which our Lord Jesus Christ wrought while he dwelt in the body in the city of Nazareth, entering on the fifth year of his age.

CHAPTER II.

ON a certain day there was a shower, and he went out of the house where his mother was, and played on the ground where the water ran down. And having made pools, the water came down, and the pools were filled with water. Then said he, I will that ye waters be clear and bright. And immediately they became so. And a certain child of Annas the Scribe coming by and carrying a willow stick, broke down the pools with the stick, and the water was spilled. And Jesus turned and said to him, Impious and lawless one, how have the pools offended thee, and why hast thou emptied them? Thou shalt not finish thy journey, and shalt be withered like the stick which thou holdest. And as he went, a little after he fell down and expired. And when the children who played with him saw it they marvelled, and went and told it to the father of him that was dead. And he ran and found his child dead, and he went away, accusing Joseph.

CHAPTER III.

AND Jesus made out of the clay twelve sparrows: and it was the Sabbath. And a certain child ran and told Joseph saying, Behold thy child is playing by the watercourse, and hath made sparrows out of the clay, which is not lawful. And when he heard it he went and said to the Child, Why dost thou do thus, profaning the Sabbath? And Jesus did not answer him, but, looking at the sparrows, he said, Go, fly away, and while ye live remember me. And at the word they flew and went off into the air. And Joseph, when he saw it, marvelled.

CHAPTER IV.

AND after some days, as Jesus was passing through the city, a boy threw a stone at him and hit him on the shoulder. And Jesus said to him, Thou shalt not

finish thy journey; and immediately he also fell down
and died. And they that happened to be there were
astonished, saying, Whence cometh this child, that
every word he speaketh forthwith becometh a deed?
But they also went away and accused Joseph, saying,
Thou canst not dwell with us in this city. But if
thou wilt, teach thy child to bless and not to curse;
for he slayeth our children, and whatever he saith
straightway cometh to pass.

CHAPTER V.

AND Joseph sat upon his seat and the child stood
before him: and taking hold of him by the ear, he
pulled it violently. And Jesus looking at him said,
It is sufficient for thee.

CHAPTER VI.

AND on the morrow, taking him by the hand, he led
him to a certain teacher, named Zacchæus, and said
to him, Teacher, take this boy and teach him letters.
And he said, Hand him over to me, brother, and I
will teach him the Scripture, and will persuade him
to bless all, and not to curse. And when Jesus heard,
he laughed and said to them, Ye say what ye know;
but I understand more than you; for before the
worlds I am, and I know when your fathers' fathers

were born, and I understand how many are the years of your lives.[1] And every one that heard was astonished. And Jesus said to them again, Ye marvel that I said to you, I know how many are the years of your lives. Verily I know when the world was created.[2] Behold, ye believe me not at present: when ye see my cross, then ye will believe that I say true. And they were amazed when they heard these things.

CHAPTER VII.

AND Zacchæus wrote the alphabet in Hebrew, and said to him, Alpha. And the child said Alpha. And the teacher said again, Alpha. And the child said the same. Then again a third time the teacher said, Alpha. Then Jesus, looking at the instructor, said, Thou that knowest not Alpha, how wilt thou teach another the Beta? And the child, beginning at Alpha, said of himself the twenty-two letters. Then again he said, Hearken, teacher, to the arrangement of the first letter, and know how many accessories and lines it hath, and marks which are common, transverse, and connected. And when Zacchæus heard such accounts of one letter, he was amazed and could not answer him; and he turned to Joseph and said, Brother, verily this child is not earth-born; therefore take him away from me.

---

[1] Comp. John viii. 56.   [2] Comp. John i. 3.

CHAPTER VIII.

AND after these things, Jesus was one day playing with other boys upon the top of a house. And one child was thrust down by another headlong to the ground and died. And when the boys who played with him saw it, they fled; and Jesus was left alone standing upon the housetop from which the boy had been pushed down. And when the parents of the dead boy learned it, they ran with weeping, and finding the boy lying dead upon the ground, but Jesus standing above, suspecting that the boy had been pushed down by him, they looked at and reviled him. And when Jesus saw this, he immediately leaped down from the house-top, and stood by the head of him that was dead, and said to him, Zeno, did I cast thee down? Arise and speak (for the boy was so called). And at the word the boy arose, and worshipping Jesus said, Lord, thou didst not cast me down, but when I was dead thou gavest me life.

CHAPTER IX.

AND a few days after, one of the neighbours, cleaving wood, cut off the sole of his foot with his hatchet, and becoming senseless was about to die. And much people running together, Jesus also came there with them. And he took hold of the wounded foot of the young man and healed him instantly, and said to him, Arise, cleave thy wood. And he arose and worshipped him, giving thanks and cleaving the wood. In like manner also, all who were there wondered and gave thanks to him.

CHAPTER X.

AND when he was six years old, his mother Mary sent him to fetch water from the well, and as he went his pitcher was broken, and, going on to the well, he spread out his garment, and drew water from the well and filled it, and he took the water and carried it to his mother. And she saw and was amazed, and embraced and kissed him.

CHAPTER XI.

AND when he came to the eighth year of his age, Joseph was ordered by a certain rich man to make a couch for him; for he was a carpenter. And he went out into the field to gather wood, and Jesus went with him. And having cut two pieces of wood, and shaped the one, he put it beside the other, and when he measured he found it too short, and on seeing this he was grieved, and sought to find another. But Jesus seeing it, saith to him, Lay these two together in order to make them equal. And

Joseph, being at a loss as to what the child meant, did what was bidden. And he saith to him again, Take firm hold of the short piece of wood; and Joseph, wondering, took hold of it. Then Jesus also took hold of the other end and pulled it, and he made it equal to the other piece, and said to Joseph: Grieve no longer, but do thy work without impediment. And when he saw, he marvelled exceedingly, and said within himself, Blessed am I, that God hath given to me such a child. And when they went away into the city, Joseph related it to Mary; and when she heard and saw the wondrous miracles of her Son, she rejoiced, glorifying him, with the Father, and the Holy Spirit, now and always, and for ever and ever. Amen.

VII

THE GOSPEL OF THOMAS. (III.)

The Latin text of this contains at the commencement certain details which are not in either of the Greek texts. It commences with the flight into Egypt, the account of which occupies chaps. i.–iii. The fourth chapter begins with an introduction answering to that at the head of the Greek copies. The Latin writer has taken no small liberty with his original, if we may judge from the longer Thomas, and has made it an object to paraphrase and expand his materials in some of the stories, while he has condensed and abbreviated others, omitting altogether two or three of them. The conclusion is not in the Greek at all. It was first published by Tischendorf from a manuscript in the Vatican library. The editor has found some fragments of another Latin text, of probably the fifth century, and more nearly agreeing with the Greek. We translate the Latin Thomas, to illustrate more fully the nature and extent of the variations to be found in the Christian Apocrypha.

THE LATIN GOSPEL OF THOMAS;

OR, THE CHILDHOOD OF JESUS, ACCORDING TO THOMAS.

CHAPTER I.

How Mary and Joseph fled with Him into Egypt.

WHEN a commotion had been raised, because a search had been made by Herod after our Lord Jesus Christ that he might slay him, then an angel said to Joseph, Take Mary and her child, and flee into Egypt from the face of those who seek to slay him. Now Jesus was two years old when he entered Egypt.

And as he walked through a corn-field, he put out his hand, and took of the ears, and put them on the fire, and crushed them, and began to eat.

Now when they had come into Egypt, they found a lodging in the house of a certain widow, and they passed one year in the same place.

And Jesus was three years old, and when he saw boys playing, he began to play with them. And he took a dry fish and put it in a bason, and ordered it to breathe, and it began to breathe. And he said again to the fish: Reject the salt which thou hast, and move in the water; and so it came to pass.[1] But the neighbours, seeing what was done, told the widow woman in whose house Mary his mother was staying; and when she heard it, she cast them out of her house in great haste.

CHAPTER II.

How a Teacher cast Him out of the city.

AND as Jesus was walking with Mary his mother through the city market-place, he looked up and saw a teacher teaching his pupils; and behold twelve sparrows which were quarrelling together fell from the wall into the lap of the teacher who was teaching the boys. But when Jesus saw it he laughed and stopped. When the teacher saw him laughing, in a great rage he said to his pupils, Go, fetch him to me. Now when they had taken him, the master took hold of his ear, and said, what hast thou seen that thou hast made merry? But he said to him, Behold master, a handful of corn. I showed it to them and scattered the corn, which, at their peril, they carry away; for it was this that they were fighting for— that they might divide the corn. And Jesus departed not thence till it was accomplished; and when this was done, the teacher began to cast him out of the city along with his mother.

[1] The fish appears to have been both salted and dried.

CHAPTER III.

How Jesus departed out of Egypt.

AND behold an angel of the Lord met Mary and said to her, Take the Child and return into the land of the Jews, for they are dead who sought his life. And Mary arose with Jesus, and they went to the city of Nazareth, which is in the proper possessions of her father. Now when Joseph went out of Egypt after the death of Herod, he took him into the desert until there should be peace in Jersusalem from those who sought the Child's life; and he thanked God that he gave him understanding, and that he found favour before the Lord God.[1] Amen.

CHAPTER IV.

What the Lord Jesus did in the city of Nazareth.

IT is glorious that Thomas the Israelite and apostle of the Lord should also tell of the works of Jesus after he came out of Egypt into Nazareth. Understand, all of you, dearest brethren, what the Lord Jesus did when he was in the city of Nazareth, which is in the first chapter.[2]

---

[1] The three preceding chapters clearly form no part of the Gospel of Thomas, although prefixed to it. Where they come from I know not.

[2] This paragraph is clearly a very slight modification of what the ancient editor found as the introduction to the book. See the copies from the Greek.

Now when Jesus was five years old, there came a great rain upon the earth, and the child Jesus walked through it: and there was a dreadful rain, which he gathered into a pool, and commanded by his word that it should become clear, and immediately it became so. Again he took of the clay which was in that pool and made of it the number of twelve sparrows. Now it was the Sabbath when Jesus did this among the Jewish children; and the Jewish children went away saying to Joseph his father, Behold thy son was playing with us, and he took clay and made sparrows, which it was not right to do on the Sabbath, and violated it. And Joseph went to the child Jesus, and said to him, Why hast thou done that which it was not right to do on the Sabbath? And Jesus, spreading out his hands, commanded the sparrows, saying, Retire aloft and fly; ye shall find death from no one: and they flew up and began with a cry to praise Almighty God. And the Jews who saw what was done were astonished, and departed, declaring the signs which Jesus did. But a Pharisee, who was there with Jesus, took an olive branch and began to disperse the pool of water which Jesus had made, and when Jesus saw this, he was troubled and said, Impious and ignorant man of Sodom, what wrong have the pools of water, my works, done to thee? Behold thou shalt become as a dry tree, nor having roots, nor leaves, nor fruit; and straightway he was withered and fell to the earth and died. And his parents carried away his dead body, and they blamed Joseph, saying, Behold what thy son hath done: teach him to pray and not blaspheme.

CHAPTER V.

How the citizens were offended against Joseph because of the deeds of Jesus.

AND a few days after, as Jesus walked with Joseph through the town, one of the children ran against him and smote him on the elbow. And Jesus said to him, Thou shalt not finish thy journey. And immediately he fell to the ground and died. Now when they saw the miracles, they cried saying, Whence is this child? And they said to Joseph, Such a child ought not to be among us. And he took him and went away. And they said to him, Depart from this place, but if thou must be with us, teach him to pray and not to blaspheme: but our sons are foolish. And Joseph called Jesus and scolded him, saying, Why dost thou blaspheme? The inhabitants cherish hatred against us. But Jesus said, I know those words are not mine, but are thine; yet I will be silent for thy sake: but let them see in their own wisdom. And immediately they who spake against Jesus were made blind. And they walked about and said, All the words which proceed from his mouth have effect. And when Joseph saw what Jesus did, he took him by the ear in a rage. But Jesus being troubled said to Joseph, It is enough for thee to see me, not to touch me. For thou knowest not who I am: but if thou knewest thou wouldst not grieve me. And although I am now with thee I was made before thee.

CHAPTER VI.

How Jesus was treated by the teacher.

THEN a certain man named Zacchæus heard all that Jesus said to Joseph, and wondering in himselt he said, I never saw such a child speaking thus. And he came to Joseph and said, Thou hast a wise child; send him to learn his letters; and when he hath been taught in the knowledge of letters, I will teach him honourably that he may not become foolish. But Joseph answered and said to him, No one can teach him save God alone. Dost thou believe that Little One will be small? Now when Jesus heard Joseph say such things, he said to Zacchæus, Verily, master, for however great things proceed from my mouth, they are true. And I was Lord before all men; but ye are aliens. For the glory of ages is given to me; nothing is given to you; for before the ages I am. And I know how many will be the years of thy life; and that thou wilt be taken into exile; as my Father hath said, that thou mayest understand that all things which proceed from my mouth are true. But the Jews who stood by and heard the words which Jesus spake, were astonished and said, We have seen such marvels, and heard such words from this Child as we never heard nor shall hear from any other man, neither from chief priests, nor doctors, nor Pharisees.[1] And Jesus answered and said to them, Why do ye wonder? Do ye account it incredible because I have spoken the truth? I know when ye and your fathers were born; and, if I tell you more, when the world was made; I know also who hath sent me to you. When the Jews heard the words which the Child spoke, they wondered at that which they could not answer. And, returning to himself, the Child exulted and said, I have spoken a proverb to you: but I know that ye are weak and ignorant.

But the teacher said to Joseph, Bring him to me; I will teach him letters. And Joseph took hold of the child Jesus, and brought him into the house of a certain teacher, where other boys were taught.[2] And the master with pleasant speech began to teach

---

[1] John vii. 46; Matt. vii. 29.

[2] About A.D. 570, Antoninus of Placentia says he went to Nazareth, "wherein are many marvels. Also there lies in the synagogue the book in which the Lord had put A, B, C. In the synagogue also there is the beam where the Lord sat with other children; this beam is moved and raised by Christians, but Jews can in no wise move it, nor does it allow itself to be carried out." From a version by myself in the Journal of Sacred Literature for January, 1866.

him letters, and wrote for him the first lesson which is from A to T, and began to caress him and to teach him. But the instructor smote the Child on the head; and the boy, when he had received the blow, said to him, I ought to teach thee, and not thou to teach me. I know the letters which thou wouldst teach me, and I know that ye are unto me as vessels out of which proceed sounds only and not wisdom.[1] And beginning the lesson, he said through the letters from A to T very rapidly. And he looked at the master and said to him, Thou who knowest not how to interpret what A is and B; how wilt thou teach others? O hypocrite, if thou knowest and wilt tell me about A, then I will tell thee about B. But when the doctor essayed to teach him about the first letter, he was not able to give him an answer. And Jesus said to Zacchæus, Hear me, doctor; understand the first letter. Observe how it hath two lines; in the middle, advancing, remaining, giving, scattering, varying, menacing: threefold and doubly mingling: like the mind at the same time having all things common.[2]

When Zacchæus saw that he so divided the first letter, he was astonished at the first letter, and at such a man and teaching, and he cried out and said, Alas for me, I am confounded; I have hired shame

---

[1] 1 Cor. xiii. 1; xiv. 7.
[2] Like the corresponding passage in others of the false Gospels, this passage is of course intentionally obscure.

to myself by means of this child. And he said to
Joseph, I pray thee earnestly, brother, take him
from me, for I cannot look at his face, nor hear his
weighty sayings. For this child can subdue fire,
and restrain the sea; for he was born before the
ages. What womb bare him, or what mother nourished him, I know not. O my friends, I am humbled
in my mind; unhappy I am mocked. I said I had
a pupil; but he is found to be my teacher. And I
cannot overcome my shame, for I am old; and I
cannot tell what to say to him. Wherefore I must
fall into great weakness, and leave this world, or depart from this city: for all have seen my shame: a
child hath deceived me. What answer can I make to
others, or what words can I repeat, since he hath
defeated me at the first letter? I am astounded, O
my friends and acquaintances; neither can I find
beginning or end in response to him. And now I
pray thee, brother Joseph, take him from me and
lead him to thy house, for he is a master, or a Lord,
or an angel. What to say, I know not.

And Jesus turning to the Jews who were with
Zacchæus, said to them, Now let all who see not, see,
and those who understand not, understand, and the
deaf hear, and let those who are dead because of me
rise again, and let me call to higher things those
who are lofty, as He who sent me to you commanded
me. Now when the child Jesus had left off speaking,

all the infirm were restored who had been made infirm through his words. And they dared not to speak to him.

CHAPTER VII.

How Jesus raised a boy.

ONE day when he went up on a certain house-top with some children, Jesus began to play with them. But one of the boys fell through the back-door, and immediately died. And when the children saw it, they all fled; but Jesus remained on the house-top. And when the parents of the boy that was dead, had come, they said to Jesus, Truly thou didst make him fall. And they laid wait for him. But Jesus going down from the house, stood over the dead child, and called with a loud voice the name of the child, Sinoo, Sinoo, arise and say if I made thee fall. And suddenly he arose and said, No, Lord. Now when his parents saw the so great miracle which Jesus did, they glorified God and adored Jesus.

CHAPTER VIII.

How Jesus healed the foot of a boy.

Now after a few days a certain boy was splitting wood in the same village, and wounded his foot. And a great crowd came to him, and Jesus came with them. And he touched the foot which was hurt, and it was immediately made well. And Jesus said to him, Arise, chop wood, and remember me. Now when the crowd saw the signs which were done with him, they adored Jesus and said, Truly we believe most certainly that thou art God.[1]

CHAPTER IX.

How Jesus brought water in his garment.

AND when Jesus was six years old, his mother directed him to draw some water. And when Jesus came to the fountain or well, there were great multitudes there and they broke his waterpot. But he took his garment with which he was clothed, and filled it with water, and brought it to Mary his mother. And when his mother saw the miracle which Jesus did, she kissed him and said, Lord, hear me, and save my son.[2]

CHAPTER X.

How Jesus sowed wheat.

Now when it was seed-time, Joseph went out to sow wheat and Jesus followed him. But when Joseph

---

[1] This shows plainly enough the writer's belief in the Deity of Jesus.
[2] This may merely be intended to show that the writer distinguished between the Deity and the humanity in Christ. The prayer is remarkable,—*salva filium meum!* Is it an interpolation?

began to sow, Jesus put out his hand, and took of the wheat as much as he could hold in his fist, and scattered it. Then Joseph came in the time of reaping, that he might reap his crop. Jesus also came, and gathered the ears which he had scattered, and they made a hundred bushels of the best corn. And he called the poor, and widows, and orphans, and bestowed on them the wheat which he had made. Of the same corn Joseph took a little for a blessing from Jesus to his house.[1]

CHAPTER XI.

How Jesus made a short piece of wood equal to a longer.

AND Jesus was eight years old. Joseph was a carpenter, and made ploughs and yokes for oxen. On a certain day a rich man said to Joseph, Master,

---

[1] The phrase "took a little for a blessing," points to the belief in what the whole system of relics rests upon. Pilgrims to the Holy Land in the sixth century "took a little for a blessing," of many things which the priests invited or allowed them to take. See for example the pilgrimage of Antoninus of Placentia, chap. xviii., etc. (translated by myself for the Journal of Sacred Literature, January, 1866). Antoninus was shown, cir. A.D. 570, the field in which Jesus produced the miraculous crop of corn. In chap. xiii., speaking of Jericho, he says, "Before the Church is the sacred field of the Lord, in which our Lord sowed corn with his own hand—sowing as much as three bushels of corn, which also is gathered twice a year; first in the month of February that it may be used at the communion at Easter; where it has been gathered it is ploughed, and gathered again with the rest of the harvest. Then it is ploughed again." The reader will compare this for himself with the version in the text. Certainly it puts a new face on the transaction, and especially the miraculous part of it. It would almost seem as if the miracle had not yet been invented; and if so,

make me a couch both useful and handsome. Now Joseph was in trouble because the wood which he had cut out for this work was too short. Jesus said to him, Be not sad. Take this wood at one end, and I at the other, and let us stretch it. Which also was done. And immediately he found it fit for what he wanted it. And he said to Joseph, Behold, make what thou wilt. Now when Joseph saw what he had done, he embraced him' and said, Blessed am I, in that God hath given me such a son.

CHAPTER XII.

How Jesus was sent to learn Letters.

AND when Joseph saw that he had such grace, and increased in stature, he thought he would send him to learn letters; and he sent him to another teacher to teach him. And the teacher said to Joseph, What letters dost thou wish the boy to be taught? Joseph answered and said, First teach him Gentile letters, and afterwards the Hebrew. Now the teacher knew him to be of excellent understanding, and received him willingly. And when he had written for him the first lesson, which is A and B, he

this false Gospel was compiled, or at least translated, at a still later date. The phrase "to take or receive for a blessing" is a Hebraism for a gift (Josh. xv. 19; 2 Kings v. 15); but the ecclesiastical application of it must be understood in a wider sense, as something with which blessing is connected,—a kind of spiritual charm, etc.

taught him for some hours. But Jesus was silent and answered nothing. Jesus said to the teacher, If thou art truly a teacher and truly knowest letters, tell me the power of A, and I will tell thee the power of B. Then, being filled with wrath, his master smote him on the head, and Jesus being angry, cursed him, and he fell suddenly and died.

And Jesus returned to his home. But Joseph directed Mary his mother not to suffer him to go out of the court of his house.

CHAPTER XIII.

How he was sent to another master.

AFTER many other days, there came another teacher, the friend of Joseph, and said to him, Send him to me, and I will teach him his letters with much kindness. And Joseph said to him, If thou art very competent take and teach him. May it be with joy! When the teacher had received him, he went with fear and great decision, and held him with exultation. And when he had come to the teacher's house, he found a book lying in the place, and he took hold of it and opened it, and did not read what was written in the book, but opened his mouth and spake by the Holy Spirit and taught the law. And all who stood there heard him attentively, and the master sat near him and heard him gladly, and entreated him to teach more. When a great crowd had gathered they heard all the holy doctrine which he taught, and the precious words, which proceeded from His mouth, who, although so young, said such things.

When Joseph heard this he was afraid, and running . . . .[1] the master where Jesus was said to Joseph, Know, brother, that I took thy child to teach or to instruct; but he is filled with much gravity and wisdom. Behold, now take him with joy to thy house, brother; for the gravity which he hath is given him of the Lord. When Jesus heard the master saying thus, he was pleased, and said, Lo, now master, thou hast spoken truly. For thy sake he must rise who was dead. And Joseph took him to his home.

CHAPTER XIV.

How Jesus delivered James from the bite of a Serpent.

Now Joseph sent James to gather stubble, and Jesus followed him. But while James was gathering stubble, a viper bit him, and he fell to the ground as if dead through the venom. And when Jesus saw it, he breathed on his wound, and immediately James was made whole, and the viper died.

---

[1] There is a gap in the construction which Dr. Tischendorf thus supplies:—"Came to the school (or door) fearing the master might die. But ——."

CHAPTER XV.

How Jesus raised a Child.

AFTER a few days, a child, his neighbour, died, and his mother greatly lamented him. Jesus hearing this went and stood over the child, and smote on his breast, and said, I say unto thee, infant, do not die, but live; and instantly the child arose. And Jesus said to the child's mother, Take thy son and give him the breast, and remember me. And the crowd who saw this miracle said, In truth this is a heavenly child, for he hath already freed many souls from death, and saved all that hoped in him.[1]

The Scribes and Pharisees said to Mary, Art thou the mother of this child? And Mary said, Truly I am. And they said to her, Blessed art thou among women,[2] for God hath blessed the fruit of thy womb, in that he hath given thee such a glorious child and such a gift of wisdom, as we never saw nor heard. Jesus rose and followed his mother. But Mary kept in her heart all the great signs which Jesus did among the people, in that he healed many sick. But Jesus increased in stature and wisdom, and all who saw him glorified God the Father Almighty, who is blessed for ever and ever. Amen.

---

[1] *Salvos fecit* may here mean 'cured' or 'healed,' as the like phrase in the Gospels (Luke vii. 50; xviii. 42; and James v. 15, where *salvabit* has the same sense).

[2] Luke i. 28.

THE GOSPEL OF THOMAS.

After all these things, I, Thomas the Israelite, have written what I saw and remembered for the Gentiles and our brethren; and many other things which Jesus did, who was born in the land of Judah. Behold the house of Israel hath seen all things from the first even to the last: what great signs and marvels Jesus did among them, very good and invisible to his father, as the Holy Scripture[1] telleth; and the prophets testified to his works among all the people of Israel. And it is he who shall judge the world according to the will of immortality,[2] for he is the Son of God in all the world. All glory and honour for ever becometh him who liveth and reigneth God through all ages for ever. Amen.

---

[1] The writer seems careful to distinguish between his work and Holy Scripture.
[2] Acts xvii. 31. The phrase "the will of immortality" is perhaps equivalent to "immortal will."

VIII.

THE ARABIC GOSPEL OF THE INFANCY.

It has often been observed that this consists of three parts, or has been drawn from three sources. Chapters i.-ix. comprise events commencing with the journey of Joseph and Mary to Bethlehem to be enrolled, and ending with the massacre of the infants by Herod. This period corresponds with the record in the Protevangelium, chapters xvii.-xxv., and the source of the narrative must be similar. It will be observed, however, that the correspondence we have noticed is anything but literal.

The second part (chapters x.-xxxv.) relates at length what is feigned to have happened during the flight into Egypt, the sojourn there, and the return. This division is the product of an extravagant imagination, and is most likely a heap of Egyptian fancies, invented and compiled very much with the intention of glorifying the Lord's mother, as the chief minister of His divine power and favour. The superstitious notions are so fully developed that the materials for this section cannot be so ancient as the rest.

The third part of the Arabic Gospel of the

Infancy (chapters xxxvi.-lv.) is somewhat conformed to the Gospel of Thomas. It records what is said to have occurred from the time when Jesus was seven years old until he was twelve, adding a general intimation respecting his life thenceforward to his thirtieth year and his baptism.

The Arabic Gospel is a compilation which may have had either an Arabic, or a Coptic, or a Syriac origin, and was probably not written till the eighth or ninth century. One can hardly see how it savours of Nestorianism however, as some have thought, since this extravagantly exalts that Mary whom the Nestorians were accused of not exalting sufficiently.

Tischendorf's Latin text was revised after the Arabic by Fleischer, and may, therefore, be relied on. The book itself was first published in Arabic and Latin by Dr. Sike in 1697.

The reader cannot fail to observe that the miracles in the second part are of a benevolent character, unlike those which breathe the malevolent spirit of the Gospel of Thomas and its congeners.

THE ARABIC GOSPEL OF THE INFANCY.[1]

CHAPTER I.

WE have found this in the book of Joseph the high priest, who lived in the time of Christ, and some have said that he is Caiaphas.[2] He saith that Jesus talked even when he was in the cradle, and said to his mother Mary, I am Jesus the Son of God, the Word, whom thou hast borne as the angel Gabriel announced to thee; and my Father hath sent me for the salvation of the world.

CHAPTER II.

Now in the 309th year of the era of Alexander, Augustus decreed that every one should be enrolled in his native place. Therefore Joseph arose and having taken Mary his spouse departed from Jeru-

---

[1] The Arabic text is preceded by the following:—
In the name of the Father, and of the Son, and of the Holy Spirit, One God.
With the help and favour of the supreme God we begin to write the book of the miracles of our Master and Lord and Saviour Jesus Christ, which is called "The Gospel of the Infancy," in the peace of the Lord. Amen.

[2] This is confirmed by Josephus (Antiq. xviii. 2, 2), who writes the name Joseph Caiphas. See also p. 230.

salem and came to Bethlehem that he might be enrolled with his family in his native city. And when they had come to a cave, Mary said to Joseph that her time to be delivered was nigh, and that she could not go into the city: but, said she, Let us enter this cave. This was done when the sun was setting. Then Joseph departed hastily to fetch a woman to attend on her. While, therefore, he was thus occupied, he saw an old woman, a Hebrew, who came from Jerusalem, and he said, Ho! blessed one, come hither and enter this cave wherein is a woman nigh to childbirth.

CHAPTER III.

THEREFORE, after sunset, the old woman and Joseph with her came to the cave, and both entered it. And lo, it was filled with lights more beautiful than the glittering of lamps and candles and brighter than the light of the sun. An infant wrapped in swaddling bands was suckling at the breast of lady Mary its mother, and laid in a manger. While they both wondered at this light, the old woman asked lady Mary, Art thou the mother of this child? And when lady Mary had assented, she said, Thou art not like the daughters of Eve. Lady Mary said, As none among children is equal to my Son, so his mother hath no equal among women. The old woman replied, My lady, I am come to gain a reward; I have been a long while afflicted with paralysis. Our lady, lady Mary, said to her, Place thy hands on the infant; which the old woman did, and was straightway restored. Then she went out saying, Henceforth will I be the handmaid and servant of this infant all the days of my life.

CHAPTER IV.

Then came shepherds, and when they had kindled a fire and enjoyed themselves a little, heavenly hosts appeared to them, praising and celebrating God most high: and as the shepherds did the same, the cave at that time was made like the temple of the world above, for celestial and terrestrial mouths glorified and magnified God, for the nativity of the Lord Christ. Now when the old Hebrew woman saw those miracles displayed, she gave thanks to God, saying, I give thanks unto thee, O God, the God of Israel, because mine eyes have seen the nativity of the Saviour of the world.

CHAPTER V.

And when the time for circumcision came, that is the eighth day, the child was to be circumcised according to the law. Therefore they circumcised him in the cave; and the old Hebrew woman took the foreskin (but others say she took the umbilical cord) and laid it up in a vase of old oil of spikenard. Now she had a son who was a perfumer, to whom she committed it, saying, Take care not to sell this vase of ointment of spikenard, even if 300 pence (*dinars*) should be offered thee for it. And this is the vase which Mary, the sinner, bought, and poured upon the head and feet of our Lord Jesus Christ, and then wiped them with the hair of her head.[1] Ten days after they took him to Jerusalem, and on the fortieth day from his birth, they brought him to the temple, and set him before the Lord and offered sacrifices for him, as is commanded in the law of Moses: Every male that openeth the womb shall be called holy to God.[2]

CHAPTER VI.

THEN the old man Simeon saw him shining as a pillar of light, when lady Mary his virgin mother rejoicing in him carried him in her arms; but angels surrounded him as a circle, praising him, as body guards standing about a king. Then Simeon came in haste to lady Mary, and spreading out his hands before her, said to the Lord Christ, Now O my Lord,

[1] Luke vii. 37; John ii. 2. This Mary is often confounded with Mary Magdalen, but wrongly. The price put upon the ointment is borrowed from John xii. 3-5.
[2] Ex. xiii. 2; Luke ii. 23.

dismiss thy servant in peace, according to what thou hast said, for mine eyes have seen thy mercy which thou hast prepared for the salvation of all peoples, a light to all nations, and a glory to thy people Israel. Hannah also, a prophetess, was present there, and came, giving thanks to God, and declaring lady Mary happy.[1]

CHAPTER VII.

AND it came to pass when the Lord Jesus was born at Bethlehem of Judah, in the time of Herod the King, behold Magi came from the east to Jerusalem, as Zerdusht had predicted: and they had with them gifts, gold, incense, and myrrh; and they worshipped him and offered unto him their gifts. Then lady Mary took one of his swaddling bands and gave it them for a little reward, and they received it from her with great honour. And the same hour there appeared unto them an angel in the form of the star which had been the guide of their way before; and following the leading of its light they departed, until they reached their own country.[2]

[1] Luke ii. 25-38.
[2] Matt. ii. 1-12. The mention of Zerdusht or Zoroaster in this chapter accords with an old Christian notion in the East, that he was the same as Balaam, and predicted the rising of the star. Some made him a disciple of Elijah, but an old priest from Oroomiah mentioned the other opinion to me as the true one. See the article *Zerdascht* in D'Herbelot's Bibliotheque Orientale. Brunet refers to the Biographie Universelle, vol. lii., and Norberg's De Zoroastre Bactriano. See, too, Hottinger's Historia Orientalis, ii. 6, 16; and also the note of Thilo, Codex Apoc., p. 139.

CHAPTER VIII.

And there came to them the kings and their princes asking what they had seen or done, how they had gone and returned, what they had brought with them. And they showed them the swaddling band which lady Mary had given them; wherefore they celebrated a festival, and kindled fire according to their custom and worshipped it, and cast the swaddling band into it, and the fire seized it and absorbed it into itself. But when the fire went out, they drew forth the swaddling band just as it was at first, as if the fire had not touched it. Therefore they began to kiss it, and to place it on their heads and eyes, saying, Verily this is undoubted truth; it is indeed a great thing that the fire could not burn or destroy it. They took it thence and with the greatest honour deposited it among their treasures.

CHAPTER IX.

Now when Herod saw that the Magi had departed and not returned to him, he sent for the priests and wise men, and said to them, Tell me where Christ is to be born. And when they had replied, At Bethlehem of Judah, he began to think of slaying the Lord Jesus Christ. Then an angel of the Lord appeared to Joseph in a dream and said, Arise, take the child and his mother, and go into Egypt.[1] Therefore he arose at cock-crowing and departed.

CHAPTER X.

WHILE he considered with himself how his journey should be performed, morning overtook him after he had made but very little way. And now he was approaching a great city wherein was an idol to which the remaining idols and divinities of the Egyptians offered gifts and vows; and a priest attended on this idol ministering to it, and as often as Satan spoke by the idol, he reported it to the inhabitants of Egypt and its borders. This priest had a son of three years old, possessed by certain demons, who said and told much, and when the demons seized him, he rent his garments and remained naked and threw stones at men. And there was an hospital in that city, dedicated to the idol; and when Joseph and lady Mary came thither, and tarried at the hospital, the citizens were greatly afraid, and all the princes and priests of idols came to the idol and said, What is this agitation and commotion which hath arisen in our land? The idol answered them: There cometh hither a God in secret, who truly is a God, neither is any God beside him worthy of worship, because he is truly the Son of God. When this land became aware of

[1] Matt. ii. 13, 14.

him it trembled, and was moved and shaken at his coming, and we are much afraid of the greatness of his power. And the same hour that idol fell, and at its fall all the inhabitants of Egypt, and others, ran together.

CHAPER XI.

But the son of the priest, when his customary affliction overtook him, entered the hospital and there met Joseph and lady Mary, from whom all the rest had fled away. And our lady, lady Mary, had washed the swaddling clothes of the Lord Christ, and spread them upon some wood. Then the boy that was a demoniac came and took one of these wrappers, and put it on his head; and the demons began to come forth out of his mouth, and fled in the form of crows and serpents. Suddenly, by command of the Lord Christ the boy was healed and began to praise God, and then to give thanks to the Lord who had healed him. When his father saw him restored to health, he said, My son, what hath befallen thee? and by what means wast thou healed? The son answered, When the demons had cast me to the ground, I went to the hospital, and there I found a noble woman with a child, whose recently washed wrappers she had laid on some wood; having taken one of them I placed it on my head, and the demons left me and fled away. And his father, greatly rejoicing because of this, said, My son, it may be that this child is the Son of the living God who created heaven and earth; for when he came to us, the idol was broken and all the gods fell, and perished through the might of his magnificence.

CHAPTER XII.

HERE was fulfilled the prophecy which saith, Out of Egypt have I called my son.[1] But Joseph and Mary, when they heard that the idol had fallen and perished, feared and trembled. Then they said, When we were in the land of Israel, Herod thought to slay Jesus, and therefore he slew all the children of Bethlehem and its borders; and there is no doubt but the Egyptians, as soon as they hear that this idol is broken, will burn us with fire.

CHAPTER XIII.

THEY departed thence and came to a place where there were robbers, who had plundered many men of their baggage and clothing, and bound them. Then the robbers heard a great noise, like the wonted noise of a magnificent king going forth from his city with an army and horsemen and drums. Being terrified thereby, the robbers abandoned all that they

[1] Hos. xi. 1; Matt. ii. 15.

had stolen. They that were captives arose, loosed the bonds of one another, and took their baggage and departed. When they saw Joseph and Mary coming thither, they said to them, Where is the king, at hearing the pompous noise of whose coming the robbers left us, so that we escaped? Joseph answered them, After us will he come.

CHAPTER XIV.

THEN they came to another city where there was a demoniac woman, whom, whenever she went out at night to fetch water, the cursed and rebel Satan oppressed. She could neither endure clothing nor stay in a house, and as often as she was bound with chains and straps, she broke them and fled naked into desolate places; and, standing in cross-roads and cemeteries, she threw stones at men, but did the worst of mischiefs to her own friends. When, therefore, the lady Mary saw her she pitied her; whereupon Satan forthwith left her, and fled in the form of a young man and departed, saying, Woe unto me from thee Mary, and from thy Son. So this woman was healed of her torment, and becoming self-conscious, she was ashamed of her nakedness, and, avoiding the sight of men, went away to her friends. And after she had put on clothing, she told her father and friends how it was; and they, being the chief people of the city, entertained lady Mary and Joseph most honourably.

CHAPTER XV.

The following day, being supplied with provision for the journey, they departed thence, and in the evening they reached another town, where a marriage was being celebrated; but, through the arts of cursed Satan and the work of enchanters, the bride was dumb, and could no longer speak. But when lady Mary entered the town, carrying her son the Lord Christ, the dumb bride saw her, and stretched out her hands towards the Lord Christ, and drew him to her and took him in her arms, and embraced him closely and kissed him, and bending over him she rocked him to and fro. Forthwith the bond of her tongue was loosed, and her ears were opened, and she gave praise and thanks to God for that he had restored her to health. And the inhabitants of that town exulted with joy that night, and thought that God and his angels had come down to them.

CHAPTER XVI.

There they stayed three days, held in honour, and living in plenty. Afterwards, being supplied with provisions, they departed from them and came to another city, wherein, because it abounded in inhabitants, they thought to pass the night. Now there was in that city an excellent woman, who, when she went to the river to wash, lo, cursed Satan in the form of a serpent leaped upon her, and twined himself about her body; and as often as night drew on, he greatly vexed her. When this woman saw my lady, lady Mary, and the Lord Christ the child in her lap, being moved with desire for him, she said to the lady Mary, O lady, give me this child that I may carry him and kiss him. So she gave him to the woman, but when he was moved towards her, Satan left her and fled away and departed from her, nor did the woman ever see him after that day. Wherefore all who were there praised the supreme God, and the woman showed them kindness liberally.

CHAPTER XVII.

THE next day the same woman took perfumed water to wash the Lord Jesus. When he was washed she took the water she had used, and poured a part of it on a girl who dwelt there (whose body was white with leprosy), and washed her with it; and the girl was instantly cleansed from her leprosy. The townspeople said, There is no doubt but Joseph and Mary and this child are gods, and not men. But when they made ready to depart from them, the girl who had been a leper came to them and begged them to take her in their company.

CHAPTER XVIII.

WHEN they had granted this to the girl she went with them. Afterwards they came into a city in which was the castle of a very famous prince, who had a house for the reception of guests. Hither they went to tarry; but the girl went and gained entrance to the wife of the prince, and finding her weeping and sad, she asked the cause of her weeping. Wonder not at my weeping, said she, for I am oppressed with a great sorrow, which I have not yet ventured to tell to anyone. Perhaps, said the girl, if you make it known and reveal it to me, I shall have a remedy for it. The wife of the prince answered, Hide it then, and tell this secret to no one. I am married to this prince, who is a king, and in whose dominion are many cities; I lived with him a long time, but he never had a son by me. But when at last I bore a son he was a leper, so he turned away from the sight of him, and said to me, Either kill him, or give him to a nurse to bring him up in some place whence no tidings of him shall ever come. Now I am a stranger to thee, and I shall never see thee again. Hence am I perplexed and oppressed with sorrow. Alas, my son! Alas, my husband! Have I not told thee, said the girl, I have found a remedy for thy affliction? which I will show thee. For I was also leprous, but God, which is Jesus, son of lady Mary, hath cured me. Now when the woman asked where the God was whom she meant, the girl said, He is with thee, he abides in the same house. But how can this be, said she, where is he? The girl replied, Behold Joseph and Mary, but the child who is with them is called Jesus, and he it is who healed me of my disease and suffering. But by what means, said she, wast thou healed of thy leprosy? Wilt thou not tell it me? Why not? said the girl. I received from his mother the water in which his body had been washed, and poured it on me, and so I am cleansed from my leprosy. Then the wife of the prince arose, and invited them to use her hospitality, and prepared a splendid feast for Joseph with a great company of men. And on the next morning she took the perfumed water in which she washed the Lord Jesus, and then with the same water washed her son whom she had brought with her, and her son was immediately cleansed from his leprosy. Therefore, giving thanks and praise to God, she said, Blessed is the mother who bore thee, O Jesus: dost thou thus purify, with the water wherewith thy body has been washed, men who are partakers of the same nature with thyself? Moreover she offered rich gifts to our lady, the lady Mary, and sent her away with much honour.

CHAPTER XIX.

AFTERWARDS they came to another city and wished to spend the night there. They went to abide therefore with a man who had been lately married, but who through magic art could not consort with his wife; and when they had passed that night with him, his bond was loosed. When daylight came and they were preparing for their journey, the husband prevented them, and made a great feast for them.

CHAPTER XX.

ON the following day they departed, and as they drew nigh to another city they saw three women coming, with weeping, out of a cemetery. On seeing them lady Mary said to the girl that accompanied them, Ask them what is their condition and what calamity has befallen them. And when they were asked by the girl they did not answer, but asked in turn, Whence are ye, and whither are ye going? for the day is now past, and night is coming on. We are travellers, said the girl, and seek a lodging wherein to pass the night. They said, Go with us, and lodge with us. They followed them therefore, and were led into a house which was new, and adorned and garnished with much furniture. Now it was wintertime, and the girl having entered the chamber of these women found them again weeping and lamenting. There stood by them a mule covered with a sumptuous cloth, sesame was placed before it, and they kissed it and gave it food. And the girl said O my ladies, What is the matter with this mule? They answered weeping and said, This mule which thou seest, was our brother, born of the same mother with us. For when our father died leaving us great wealth, we who had this only brother endeavoured to secure his marriage, and arranged a wedding for him after the manner of men. But the women, being moved with envy of one another, placed a charm upon him unknown to us, and one night, a little before daylight, when the doors of our house were shut, we saw that this our brother had been changed into a mule, such as thou now seest him. But we, in sorrow, as thou seest, having no father by whom we may be comforted, have left untried no learned magician or enchanter in the world, without sending for him; but it has profited us nothing. Now whenever our hearts are oppressed with grief, we rise and go with our mother, and after we have wept at the tomb of our father, we return.

CHAPTER XXI.

WHEN the girl had heard this, she said, Be of good cheer, and weep not: for a remedy for your trouble is at hand; yea, it is with you and within your house: for I also was a leper, but when I saw that woman and with her this little child whose name is Jesus, I poured upon my body the water with which my mother had washed him, and I was healed. Now I know that he can heal your affliction also. But arise, go to my lady Mary, and when she is brought into your house reveal your secret to her, suppliantly entreating her to have pity on you. And when the women heard what the girl said, they went in haste to my lady Mary, and brought her to them, and sat down before her weeping and saying, O our lady, lady Mary, have pity on thy servants, for there is no one older than ourselves, or head of the family surviving, nor is there father or brother to take care of us: but this mule which thou seest was our brother, whom the women by a charm have made what thou seest. We pray thee, therefore, have pity on us. Then lamenting their lot, lady Mary lifted up the Lord Jesus and put him on the back of the mule, and herself wept along with the women; and to Jesus Christ she said, Alas, my son, heal this mule by thy great power, and make him a man endued with reason as he was formerly. When these words proceeded from the mouth of my lady, lady Mary, the mule changed its form, and became a man, a young man, who was whole without any blemish. Then he and his mother and sisters adored my lady, lady Mary, and began to kiss the Child, holding him above their heads, saying, Blessed is thy mother, O Jesus, O Saviour of the world ; blessed are the eyes which enjoy the happiness of beholding thee.

CHAPTER XXII.

THEN both the sisters said to their mother, Our brother indeed, by the help of the Lord Jesus Christ and the salutary intervention of this girl, who made known to us Mary and her son, is restored to human form. But now since our brother is unmarried, it is meet that we should give him to marry this damsel their servant. When they asked this of lady Mary, and she had given them her consent, they prepared a splendid wedding for the girl, and their sorrow being turned into joy, and their mourning into dancing, they began to be glad, to rejoice, to exult, and to sing, for great joy adorning themselves in raiment most splendid and pure. Then they began to repeat hymns and praises, and to say, O Jesus, son of David, who changest sorrow into joy, and lamentations into gladness ! And Joseph and Mary remained there ten days. Then they departed, receiving great honours from these people, who bade them farewell, and returned weeping from bidding farewell, especially the damsel.

CHAPTER XXIII.

HAVING departed thence, when they had come into a desert country, and heard that it was haunted by robbers, Joseph and lady Mary thought to pass through this region by night. But as they went, behold they saw two robbers lying in the way, and with them a multitude of robbers who were their companions, asleep. Now the two robbers upon whom they came were Titus and Dumachus. So Titus said to Dumachus, I pray thee suffer these persons to depart freely, and so that our companions observe them not. But when Dumachus refused, Titus said again, Take to thee from me forty drachmas, and hold this pledge. At the same time he held out to him his girdle with which he was girded, that he should not open his mouth nor speak. And when my lady, lady Mary, saw that the robber showed kindness to them, she said to him, The Lord God shall sustain thee with his right hand, and give thee remission of sins. And the Lord Jesus answered and said to his mother, After thirty years, O mother, the Jews will crucify me at Jerusalem, and these two robbers will be lifted on the cross with me, Titus at my right hand and Dumachus at my left, and after that day Titus shall go before me into Paradise.[1] And when she had said, God avert this from thee my son,

[1] Luke xxiii. 39–43.

they went thence to a city of idols which, when they approached, was changed into heaps of sand.

CHAPTER XXIV.

HENCE they proceeded to the sycamore tree which is now called Matarea, and the Lord Jesus produced a fountain in Matarea, wherein lady Mary washed her garment. Now from the sweat of the Lord Jesus which he there let drop the balsam came forth in that region.[1]

CHAPTER XXV.

THENCE they went down to Memphis, and having seen Pharaoh,[2] they staid three years in Egypt; and the Lord Jesus wrought very many miracles in Egypt, which are not found written either in the Gospel of the Infancy or in the Perfect Gospel.

CHAPTER XXVI.

BUT after three years he returned from Egypt,

[1] Matarea, or Matarééh, lies a few miles N.E. of Cairo, and is supposed to be the ancient Heliopolis. Sir J. G. Wilkinson says the water of the Fountain of the Sun is reported to have been salt until Joseph and Mary made it fresh. A sycamore tree is shown there under which they say the holy family rested. As for the balsam trees, Cleopatra is reported to have had them transplanted here from Judea. The tradition of the text only partially coincides with the many versions of it reported by pilgrims and travellers.

[2] Memphis may have been visited; but who was Pharaoh? Egypt was then under Roman rule.

and came back: and when they drew nigh to Judea, Joseph was afraid to enter it, but hearing that Herod was dead, and Archelaus his son had succeeded in his stead, he was still afraid, but he went into Judea. And an angel of God appeared to him and said, O Joseph, go into the city of Nazareth, and there abide.

It is truly wonderful that the Lord of regions was thus borne and carried about through the regions.

CHAPTER XXVII.

AFTER this, having entered the city of Bethlehem, they saw there many and sore afflictions distressing the eyes of infants, who died in consequence. There was there a woman who had a sick son whom, being already nigh unto death, she brought to my lady, lady Mary, who saw her while she was washing Jesus Christ. Then said the woman, O my lady Mary, regard this my son who suffereth grievous pain. And when lady Mary heard her she said, Take a little of this water with which I have washed my son, and sprinkle him with it. So she took a little of the water, as lady Mary had said, and poured it on her son; and having done this his pain ceased, and when he had slept a little, he afterwards awoke from sleep safe and sound. His mother rejoicing at this brought him again to lady Mary. And she said to her, Give thanks to God, that he hath healed thy son.

CHAPTER XXVIII.

THERE was there another woman, the neighbour of her whose son had just been healed. Her son being afflicted with the same disease, and his eyes being now almost blinded, she lamented night and day. The mother of the child that was healed said to her, Why dost thou not carry thy son to lady Mary, as I carried my son to her, when he was nigh unto death, and he was made well by the water wherewith the body of her son Jesus had been washed? When the woman had heard this from her, she too went, and having received some of the same water washed her son with it, and his body and eyes immediately became well. Her also, lady Mary, when she had taken her son to her, and told her all that had happened, commanded to give thanks to God for the restoration of her son to health, and not to tell the matter to any one.

CHAPTER XXIX.

THERE were in the same city two women, the wives of one man, and each of them had a son ill of fever. One of these was called Mary, and the name of her son was Cleopas. This woman arose, and taking her son went to my lady, lady Mary, the mother of Jesus, and offering her a beautiful cloak, said, O my lady Mary, receive from me this cloak, and give me for it one swaddling band. This Mary did, and the mother of Cleopas went away and dressed her son in a shirt made out of it. Thus was his disease healed; but the son of her rival died. Hence enmity arose between them, and since on alternate weeks they managed the affairs of the household, and on one occasion the turn of Mary the mother of Cleopas came on, she heated the oven to bake bread, and went away to fetch the dough she had kneaded, leaving her son Cleopas at the oven. Her rival seeing him alone—the oven being hot with the fire that was burning—she took him and threw him into the oven, and withdrew from the place. When Mary came back and saw her son Cleopas lying in the middle of the oven laughing, and the oven cold, as if no fire had been put into it, she knew that her rival had thrust him into the fire. She took him out therefore and carried him to the lady, my lady Mary, and told her what had happened. And she said, Keep silence, and tell this to no one; for I fear for thee if thou divulge it. Afterwards her rival went to the well to draw water, and seeing Cleopas near the well playing, and no one nigh, she took him and thrust him into the well, and went home. When men came to fetch water from the well, they saw the boy sitting on the surface of the water, so they went down and brought him out. But great admiration of the child seized them and they praised God. Then came his mother, and weeping, brought him that had been taken out

to my lady, lady Mary, and said, O my lady, see
what my rival hath done to my son, and how she
hath thrust him into the well; it is impossible that
she should not sometime destroy him. Lady Mary
said to her, God will avenge thee upon her. Afterwards when her rival went to draw water at the well,
her feet became entangled in the rope and she fell
into the well. Men came to draw her out indeed, but
they found her head bruised and her bones broken.
So she died a bad death, and that saying was fulfilled
in her,—They dug a well deep, but they fell into the
pit which they had prepared.[1]

CHAPTER XXX.

ANOTHER woman there had two sons who fell sick,
and one died but the other lived: so his mother took
him up and, weeping, brought him to my lady, lady
Mary, and said, O my lady, help and succour me.
For I had two sons, one of whom I have now buried,
but the other is nigh unto death. See how I will
beg and pray to God. And she began to say, O Lord,
thou art kind and merciful and good; thou gavest
me two sons, but since thou hast taken one of them
away, leave me at least this one. Therefore lady
Mary, seeing the violence of her weeping pitied her,
and said, Put thy son in my son's bed and cover him

[1] Ps. vii. 15; lvii. 6.

with his clothes. And when she had put him in the bed in which Christ was lying, and he was already dead and had closed his eyes, as soon as the smell of the garments of the Lord Jesus Christ reached the boy, he opened his eyes and, calling his mother with a loud voice, asked for bread, which he swallowed when he received it. Then said his mother, O lady Mary, now I know that the power of God dwelleth in thee, so that thy Son healeth men who are partakers of the same nature with himself, after they have touched his garments. This boy that was healed is he who in the Gospel is called Bartholomew.[1]

CHAPTER XXXI.

MOREOVER there was there a leprous woman who came to my lady, lady Mary, the mother of Jesus, and said, My lady, help me. But the lady Mary answered, What kind of help dost thou seek? is it gold or silver? or that thy body may be cleansed from leprosy? But the woman answered, Who can give me this? Lady Mary said, Wait a little, until I have washed my son Jesus and laid him in bed. The woman waited as Mary told her; and when she had put Jesus to bed, she held out the water with which she had washed his body, saying, Take a little of this water and pour it on thy body. When she had done

[1] Matt. x. 3.

THE ARABIC GOSPEL OF THE INFANCY. 197

this, she was straightway cleansed, and praised God, and gave thanks to him.

CHAPTER XXXII.

AND after she had staid three days with her she departed, and going into the city saw there a chief man who had married the daughter of another chief man; but when he saw the woman he perceived between her eyes the mark of leprosy like a star; so the marriage had been dissolved and annulled. And seeing them in that state, oppressed with sorrow and weeping, the woman asked of them the cause of their weeping. And they said, Inquire not after our condition, for we cannot tell our trouble to any mortal, or reveal it to any. But she was urgent, and begged them to commit it to her, for perhaps she could show them its remedy. When therefore they showed her the girl and the sign of leprosy which appeared between her eyes, as she saw it the woman said, I also, whom you see here, suffered from the same disease, when on some business, which I had, I went to Bethlehem. There entering a cave I saw a woman named Mary, whose son was one called Jesus; and when she saw that I was leprous she had pity on me, and gave me the water with which she had washed the body of her Son. I poured it on my body, and I became clean. Therefore, the women said to her, wilt thou,

O lady, arise and go with us and show us my lady, lady Mary? She assented, and they arose and went to my lady, lady Mary, bearing splendid gifts with them. And when they had entered and offered her the gifts, they showed her the leprous girl whom they had brought with them. Therefore, the lady Mary said, The mercy of the Lord Jesus Christ descend upon you. And giving to them also a little of the water with which she had washed the body of Jesus Christ, she commanded the unfortunate one to be washed with it. And when they had done this, she was forthwith healed; and they, and all who stood by, praised God. Therefore they returned to their own city rejoicing, and praising the Lord for it. Now when the chief man heard that his wife was healed, he took her to his house and made a second wedding, and gave thanks to God for the recovered health of his wife.

CHAPTER XXXIII.

There was also there a damsel who was afflicted by Satan; for that cursed one, in the form of a huge dragon, from time to time appeared to her, and prepared to swallow her up; he also sucked out all her blood, so that she remained like a corpse. As often as he approached her, she, with her hands clasped above her head, would scream and say, Alas, Alas, for me, that no one is here to deliver me from this most wicked dragon! Now her father and mother, and all who were about her, or saw her, pitied her lot; and men stood in confusion around her, and all wept and lamented, especially when she herself wept and said, O my brethren and friends, is there no one to deliver me from this murderer? But the daughter of the prince, who had been healed of her leprosy, hearing the voice of the damsel, went up to the roof of her castle and saw her with her hands clasped above her head weeping, and all the groups of those who stood around likewise weeping. Therefore she asked the husband of this demoniac whether the mother of his wife was living. When he had said that both her parents were alive, she said, Call her mother to me. When she saw her come, after being called by him, she said, Is this distracted young woman thy daughter? Yea, O lady, said the sad and weeping woman, she is my daughter. The prince's daughter answered, Hide my secret: for I confess to thee that I was a leper, but now lady Mary, the mother of Jesus Christ, hath healed me. But if thou wouldst have thy daughter healed, take her to Bethlehem and seek out Mary, the mother of Jesus, and be sure thy daughter will be healed; and I am sure thou wilt return hither rejoicing with thy daughter in good health. The woman as soon as she heard the saying of the prince's daughter, immediately took her daughter with her, and, proceeding to the place indicated, went to my lady, lady Mary, and revealed to her her daughter's condition. Having heard her statement lady Mary gave her a little of the water in which she had washed the body of her son Jesus, and commanded her to pour it on the body of her daughter. She gave her also a strip of the clothes of the Lord Jesus, and said, Take this strip of cloth and show it to thy enemy as often as thou seest him. And she dismissed them with a salutation.

CHAPTER XXXIV.

WHEN therefore they had departed from her and returned to their own country, and the time came in which Satan was wont to assail her, at that time the accursed one appeared to her in the form of a huge dragon, at the sight whereof the girl was afraid. But her mother said, Fear not, O daughter, suffer him to approach thee, and then show to him the strip of cloth which my lady Mary gave us, and we shall see what will happen. When therefore Satan like a terrible dragon came nigh, the body of the girl shuddered for fear of him; but as soon as she took out the strip of cloth, and put it on her head, and covered her eyes with it, flames and flashes began to blaze out of the strip of cloth, and to dart at the dragon. O the great miracle which was wrought as soon as the dragon saw the strip of cloth of the Lord Jesus, from which fire shone out, and darted at his head and eyes! With a loud voice he cried out, What have I to do with thee, O Jesus, son of Mary? Whither shall I flee from thee? With great dread, turning his back, he departed from the girl, and never after appeared to her. And the girl had rest from him, and gave praise and thanks to God, and with her all who were present at the miracle.

CHAPTER XXXV.

In the same place there dwelt another woman whose son was vexed by Satan. He, Judas by name, whenever Satan seized him, bit all who approached him; and if he found no one near him he bit his own hands and other members. Therefore, the mother of this unfortunate one, hearing the fame of lady Mary and her son Jesus, arose and took with her her son Judas to my lady Mary. Meanwhile James and Joses had taken away the child Lord Jesus to play with other children; and after leaving home they had sat down and the Lord Jesus with them. Judas the demoniac came nigh and sat down at the right of Jesus; and then being assaulted by Satan as he was wont to be, he sought to bite the Lord Jesus, but he could not, yet he struck the right side of Jesus, who for this cause began to weep. Forthwith Satan went forth out of the boy in form like a mad dog. Now this boy, who struck Jesus, and from whom Satan went out in the form of a dog, was Judas Iscariot, who betrayed him to the Jews, and that side of him on which Judas had smitten him, the Jews pierced with a spear.[1]

CHAPTER XXXVI.

Now when the Lord Jesus had accomplished seven years from his nativity, on a certain day he was with other boys of the same age. Now they were playing with clay, out of which they made figures of asses, oxen, birds, and other animals, and each one, glorying in his skill, praised his own work. Then the Lord Jesus said to the boys, the figures which I have made I will command to walk. Being asked by the boys whether then he was the son of the Creator, the Lord Jesus commanded them to walk, and they straightway began to jump about: then, when he gave them leave, they stood still again. Now he had made figures of birds and sparrows, which flew when he bade them fly, and stood still when he bade them stand, and ate and drank when he offered them food and drink. After the boys went and told these things to their parents, their fathers said to them, Beware, O sons, of keeping company with him again; for he is a sorcerer; therefore flee him and avoid him, and henceforth play with him no more.

[1] Matt, x. 4; John xix. 34.

CHAPTER XXXVII.

On a certain day, as the Lord Jesus was running about and playing with the boys, he went by the shop of a dyer, whose name was Salem; and he had in his shop many cloths which he was going to dye. The Lord Jesus therefore entering the shop of the dyer took all these cloths and cast them into a vessel full of Indian blue. When Salem came and saw the cloths spoiled, he began to cry out with a loud voice and to scold the Lord Jesus, saying, O son of Mary, what hast thou done to me? Thou hast rendered me dishonourable among all my townsmen; for every one wished for the colour that suited him, but thou hast come and ruined all. The Lord Jesus answered, Of whatever cloth thou wishest the colour changed, I will change it for thee, and he began at once to take the cloths out of the vessel, each of them dyed the colour which the dyer desired, until he had drawn them all out. The Jews who saw this miracle and prodigy praised God.[1]

CHAPTER XXXVIII.

Now Joseph went about through all the city and took with him the Lord Jesus, since men sent for him on account of his craft, to make for them doors,

---

[1] This tradition is still current in Persia and other Eastern countries.

and milk-pails, and couches, and boxes. And the Lord Jesus was with him wherever he went. Therefore as often as Joseph had to make any of his work a cubit or a span longer or shorter, wider or narrower, the Lord Jesus used to stretch out his hand towards it, and when this was done it became such as Joseph wished; and there was no need for him to do anything with his own hand; for Joseph was not very skilful as a carpenter.

CHAPTER XXXIX.

On a certain day the king of Jerusalem sent for him and said, Joseph, I wish thee to make me a throne of the measure of the place where I have been used to sit. Joseph obeyed, and immediately after he put his hand to the work; he remained two years in the palace, until he had finished making the throne. But when he had it removed into its place, he perceived that on each side it was two spans shorter than the proper measure. On seeing this the king was angry with Joseph; and Joseph, being greatly afraid of the king, passed the night supperless and tasting nothing whatever. Then he was asked by the Lord Jesus why he was afraid? Because, said Joseph, I have lost all that I have done for two years. The Lord Jesus said to him, Fear not, nor lose heart, but take thou one side of the throne, and I will take the other, to set it right. And when Joseph had done as the Lord Jesus had said, and each had pulled on his own side, the throne was made right, and brought to the exact measure of the place. When this prodigy was seen, they who were present were amazed, and praised God. Now the wood of the throne was of that kind which was celebrated in the time of Solomon, the son of David; that is, variegated and diversified.

CHAPTER XL.

ANOTHER day the Lord Jesus went out into the street, and seeing some boys who had met to play, he followed them; but the boys hid themselves from him. Therefore when the Lord Jesus had come to the door of a certain house, and saw the women who stood there, he asked them whither the boys had gone. And when they told him that there was nobody there, the Lord Jesus said again, What are these whom ye see in the vault? They answered that they were kids of three years old. And the Lord Jesus cried aloud and said, Come out here, O kids, to your shepherd! Then the boys came out, having the form of kids, and began to skip about him. When they saw it the women wondered greatly, and, being seized with fear, they suppliantly and in haste adored the Lord Jesus, saying, O our Lord Jesus, son of Mary, thou art indeed the Good Shepherd of Israel; have pity on thy handmaids who stand before thee and never doubted; for, O our Lord, thou hast come to heal, and not to destroy. But when the Lord Jesus had answered, that the children of Israel were like Ethiopians among the nations, the women said, Thou Lord, knowest all things, and nothing is hidden from thee; but now we pray thee, and from thy kindness we ask, that thou wouldst restore these boys, thy servants, to their former condition. The Lord Jesus therefore said, Come, boys, let us go and play; and immediately, while the women stood there, the kids were changed into boys.

CHAPTER XLI.

Now in the month of Adar, Jesus assembled the boys as if he were their king; they strewed their garments on the ground, and he sat upon them. Then they put on his head a crown wreathed of flowers, and, like attendants waiting on a king, they stood in order before him on his right hand and on his left. And whoever passed that way, the boys took him by force, saying, Come hither and adore the king, and then proceed on thy way.

CHAPTER XLII.

MEANWHILE, as these things were going on, there

came up men who were carrying a boy. For this boy had gone to the mountain, with others of his age, to seek for wood; and when he had found there a partridge's nest, and put out his hand to take the eggs from it, a poisonous serpent from the middle of the nest wounded him, so that he cried out for help. When his companions came near in haste, they found him lying on the ground like one dead, and then his relatives came and lifted him up to carry him into the town. But when they had come to the place in which the Lord Jesus was sitting as the king, and the other boys standing round as his attendants, the boys went in haste to meet him who was bitten by the serpent, and said to his friends, Come and salute the king. But when they would not come, because of the sorrow in which they were, the boys took them by force against their will. And when they had come to the Lord Jesus, he asked them why they were carying this boy. And when they replied that a serpent had bitten him, the Lord Jesus said to the boys, Let us go and kill the serpent. And when the parents of the boy asked that they would let them depart, for their son was at the point of death, the boys answered and said, Have ye not heard what the king hath said: Let us go and kill the serpent? And will ye not obey him? And so against their will they took the litter back. And when they had come to the nest, the Lord Jesus said, Is this the serpent's place? And when they said it was, the serpent, being called by the Lord, came forth without delay, submitting himself to him. And he said, Go and suck out all the venom which thou hast infused into this boy. The serpent therefore crawled to the boy and sucked out all its venom. Then the Lord Jesus cursed him: whereupon he was instantly rent asunder; and the boy, being stroked by the hand of the Lord Jesus, became well again. And when he began to weep, the Lord Jesus said, Weep not, for hereafter thou shalt be my disciple. And this was Simon the Cananite, of whom mention is made in the Gospel.[2]

CHAPTER XLIII.

On another day, Joseph had sent his son James to gather wood, and the Lord Jesus had joined him as a companion. And when they came to the place in which the wood was, and James began to gather it, behold a noxious viper bit his hand, so that he began to cry out and weep. The Lord Jesus, therefore, seeing him in this condition, came to him and breathed on the place where the viper had bitten him; whereupon he was instantly healed.

CHAPTER XLIV.

One day when the Lord Jesus was again among

[1] *Cananite*, a Syriac word synonymous with *Zelotes*.
[2] Matt. x. 4.

the boys who were playing on a housetop, one of the boys fell down from above and immediately died. Now the other boys fled, and the Lord Jesus alone remained on the housetop. And when the kindred of the boy had come, they said to the Lord Jesus, Thou hast pushed our son headlong from the housetop. And as he denied it, they called out, saying, Our son is dead, and this is he who killed him. The Lord Jesus said to them, Do not blame me: but if ye believe not me, come and let us ask the boy himself, and let him bring the truth to light. Then the Lord Jesus came down, and, standing over him that was dead, he said in a loud voice, Zeno, Zeno, who cast thee down from the housetop? Then he that was dead answered, saying, Lord, thou didst not cast me down; but such a one pushed me off. And when the Lord Jesus had bidden those who stood there to observe his words, all who were present praised God for this miracle.

CHAPTER XLV.

MY lady, Lady Mary, once commanded the Lord Jesus to go and fetch her some water from the well. But when he went to bring the water, his waterpot, which was already filled, was shattered and broken. But the Lord Jesus spread out his handkerchief, and took the water he had gathered up to his mother, who marvelled at the act. But she laid up and stored in her heart all that she saw.

CHAPTER XLVI.

AGAIN, another day, the Lord Jesus was at the water-side with some boys, and they made little pools again. Now the Lord Jesus had made twelve sparrows and ranged them three on each side about his pool. And it was the Sabbath day. So the son of Ananias, a Jew, coming up and seeing them doing such things, was angry and indignant. Do you, then, said he, make figures of clay on the Sabbath day? And, running up in haste, he destroyed their pools. Now when the Lord Jesus had clapped his hands over the sparrows he had made, they flew away chirping. Then the son of Ananias came also to the pool of Jesus, and kicking it down with his shoes, the water ran out of it. And the Lord Jesus said to him, As that water hath disappeared, so also thy life shall disappear; and immediately the boy withered away.

CHAPTER XLVII.

AT another time when the Lord Jesus was returning home with Joseph in the evening, he met a boy, who ran and thrust him so violently that he fell down. The Lord Jesus said to him, As thou hast thrown me down, so shalt thou fall and not rise; and the same hour the boy fell down and breathed his last.

CHAPTER XLVIII.

MOREOVER there was at Jerusalem one named Zacchæus, who was a teacher of boys. He said to Joseph, Joseph, why dost thou not bring me Jesus to learn letters? Joseph gave him his consent, and reported this to lady Mary. So they brought him to the master, who, as soon as he saw him, wrote the alphabet for him, and bade him say Aleph; and when he had said Aleph, the master ordered him to say Beth; and the Lord Jesus said to him, Tell me first the meaning of the letter Aleph and then I will say Beth. And when the master threatened to flog him, the Lord Jesus explained to him the meanings of the letters Aleph and Beth; also which forms of the letters were straight, which crooked, which drawn spirally, which marked with points, which were without them, and why one letter came before another; and he began to tell and explain many other things which the master himself had never heard, nor had read in any book. Moreover, the Lord Jesus said to the master, Attend, that I may tell thee. And he began clearly and distinctly to repeat Aleph, Beth, Gimel, and Daleth, as far as Tau. The master, wondering at this, said, I think this boy was born before

Noah; and, turning to Joseph, he said, Thou hast brought to me to be taught a boy that is wiser than all teachers. To lady Mary also he said, There is no need of instruction for this thy son.

CHAPTER XLIX.

Then they brought him to another and more learned master; and when he saw him he said, Say Aleph, and when he had said Aleph, the master ordered him to say Beth. The Lord Jesus answered and said to him, Tell me first the meaning of the letter Aleph, and then I will say Beth. When the master had lifted up his hand and struck him, his hand immediately withered, and he died. Then Joseph said to lady Mary, Henceforth we will not let him go out of the house, for whoever opposeth him is punished with death.

CHAPTER L.

And when he was twelve years old they took him to Jerusalem to the feast. But when the feast was over they, indeed, returned, but the Lord Jesus remained in the Temple among the doctors and elders and learned men of the sons of Israel; and he asked them sundry questions about the sciences, and they answered him in turn.[1] Now he said to them, Whose

[1] Luke ii. 42–47.

son is Messiah? They answered him, The Son of David. Wherefore then, said he, doth he in spirit call him his Lord, when he saith, The Lord said unto my Lord, sit thou on my right hand, that I may bring down thy enemies to the footprints of thy feet?[1] Again the chief of the doctors said to him, Hast thou read the scriptures? The Lord Jesus said, Both the scriptures and the things which are contained in them. And he explained the scriptures and the law and the precepts, and the statutes and the mysteries which are contained in the books of the prophets—things which the understanding of no creature attains unto. The doctor said, therefore, Heretofore I have not acquired nor heard such wisdom; what, thinkest thou, will that boy be?

CHAPTER LI.

AND since there was there a philosopher skilled in astronomy, and he asked the Lord Jesus whether he had studied astronomy, the Lord Jesus answered him and expounded the number of the spheres and celestial bodies, and their natures and operations, their opposition, trine, quartile, and sextile aspect, their direct course and retrogression, degrees and the sixtieths of degrees, and other things which reason does not attain unto.

[1] Matt. xxii. 42-45 · Ps. cx. 1.

CHAPTER LII.

There was also among those philosophers one who was excellently skilled in the handling of natural things; and when he asked the Lord Jesus whether he had studied medicine, he answered and explained to him physics and metaphysics, hyperphysics and hypophysics; the virtues of the body; also the humours and their effects; also the number of the members and bones, veins, arteries, and nerves; also the effect of heat and dryness, of cold and moisture, and what might arise out of them; what the operation of the soul upon the body, and its senses and virtues; and the operation of the faculty of speaking, of anger, and of desire; finally, conjunction and disjunction, and other things which the intellect of no creature attains unto. Then the philosopher arose and adored the Lord Jesus, and said, O Lord, from this time I will be thy disciple and servant.

CHAPTER LIII.

While they were conversing together of these and other things, my lady, lady Mary, came in after she had gone about with Joseph seeking him for three days. Therefore seeing him sitting among the doctors, and asking and answering them by turns, she said to him, My son, why hast thou dealt so with us? Lo, I and thy father have sought thee with much trouble. And he said, Why do ye seek me? Know ye not that I must be occupied in the house of my Father? But they understood not the words which he said to them. Then the doctors asked Mary whether this was her son, and on her assenting, they said, How happy thou art, who hast given birth to such a one as he! But he returned with them to Nazareth, and obeyed them in all things. And his mother laid up all those things in her heart. But the Lord Jesus advanced in stature and wisdom, and in favour with God and men.[1]

CHAPTER LIV.

AND from that day he began to hide his concealed and secret miracles[2] and to study the law, until he accomplished his thirtieth year, when the Father publicly declared him at the Jordan by this voice sent down from heaven: "This is my beloved Son in whom I am well pleased;" the Holy Spirit being present in the form of a white dove.[3]

CHAPTER LV.

THIS is He whom we suppliantly adore, who gave to us being and life, and took us from our mothers'

[1] Luke ii. 46-52.   [2] Cf. John ii. 11.
[3] Matt. iii. 13-17; Luke ii. 21-23.

wombs; who, for our sake, took upon him a human body and redeemed us, that eternal mercy might embrace us, and that he might show us his clemency in liberality and beneficence, and generosity and benevolence. To him be the glory and goodness and power and dominion from henceforth unto eternal ages. Amen.

Here ends the whole of the Gospel of the Infancy, with the help of God most high, according to what we found in the original.

THE CORRESPONDENCE BETWEEN ABGAR AND JESUS, ETC.

It seems proper to insert in this place a few minor compositions, which belong, chronologically, to the period of our Saviour's ministry.

1. *The Correspondence between Abgar, King of Edessa, and Jesus.*—This is inserted by Eusebius at the end of Book I. of his Ecclesiastical History, as derived from the original Syriac in the archives of Edessa. Recent discoveries of what seems to be a further portion of the same document, have led me to believe that the correspondence was forged about the middle of the third century.

2. *The Epistle of Lentulus.*—I consider this not very ancient. It first appears attached to a printed edition of the works of Anselm and may be regarded as a modification of preceding attempts to determine the personal appearance of Jesus. The composition of it almost certainly falls between the age of Nicephorus (14th cent.), and the year 1500. No such person as Lentulus occupied the position indicated

by this letter at the time to which it refers. Yet the name is common in the consular lists of the ages preceding and following the birth of Christ, and probably this is the reason of its adoption by the writer, who composed it in Latin.

3. *The Prayer of Jesus, the Son of Mary.*—Selden first published this in Arabic and Latin; and it was reprinted with an English version by Jeremiah Jones. It is a purely Mohammedan fiction, and but for its brevity I would scarcely have admitted it.

4. *The Story of Veronica.*—Under this head I give an extract from the chronicle of John Malela, who wrote about 600 A.D. The passage is chiefly remarkable for a pretended petition addressed to Herod by Veronica. The monument which she is said to have erected is described by Eusebius (Hist. Eccles. 7, 18). Its later history is narrated by Sozomen (Hist. Eccles. 5, 20). Upon the character of the story told by Malela, no observation is required, as it is so palpably apocryphal. I may add that while Eusebius describes the monument as consisting of two figures, said to represent Christ and the woman, he regards it as a heathenish affair, and is careful not to identify such things with Christianity.

THE LETTER OF ABGAR TO JESUS.

Copy of a letter that was written by Abgar the King to Jesus, and was sent to him by the hand of Ananias the tabellarius to Jerusalem.

ABGAR UCHOMO, chief of the land, to Jesus, the good Redeemer, that hath appeared in the land of Jerusalem: Greeting.

I have heard of thee and of the healing which is performed by thy hands without medicines and herbs. For, as it is said, thou makest the blind to see, and the lame to walk, and thou cleansest the lepers, and thou castest out unclean spirits and demons, and those that are tormented with lingering diseases thou healest, and the dead thou raisest up.[1] And when I heard all these things of thee, I settled in my mind one of two things: either that thou art God who camest down from heaven and dost these things, or that thou art the Son of God and dost these things. For this cause, therefore, I have written to ask of thee that thou wouldest trouble thyself to come to me, and heal this sickness which I have.[2] For I have also heard that the Jews murmur against thee, and wish to injure thee. Now I have a small and beautiful city which is sufficient for both.

[1] Matt. xi. 5.   [2] Cf. Luke vii. 6.

THE LETTER OF JESUS TO ABGAR.

Copy of the things which were written by Jesus, by the hand of Ananias the tabellarius to Abgar, chief of the land.

BLESSED is he that believeth in me when he hath not seen me.[1] For it is written concerning me that they who see me would not believe in me, and they who see me not would believe and be saved.[2] Now as for this that thou hast written to me, that I would come to thee, it behoveth that I should accomplish here everything because whereof I have been sent.[3] And after I have accomplished it, then I shall be taken up to Him that sent me. And when I am taken up I will send thee one of my disciples to heal thy sickness; he shall also give salvation unto thee and to them that are with thee.[4]

---

[1] John xx. 29.
[2] Is. vi. 10; lii, 15; John ix. 39.
[3] Matt. iii. 15; John v. 36; ix. 4.
[4] Luke i. 77; xix. 9; Acts xi. 14; xvi. 31.

THE LETTER OF LENTULUS.

LENTULUS, president of the people of Jerusalem, to the Roman Senate and People: Greeting.

THERE has appeared in our times, and still is, a man of great virtue named Christ Jesus, who is called by the Gentiles a prophet of truth, whom his disciples call the Son of God, raising the dead and healing diseases. He is a man of lofty stature, handsome, having a venerable countenance which the beholders can both love and fear. He has wavy hair, rather crisp, of a bluish tinge, and glossy, flowing down from his shoulders, with a parting in the middle of the head after the manner of the Nazarenes.[1] His forehead is even and very serene, and his face without any wrinkle or spot, and beautiful with a slight blush. His nose and mouth are without fault; he has a beard abundant and reddish, of the colour of his hair, not long but forked. His eyes are sparkling and bright. He is terrible in rebuke, calm and loving in admonition, cheerful but preserving gravity, has never been seen to laugh

---

[1] The writer has here evidently confounded *Nazarenes* with *Nazarites*.

but often to weep. Thus, in stature of body, he is tall; and his hands and limbs are beautiful to look upon. In speech he is grave, reserved, and modest; and he is fair among the children of men.[1] Farewell.

PRAYER OF JESUS, SON OF MARY:

Peace be upon them!

He said,—O God, I am not able to extirpate (or overcome) that which I abhor, nor have I attained the good which I desired; but others, and not I, have their reward in their hands. But my glory abideth in my work; nor is any poor man poorer than I am. O God most high, grant me pardon. O God, suffer not mine enemy to reproach me; nor let my friend contemn me; nor add affliction to my religion; nor let the world be my chief aim; nor set him over me who shall not pity me, for thy mercy's sake, O most merciful of the merciful.

[1] Ps. xlv. 2.

THE STORY OF VERONICA.

In the fifteenth year of the reign of Tiberius, in the consulate of Albanus and Nerva, St. John the Forerunner began to preach the baptism of repentance, and to baptize, according to the prophetic utterance, and there went forth to him all the Jewish region. And, moreover, our Lord Jesus Christ wrought the beginning of salvation; being baptized by the same John the Forerunner when he came to be about thirty years old, and doing miracles. He was baptized in the Jordan, a river of Palestine, on the 6th of the month Audynæus or January, at the tenth hour of the night, in the consulship of Rufus and Rubellio. From that time also John the Baptist was manifest to men. And Herod the king, the brother of Philip, who was tetrarch or king of the region of Trachonitis, beheaded him in the city of Sebaste, on the 8th before the calends of June, in the consulship of Flacco and Rufinus, because of Herodias his wife; for John said to him, "It is not lawful for thee to have the wife of thy brother," as in the divine Scriptures these things are recorded. This same king Herod, the second brother of Philip, being grieved because of John, went away from the city of Sebaste to Paneas, a city of Judea. And there came to him a certain very wealthy woman, Veronica by name, who dwelt in the same city of Paneas, who wished, as having been healed by Jesus, to erect a monument to him, and not daring to do this without royal order, she offered a petition to the said king Herod, asking to erect a monument to the Saviour Christ in the same city,—which petition runs thus:

To the august Herod, tetrarch and legislator both of Jews and Greeks, king of the region of Trachonitis, humble petitions from Veronica, an honourable woman of the city of Paneas.

Justice and kindness, and all other virtues surround thy divine brow. Wherefore, I also, knowing this, come with good hope to obtain altogether my requests.[1] But what is the aim of the present preface, the following account will inform thee.

Having from my childhood been afflicted with an issue of blood, I went to the physicians and expended my living and wealth, and found no cure; but hearing of the cures of the wonderful Christ, who raises the dead, restores sight to the blind, casts out demons from mortals, and heals with a word all who pine away in sickness, therefore I too ran to him as to a God. Observing the multitude which surrounded him, and fearing to tell him my incurable

[1] Cf. Acts xxiv. 2-4, 10.

THE STORY OF VERONICA.

disease, lest turning away from the loathsomeness of my affliction, he should be angry with me, and the stroke of my disease come worse upon me, I thought with myself that if I could take hold of the hem of his garment I should be altogether healed; and secretly entering the multitude around him, I stole a cure by touching his hem,—the fountain of my blood stayed, and suddenly I became well. But he the more, as foreknowing the purpose of my heart, cried out, "Who hath touched me? for power is gone out of me;" and I, turning pale, and groaning, supposing the disease would return upon me more violently, falling before him flooded the ground with tears, confessing my daring. But he, being good, had compassion on me, and confirmed my cure, saying, "Daughter, take heart, thy faith hath delivered thee; go in peace."[1] So also do thou, O august one, grant her earnest petition to the petitioner.

And king Herod, hearing these things from the petition, was astonished at the miracle; and being afraid at the mystery of the healing, said, "This cure which hath befallen thee, O woman, is worthy of a very great monument. Therefore, go and erect unto him such a monument as thou wilt, honouring by thy zeal him that healed thee."

And immediately after this, Veronica, who before

[1] Matt. ix., 20-22. Mark v., 25-34. Luke viii., 43-48.

had the issue of blood, erected in the midst of her own city, Paneas, unto our Lord and God, Jesus Christ, a monument of molten brass, mingling therewith a certain portion of gold and silver,—which monument remains in the city of Paneas until now, having been removed a long time ago from the place where it stood in the middle of the city into the holy house of prayer.

This document I found in the same city of Paneas in the possession of a certain Bassus, who had become a Christian from among the Jews. There was also together with it, a life of all the kings who formerly reigned in the Jewish region.[1]

[1] Chronographia, lib. x. pp. 304–308. Ed. Hod. Ox. 1691. Additional notices of Veronica will be found in the Latin Gospel of Nicodemus, and also towards the end of this volume in "The Death of Pilate" and "The Saviour's Revenge."

IX.

THE GOSPEL OF NICODEMUS, OR ACTS OF PILATE.

THIS may be designated a supplementary gospel. Those which precede are mainly preliminary to the Evangelical narratives, of which the last scenes are here the starting point. The book professes to record the trial, crucifixion, burial, resurrection, and ascension of Christ; the miraculous and wonderful incidents which attended those events, and the conduct pursued by the friends and enemies of the Saviour. Inasmuch as the Gospels lie at the basis, and the writer was a person generally well informed, the truthful element in this composition is more marked than in any of the preceding. Whether the writer had any authentic documents of an official character to assist him is more than can be affirmed; it seems more likely that he used current traditions and with the help of the Gospels, reduced them as far as possible to an appearance of truth. We know that as early as the time of Justin Martyr there were extant Acts of Pilate, which that father regarded as genuine, and which may have been so for anything we can tell. But the Greek text here translated is avowedly not earlier than the time of Valentinian, as appears in the Prologue.[1] The phraseology is barbarous. It is unknown in what language it was primarily written. The author may have been a converted Jew who wrote in Greek.

The book has been often printed both in Latin and in Greek, and Tischendorf gives three recensions of it. The one which immediately follows is often connected with a supplement of later date, which I have called Part II.

It is perhaps the most famous of the New Testament Apocrypha, and its merits, such as they are, have attracted to it much attention. Although it largely uses the genuine Gospels, it omits important details which they exhibit, and in many other ways it departs widely from them. The marvellous incidents in it are partly pure fictions, and apparently imitations from the Apocalypse and other portions of Scripture. Tischendorf would ascribe its origin to the second century.

---

[1] The Prologue varies in the copies; some want it altogether, and some have it at the end of the book.

THE GOSPEL OF NICODEMUS, OR ACTS OF PILATE (I.)

Acts of our Lord Jesus Christ wrought in the time of Pontius Pilate.

PROLOGUE.

I, ANANIAS, a provincial warden, being a disciple of the law, from the divine Scriptures recognised our Lord Jesus Christ, and came to him by faith, and was also accounted worthy of holy baptism. Now when searching the records which were made in the time of our Lord Jesus Christ, which the Jews laid up under Pontius Pilate, I found that these records were written in Hebrew, and by the good pleasure of God I translated them into Greek for the information of all who call on the name of our Lord Jesus Christ, under the government of our lord Flavius Theodosius, the 17th year, and in the 6th consulate of Flavius Valentinianus, in the 9th indiction.[1]

[1] The dates given in the consular tables do not agree in all editions, but I do not find any in which the seventeenth of Theodosius and the sixth of Valentinian come together. The seventeenth consulate of Theodosius is by some placed in A.D. 441, and the fifth of Valentinian in 442; while the eighteenth of Theodosius falls in 446, and the sixth of Valentinian in 447. The ninth indiction, according to Dufresnoy, falls in 441. We may therefore correct the text by reading the seventeenth consulate of Theodosius, and the fifth of Valentinian, which would be A.D. 441-2. The Coptic has the fifth of Valentinian, and the Latin the eighteenth of Theodosius.

All therefore who read and copy into other books remember me and pray for me, that God may be propitious to me, and be gracious to my sins which I have committed against him.[1]

Peace to those who read and those who hear, and to their servants. Amen.

In the 15th year of the government of Tiberius Cæsar, king of the Romans; and of Herod, king of Galilee, the 19th year of his reign, on the 8th before the calends of April, which is the 25th of March; in the consulship of Rufus and Rubellio; in the 4th year of the 202nd Olympiad, when Joseph Caiaphas was high priest of the Jews.[2]

Whatsoever, after the cross and passion of our Lord Jesus Christ, the Saviour God, Nicodemus recorded and wrote in Hebrew, and left to posterity, is after this fashion.[3]

---

[1] Ancient scribes were very much in the habit of putting in requests for the prayers of their readers.

[2] The fifteenth of Tiberius is the date of our Lord's baptism (Luke iii, 1), but some ancient writers also give it as the date of the crucifixion, which is an error. For the nineteenth of Herod we must substitute the thirty-second, [Lewin's Fasti, p. 173]. Rufus and Rubellio may have been the consuls in the fifteenth of Tiberius, but were not when our Lord suffered. The fourth year of Olympiad 202 answers to the nineteenth of Tiberius. The phrase Joseph Caiaphas is justified in the note at p. 172. The placing of our Lord's arrest on March 25, is in harmony with several early authorities, but Clement of Alexandria mentions some who referred it to three or four months later in the year. The paragraph which contains these indications of time is found in many copies, but not in all.

[3] The ascription of this book to Nicodemus and a Hebrew original is evidence that it was not supposed to be the *Acts of Pilate* referred to by Justin Martyr and Tertullian.

CHAPTER I.

For the chief priests and scribes having taken counsel, Annas, and Caiaphas, and Semes, and Dathaes, and Gamaliel, Judas, Levi, and Nephthalim, Alexander and Jaeirus,[1] and the rest of the Jews, came to Pilate, accusing Jesus of many deeds, saying, We know this man that he is the son of Joseph the carpenter, born of Mary, and he saith that he is the Son of God and a king: moreover he profaneth the Sabbaths, and wisheth to abolish the law of our fathers. Pilate saith, And what is it that he doeth and wisheth to abolish? The Jews say, We have a law that no one shall heal on the Sabbath; but he by evil arts hath healed on the Sabbath the lame, and mutilated, and withered, and blind, and paralytic, deaf and demoniacs. Pilate saith to them, By what evil arts? They say to him, He is a magician, and by Beelzebub, prince of the demons, he casteth out demons; and they are all subject to him. Pilate saith to them, It is not possible to cast out demons by an unclean spirit, but by the God Esculapius.

The Jews say unto Pilate, We request thy majesty that he may be set before thy judgment seat and be heard. And Pilate calling them saith, Tell me, how can I who am a governor try a king? They say to

[1] The copies and versions differ exceedingly about these names.

him, We do not say that he is a king, but he saith he is one. And Pilate having called the officer[1] saith to him, Let Jesus be brought with gentleness. And the officer went out and having recognised him worshipped him, and taking a scarf[2] in his hand spread it on the ground, and said to him, Lord, walk here, and come in, for the governor calleth thee. And the Jews seeing what the officer did cried out against Pilate, saying, Why didst thou not order him by a crier to come in, rather than by an officer?[3] For when the officer saw him he worshipped him, and spread his scarf on the ground and made him walk on it like a king.

And Pilate called the officer and said to him, Why hast thou done this, and spread thy scarf on the ground and made Jesus walk upon it? The officer saith to him, My lord governor, When thou sentest me to Jerusalem to Alexander,[4] I saw Him sitting on an ass, and the children of the Hebrews held boughs in their hands and cried out, and others spread out their garments, saying, Save now, thou who art in the highest: blessed is he that cometh in the name of the Lord.[5]

The Jews cried out, and said to the officer, The

---

[1] The word is here the latin *cursor*, a messenger.
[2] The copies differ about the words I render 'scarf', but it seems to have been a loose wrapper.
[3] A *præco* rather than a *cursor*.
[4] I do not know what Alexander is meant.
[5] Matt., xxi, 8, 9.

children of the Hebrews cried out in Hebrew; whence hast thou the Greek? The officer saith to them, I asked one of the Jews and said, What is it that they cry out in Hebrew? And he explained to me. Pilate saith to them, How did they cry out in Hebrew? The Jews said to him, *Hosanna membrome, barouchamma Adonai*.[1] Pilate saith to them, And how is Hosanna and the rest interpreted? The Jews say unto him, Save now, thou that art in the highest: Blessed is he that cometh in the name of the Lord. Pilate saith to them, If ye bear witness that these words were spoken by the children, how hath the officer done wrong?[2] And they were silent. The governor saith to the officer, Go and bring him in what manner thou wilt. And the officer went out and did the same as before, and said to Jesus, Lord, enter, the governor calleth thee.

And when Jesus entered, and the standard-bearers holding the standards, the tops of the standards bowed down and worshipped Jesus. And when the Jews saw the manner of the standards, how they bowed down and worshipped Jesus, they cried out exceedingly against the standard-bearers. And Pilate said to the Jews, Do ye not marvel how the banners bowed down and worshipped Jesus? The Jews said to Pilate, We saw how the standard-bearers bowed

---

[1] *Hoshia na bamromim: baruch habbā (b'shem) Adonai.* Ps. cxviii. 26.
[2] The preceding story does not savour much of a Hebrew original!

down and worshipped him. And the governor called the standard-bearers and said to them, Why did ye do so? They said to Pilate, We are Greeks and wait upon the gods, how could we worship him? but as we were holding the banners they bowed down of themselves and worshipped him.

Pilate said to the chiefs of the synagogues and the elders of the people, Choose ye strong and powerful men, and let them hold the standards, and let us see if they bow down of themselves. And the elders of the Jews took twelve strong and powerful men, and made six together hold the standards, and they stood before the judgment-seat of the governor. And Pilate saith to the officer, Take him out of the prætorium, and bring him in again in what manner thou wilt. And Jesus and the officer went out of the prætorium. And Pilate called those who before held the banners, and saith to them, I have sworn by the salvation of Cæsar that if the standards do not bow down when Jesus entereth I will cut off your heads. And the governor gave order the second time that Jesus should come in. And the officer did the same as before, and earnestly entreated Jesus to tread upon his scarf. And he trod on it, and came in. And as he entered the standards bowed down again and worshipped Jesus.

CHAPTER II.

And when Pilate saw it he was afraid and sought to rise up from the judgment seat. And while it was yet in his mind to rise, his wife sent to him, saying, Have nothing to do with this just man, for I have suffered very much because of him in the night.[1] And Pilate, having called the Jews, said to them, Ye know that my wife is religious, and inclined to practise Judaism with you. They said unto him, Yea, we know it. Pilate saith to them, Behold, my wife hath sent to me, saying, Have nothing to do with this just man, for I have suffered very much because of him in the night. But the Jews answered and said to Pilate, Did we not tell thee that he is a magician? Behold he hath sent a dream to thy wife.

And Pilate called Jesus and said to him, What do these testify against thee? Dost thou say nothing? And Jesus said, Except they had power they would have said nothing. For every one of them hath power over his own mouth to speak both good and evil. They will see.

And the elders of the Jews answered and said to Jesus, What shall we see? first, that thou wast born

---

[1] Matt. xxvii. 19. This message is hinted at in the letter of Pilate to Herod, which will be found lower down.

of fornication; secondly, that thy birth in Bethlehem became the slaughter of babes; thirdly, that thy father Joseph and thy mother Mary fled into Egypt because they had no confidence with the people.

Some of the pious among the Jews who stood by said, We do not say that he was born of fornication, but we know that Joseph was espoused to Mary, and he was not born of fornication. Pilate said to the Jews, who said he was born of fornication, This saying of yours is not true; because the betrothal had taken place, as also your fellow countrymen say. Annas and Caiaphas say to Pilate, All the multitude of us cry out and do not believe that he was born of fornication:[1] these are proselytes and his disciples. And Pilate called Annas and Caiaphas and said to them, What are proselytes? They said to him, They were born the children of Greeks, and have now become Jews. Those who said he was not born of fornication, Lazarus, Asterius, Antonius, James, Amnes, Zera, Samuel, Isaac, Phinehas, Crispus, Agrippa, and Judas,[2] said, We have not become proselytes, but are children of Jews, and speak truth. And at the espousals of Joseph and Mary we were present.

And Pilate called these twelve men who said he was not born of fornication, and said to them, I ad-

---

[1] The context seems to require either, 'And we do believe', or 'Do we not believe?'
[2] The copies vary in this list of names.

jure you, by the salvation of Cæsar, is that true which ye say, that he was not born of fornication? They say to Pilate, We have a law not to swear, because it is sin; but they will swear that it is not as we said, and we are liable to death. Pilate saith to Annas and Caiaphas, Answer ye nothing to these things? Annas and Caiaphas say to Pilate, These twelve believe that he was not born of fornication; all the multitude of us proclaim that he was born of fornication, and is a magician, and calleth himself the Son of God and a king, and we believe him not.

And Pilate commanded all the multitude to go out, except the twelve men who said that he was not born of fornication, and commanded Jesus to be taken out. And Pilate saith to them, On what account wish they to slay him? They say unto him, They are jealous because he healeth on the sabbath. Pilate saith, For a good work do they wish to slay him? They say unto him, Yea.

CHAPTER III.

AND Pilate was filled with anger, and went out of the prætorium and saith to them, I call the sun to witness that I find no fault in this man. The Jews answered and said to the governor, If this man was not an evil doer, we should not have delivered him to thee. And Pilate said, Take ye him and judge him according to your law. The Jews said to Pilate, It is not lawful for us to put any one to death. Pilate said, Did God command you not to kill, but me to kill?

And Pilate went in again to the prætorium, and called Jesus aside, and said to him, Art thou the king of the Jews? Jesus answered Pilate, Dost thou speak this of thyself, or have others said it to thee of me? Pilate answered Jesus, Am I also a Jew? Thine own nation and the chief priests have delivered thee to me. What hast thou done? Jesus answered, My kingdom is not of this world: for if my kingdom was of this world, my servants would have fought for me that I should not be delivered to the Jews; but now my kingdom is not from hence. Pilate said to him, Art thou then a king? Jesus answered him, Thou sayest; for I am a king: for this was I born, and I am come that every one who is of the truth should hear my voice. Pilate saith unto him, What is truth? Jesus saith to him, Truth is from heaven. Pilate saith, Is truth not upon earth? Jesus saith to Pilate, Thou seest how they who say the truth are judged by those who have power upon earth.

CHAPTER IV.

AND leaving Jesus within the prætorium, Pilate went out to the Jews, and saith unto them, I find no fault in him. The Jews say unto him, This man said, I can destroy this temple, and build it in three days. Pilate saith, What temple? The Jews say, That which Solomon[1] built in forty and six years, but he speaketh of destroying and building it in three days. Pilate saith to them, I am guiltless of the blood of this just man: ye will see. The Jews say, His blood be upon us, and upon our children.

And Pilate having called the elders and priests and Levites, said to them privately, Do not thus, for ye have accused him of nothing worthy of death; for your accusation is for healing, and the profanation of the sabbath. The elders and priests and Levites say, If any one speaks evil against Cæsar, is he worthy of death or no? Pilate saith, He is worthy of death. The Jews say to Pilate, If any one speaketh evil against Cæsar, he is worthy of death; but this man hath spoken blasphemy against God.

And the governor commanded the Jews to go out from the prætorium, and calling Jesus, he saith to him, What shall I do to thee? Jesus saith to Pilate, As it hath been given thee. Pilate saith, How has it been given? Jesus saith, Moses and the Prophets spake beforehand of my death and resurrection. And the Jews who observed and heard said to Pilate, What more wouldst thou hear than this blasphemy? Pilate saith to the Jews, If this saying is blasphemous,

[1] This is of course a blundering paraphrase of John ii. 20.

take ye him for blasphemy, and lead him away to your synagogue, and judge him according to your law. The Jews say to Pilate, Our law maintains that if a man sin against a man, he is worthy to receive forty stripes save one; but he that blasphemeth against God, is to be stoned with stones.[1]

Pilate saith to them, Take ye him and be avenged upon him in what manner ye will. The Jews say to Pilate, We wish that he should be crucified. Pilate saith, He doth not deserve to be crucified.

And as the governor looked round at the multitudes of Jews who stood about, he saw many of the Jews weeping, and he said, All the multitude doth not wish him to die. The elders of the Jews said, For this cause all the multitude of us have come, that he may die. Pilate saith to the Jews, Wherefore should he die? The Jews say, Because he said that he was the Son of God and a King.

CHAPTER V.

AND a certain man named Nicodemus, a Jew,[2] stood before the governor and said, I entreat thee, worshipful one, bid me say a few words. And Pilate said, Speak. Nicodemus saith, I said to the elders and the

---

[1] Deut. xxv. 3; 2 Cor. xi. 24; Lev. xxiv. 10-16.
[2] It is hardly to be imagined that Nicodemus would have introduced himself in this way, had he been the author of the book. John iii. 1 vii. 50; xix. 39.

THE GOSPEL OF NICODEMUS. 241

priests and Levites and all the multitude of the Jews in the synagogue, What seek ye with this man? This man doth many signs and wonders, such as no other did or will do. Release him, and wish no evil against him. If the miracles which he doth are of God, they will stand; but if of men, they will come to nought.[1] For Moses also, when sent from God into Egypt, wrought many signs which God commanded him to do before Pharoah, King of Egypt. And there were men there, Jannes and Jambres, physicians of Pharaoh, and they also did not a few signs such as Moses did, and the Egyptians esteemed them as gods, that is Jannes and Jambres.[2] And since the signs which they did were not of God, they perished, both they and those who believed in them. Now, therefore, release this man, for he is not deserving of death.

The Jews said to Nicodemus, Thou art his disciple, and makest a defence for him. Nicodemus saith to them, Is the governor also his disciple, and is he making a defence for him? Hath not Cæsar appointed him to this dignity? And the Jews were very angry, and gnashed their teeth against Nicodemus. Pilate saith to them, Why do ye gnash your teeth against him, when ye hear the truth? The Jews say to Nicodemus, Mayest thou receive his truth

---

[1] Cf. Acts v. 35.
[2] 2 Tim. iii. 8. The names of Jannes and Jambres are introduced into the Targum of Palestine at Exod. vii. 11.

and his portion! Nicodemus saith, Amen, amen; may I receive as ye have said!

CHAPTER VI.

AND one of the Jews starting up, asked the governor that he might say a word. The governor saith, If thou wilt speak, speak. And the Jew said, I lay thirty-eight years on my bed in pain and affliction. And when Jesus came, many demoniacs and persons suffering various diseases were healed by him, and some young men had pity on me, and carried me with my bed, and took me to him; and when Jesus saw me, he had compassion, and said the word to me, Take up thy bed and walk: and I took up my bed and walked. The Jews said to Pilate, Ask him what day it was when he was healed. He that was healed said, On the sabbath.[1] The Jews said, Did we not tell thee so, that on the sabbath he healeth and casteth out demons?

And another Jew starting up, said, I was born blind; I heard a voice, but saw no person; and as Jesus passed by, I cried with a loud voice, Have pity on me, Son of David; and he had pity on me, and placed his hands upon my eyes, and immediately I saw. And another Jew leaping up, said, I was a cripple, and he made me straight with a word.[2] And

[1] John v. 5-9.   [2] John ix. 1-12; Mark viii. 22-26.

another said, I was a leper, and he healed me with a word.[1]

CHAPTER VII.

AND a certain woman cried out from a distance and said, I had an issue of blood, and I touched the hem of his garment, and my issue of blood, which had been for twelve years, was stayed.[2] The Jews said, We have a law not to admit a woman to witness.[3]

CHAPTER VIII.

And others, a multitude both of men and of women, cried and said, This man is a prophet, and demons are subject unto him. Pilate said to those who said that demons were subject to him, Why were your teachers not also subject to him? They say unto Pilate, We know not. And others said, That he raised up Lazarus from the sepulchre when he had been dead four days.[4] And the governor, becoming afraid, said to all the multitude of the Jews, Why will ye shed innocent blood?

---

[1] Matt. viii. 1-4; Mark i. 40-45.
[2] Matt. ix. 20-26; Luke viii. 43-48.
[3] The Jews did not allow a woman as a witness. Otho's Lex. Rab. *s.v.* Testimonium.
[4] John xi. 1-16.

CHAPTER IX.

AND calling Nicodemus and the twelve men who said that he was not born of fornication, he said to them, What shall I do? for there is a sedition among the people. They said to him, We know not; they will see. Pilate called again all the multitude of the Jews, and said, Ye know that it is a custom with you at the feast of unleavened bread, to deliver up to you a prisoner; I have a condemned prisoner in the gaol, a murderer called Barabbas, and this Jesus who stands before you, in regard to whom I find no fault in him. Which will ye that I deliver to you? And they cry out, Barabbas. Pilate saith, what then shall we do with Jesus, who is called Christ? The Jews say, Let him be crucified. Others said, Thou art not Cæsar's friend, if thou discharge him; for he said that he was the Son of God and a king: thou wishest him to be king therefore, and not Cæsar.

And Pilate was angry, and said to the Jews, Your nation is always seditious, and ye speak against your benefactors. The Jews say, What benefactors? He saith to them, Your God led you out of Egypt from hard bondage, and delivered you through the sea as through dry land, and fed you in the wilderness with manna, and gave you quails, and gave you water to drink from a rock, and gave you a law; and amid all these things, ye provoked your God to anger, and sought after a molten calf: and angered your God, and he sought to slay you, and Moses made supplication for you, and ye died not.[1] And now ye exclaim against me, that I hate the king.

And he rose from the judgment seat and sought to go out. And the Jews cried out, saying, We know that Cæsar is king and not Jesus. For the Magi also offered gifts to him as to a king. And when Herod heard from the Magi that a king was born, he sought to put him to death. But when his father Joseph knew it he took him and his mother, and they fled into Egypt. And when Herod heard it, he destroyed the Hebrew children that were born in Bethlehem.

And when Pilate heard these words he was afraid. And Pilate caused the multitudes to keep silence, for they cried out; and he said, So this is he whom Herod sought? The Jews said, Yea, this is he. And Pilate took water, and washed his hands before the sun, saying, I am innocent of the blood of this just man: see ye to it. The Jews cried out again, His blood be upon us, and upon our children.

Then Pilate commanded the curtain of the judgment seat where he sat to be drawn, and said to

---

[1] Pilate's knowledge of the Old Testament has much increased since he asked about 'Hosanna' etc., earlier in the book!

Jesus, Thine own nation hath convicted thee as a king; therefore I have declared that thou shalt first be scourged after the custom of the pious kings, and then be fastened upon the cross in the garden where thou wast taken: and let Dysmas and Gestas the two malefactors be crucified with thee.

CHAPTER X.

AND Jesus went out of the prætorium, and the two malefactors with him; and when they came to the place they stripped him of his garments, and put about him a linen cloth, and they put a crown of thorns on him about his head. And they crucified him: and at the same time they hanged the two malefactors with him. And Jesus said, Father, forgive them, for they know not what they do. And the soldiers parted his garments. And the people stood beholding him. And the chief priests and the rulers with them derided him, saying, He saved others, let him save himself: if he is the Son of God, let him come down from the cross. And the soldiers mocked him, coming and offering him vinegar and gall, and said, Thou art the King of the Jews; save thyself.

And after the sentence, Pilate commanded that for a title his accusation should be written up, in Greek, Roman, and Hebrew letters, as the Jews said, He is King of the Jews.

And one of the malefactors that were hanged, spake to him, saying, If thou art the Christ, save thyself and us. And Dysmas answered and rebuked him, saying, Dost thou not fear God, because thou art in the same condemnation? and we, indeed, justly; for we receive our deserts for what we have done; but he hath done no evil. And he said to Jesus, Lord, remember me in thy kingdom. And Jesus said to him, Verily, verily, I say unto thee, That to day thou art with me in Paradise.

CHAPTER XI.

AND it was about the sixth hour, and darkness was upon the earth until the ninth hour, for the sun was darkened; and the veil of the temple was rent in the midst. And calling with a loud voice, Jesus said, Father, *Baddakh ephkid rouel*,[1] which is interpreted, Into thy hands I commend my spirit. And having said this he gave up the ghost. And when the centurion saw what had happened, he glorified God, saying, This man was just. And all the multitudes who were present at that sight, seeing what had happened, returned, smiting their breasts.

And the centurion reported to the governor what was done. And when the governor heard, and his wife, they were very sorrowful, and neither ate nor

[1] More correctly *Beyadka aphkid ruchi*. Luke xxiii. 46; Ps. xxxi. 5.

drank that day. And Pilate sent for the Jews and said to them, Have ye seen what has happened? And they said, An eclipse of the sun has happened in the usual manner.

And his acquaintance stood afar off, and the women who came with him out of Galilee beholding these things. And a certain man, Joseph by name, a councillor, who was of the city of Arimathea, and himself also expected the Kingdom of God, the same came to Pilate and asked for the body of Jesus. And he took it down and wrapped it in a clean linen cloth, and placed it in a sepulchre hewn in stone, wherein no one was yet lying.

CHAPTER XII.

AND when the Jews heard that Joseph had asked the body of Jesus, they sought for him, and for the twelve who said that Jesus was not born of fornication, and Nicodemus, and many others besides, who had risen up before Pilate, and made known his good works. And whereas they were all hidden, Nicodemus alone was seen by them, because he was a ruler of the Jews. And Nicodemus said to them, How came ye into the synagogue? The Jews say unto him, How camest thou into the synagogue? for thou art a witness for him; and be his lot with thee in the world to come. Nicodemus saith, Amen, amen.

And in like manner also Joseph came forth, and said to them, Why were ye offended at me, because I asked for the body of Jesus? behold I have placed him in my new sepulchre, have wrapped him in clean linen, and have rolled a stone to the door of the sepulchre. And ye have not done right against that just one, because ye repented not of crucifying him, but even pierced him with a spear. And the Jews took hold of Joseph, and commanded him to be kept safely until the first day of the week, and said to him, Know that the time doth not permit us to do anything against thee, because the Sabbath is dawning: and know that thou shalt not be counted worthy of burial, but we will give thy flesh to the birds of heaven. Joseph saith to them, This is the saying of the boasting Goliath, who reproached the living God and the holy David.[1] For God said by the prophet, Vengeance is mine, and I will repay saith the Lord.[2] And now he that is uncircumcised in the flesh, but circumcised in his heart, hath taken water and washed his hands before the sun, saying, I am innocent of the blood of this just man; see ye too it. And ye answering Pilate said, His blood be upon us and upon our children; and now I fear lest the anger of the Lord should come upon you and your children, as ye said. And when the Jews heard these words they were vexed in soul, and taking hold of Joseph they

[1] 1 Sam. xvii. 4-43. [2] Deut. xxxii. 35; Rom. xii. 19.

arrested him and shut him in a house where there was no window, and guards were stationed at the door, and they sealed the door where Joseph was shut up.

And on the Sabbath the rulers of the synagogue and the priests and the Levites made a decree, that all should be present in the synagogue on the first day of the week. And rising early in the morning, all the multitude took counsel in the synagogue by what death they should kill him. And when the council was seated, they commanded him to be brought with much dishonour. And when they opened the door they found him not. And all the people was astonished; and they were amazed because they found the seals sealed, and because Caiaphas had the key. And they no more dared to lay hands on them who spake for Jesus before Pilate.

CHAPTER XIII.

AND while they were still sitting in the synagogue, and wondering about Joseph, certain of the guard came, whom the Jews had asked of Pilate to keep the tomb of Jesus, that his disciples might not come and steal him. And they reported and told to the rulers of the synagogue and the priests and the Levites, what had happened: how there was a great earthquake, and we saw an angel coming down from heaven, and he rolled away the stone from the mouth of the sepulchre, and sat upon it; and he shone like snow and like lightning; and we, being greatly afraid, lay as if we were dead. And we heard the voice of the angel talking with the women who waited by the tomb,—Fear ye not; for I know that ye seek Jesus who was crucified. He is not here: he is risen, as he said. Come, see the place were the Lord lay; and go forth quickly, and tell his disciples that he is risen from the dead, and is in Galilee.

The Jews said, With what women did he talk? The men of the guard said, We know not who they were. The Jews said, At what hour was it? The men of the guard said, At midnight. The Jews said, And why did ye not lay hold upon them? The men of the guard said, We were like dead men for fear, not expecting to see the light of day, and how could we lay hold upon them? The Jews said, As the Lord liveth, we do not believe you. The men of the guard said to the Jews, Ye have seen so great signs in that man, and have not believed, and how can ye believe in us? For ye have well sworn, that the Lord liveth, for also he liveth. They of the guard said again, We have heard that ye shut up him that asked for the body of Jesus, and sealed the door, and when ye opened it ye found him not; therefore produce him that ye kept, and we will give up Jesus. The Jews said, Joseph went away to his own city. They of the guard said to the Jews, And Jesus arose as we heard from the angel, and is in Galilee.

And the Jews hearing these words were greatly afraid, saying, Lest this report should be heard, and all men should incline to Jesus. And the Jews, calling a council, put down much money and gave to the soldiers, saying, Say, While we slept his disciples came by night and stole him. And if this should be heard by the governor, we will persuade him and keep you from trouble. And they took it and said as they were taught.

CHAPTER XIV.

AND Phinehas a priest, and Adas a teacher, and Aggæus a Levite, coming from Galilee to Jerusalem, declared to the rulers of the synagogue, and the priests and the Levites, We saw Jesus with his disciples, sitting on the mount which is called Mamilk,[1] and he said to his disciples, Go into all the world and preach to every creature; he that believeth and is baptised shall be saved, and he that believeth not shall be condemned. And these signs shall follow them that believe: in my name they shall cast out

[1] The explanation of Mamilk is to be sought for from Jewish writers. The word seems to be a corruption of Malek or Melek, *a king*. The name Mount Melek was applied by the Rabbins to the hill country of Judah; but our author has not only identified the Mount of Olives with Mount Melek, but located it in Galilee.

demons, they shall speak with new tongues, they shall take up serpents, and if they drink any deadly thing it shall not hurt them; upon the sick they shall lay hands and they shall be well.[1] While Jesus was yet speaking to his disciples, we saw him taken up into heaven.

The elders and priests and Levites said, Give glory to the God of Israel; and make acknowledgment to him if ye have heard and seen these things which ye relate. Those who reported them said, As the Lord God of our Fathers Abraham, Isaac, and Jacob liveth, we heard these things, and saw him taken up into heaven. The elders and priests and Levites said unto them, Have ye come to proclaim this to us, or have ye come to pay a vow to God? And they said, To pay a vow to God. The elders and chief priests and Levites said to them, If ye have come to pay a vow to God, why these trifles with which ye have trifled before all the people?

And Phineas the priest, and Adas the teacher, and Aggæus the Levite, said to the rulers of the synagogue and priests and Levites, If these things which we have told and seen are sin, behold we are before you; do to us according to what is good in your eyes. And taking the law they made them swear that they would tell no one these words any more. And they gave them to eat and drink, and sent them out of the

[1] Mark xvi. 15.

city, after bestowing money upon them, and three men with them, and they removed them back to Galilee.

And when those men were gone into Galilee, the chief priests and rulers of the synagogue, and elders, assembled in the synagogue, shutting the gate, and they lamented with a great lamentation, saying, Hath this sign come to pass in Israel? And Annas and Caiaphas said, Why are ye troubled? Why do ye weep? Know ye not that his disciples gave much gold to the guards of the tomb, and taught them to say that an angel came down and rolled away the stone from the door of the sepulchre? And the priests and elders said, Be it that his disciples stole the body; but how did the soul enter the body, and how abideth he in Galilee? And they, being scarcely able to give an answer to these things, said, It is not lawful for us to believe the uncircumcised.

CHAPTER XV.

And Nicodemus arose and stood before the council, saying, Ye speak aright. Ye know O people of the Lord, that the men who came down from Galilee fear God, are men of substance, hating covetousness, men of peace. And they spake with an oath, saying, We saw Jesus at Mount Mamilk,[1] with his disciples, and he

---

[1] See note to chapter xiv.

taught what we heard from him, and we saw him taken up into heaven. And no one asked them in what manner he was taken up. For as the Book of the Holy Scriptures hath taught us, Elijah also was taken up into heaven; and Elisha called with a loud voice, and Elijah cast his sheepskin upon Elisha; and Elisha cast his sheepskin upon the Jordan, and passed over, and came to Jericho. And the children of the prophets met him, and said, Elisha, where is thy master Elijah? and he said, He was taken up into heaven. And they said to Elisha, Hath a spirit seized him and cast him upon one of the mountains? Let us take our young men with us and seek him. And they persuaded Elisha, and he went with them. And they sought him three days, and found him not, and knew that he was taken up.[1] . And now hear me, and let us send through all the border of Israel, and see whether the Christ hath been taken up by a spirit, and cast upon one of the mountains. And this saying pleased them all. And they sent through all the border of Israel, and sought for Jesus, and found him not. But they found Joseph at Arimathea: and no one dared lay hold upon him.

And they brought word to the elders and the priests and the Levites, saying, We went through all the border of Israel, and found not Jesus: but we found Joseph at Arimathea. And when they heard

[1] 2 Kings ii. 1-18

of Joseph they rejoiced, and gave glory to the God of Israel. And the rulers of the synagogue, and the priests and the Levites took counsel in what manner they might meet with Joseph, and took a sheet of paper, and wrote to Joseph, thus:—

"Peace be unto thee. We know that we have sinned against God, and against thee, and we have prayed to the God of Israel that thou wouldest deign to come to thy fathers, and to thy children, because we are all troubled; for when we opened the door, we found thee not. And we know that we devised an evil counsel against thee, but the Lord undertook for thee, and the Lord himself scattered our counsel which was against thee, honoured father Joseph."

And they chose out of all Israel, seven men, friends to Joseph, with whom Joseph also was acquainted. And the rulers of the synagogue, and the priests and the Levites, said to them, See ye; if he receiveth and readeth our epistle, ye know that he will come to us along with you: but if he doth not read it, ye know that he is offended with us, and ye shall salute him in peace, and return to us. And they blessed the men and sent them away. And the men came to Joseph, and bowed down to him, and said to him, Peace be unto thee. And he said, Peace be to you, and to all the people of Israel. And they gave him the roll of the epistle. And Joseph received, and read, and folded the epistle, and blessed God, and said, Blessed be the Lord God, who hath delivered Israel from shedding innocent blood; and blessed be the Lord, who sent his angel, and protected me under his wings. And he set a table before them, and they ate, and drank, and slept there.

And they rose early and prayed. And Joseph saddled his ass, and went with the men, and they came to the holy city, Jerusalem. And all the people met Joseph, and cried, Peace be unto thee at thy coming in. And he said to all the people, Peace be unto you. And he kissed them. And the people prayed with Joseph, and were astonished at the sight of him. And Nicodemus received him into his house, and made a great supper, and invited Annas, and Caiaphas, and the elders, and the priests, and the Levites, to his house. And they rejoiced, both eating and drinking with Joseph. And when they had sung hymns, every one went to his own home. But Joseph abode at the house of Nicodemus.

And on the morrow, which was the preparation, the rulers of the synagogue, and the priests and the Levites, came early to the house of Nicodemus, and Nicodemus met them, and said, Peace be unto you. And they said, Peace be unto thee, and unto Joseph, and to all thy house, and to all the house of Joseph. And he took them into his house. And all the assembly sat, and Joseph sat between Annas and Caiaphas. And no one dared to speak to him a word. And Joseph said, Wherefore have ye called for me? And they signified to Nicodemus to tell Joseph. And Nicodemus opened his mouth, and said to Joseph, Father, thou knowest that the honourable teachers, and priests and Levites seek to learn something from thee. And Joseph said, Ask. And Annas and Caiaphas took the law, and made Joseph swear, saying, Give glory to the God of Israel, and give confession to him. Because when Achan[1] was sworn by the prophet Joshua,[2] he did not forswear himself, but told him all, and hid nothing from him. Thou, therefore, hide not anything from us. And Joseph said, I will not hide from you one word. And they said to him, We were exceedingly grieved that thou didst ask for the body of Jesus, and didst wrap it in clean linen, and didst lay him in a sepulchre. And for this cause we secured thee in a house wherein there was no window, and we put locks and seals upon the doors, and guards watched where thou wast confined. And when we opened it on the first day of the week, we found thee not, and were greatly troubled. And astonishment fell upon all the people of the Lord until yesterday. And now tell us what befel thee.

And Joseph said, On the preparation, about the tenth hour, ye put me in prison, and I remained so all the sabbath. And about midnight, as I stood and prayed, the house wherein ye shut me was sus-

[1] Gr. Achar.   [2] Gr. Jesus; Josh. vii. 19-20.

pended[1] by the four corners, and I saw, as it were, a flash of light in my eyes. And being afraid, I fell to the ground. And some one took me by the hand, and removed me from the place where I had fallen, and a quantity of water was poured out (upon me) from my head to my feet; and a smell of myrrh came to my nostrils. And he wiped my face, and kissed me, and said to me, Fear not Joseph; open thy eyes, and see who it is that talketh with thee. And looking up, I saw Jesus. And being afraid, I thought it was an apparition, and said the commandments.[2] And he said them with me. And as ye know, if an apparition meeteth a man, and heareth the commandments, it taketh to flight. And seeing that he said them with me, I said to him, Rabbi Elias. And he said to me, I am not Elias. And I said to him, Who art thou, Lord? And he said to me, I am Jesus, whose body thou didst beg from Pilate; and thou didst wrap me in clean linen, and didst put a napkin upon my face, and didst lay me in thy new tomb, and didst roll a great stone to the door of the sepulchre. And I said to him that talked with me, Show me the place where I laid thee. And he took me, and showed me the place where I laid him: and the

[1] Comp. Acts x. 11; This idea reached its fullest development in the legend of the Virgin's house removed by angels from Nazareth to Loretto: a fiction of which we first read in the fifteenth century.
[2] Some formula was probably enjoined to be repeated on such occasions, as a kind of charm. Thilo thinks it was the Decalogue.

linen cloth lay therein, and the napkin which was upon his face; and I knew that it was Jesus. And he took me by the hand, and set me, the doors being shut, inside my house, and he led me to my couch, and said to me, Peace be to thee. And he kissed me, and said to me, Go not out of thine house for forty days; for behold, I go into Galilee, unto my brethren.

CHAPTER XVI.

AND when the rulers of the synagogue, and the priests and the Levites heard these words from Joseph, they became as dead men, and fell to the ground, and fasted until the ninth hour. And Nicodemus and Joseph comforted Annas and Caiaphas, the priests and the Levites, saying, Arise and stand upon your feet, and taste bread, and strengthen your souls, for to-morrow is the sabbath of the Lord. And they arose and prayed to God, and ate and drank, and went every man to his house.

And on the sabbath, our teachers, and the priests and Levites, sat and questioned with one another, and said, What is this wrath which has come upon us? for we know his father and his mother. Levi a teacher, saith, I know his parents fear God, and neglect not prayer, and give tithes thrice a year. And when Jesus was born, his parents brought him to this place, and offered sacrifices and whole burnt offerings to God. And the great teacher Simeon took him into his arms, and said, Now Lord, lettest thou thy servant depart, according to thy word, in peace; because mine eyes have seen thy salvation, which thou hast prepared before the face of all people; a light to lighten the Gentiles, and the glory of thy people Israel. And Simeon blessed them, and said to Mary, his mother, I tell thee good tidings concerning this child. And Mary said, Good, my lord. And Simeon said to her, Good: behold he is set for the fall and rising again of many in Israel, and for a sign which shall be spoken against; and a sword shall pierce through thy own soul also, that the thoughts of many hearts may be revealed.[1]

They say unto Levi the teacher, How knowest thou these things? Levi saith to them, Know ye not that from him I learned the law? The assembly say to him, We would see thy father. And they sent for his father. And when they asked him, he said to them, Why did ye not believe my son? The blessed and righteous Simeon himself taught him the law. The assembly saith to Rabbi Levi, Is the word true which thou hast spoken? And he said, It is true. And the rulers of the synagogue, and the priests, and the Levites, said among themselves, Come, let us send into Galilee, to the three men who came and told us about his teaching, and his ascension, and let them

[1] Luke ii. 25-35.

tell us how they saw him taken up. And this saying pleased them all. And they sent the three men who had already gone into Galilee with them, and said to them, Say to Rabbi Adas, and Rabbi Phinehas, and Rabbi Aggæus, Peace be to you, and all that are with you. Because there is much enquiry in the Sanhedrim, we have sent to you, to call you to this holy place, Jerusalem.

And the men went into Galilee, and found them sitting, and meditating upon the law, and they greeted them in peace. And the men who were in Galilee, said to them that had come to them, Peace be upon all Israel. And they said, Peace to you. And again they said to them, Wherefore are ye come? And they who were sent said, The Sanhedrim in the holy city Jerusalem call you. And when the men heard that they were asked by the Sanhedrim, they prayed to God, and sat down with the men, and ate, and drank, and arose and went in peace to Jerusalem.

And on the morrow the Sanhedrim sat in the synagogue, and asked them, saying, Did ye truly see Jesus sitting on the mount Mamilk, as he taught his eleven disciples, and did ye see him taken up? And the men answered them, and said, As we saw him taken up, so also we said.

Annas saith, Take them apart, and let us see if their report agreeth. And they took them apart.

And they called Adas first, and said to him, How sawest thou Jesus taken up? Adas saith, While he was sitting on the mount Mamilk, and teaching his disciples, we saw a cloud overshadowing him, and his disciples; and the cloud bore him up into heaven, and his disciples lay on their faces upon the ground. And they called Phinehas the priest, and asked him also, saying, How sawest thou Jesus taken up? And he said the same. And again they asked Aggæus, and he said the same. And the Sanhedrim said, The law of Moses, declareth, By the mouth of two or three, every word shall be established. Buthem, a teacher, said, It is written in the law, And Enoch walked with God, and was not, because God took him.[1] Jairus, a teacher, said, And we have heard of the death of holy Moses, and we saw it not. For it is written in the law of the Lord, And Moses died, by the word of the Lord, and no man knoweth his sepulchre, unto this day.[2] And Rabbi Levi said, What did Rabbi Simeon say, when he saw Jesus? Behold he is set for the fall and rising again of many in Israel, and for a sign which shall be spoken against.[3] And Rabbi Isaac said, It is written in the law, Behold, I send my angel before thy face, who shall go before thee, to preserve thee in every good way, because my name is called upon it.[4]

---

[1] Gen. v. 24; Heb. xi. 5.   [2] Deut. xxxiv. 5, 6.
[3] Luke ii. 34.   [4] Ex. xxiii. 20, 21; Mal. iii, 1.

Then Annas and Caiaphas said, Ye have rightly told what is written in the law of Moses, that no man saw the death of Enoch, and no man mentioned the death of Moses. But Jesus gave account to Pilate, and we saw him receiving blows, and spittings in his face; and the soldiers put a crown of thorns upon him, and he was scourged, and received sentence from Pilate, and was crucified on Calvary, and two robbers with him, and they gave him to drink vinegar and gall; and Longinus, the soldier, pierced his side with a spear, and Joseph our honourable father, begged his body; and as he saith, he arose; and as the three teachers say, We saw him taken up to heaven; and Rabbi Levi hath spoken, attesting what was uttered by Rabbi Simeon, and that he said, Behold he is set for the fall and rising again of many in Israel, and for a sign to be spoken against.[1] And all the teachers said to all the people of the Lord, If this is from the Lord, and it is marvellous in your eyes,[2] ye shall know assuredly, O house of Jacob, that it is written, Cursed is everyone that hangeth on a tree.[3] And another Scripture teacheth, The gods which made not heaven and earth, shall perish.[4] If his memorial is unto the year,[5] which is called Jobel,

---

[1] Luke ii. 34.   [2] Ps. cxviii. 23.
[3] Deut. xxi. 23; Gal. iii. 13.   [4] Jer. x. 11.
[5] The Greek text is ἕως τοῦ σόμμου which Dr. Tischendorf confesses he does not understand. It is a barbarous representation of the phrase " until the *year* of *jubilee*," which frequently occurs in Lev. xxv. By

know ye that he will prevail for ever, and hath raised up for himself a new people. Then the rulers of the synagogue, and the priests, and the Levites, made declaration to all Israel, saying, Cursed is that man, who shall worship the work of man's hands, and cursed is the man, who shall worship the creatures, more than the Creator. And all the people said, Amen, amen.[1]

And all the people sang hymns to the Lord, and said, Blessed be the Lord, who hath given rest to his people Israel, according to all that he spake. Not one word hath failed of all his good words, which he spake to Moses his servant. May the Lord our God be with us, as he was with our fathers. May he not suffer us to perish. And may he not suffer us to fall away from inclining our hearts towards him, from walking in all his ways, from keeping his commandments, and his ordinances, which he commanded to our fathers. And the Lord shall be king over all the earth in that day. And there shall be one Lord, and his name one. The Lord is our king: He shall save us. There is none like unto thee, O Lord; great art thou, O Lord, and great is thy name. In

---

σώμμου the writer meant שָׁנָה (*shanah*), a year. Jobel is merely the Hebrew word for *jubilee* in Greek letters. The copies vary considerably about the reading, but I ascribe this to the inability of the scribes to solve the difficulty, and do not hesitate to prefer the reading of Dr Tischendorf

[1] Deut. xxvii. 15; Rom. i. 25.

thy power heal us, O Lord, and we shall be healed. Save us, O Lord, and we shall be saved. For we are thy portion, and thine heritage. And the Lord shall not cast off his people, for his great name's sake, for the Lord hath begun to make us his people.[1]

And having sung hymns, they went every man to his house, glorifying God, for his is the glory, for ever and ever.[2] Amen.

[1] 1 Chr. xxiii. 25; Josh. xxi. 45; 1 Kings viii. 56, 57, 58; Ex. xii. 23; Zech. xiv. 9; Is. xxxiii. 22; Ps. lxxxvi. 8; Jer. xvii. 14; Deut. xxxii. 9; Ps. xciv. 14; 1 Sam. xii. 22.
[2] 2 Peter iii. 18.

THE GOSPEL OF NICODEMUS, OR ACTS OF PILATE (II.)

Narrative of the Passion of our Lord Jesus Christ, and of his holy Resurrection.

COMPILED BY A JEW NAMED ÆNEAS; TRANSLATED FROM THE HEBREW TONGUE INTO THE ROMAN BY NICODEMUS, A ROMAN TOPARCH.[1]

AFTER the kingdom of the Hebrews was abolished, four hundred years had passed away, and the Hebrews were tributaries under the government of the Romans, the king of the Romans appointing for them a king; Tiberius Cæsar at length wielded the Roman sceptre, and in the eighteenth year of his reign he appointed as king in Judea, Herod, the son of that Herod who slew the infants in Bethlehem, and he had Pilate for governor in Jerusalem; Annas

[1] It will be observed that here Nicodemus is a Roman, and only the translator of a book written by Æneas. Part of the preface seems to indicate that it was the work of a contemporary, but part of it suggests more truly that it was done in after times. The Greek text, from which this second version of Nicodemus is made, seems to be less ancient than the first, and to have been revised and polished by its editor. I suppose the name of Æneas not to be older than the account of the Journey to the Underworld, which has been added to the original composition, and follows the present recension of Nicodemus as Part II.

and Caiphas also holding the high-priesthood of Jerusalem; Nicodemus, a Roman toparch, called unto him a Jew, named Æneas, and asked him to write what was done in Jerusalem, concerning Christ, in the times of Annas and Caiaphas; which also the Jew did, and delivered it unto Nicodemus, who straightway translated it from the Hebrew copy into Roman language. Now the matter of the history is this:—

CHAPTER I.

Our Lord Jesus Christ wrought many, and great, and extraordinary miracles in Judea, and was therefore viewed with jealousy by the Hebrews, when Pilate was governor at Jerusalem, and Annas and Caiaphas were chief priests. So Judas, Levi, Nephthalim, Alexander, Syrus, and many other of the Jews came to the chief priests, speaking against Christ. And the chief priests sent them to tell these things to Pilate. And they went away, and said to him, A man who hath a father called Joseph, and a mother Mary, goeth about in this city, and calleth himself a king, and the Son of God, and although a Jew, overthroweth the Scriptures, and breaketh the sabbaths. Pilate therefore enquired of them, in what manner he broke the sabbaths. And they answered, saying, He healeth the sick on the sabbath. Pilate saith, If he maketh the sick whole, he doeth no evil. They say to him, If he wrought his cures aright, the evil would be small; but he performeth them by using magic, and having demons with him. Pilate saith, To heal the sick is not a diabolical work, but a gift from God.

The Hebrews said, We pray thy majesty to summon him, that thou mayest examine thoroughly what we say. Pilate therefore, throwing off his robe, gave it to one of his servants, saying, Go and show this to Jesus, and say to him, Pilate the governor calleth thee to come to him. So the servant departed, and finding Jesus, he called to him, spreading upon the ground the robe of Pilate, and inviting him to walk upon it. The Hebrews seeing this, and being greatly offended, came to Pilate, murmuring against him how that he had counted Jesus worthy of so great honour.

And he enquired of the servant that was sent, why he had done so. And the servant answered, When thou sentest me to Alexander the Jew, I met with Jesus, as he entered the gate of the city, sitting upon an ass; and I saw the Hebrews that they strewed their garments in the way, and the ass walked upon the garments; and others cut down branches; and they came out to meet him, and cried, Hosanna in the highest! Thus, therefore, it became me also to do.

On hearing these words, the Jews said to him,

Thou who art a Roman, how knewest thou what was said by the Hebrews? The servant answered, I asked one of the Hebrews, and he told it to me. Pilate said, What meaneth Hosanna? The Jews said, Save us, Lord. Pilate answered, Seeing ye confess that your children spake thus, how do ye now accuse, and say against Jesus that which ye say? And the Jews were silent, and could answer nothing.

Now when Jesus came to Pilate, the soldiers of Pilate worshipped him. And there stood also others before Pilate, holding the standards. And when Jesus came, the standards also bowed down and worshipped him. As Pilate therefore wondered at what had happened, the Jews said to him, Lord, the standards did not worship Jesus, but the soldiers who hold them carelessly.

Pilate saith to the ruler of the synagogue, Choose out twelve strong men, and give them the standards to hold them firmly. And when this was done, Pilate commanded the servant to take Jesus out, and bring him in again. And as he came in, the standards again bowed down, and worshipped him. Therefore, Pilate wondered greatly. And the Jews said, He is a magician, and therefore he doeth these things.

CHAPTER II.

PILATE saith to Jesus, Hearest thou what these

testify against thee, and answerest not? Jesus answered and said, Every man hath power to speak what he will, whether good or evil; therefore these, having the power, say what they will.

The Jews said to him, What have we to say concerning thee? first, that thou wast born of sin; secondly, that on account of thee, when thou wast born, they slew the infants; thirdly, that thy father and thy mother fled into Egypt, wherefore they had no boldness before the people.

To these things, the Jews who were there present, and were pious men, answered and said, We say that his birth was not of sin, for we know that Joseph received his mother Mary, according to the rule of espousals, to keep her. Pilate said, Therefore ye lie who say that his birth was of sin. They say again to Pilate, All the people testify that he is a magician. The pious Jews answered, and said, We were present at the espousal of his mother, and we are Jews, and we know his whole conduct; but that he is a magician, this we do not know. Now the Jews who said this, were these: Lazarus, Astharius, Antonius, James, Zarah, Samuel, Isaac, Phinehas, Crispus, Dagrippus, Amesa, and Judas.

Therefore, Pilate saith to them, I will that ye swear by the life of Cæsar, whether the birth of this man was without sin. They answered, Our law ordaineth that we should swear nothing, because an oath is a great sin. Yet by the life of Cæsar, we swear that his birth was without sin; and if we lie, command that we all be beheaded. And when they said these things, the Jews who accused him, answered Pilate, and said, And dost thou believe these twelve Jews alone, more than the whole multitude, and us, who know well that he is a magician, and a blasphemer, and calleth himself the Son of God?

Then Pilate commanded all to go out of the prætorium, except only the twelve spoken of, and when this was done, Pilate saith to them privately, As for this man, it appeareth that, for envy and madness, the Jews wish to slay him. For they accuse him of one thing, that he breaketh the sabbath. But he then doeth a good work, because he healeth the sick. This is no cause for condemning the man to death. And the twelve said to him, Yea, lord, thus it is.

CHAPTER III.

THEREFORE, Pilate went out in anger and wrath, and he said to Annas and Caiaphas, and the multitude who brought Jesus, I hold the sun to witness that I find no fault in this man. The multitude answered, If he were not a sorcerer, and a magician, and a blasphemer, we should not have brought him to thy majesty. Pilate said, Try him yourselves; and since ye have a law, as your law saith, so do. The

Jews said, Our law doth not permit us to put any man to death. Pilate saith, If ye are unwilling to put him to death, how much more am I!

Then Pilate returned into the palace, and said to Jesus, Tell me, art thou the king of the Jews? Jesus answered, Dost thou say this, or did the other Jews say this to thee, that thou shouldst ask me? Pilate said, And am I a Hebrew? I am not a Hebrew; thine own people, and the chief priests, delivered thee into my hands; tell me then, if thou art king of the Jews. Jesus answered, My kingdom is not in this world; for if my kingdom was in this world, my soldiers would not be unconcerned, that I am arrested; therefore, my kingdom is not in this world. Pilate saith, Art thou then a king? Jesus said, Thou sayest: for this was I born, namely, to bear witness to the truth, and if any one is a man of truth, he believeth my word, and doeth it. Pilate saith, What is truth? Jesus answered, Truth is from heaven. Pilate saith, Is not truth on earth? Christ saith, I am the truth; and how is truth judged on earth, by those who have earthly power!

CHAPTER IV.

THEREFORE, Pilate leaving Jesus alone, went out, and said to the Jews, I find no fault in this man. The Jews answered, May we tell thy majesty what he himself said? He said, I am able to destroy the temple of God, and to build it in three days. Pilate saith, And what sort of temple did he say he could destroy? The Hebrews said, The temple of Solomon, which Solomon was forty-six years building.

Pilate saith privately to the chief priests and scribes and Pharisees, I entreat you, do nothing evil to this man; for if ye do evil to him, ye will deal unjustly. For it is not just that such a man should die, who hath done great good to many men. They said to Pilate, If he who hath dishonoured Cæsar is worthy of death, my lord, how much rather is this man who dishonoureth God?

Then Pilate gave order, and they all went out. Then saith he to Jesus, What wilt thou that I should do to thee? Jesus saith to Pilate, Do unto me as it is ordained. Pilate saith, How is it ordained? Jesus answered, Moses and the prophets wrote that I should be crucified and should rise again. The Hebrews who heard him, said to Pilate, Why seek ye to hear from him greater insult against God? Pilate saith, This is no word of insult against God, since it is written in the books of the prophets.[1] The Jews said, Our Scripture saith, If a man offend against a man, as if he revile him, he is worthy to

---

[1] Pilate's appeal to the Scriptures implies, either that he was acquainted with them, or, that he believed Christ's affirmation. The Jews do not refute, but evade the point.

receive forty strokes with a stick; but if he revile God, to be stoned.[1]

Then came a messenger from Procla the wife of Pilate unto him, and the message said, Take heed that thou suffer not any evil to happen to the good man Jesus; for this night I have seen terrible dreams on account of him. And Pilate gave an answer to the Hebrews, saying, If ye regard as an insult to God, the words which ye say Jesus said, take him, and judge ye according to your law. The Jews said to Pilate, We will that thou shouldst crucify him. Pilate saith, This is not good.

And Pilate, turning towards the people, saw many weeping, and he said, It seemeth to me that it is not the will of all the people that this man should die. The priests and scribes said, For this cause have we brought all the people, that thou mightest receive full assurance that they all wish for his death. Pilate saith, What evil hath he done? The Hebrews said, He saith that he is a king and the Son of God.

CHAPTER V.

Then a pious Jew, named Nicodemus, standing in the midst, said to Pilate, I pray thy majesty to suffer me to say some few words unto thee. Speak, said Pilate. Nicodemus said, I said to the priests and Levites

[1] Deut. xxv. 3; Lev. xxiv. 16.

and scribes, and the people when I was in the synagogue, What matter have ye against this man? This man doeth many miracles, such as man never did, nor will do. Therefore, let him go, and if what he doeth is from God, it will stand; but if it is of men, it will be destroyed.[1] As it came to pass, also, when God sent Moses into Egypt, and Pharaoh king of Egypt said to him, that he should do a miracle, and he did it. Then Pharaoh also had two magicians, Jannes and Jambres, and they too did miracles, using magic art, but not such as Moses did. And the Egyptians esteemed these two magicians as gods; but, because they were not of God, what they did came to nought. This Jesus, therefore, hath raised Lazarus, and he is alive. For this cause I pray thee, my lord, not to suffer this man to be put to death.

The Hebrews were angry against Nicodemus, and said to him, Receive the truth of Jesus and have thy part with him. Nicodemus saith, Amen, Amen, be it unto me as ye say.

CHAPTER VI.

When Nicodemus had said these things, another Hebrew arose, and saith to Pilate, I pray thee my lord Pilate, hear me also. Pilate answered, Say what thou wilt. The Hebrew saith, I lay sick upon

---

[1] Acts v. 38. These words were Gamaliel's, about the apostles.

my bed thirty-eight years, and seeing me he was grieved, and said to me, Arise, take up thy bed and depart to thine house; and as he said to me the word I arose and walked. The Hebrews said, Ask him on what day of the week this was done. He saith, On the sabbath.[1] The Jews said, And therefore we say truly that he keepeth not the sabbath.

Again, another standing in the midst said, I was born blind, and as Jesus went along the way I called to him, saying, Have mercy on me, Lord, Son of David; and he took clay and anointed mine eyes, and immediately I saw.[2] Another said, I was a cripple, and seeing him I cried, Have mercy on me, Lord, and he took me by the hand, and immediately I arose.[3] Another said, I was a leper, and he healed me by a word alone.[4]

CHAPTER VII.

THERE was found there also, a woman named Veronica.[5] And she said, I was twelve years with an

[1] John v. 5-9. [2] John ix. 6.
[3] Matt. ix. 1-7; cf. Acts iii. 7. [4] Luke xvii. 13.
[5] The Greek is Beronice, but the Latin Veronica seems to be the original. The name has reference to a supposed likeness of Christ, and was often applied to the likeness itself. 'The likeness of the Lord, which is called Veronica—Veronica is the *true picture* of the Lord,' says Gervase of Tilbury. The word is said not to be a corruption of Berenice, but of *Vera Icon*, 'a true likeness.' According to one story, Veronica is the name of a woman who *received* from Jesus his portrait, upon a handkerchief or napkin. They still pretend to exhibit this at Rome and elsewhere, for like many relics, it has '·increased and

issue of blood, and I only took hold of the edge of his garment, and was immediately healed.[1] The Jews said, The law doth not admit the testimony of a woman.

CHAPTER VIII.

OTHER men cried, This man is a prophet, and the demons fear him. Pilate saith, And how is it that the demons did not thus fear your parents also? They say, We know not. Others again said, By a word only he raised up Lazarus, who had been four days in his sepulchre. Pilate, therefore, hearing of the resurrection of Lazarus was afraid, and saith to the people, Wherefore will ye shed the blood of a just man?

CHAPTER IX.

THEN he called Nicodemus and the twelve pious Jews, and said to them, What say ye that I should do, for the people are in a commotion? They say, We know not: do what thou wilt. But whatever the people do, they do unrighteously, in order to destroy him. Pilate went out again, and saith to the

---

multiplied.' According to another legend, the woman mentioned in our text *made* an image or representation of Jesus at Paneas. See the Story of Veronica, pp, 218, 223. Also, the Death of Pilate; and the Saviour's Revenge, near the end of this volume.

[1] Matt. ix. 20-22.

people, Ye know that at the feast of unleavened bread it is customary for me to liberate for your sake one of the criminals confined in prison. Now I have a malefactor in gaol, a robber, called Barabbas, and I have Jesus, who hath never done evil. Which therefore of the two will ye that I should release to you? The people answered, Release unto us Barabbas. Pilate saith, What then shall I do with Jesus? They say, Let him be crucified. Again, others of them cried out, If thou dost release Jesus, thou art not the friend of Cæsar, because he calleth himself the Son of God and a king; and if thou settest him at liberty, he becometh a king, and will take Cæsar's kingdom.

Therefore, Pilate was angry, and said, Your race was always slanderous and unbelieving, and ye have been always the adversaries of your benefactors. The Hebrews said, And who were our benefactors? Pilate saith, God, who delivered you from the hands of Pharaoh, and led you over the Red Sea, as on dry ground, and fed you with quails, gave you water to drink from the dry rock, and gave you a law, which ye broke by denying God, and if Moses had not stood to plead with God ye would have perished with a bitter death. Therefore, ye have forgotten all these things. And so, also, now ye say that I love not Cæsar at all, but have hatred towards him, and wish to plot against his government.

And having said these things Pilate arose from his seat with anger, wishing to escape from them. Therefore the Jews cried out saying, We wish Cæsar to govern us, not Jesus, because Jesus received gifts from the magi.[1] And Herod also heard this, that he would be a king, and wished to put him to death, and on this account, sent and slew all the infants in Bethlehem. And for this cause also, Joseph his father, and his mother, through fear of him fled into Egypt.

Pilate therefore, having heard this, commanded all the people to keep silence, and said, So then this is the Jesus whom Herod sought to slay? They say unto him, Yea. Pilate, therefore, having learned that he was of the jurisdiction of Herod, as though descended from the race of the Jews, sent Jesus to him. And when Herod saw him, he rejoiced greatly, for of a long time he had desired to see him, having heard of the miracles which he did. Therefore, he arrayed him with white garments; then he began to question him. But Jesus gave him no answer. And Herod, who wished to see a miracle of some kind wrought by Jesus, and not seeing one, but that he gave him no answer to what was said, sent him back at once to

---

[1] An ingenious distortion, or application of Matt. ii. 11, where, however, the Greek has δῶρα, and not χαρίσματα as here,—an important difference. What follows about Christ's being sent to Herod is mainly an addition to the older form of the book.

Pilate.[1] Seeing this, Pilate commanded his servants to bring water. Therefore, washing his hands with the water, he said to the people, I am innocent of the blood of this good man. Ye will see that he is unjustly put to death, for neither have I found fault in him, nor yet Herod; for which cause he sent him back to me again. The Jews said, His blood be upon us and upon our children![2]

Then Pilate sat on his seat to pronounce sentence. He gave order therefore, and Jesus came before him. And they brought a crown of thorns and put it on his head, and a reed in his right hand. Then he pronounced sentence, and said to him, Thy nation saith and witnesseth of thee, that thou desirest to be a king. Therefore I ordain that they first smite thee with a rod forty stripes, as the laws of the kings ordain: and that they mock thee; and lastly, that they crucify thee.

CHAPTER X.

WHEN, therefore, sentence was declared by Pilate to this effect, the Jews began to smite Jesus, some with sticks, some with their hands, and some with their feet; and some also spat in his face. Then, straightway, having prepared the cross and given it to him, they made haste to set out. And going thus,

[1] Luke xxiii. 6-11.   [2] Matt. xxvii. 25.

and bearing the cross, he came unto the gate of the city of Jerusalem. When, therefore, because of the many blows and the weight of the cross, he could not walk, the Jews through the desire which they had to crucify him as soon as possible, took the cross from him and gave it to one who met them, named Simon, who also had two sons, Alexander and Rufus: and he was of the city of Cyrene. Therefore they gave the cross to him, not as pitying Jesus and lightening his burden, but desiring, as hath been said, to put him to death more speedily.

And John, one of his disciples, followed him there.

Then he fled, and went to the mother of God,[1] and said to her, Where wast thou, that thou didst not come and see what was done? She answered, What is it that was done? John said, Know that the Jews have taken my master by force and now lead him away to crucify him. When his mother heard this she cried with a loud voice, saying, My son, my son, what evil hast thou done, that they lead thee away to crucify thee? She arose, as one benighted, and went weeping along the road. The women also followed her, Martha, and Mary Magdalene, and Salome, and other virgins. And John also was with her. When therefore they overtook the multitude, the mother of

---

[1] Gk. τὴν θεοτόκον. The use of this expression is a strong indication of the late date of this part of the composition. The whole paragraph is wanting in some copies, and is an interpolation.

God said to John, Where is my son? John saith, Seest thou him who beareth the crown of thorns, and hath his hands bound? When the mother of God heard this, and saw him, she fainted, and fell backward to the earth, and lay a considerable time. And the women who followed her stood around her and wept. And when she revived and arose, she cried with a loud voice, saying, My lord, my son, whither is the beauty of thy form departed? How shall I bear to see thee suffering such things? And saying this, she tore her face with her nails and smote her breast. Whither have passed, said she, the good deeds which thou didst in Judea? What evil hast thou done to the Jews. Thus then the Jews who saw her weeping and crying out came and drove her out of the way. But she was not persuaded to flee, but continued saying, Slay me first, O lawless Jews.

Then they retired to the place called Cranium, which was paved with stones, and there the Jews set up the cross. Then they stripped Jesus, and the soldiers took his garments and divided them among themselves, and they put upon him a scarlet cloth; and raised him up and fastened him on the cross at the sixth hour of the day. After this they also lifted up two robbers, one on his right hand and one on his left.

Then the mother of God, standing and beholding,

cried with a loud voice, saying, My son, my son. And Jesus turning to her and seeing John near her, and weeping with the rest of the women, said, Behold, thy son. Then saith he also to John, Behold, thy mother. And she wept exceedingly, saying, Therefore do I weep for thee, my son, because thou art suffering unjustly; for the lawless Jews have delivered thee to a bitter death. Without thee, my son, what will become of me? How shall I live without thee? What life shall I lead? Where are thy disciples who boasted they would die with thee? Where are those who were healed by thee? How is it that no one was found to help thee? And looking at the cross she said, Bow down O cross, that I may embrace my son, and kiss my son, whom at this breast strangely I nourished as one who knew not man. Bow down O cross, I wish to embrace my son. Bow down O cross, that as a mother I may converse with my son. When the Jews heard these things they came and drove away both her and the women and John to a distance.[1]

Then Jesus cried with a loud voice, Father, reckon not this sin unto them; for they know not what they do. Then saith he, I thirst. And straightway one of the soldiers ran and took a sponge and filled it with gall and vinegar mingled, and putting it upon

[1] The preceding paragraph is another interpolation. It is much longer in some copies.

a reed, he gave it to Jesus to drink. And when he had tasted it he would not drink. And the Jews who stood and saw, ridiculed him and said, If thou saidst truly that thou art the Son of God, come down from the cross, and immediately, that we may believe in thee. Others said in ridicule, He saved others, he helped others, and he healed the sick, the paralytic, lepers, demoniacs, blind, lame, all but dead, and he cannot help himself.

So also the robber who was crucified at his left side said to him, If thou art the Son of God, come down and save both thyself and us. His name was Gistas. But he that was crucified at his right side, Dysmas by name, reproached the other robber, saying, Wretched and miserable one, dost thou not fear God? We suffer what we deserve for what we have done; but he hath done no evil at all. And turning to Jesus, he saith to him, Lord, when thou shalt reign, forget me not. And he said unto him, To day, I tell thee truth, that I have thee with me in paradise.

CHAPTER XI.

THEN Jesus, having cried with a loud voice, Father, into thine hands will I commit my spirit, expired. And immediately the rocks were to be seen rent, for there was an earthquake in all the land, and because the earthquake was violent and great, even the rocks were rent: and the tombs of the dead were opened; and the veil of the temple was rent; and there was darkness from the sixth hour until the ninth. And when all these things came to pass the Jews were afraid, and said, Truly this man was righteous: and Longinus, the centurion, stood and said, Truly, this was the Son of God.[1] Others who came and saw him, smote upon their breasts for fear, and returned back again.

Now the centurion, observing all these marvels went away to Pilate and related them. And when he heard he wondered and was amazed, and through his fear and sorrow he would neither eat nor drink that day. And he gave notice, and there came to him all the council, after the darkness was passed away, and he said to the people, Ye saw how the sun was darkened, ye saw how the veil was rent. Truly, I did well in that I was not at all eager to put this good man to death. But the evil doers said to Pilate, Such a darkness is an eclipse of the sun, as it hath happened also at other times. Then say they to him, We hold the feast of unleavened bread to-morrow, and we intreat thee, since they who have been crucified still breathe, that their bones may be broken,

---

[1] The name Longinus, given to the centurion, is an addition to the earlier text, which has been altered throughout, both by additions and by omissions. This chapter especially has received all sorts of developments.

and that they may be taken down. Pilate said, This shall be done. Therefore he sent soldiers, and they found the two robbers still breathing, and they brake their legs; but finding Jesus dead, they did not touch him, save that a soldier speared him in the right side, and immediately there came out blood and water.

Now towards evening, when the preparation was come, Joseph, a high-born and wealthy man, a pious Jew, finding Nicodemus, whose speech had already betrayed him, saith to him, I know that thou lovedst Jesus when he was living, and didst gladly hear his words, and I saw thee contending with the Jews for him. Therefore, if it seemeth good to thee, let us go to Pilate and beg the body of Jesus for burial, for it is a great sin that he should lie unburied. I am afraid, saith Nicodemus, lest if Pilate be angry, I should suffer some mischief. But if thou shouldst go alone and ask, and shouldst receive the dead one, then I too will accompany thee, and will perform all that is necessary for the funeral. When Nicodemus had said this, Joseph lifted up his eyes to heaven, and prayed that he might not fail in his request, and went to Pilate, and having saluted him, sat down. Then he saith to him, I pray thee, my lord, if I ask anything which seemeth to thy majesty unreasonable, not to be angry with me. And he said, And what is it that thou askest? Joseph saith, Jesus, the good man whom through envy the Jews have carried away to crucifixion, I beseech thee to give me him for burial. Pilate saith, And what hath happened, that when he hath been witnessed against by his own nation for magic arts, and hath been suspected of seizing the kingdom of Cæsar, and hath therefore been given up to death by us, we should give order for him to be honoured again when he is dead? And Joseph, being very sorrowful and weeping, fell at the feet of Pilate, saying, My lord, let no jealousy of the dead possess thee. For, in death, every fault must perish with a man. But I know thy majesty, how anxious thou wast not to crucify Jesus, and what thou saidst to the Jews for him, at one time persuading, and at another time angry, and afterwards how thou didst wash thy hands, and didst declare thou hadst no part at all with those who wished him to be put to death. On all which accounts I entreat thee that my request may not be rejected. Pilate, therefore, seeing Joseph thus urgent and entreating, and weeping, raised him up, saying, Go, I grant thee such a one that is dead; take him and do what thou wilt.

And then Joseph, having given thanks to Pilate, and kissed his hands and his robes, went out rejoicing in heart, because he had obtained what was desired, but having his eyes yet filled with tears: thus, while sorrowing, he had joy. He went away to Nicodemus, therefore, and told him all that had happened. Then, when they had bought a hundred pounds of myrrh

THE GOSPEL OF NICODEMUS, (II.)   289

and aloes, and a new sepulchre,[1] with the mother of God, and Mary Magdalene, and Salome, with John and the other women, they wrapped him in a white linen cloth, according to the custom, and laid him in the tomb.

And the mother of God said, weeping, How shall I not bewail thee, my son? how shall I not tear my face with my nails? This, my son, is that which the old man Simeon foretold to me, when I took thee into the temple, a babe of forty days old. This is the sword which now pierceth through my soul. My sweetest son, who shall stay my tears? None at all, but only thou, if, as thou saidst, thou shalt rise again on the third day.

Mary Magdalene said, weeping, Hearken O peoples tribes, and tongues, and learn to what a death the lawless Jews have delivered him that had wrought for them countless benefits. Hearken and wonder. Who will cause these things to be heard throughout all the world? I will go alone to Cæsar in Rome; I will make known to him what evil Pilate hath done by yielding to the lawless Jews. Thus also Joseph lamented, saying, Alas for me! sweetest Jesus, dear and most unfortunate of men, if one must call thee a

[1] They bought a new sepulchre, says this writer, in direct contradiction to the Gospels, which teach us that the sepulchre was already Joseph's own. Matt. xxvii. 57-60. Most of the particulars in this account of the burial are fictitious, and were added not earlier than the second part about the Descent into the Underworld.

man, who has done such marvels as man never did. How shall I perform thy obsequies? how shall I bury thee? Now ought they too to be present whom thou didst feed with a few loaves: for thus I should not have seemed to be wanting in honour.

Then Joseph with Nicodemus went home: likewise also the mother of God, with the women, John also accompanying them.[1]

CHAPTER XII.

When the Jews learned that these things had been done by Joseph and Nicodemus they were greatly moved against them; and the chief priests, Annas and Caiaphas, admonished Joseph, and said to him, Wherefore hast thou performed these obsequies for Jesus? Joseph saith, I know that Jesus was a just and true and good man in all respects, and I know also, that ye through envy devised his murder; and for this cause I performed his funeral. Then the chief priests were angry and seized Joseph and cast him in prison, and said unto him, If we did not keep the feast of unleavened bread to-morrow, we would have put thee to death to-morrow, as we did him; but for the present, being kept in confinement,

---

[1] The mention of John in this story of the burial seems to have a motive, but I cannot say what it is: probably, John was pre-eminent among the saints, honoured where this adaptation of Nicodemus was produced. Peter on the contrary, is studiously kept out of sight, if we except the allusion at page 284, lines 10, 11.

early on the Lord's day[1] thou shalt be delivered to death. Thus they said, and sealed with a seal the prison, which was fastened with all manner of bolts and locks.

Thus, then, when the preparation was finished, early on the Sabbath the Jews went to Pilate, and said to him, Lord, that deceiver said that after three days he would rise again. Lest therefore his disciples should steal him by night and deceive the people by such a falsehood, command that his sepulchre should be guarded. Pilate therefore, on this, gave them five hundred soldiers,[2] who also were set about the sepulchre to guard it, and they put seals upon the stone of the sepulchre.

Therefore, when the day began to break on the Lord's day, the chief priests and the Jews held a council, and sent to bring Joseph out of prison in order to put him to death; but on opening it they found him not. And they wondered at this, how when the doors were shut and the locks secure, and the seals remaining, Joseph was not to be seen.

---

[1] That the Jews should speak of the Lord's day before it was instituted is an amusing anachronism, but worthy of notice, as a fresh evidence of the utter disregard of truth and consistency with which these apocrypha have been made up.

[2] Pilate, most likely, did not appoint a guard of more than four or five soldiers—hundreds are easily written. The paragraph is one of the interpolations.

CHAPTER XIII.

Hereupon, one of the soldiers who guarded the tomb, came and said in the synagogue, Know that Jesus is risen! The Jews said, How? And he said, First there was an earthquake; then an angel of the Lord bearing lightning came from heaven and rolled away the stone from the sepulchre, and sat upon it. And through fear of him all we soldiers became as dead men, and could neither flee nor speak. And we heard the angel saying to the women who came there to see the sepulchre, Fear not; for I know that ye seek Jesus. He is not here, but is risen, as he foretold you. Stoop down and see the sepulchre where his body lay. But go and tell his disciples that he is risen from the dead: and let them go into Galilee, for there shall they find him. Therefore, I tell you this beforehand.

The Jews said to the soldiers, Who were the women who came to the sepulchre, and why did ye not lay hold of them? The soldiers said, Because of fear, and the sight alone of the angel, we could neither speak nor move. The Jews said, As the God of Israel liveth, we believe nothing that ye say. The soldiers said, Jesus performed so great miracles and ye believed not, and will ye now believe us? Ye say truly that God liveth, and in very truth He liveth whom ye crucified. We have heard moreover that ye had Joseph shut in the prison, and that ye afterwards opened the doors and found him not. Do ye then give up Joseph, and then we will also give you Jesus. The Jews said, Joseph who escaped from prison ye will find at Arimathea, his own place. And the soldiers said, Go ye also into Galilee, and ye will find Jesus, as the angel said to the women.

Hereupon the Jews were afraid, and said to the soldiers, See that ye tell this matter to no one, or all will believe in Jesus. On which account, also, they gave them much money. And the soldiers said, We are afraid lest Pilate should hear that we have received money, and should put us to death. But the Jews said, Take it, and we pledge ourselves to give to Pilate an answer for you; only, say that ye slept, and that in your sleep the disciples of Jesus came and stole him out of the sepulchre. Therefore the soldiers took the money, and said as they were told. And until this day the same false report is spoken among the Jews.

CHAPTER XIV.

AND after a few days, three men came from Galilee to Jerusalem. One of them was a priest, Phinehas by name, another was a Levite, by name Aggæus, and the other was a soldier,[1] by name Adas. These came to the chief priests, and said to them, and to the people, Jesus, whom ye crucified, we have seen in Galilee, with his eleven disciples, at the mount of Olives, teaching them, and saying, Go ye into all the world, and preach the Gospel; and whoso believeth and is baptised, shall be saved, but whoso believeth not, shall be condemned. And having said this, he ascended to heaven.[2] And we saw, both we and many others of the five hundred who were there.[3]

And when the chief priests and Jews heard these things they said to the three men, Give glory to the God of Israel, and repent of the falsehoods ye tell. They answered, As the God of our fathers liveth, of Abraham, Isaac, and Jacob, we lie not, but tell you the truth. Then spake the chief priest, and they brought the Old Testament of the Hebrews from the temple, and he made them swear, and giving them also money, he sent them to another place that they might not proclaim the resurrection of Christ in Jerusalem.

When, therefore, such sayings had been heard by all the people, the multitude assembled in the temple, and there was a great tumult. For many said, Jesus is risen from the dead, as we hear, and why did ye crucify him? But Annas and Caiaphas said, Believe

---

[1] In the earlier version of the book Adas is called a teacher.
[2] Mark xvi. 16.
[3] 1 Cor. xv. 6.

not, O Jews, what the soldiers say; nor believe that they saw an angel descending from heaven. For we gave money to the soldiers not to tell such things to any one; and so also, the disciples of Jesus gave them money, to say that Jesus is risen from the dead.

CHAPTER XV.

NICODEMUS said, O children of the people of Jerusalem, the prophet Elijah ascended to the height of heaven with a fiery chariot, and it is not incredible if Jesus also is risen; for the prophet Elijah was a pre-figuration of Jesus, in order that ye should not disbelieve when ye heard that Jesus was risen. I therefore say and advise that we ought to send soldiers into Galilee, where the men testify that they saw him with his disciples, in order that they may go about and find him, and so that we may seek from him forgiveness for the evil which ye did to him. This saying pleased them, and they chose out soldiers, and sent them into Galilee: and Jesus they found not; but they found Joseph at Arimathea.

When, therefore, the soldiers returned, and the chief priests learned that Joseph was found, they assembled the people, and said, What shall we do to Joseph, that he may come to us? So when they had taken counsel, they wrote him a letter to this effect:

Father Joseph: Peace to thee, and to all thine house, and to thy friends. We know that we have offended against God, and against thee, his servant. Therefore we entreat thee to come hither to us thy children; for we have wondered much how thou didst escape from prison, and we truly say that we took evil counsel against thee. But God, who saw that we took unjust counsel against thee, delivered thee out of our hands. Nevertheless, come to us; for thou art the honour of our people.

The Jews sent this letter to Arimathea with seven soldiers, friends of Joseph, who went and found him, and addressed him respectfully, as they were bidden, and gave him the letter. And when he had received and read this, he glorified God, and bade the soldiers welcome, and when the table was set, he ate and drank with them all day and night.

And on the morrow he went with them to Jerusalem. And the people came out to meet him, and bade him welcome. And Nicodemus received him into his house. And on the day following, both Annas and Caiaphas, the chief priests, invited him to the temple, and said to him, Give glory to the God of Israel, and tell us the truth. For we know that thou didst bury Jesus, and for this we apprehended thee, and shut thee in prison. Afterwards, when we sought to bring thee out in order that thou mightest be put to death, we found thee not, and we marvelled, and were greatly afraid;

nevertheless, we prayed to God that we might find and ask thee. Therefore, tell us the truth.

Joseph said to them, On the evening of the preparation, when ye secured me in prison, I betook myself to prayer all the night, and all the day of the sabbath. And at midnight I saw the prison house, that four angels lifted it up, holding it by the four corners. And Jesus entered like lightning, and through fear of him I fell to the ground. Therefore, taking me by the hand, he raised me, saying, Fear not, Joseph. Then he embraced and kissed me, and said, Turn and see who I am. Therefore, I turned and looked and said, Lord, I know not who thou art. He saith, I am Jesus, whom thou didst bury the day before yesterday. I said to him, Show me the sepulchre, and then I will believe. Therefore he took me by the hand, and led me away to the sepulchre, which was open. And when I saw the linen clothes and the napkin, and knew, I said, Blessed is he that cometh in the name of the Lord, and worshipped him. Then he took me by the hand, the angels also following, and led me to Arimathea, to my house, and saith unto me, Abide here for forty days. For I go unto my disciples, that I may instruct them to preach my resurrection.

CHAPTER XVI.

WHEN Joseph had said these things, the chief

priests cried unto the people, We know that Jesus had both father and mother; how shall we believe that he is the Christ? One of the Levites answered and said, I know the family of Jesus, honest men, greatly addicted to the service of God, and receiving tithes of the people of the Jews.[1] And I also know Simeon, the old man, that he took him when he was a babe, and said to him, Now lettest thou thy servant depart, O Lord.

The Jews said, Let us find the three men who saw him at the mount of Olives, that we may ask them and learn the truth more accurately. And they found and brought them before all, and made them swear to tell the truth. And they said, As the God of Israel liveth, we saw Jesus at the mount of Olives, alive, and ascending into heaven.

Then Annas and Caiaphas separated the three from one another, and asked them privately and singly. They agreed therefore in their speech, and the three spoke the same thing. The chief priests answered and said, Our scripture saith that every word shall be established with two or three witnesses.[2] Joseph therefore hath confessed that he performed his funeral rites, and buried him, along with Nicodemus, and how it is the truth that he hath risen.

---

[1] This receiving of tithes by the family of Jesus is a fiction with no possible foundation.
[2] Deut. xvii. 6; Matt. xviii. 16.

THE GOSPEL OF NICODEMUS.

THE SECOND PART: OR,

THE DESCENT OF CHRIST TO THE UNDERWORLD.

CHAPTER I. (XVII.)[1]

Joseph saith, And why marvel ye that Jesus hath risen? This is not wonderful; but it is wonderful that he arose not alone, but that he also raised many other dead, who appeared unto many in Jerusalem. And if ye know not the others, Simeon at least, who took Jesus (in his arms), and his two sons, whom he raised again, them at least ye know. For we buried them a short time ago, but now their tombs are seen open and empty, and they are living, and abiding in Arimathea. Therefore they sent men and found their sepulchres open and empty. Joseph saith, Let us go to Arimathea, and let us find them.

Then the chief priests, Annas and Caiaphas, arose,

---

[1] Two sets of numbers are prefixed to the chapters of this second part, because it is written merely as a continuation of the former in the copies which contain it.

and Joseph, and Nicodemus, and Gamaliel, and others with them, and went to Arimathea, and found those whom Joseph said. Therefore they offered prayer, and saluted one another. Then they came with them to Jerusalem, and brought them into the synagogue, and shut the doors, and placed in the midst the Old Testament of the Jews, and the chief priests said unto them, We wish you to swear by the God of Israel and Adonai, and thus that ye may tell the truth, how ye arose, and who raised you from the dead.

When the men who had risen heard this, they made upon their faces the sign of the cross,[1] and said to the chief priests, Give us paper and ink and a pen. They brought them therefore; and they sat down and wrote thus—

CHAPTER II. (XVIII.)

O Lord Jesus Christ, the resurrection and the life of the world, give us grace that we may rehearse thy resurrection, and thy wonderful works which thou didst in Hades. We, therefore, were in Hades with all those who fell asleep from the beginning. Now at the hour of midnight, upon those dark places, there arose as it were the light of the sun, and

---

[1] This notion of the sons of Simeon crossing themselves, refers to a practice at least as old as the time of Tertullian (De Corona Milit. 2).

shone, and we were all lighted up and saw one another. And immediately our father Abraham was united with the patriarchs and the prophets, and they were together filled with joy, and said to one another, This light is from a great illumination. The prophet Isaiah, who was there, said, This light is from the Father, and the Son, and the Holy Spirit, concerning whom I prophesied while I was yet alive, saying, The land of Zebulun, and the land of Nephthalim, the people which sitteth in darkness hath seen a great light.[1]

Then came into the midst another, an ascetic from the desert, and the patriarchs said to him, Who art thou? And he said, I am John, the last of the prophets, who made straight the ways of the Son of God, and preached to the people repentance for remission of sins. And the Son of God came unto me; and when I saw him from afar I said to the people, Behold, the Lamb of God, who taketh away the sin of the world.[2] And with my hand I baptised him in the river Jordan, and I saw, also, as it were, a dove, the Holy Spirit coming upon him; and I heard also the voice of God and the Father saying thus, This is my beloved Son in whom I am well pleased. And for this cause he sent me also to you, that I might preach how the only begotten Son of God cometh hither, that whoever believeth in him

[1] Is. ix. 1, 2. [2] Matt. iii. 3, 11; Mark i. 4; John i. 36

shall be saved, but whoso shall not believe in him shall be condemned.[1] Therefore, I say, to all of you: whereas ye see him, that ye should all worship him, because, now only have ye time of repentance for your worship of idols in the vain world above, and for the sins ye have committed: but at another time this cannot be.

CHAPTER III. (XIX.)

THEREFORE, while John was thus teaching those who were in Hades, and the first made and first father Adam heard it, he saith to his son Seth, My son, I wish thee to tell the forefathers of the race of men, and to the prophets, whither I sent thee when I was about to die. And Seth said, Prophets and patriarchs, hearken. When my father Adam, the first made, was about to die, he sent me to offer prayer to God very near the gate of Paradise, that he would guide me by an angel to the tree of mercy, and let me take oil and anoint my father, and that he might recover from his sickness. Which also I did. And after my prayer the angel of the Lord came and said to me, Seth, what dost thou ask? dost thou ask the oil which restoreth the sick, or the tree which poureth forth such oil, because of the sickness of thy father? This is not now to be found. Go, therefore, and tell

[1] Mark xvi, 16.

thy father that, after 5500 years are accomplished from the creation of the world, then shall descend upon earth, the only begotten Son of God, being made man, and He shall anoint him with such oil, and he shall rise again, and with water and with the Holy Spirit He shall wash both him and his descendants, and then shall he be healed of all sickness: but now this cannot be.[1]

When the patriarchs and the prophets heard this they rejoiced greatly.

CHAPTER IV. (XX.)

Now while they were all in so great joy, Satan, the inheritor of darkness, came and said to Hades, All-devouring and insatiate one, hear my words. From the race of the Jews, there is one called Jesus, naming himself the Son of God, but being a man, the Jews through our joint exertions have crucified him. And now that he is dead, be ready that we may bind him safely here. For I know that he is a man, and I also heard him saying My soul is very sorrowful, unto death.[2] He wrought me many evils also in the world above while he conversed with mortals. For

---

[1] This legend of Seth seems to have been borrowed from a Jewish source, and adapted to Christian uses. The reader will find something more about it in the preliminary essay.
[2] Mark xiv. 34.

where he found my servants he persecuted them, and the men whom I made halt, blind, lame, lepers, and the like, he healed by his word alone. And when I had made many ready for burial, even them, by a word alone, he made alive again.

Hades saith, And is he so mighty as to be able to do such things by a word alone? or canst thou resist him who is such? It seemeth to me no one will be able to resist him who is such. But if thou sayest thou heardest him fearing death, he said this mocking and laughing at thee, wishing to seize thee with a mighty hand; and woe, woe, unto thee for evermore.

Satan saith, All-devouring and insatiate Hades, wast thou so afraid when thou heardest of our common foe? I feared him not, but I wrought upon the Jews, and they crucified him, and gave him gall and vinegar to drink. Be ready, therefore, to hold him firmly when he cometh.

Hades answered, Inheritor of darkness, son of perdition, Devil, thou hast but now told me that many whom thou preparedst for burial he by a word alone did make alive: and if he delivered others from burial, how and by what power shall he be held by us? Now a short time ago I swallowed a certain dead man, Lazarus by name, and a little after, one of the living, by a word alone, forcibly drew him out of my bowels. Now I think it was he of whom thou speakest. Therefore, if we receive him here, I fear we may run a risk even in regard to the rest; for lo! I see that all whom I have ever swallowed are in commotion, and my belly[1] is in pain. And Lazarus, who was snatched beforehand from me, seemeth to me no good sign; because he flew away from me, not like a dead man, but like an eagle; so quickly did the earth cast him forth. Wherefore, I conjure thee, both for thy benefit and for mine, not to bring him hither; for I think that he is coming here, in order to raise up all the dead. And this I say to thee, By the darkness which we keep, if thou dost bring him hither, none of the dead will be left to me.

CHAPTER V. (XXI.)

WHILE Satan and Hades were talking thus with each other, there came a great voice like thunder, saying, Lift up your gates, O ye rulers, and be ye lifted up, eternal gates, and the King of Glory shall come in.[2] And when Hades heard, he said to Satan, Go forth, if thou art able, and resist him. Therefore Satan went forth. Then saith Hades to his demons, Secure well and firmly the brazen gates, and the iron bars, and hold down my bolts, and stand upright and

---

[1] Jonah ii. 2.   [2] Ps. xxiv. 7.

watch everything : for if he should enter here, woe will seize us.

On hearing these things, the forefathers all began to reproach him, saying, All-devouring and insatiate, open, that the King of Glory may come in. David the prophet saith, Knowest thou not, O blind one, that when I was living in the world, I predicted this voice, Lift up your gates, O ye rulers? Isaiah said, Through the Holy Spirit, when I foresaw this, I wrote, The dead shall arise, and they that are in the tombs shall be raised, and those who are in the earth shall be glad, And, Where is thy sting, O Death? where is thy victory, O Hades?[1]

The voice, therefore, came again, saying, Lift up the gates. Hades, hearing the voice a second time, answered, as forsooth not knowing, and said, Who is this King of Glory? The angels of the Lord said, The Lord strong and mighty, the Lord mighty in battle. And immediately, at this word, the brazen gates were broken, and the iron bars were crushed, and all the dead that were bound were loosed from their bonds, and we[2] with them. And the King of Glory entered as a man, and all the dark places of Hades were lighted up.

---

[1] Is. xxvi. 19; Hos. xiii. 14.
[2] That is, the two sons of Simeon, who are supposed to write the story.

CHAPTER VI. (XXII.)

HADES straightway cried, We are conquered; woe unto us. But who art thou that hast so great authority and power? And what art thou, who comest hither without sin—seeming small, and able to do great things, humble and high, servant and Lord, soldier and king, who hast authority over the dead and the living? Thou wast nailed to the cross, and wast laid in the tomb, and now thou art free, and hast dissolved all our power. Art thou, then, the Jesus, of whom the chief ruler Satan said to us, That through the cross and death thou art about to inherit all the world?

Then the King of Glory seized the chief ruler Satan by the head, and delivered him to the angels, and said, Bind with irons his hands and feet and neck and mouth. Then he delivered him to Hades, and said, Take him and keep him safely until my second coming.

CHAPTER VII. (XXIII.)

AND Hades took Satan, and said to him, Beelzebub, inheritor of fire and punishment, enemy of the saints, by what necessity hast thou contrived that the King of Glory should be crucified, that he might come hither and spoil us? Turn and see that none of the dead is left in me; but all that thou didst gain by the tree of knowledge, thou hast lost it all by the tree of the cross; and all thy joy is changed into grief; and thou, that didst wish to put to death the King of Glory, hast put thyself to death. For since I have received thee to keep thee safely, thou wilt learn by experience what evils I shall do to thee. O chief devil, the beginning of death, the root of sin, the end of all evil! what evil didst thou find in Jesus, to procure his destruction? How didst thou dare to do so great evil? How didst thou study to bring down to this darkness such a man, through whom thou art deprived of all that ever died?

CHAPTER VIII. (XXIV.)

WHILE Hades thus discoursed with Satan, the King of Glory opened his right hand, and took hold of the first father Adam, and raised him. Then he turned and said to the rest, Come with me all ye who have died through the tree which he touched. For behold, I raise you all up again through the tree of the cross. Moreover, he sent them all out; and the first father Adam appeared, filled with satisfaction, and said, I give thanks unto thy majesty, O Lord, because thou hast brought me from the lowest Hades.[1] So also all the prophets and the saints said, We give thee thanks, O Christ, Saviour of the world, because thou hast brought back our life from destruction.[2]

And when they had said these things, the Saviour blessed Adam on the forehead with the sign of the cross; and he did this also to the patriarchs and the prophets, and martyrs and forefathers, and took them and sprang up out of Hades. And as he went, the holy fathers followed him, chanting, and saying, Blessed is He that cometh in the name of the Lord,[3] Alleluia: to him be glory from all the saints.

CHAPTER IX. (XXV.)

THEN He went to Paradise, holding the forefather Adam by the hand, and delivered him, and all the righteous, to the archangel Michael. When, therefore, they entered the gate of Paradise, two aged men met them, to whom the holy fathers said, Who are ye, who have not seen death, and have not descended into Hades, but inhabit Paradise in body and soul? One of them answering, said, I am Enoch, who pleased God, and was translated hither by him; and this is Elijah the Tishbite; and we are to live until the end of the world: and then we are to be sent by God to resist Antichrist, and

[1] Ps. lxxxvi. 13.   [2] Ps. ciii. 4.   [3] Ps. cxviii. 26

to be slain by him, and after three days to rise again, and to be caught up in clouds to meet the Lord.[1]

CHAPTER X. (XXVI.)

WHILE they were saying these things, there came another lowly man, and bearing a cross upon his shoulders; and the holy fathers said to him, Who art thou, having the appearance of a robber, and what is the cross which thou bearest upon thy shoulders? He answered, As ye say, I was a robber and a thief in the world, and therefore the Jews seized me and delivered me to the death of the cross, with our Lord Jesus Christ. As he was hanging upon the cross I believed in him, seeing the miracles which were done; and I called upon him, and said, Lord, when thou shalt reign, forget not me. And straightway he said to me, Verily, verily, I say unto thee, to day thou shalt be with me in Paradise. Therefore, bearing my cross I came to Paradise, and finding the archangel Michael, I said to him, Our Lord Jesus, who was crucified, hath sent me hither; lead me, therefore, into the gate of Eden. And the flaming sword, seeing the sign of the cross, opened unto me, and I came in. Then saith the archangel to me, Wait a little, for Adam, the forefather of the race of men,

[1] 1 Thess. iv. 17; Rev. xi. 3-12; 1 John ii. 18; iv. 3.

is coming with the righteous, that they also may enter in. And now seeing you, I am come to meet you.

On hearing these things, the saints all cried with a loud voice, Great is our Lord, and great is his power.[1]

CHAPTER XI. (XXVII.)

ALL these things we two brothers saw and heard; and we were sent by Michael the archangel, and were appointed to preach the resurrection of the Lord, but first to go to Jordan and be baptised; whither also we went, and were baptised along with other dead who had risen; and afterwards we came to Jerusalem, and celebrated the Passover of the resurrection.[2] But now, not being able to remain here, we are going away. And may the love of God and the Father, and the grace of our Lord Jesus Christ, and the communion of the Holy Spirit be with you all.[3]

When they had written these things, and closed the books, they gave half to the chief priests, and half to Joseph and Nicodemus. And immediately they vanished: unto the glory of our Lord Jesus Christ. Amen.

---

[1] Ps. cxlvii. 5.

[2] The brothers do not say who baptised them at the Jordan. Their keeping the Passover of the resurrection at Jerusalem raises a difficulty which I do not care to discuss.

[3] 2 Cor. xiii. 14

THE LATIN GOSPEL OF NICODEMUS,

Part I.,

OR, ACTS OF PILATE.

I, Æneas, was at first a protector of the Hebrews, and a follower of the law ; then the Saviour's grace and his great gift apprehended me, and I knew Christ Jesus in Holy Scripture, I came to him, and embraced his faith, that I might become worthy of his holy baptism. First of all I sought for the records, written in those times, concerning our Lord Jesus Christ, which the Jews published in the age of Pontius Pilate, and we found them in Hebrew writings, drawn up in the age of our Lord Jesus Christ; but I translated them into Gentile speech during the reign of the eminent Theodosius, in his seventeenth consulship, and Valentinian, the fifth time consul, in the ninth indiction.[1] All ye who read this book, and copy into other documents, be mindful of me, and pray for me, Æneas, the least of the servants of the Lord, that he may be merciful to

---

[1] See note, p. 229.

LATIN GOSPEL OF NICODEMUS. 313

me, and forgive my sins which I have committed against him. Peace be to all who read these things, and to all their house for ever. Amen.

Now it came to pass in the nineteenth year of the reign of Tiberius Cæsar, emperor of the Romans, and of Herod, the son of Herod king of Galilee, the nineteenth year of his dominion, on the eighth of the kalends of April, which is the twenty-fifth day of the month of March, in the consulate of Rufinus and Rubellio, in the fourth year of the 202nd Olympiad, under the chief priests of the Jews, Joseph and Caiaphas: the great things done by the chief priests and the other Jews, which Nicodemus recorded after the cross and passion of the Lord, and which Nicodemus himself committed to Hebrew writing.

CHAPTER I.

Annas and Caiaphas, Summas and Datam, Gamaliel, Judas, Levi, Nephthalim, Alexander and Jairus, and the rest of the Jews came to Pilate, accusing the Lord Jesus Christ of many things, and saying, We know that he was born the son of Joseph the carpenter by Mary, and he saith he is the Son of God and a king: not only this, but he also breaketh the sabbath, and wisheth to abolish the law of our fathers. Pilate saith, What are the things which he doth, and would thereby abolish the law? The Jews say, We have a law that no one should heal on the sabbath; but he on the sabbath, by evil arts, healeth the lame and the humpbacked, the blind, the paralytic, the leprous, and demoniacs. Pilate saith to them, By what evil arts? They say to him, He is an evil doer, and casteth out demons by Beelzebub, the prince of the demons, and they all are subject to him. Pilate saith to them, It is not for an unclean spirit to cast out demons, but for the god Scolapius.[1]

The Jews said, We pray thy majesty to set him to be examined before thy judgment seat. Pilate called the Jews to him, and said unto them, Tell me how can I, who am a procurator, examine a king? They say unto him, We do not say that he is a king, but he saith that he is. Therefore, Pilate called a messenger, and said to him, Let Jesus be brought with gentleness. And the messenger went out and adored him, when he recognised him, and spread upon the ground the vestment which he carried in his hand, saying, Lord, walk upon this and enter, for the procurator calleth for thee. But the Jews, seeing what the messenger did, cried out against Pilate saying, Why didst thou not cause him to enter by the summons of a herald, and not by a messenger? For when the messenger saw him he adored him, and the vestment which he held in his hand he spread before him on

[1] Literally 'the god of Scolapii,' but 'in deo Scolapii' are to be understood as if in apposition. Thus, for 'Urbs Roma,' 'the city Rome,' we say 'the city *of* Rome.' Scolapius is of course Æsculapius.

the ground, and said to him, Lord, the procurator calleth for thee.

Now Pilate, summoning the messenger, said to him, Why hast thou done this, and honoured Jesus who is called Christ? The messenger said to him, When thou sentest me to Jerusalem to Alexander, I saw him sitting on an ass, and the children of the Hebrews broke off branches from the trees and strewed them in the way; and some held branches in their hands; and some strewed their garments in the way, crying and saying, Save, then, thou who art in the highest; blessed is he that cometh in the name of the Lord.

The Jews cried out and said against the messenger, The children of the Hebrews cried out in Hebrew; how is it for thee, a Gentile, to know this? The messenger said to them, I asked one of the Jews and said, What is that which they cry out in Hebrew? and he explained it to me. Pilate said to them, How did they cry out in Hebrew? The Jews said, Hosanna in the highest. Pilate saith to them, How is Hosanna in the highest interpreted? They say unto him, Save us, thou who art in the highest. Pilate saith to them, If ye confirm the words and sayings with which the children cried out, what sin hath the messenger committed? And they were silent. The procurator, therefore, said to the messenger, Go out and bring him in as thou wilt. And the messenger went out and did as before, and said to Jesus, Lord, come in, for the procurator calleth for thee.

Now when Jesus entered, and the standard-bearers were bearing the standards, the tops of the standards bowed down of themselves and worshipped Jesus. But the Jews, seeing how the standards bowed themselves and worshipped Jesus, cried out still more against those who bore the standards. So Pilate said to the Jews, Marvel ye not how the standards bowed themselves and worshipped Jesus? The Jews said to Pilate, We saw how the men who bear the standards bowed and worshipped Jesus. And the procurator called the standard-bearers, and said unto them, Why have ye done thus? They said unto Pilate, We are Gentiles, and servants of the temples; how should we worship him? for as we were holding the ensigns they bowed themselves of their own accord, and worshipped him.

Pilate said unto the rulers of the synagogue, and the elders of the people, Choose ye strong and powerful men, and let them hold the standards, and let us see if they bow of themselves. So the elders of the Jews took twelve most strong and powerful men, and made them hold the standards by six and six, and they stood before the judgment seat of the procurator. Pilate saith to the messenger, Take out Jesus from the prætorium, and bring him in again in any way thou wilt. And Jesus and the messenger went outside the prætorium. And Pilate called those who held the standards before, and said to them, By the safety of Cæsar, if the standards do not bow themselves when Jesus entereth, I will cut off your heads. And the procurator commanded Jesus to enter the second time. And the messenger did the same as before, and greatly entreated Jesus to go up, and walk upon his vestment. And He walked upon it and came in. But as Jesus entered, immediately the standards bowed themselves and worshipped Jesus.

CHAPTER II.

Now when Pilate saw it, fear took hold of him, and he forthwith wished to rise up from the judgment seat. And while he thought thus, to rise up and depart, his wife sent unto him, saying, Have nothing to do with that just man; for I have this night suffered many things because of him. And Pilate called the Jews, and said to them, Ye know that my wife is a worshipper of God, and rather accordeth with you in Judaism. The Jews say unto him, It is so, and we know it. Pilate saith to them, Behold, my wife hath sent to me saying, Have nothing to do with that just man; for I have this night suffered many things because of him. The Jews answered and said unto Pilate, Have we not told thee that he is a magician? behold, he hath sent a phantom of dreams to thy wife.

Pilate called Jesus and said to him, What is it that these testify against thee? and sayest thou nothing to them? And Jesus answered, If they had not power they would not speak. Every one hath power over his own mouth, to speak good and bad: they will see.

So the elders of the Jews answered and said to Jesus, What shall we see? First, that thou art born of fornication; secondly, that at thy nativity at Bethlehem there was made a slaughter of infants; thirdly, that thy father Joseph, and thy mother Mary fled into Egypt, because they had no confidence in the people.

Certain of the Jews who stood by, being well disposed, said, We say not that he was born of fornication, but we know that Mary was espoused to Joseph, and he was not born of fornication. Pilate said to the Jews who said he was born of fornication, This your speech is not true, because the espousals were celebrated, as these men of your nation say. Annas and Caiaphas say unto Pilate, We say with all the multitude that he was born of fornication and is a malefactor; but these are proselytes and his disciples. And Pilate, calling to Annas and Caiaphas saith to them, What are proselytes? They say unto him, They were born children of the Gentiles, and are now become Jews. Those who bore witness that Jesus was not born of fornication, Lazarus and Asterius, Antonius and Jacob, Annes and Azaras, Samuel and Isaac, Phinehas and Crispus, Agrippa and Judas, answered, We are not proselytes, but were born children of the Jews, and speak the truth; for we were present at the espousals of Mary.

So Pilate called unto him these twelve men who proved that Jesus was not born of fornication, and he said unto them, I adjure you by the safety of Cæsar, tell me if it is true that Jesus was not born of fornication. They say unto Pilate, We have a law not to swear, because it is sin; but let them swear by the safety of Cæsar that it is not as we say, and we are deserving of death. Then said Pilate to Annas and Caiaphas, Answer ye nothing to those things which these men testify? Annas and Caiaphas say unto Pilate, These twelve are believed that he was not born of fornication: all we people cry that he was born of fornication, and is a malefactor, and saith that he is the son of God and a king; and we are not believed.

And Pilate commanded all the multitude to go out, except the twelve men who said that he was not born of fornication, and he commanded Jesus to be set apart from them. And Pilate said to them, Wherefore wish the Jews to slay Jesus? They say unto him, They are jealous because he healeth on the sabbath.

Pilate said, For a good work do they wish to slay him? They say unto him, Yea, lord.

CHAPTER III.

PILATE being filled with fury went out of the prætorium and said to them, I take the sun to witness that I find not one fault in this man. The Jews answered and said to the governor, If he had not been a malefactor we should never have delivered him unto thee. Pilate saith to them, Take ye him and judge him according to your law. The Jews answered, It is not lawful for us to put any one to death. Pilate saith to them, God hath said to you that ye should not put any one to death; hath he then said to me that I should kill?

Having entered the prætorium again, Pilate called Jesus unto himself privately and said to him, Art thou king of the Jews? Jesus answered Pilate, Dost thou speak this of thyself? or have others said it to thee concerning me? Pilate answered, Am I a Jew? thine own nation and the chief priests have delivered thee unto me: what hast thou done? Jesus answered and said, My kingdom is not of this world. If my kingdom had been of this world, my servants would by all means have contended that I should not be delivered to the Jews. But now my kingdom is not from hence. Pilate said to him, Art thou therefore a king? Jesus saith to him, Thou sayest; for I am a king. For on this account was I born, and for this I came, that I should bear witness for the truth, and every one who is of the truth heareth my voice. Pilate saith unto him, What is truth? Jesus saith, Truth is from heaven. Pilate saith, Is truth not on earth? Jesus saith to Pilate, Observe how they who say the truth are judged by those who have power on earth.

CHAPTER IV.

PILATE therefore, leaving Jesus within the prætorium, went out to the Jews and said to them, I find not one fault in him. The Jews say to him, He said, I can destroy this temple, and raise it up again in three days. Pilate said to them, What temple? The Jews say to him, That which Solomon built in forty-six years; and he speaketh of destroying and building it in three days. Pilate saith to them, I am innocent of the blood of this man: Ye shall see to it. The Jews say to him, His blood be on us and on our children.

But Pilate called the elders and priests and Levites and said to them privately, Do not so: for though ye accuse him I have found him in no wise worthy of death, not even for healing and the violation of the Sabbath. The priests and Levites and elders say,

Tell us, if one hath blasphemed Cæsar, is he worthy of death or no? Pilate saith to them, He is worthy to die. The Jews answered him, How much more is he worthy to die who hath blasphemed God?

Now the governor commanded the Jews to go out of the prætorium, and calling Jesus he said to him, What shall I do to thee? Jesus saith to Pilate, As it is allowed. Pilate saith, How is it allowed? Jesus saith, Moses and the prophets preached beforehand of my death and resurrection. Now when the Jews heard this they said to Pilate, Why further desirest thou to hear the blasphemy? And Pilate said, If this saying is blasphemous, take ye him, and lead him to your synagogue, and judge him according to your law. The Jews say to Pilate, Our law containeth this, If a man sinneth against man, he is worthy to receive forty stripes save one; but he that blasphemeth against God is to be stoned.

Pilate saith to them, Therefore judge him according to your law. The Jews say to Pilate, We wish him to be crucified. Pilate saith to them, He deserveth not to be crucified.

Now the governor looking at the people of the Jews standing round, saw very many of the Jews weeping, and he said, All the multitude doth not wish him to die. The elders say to Pilate, The whole multitude of us have come for this that he may die. Pilate saith to the Jews, What hath he done that he should die? They say to him, Because he said that he is the Son of God and a King.

CHAPTER V.

But a certain man named Nicodemus, who was a Jew, stood before the governor and said, I beseech thee mercifully to bid me say a few words. Pilate saith to him, Say on. Nicodemus saith, I have said to the elders and priests and Levites and all the multitude of the Jews in the synagogue, What have ye to do with this man? This man doth many miracles and signs which no man hath done or can do. Dismiss him and do nothing evil against him. If the signs which he doeth are of God, they will stand, but if of men they will be brought to nought. For Moses also, when sent of God into Egypt, did many signs, which God commanded him to do before Pharaoh king of Egypt. And the evil-doers Jamnes and Mambres were there healing, and they also did the signs which Moses did, but not all of them, and the Egyptians esteemed them as gods, both Jamnes and Mambres. And because the signs which they did were not of God, both they themselves perished, and those who believed them. And now dismiss this man, for he is not worthy of death.

The Jews say to Nicodemus, Thou art become his disciple, and makest a plea for him. Nicodemus saith unto them, Is the governor also become his disciple, and doth he make a plea for him? Hath not Cæsar appointed him to this dignity? Now the Jews were raging and gnashing their teeth against Nicodemus. Pilate saith to them, Why do ye gnash your teeth against him when ye hear the truth? The Jews say to Nicodemus, Receive his truth and a portion with him. Nicodemus saith, Amen, amen, amen, may I receive as ye have said.

CHAPTER VI.

Now a certain other of the Jews, starting up, asked the governor that he might say a word. The governor saith, What thou wilt say, say. He said, I lay eight-and-thirty years infirm in my bed in the greatest pain. And when Jesus came, many demoniacs and persons seized with divers infirmities were healed by him. And certain young men pitied me and carried me in my bed and placed me before him. And when Jesus saw, he had pity on me and said this word to me, Take up thy bed and walk. And immediately I was made whole, and took up my bed and walked. The Jews say unto Pilate, Ask him what day it was when he was healed. He said, The Sabbath. The Jews said, Have we not thus declared, that on the Sabbath he healeth and casteth out demons?

And a certain other Jew, starting up, said, I was born blind, I heard a voice and saw nobody. And as Jesus passed by, I cried with a loud voice, Son of David, have mercy on me. And he had mercy on me, and put his hands upon my eyes, and immediately I saw.

And another Jew, starting up, said, I was bowed down and he made me upright with a word.

And another said, I was leprous, and he healed me with a word.

CHAPTER VII.

Also a woman, named Veronica, called out from a distance to the governor, I had an issue of blood twelve years, and I touched the hem of his garment, and immediately the issue of my blood stayed. The Jews say, We have a law that a woman shall not come to bear witness.

CHAPTER VIII.

And certain others, a multitude of men and women, cried out, saying, This man is a prophet, and the demons are subject unto him. Pilate saith to those who said, The demons are subject unto him, And why are your teachers not subject unto him? They say to Pilate, We do not know. And others said to Pilate that he raised up Lazarus from the tomb after he had been dead four days. When the governor heard this, he trembled, and said to all the multitude of Jews, Why do ye wish to shed innocent blood?

CHAPTER IX.

AND Pilate called Nicodemus and the twelve men who said he was not born of fornication, and said to them, What shall I do? for there is a sedition among the people. They say unto him, We know not: let them see to it. Pilate again called all the multitude of the Jews and said, Ye know that it is a custom with you on the day of unleavened bread that I should release unto you one that is bound. I have a notable criminal in prison, a murderer called Barabbas, and Jesus who is called Christ, in whom I find no cause of death. Which will ye that I release unto you? And they all cried, saying, Release Barabbas unto us. Pilate saith unto them, What then shall I do with Jesus who is called Christ? They all say, Let him be crucified. The Jews said again, Thou art not the friend of Cæsar if thou dost release him, for he said he was the Son of God and a king; except thou wishest him to be king, and not Cæsar.

Then Pilate, filled with anger, said to them, Your

race hath always been seditious, and ye have been opposed to them that have been for you. The Jews answered, Who are for us? Pilate saith to them, Your God who snatched you from the hard servitude of the Egyptians, and led you out of Egypt through the sea, as by dry land, and fed you in the desert with manna and quails, and brought forth water from the rock for you and gave you drink, and gave a law unto you: and amid all these things ye provoked your God, and sought for you a molten calf as your God. And ye did anger your God, and he meant to slay you; and Moses prayed for you that ye might not die. And now ye say that I hate the king.

And rising from the tribunal he sought to go out. But the Jews cried and said to him, We know that Cæsar and not Jesus is king. For the magi also offered him gifts as a king, and when Herod heard from the magi that a king was born, he wished to slay him. But this becoming known, Joseph, his father, took him and his mother, and they fled into Egypt; and on hearing it, Herod slew all the infants of the Jews born in Bethlehem.

Pilate was afraid when he heard these words: and when silence was made among the people, who were shouting, Pilate said, Is this he whom Herod sought after? They say to him, It is he. And Pilate took water and washed his hands before the people, saying, I am innocent of the blood of this just man; ye will see. The Jews shouted again, saying, His blood be upon us and upon our children.

Then Pilate commanded the curtain to be drawn, and said to Jesus, Thine own nation complain of thee as a king: therefore I have decreed that thou shalt first be scourged according to the statutes of the emperors, and then be crucified upon a cross.

CHAPTER X.

AND when Jesus had been scourged he delivered him to the Jews to be crucified, and two robbers with him, one named Dismas and another named Gestas. And when they came to the place, they stripped him of his garments, and girded him with a linen cloth, and put a crown of thorns upon his head. Likewise also they hung up the two robbers with him, Dismas on the right, and Gestas on the left. And Jesus said, Father, forgive them, for they know not what they do. And the soldiers parted his garments amongst them. And the people stood waiting. And the chief priests and their judges derided him, saying among themselves, He saved others, now let him save himself; if he is the Son of God, let him come down from the cross. And the soldiers mocked him, falling down before him, and offering him vinegar with gall, and saying, If thou art king of the Jews, deliver thyself.

Now after the sentence Pilate commanded a title to be written in Hebrew, Greek, and Latin letters according to what the Jews had said:—THIS IS THE KING OF THE JEWS.

Now one of the robbers that were hanging, Gestas by name, said to him, If thou art Christ, deliver thyself and us. But Dismas, answering, rebuked him saying, Dost thou not even fear God, who art in this condemnation? for we, indeed, justly and worthily receive the things we have done; but he hath done no evil. And he said to Jesus, Lord, remember me in thy kingdom. And Jesus said to him, Verily I say unto thee, that to-day thou shalt be with me in Paradise.

CHAPTER XI.

Now it was about the sixth hour, and darkness came upon all the earth and the sun was obscured, and the veil of the temple was rent in the midst; and he cried with a loud voice and said, Father, into thy hands I commend my spirit. And, having said this, he expired. And the centurion, seeing what was done, glorified God, saying, This man was just. And all the people, who were present at that sight, seeing what was done, smote their breasts and returned.

Then the centurion reported to the governor what was done. And the governor and his wife, on hearing it, were greatly grieved, and neither ate nor drank that day. And Pilate, calling the Jews, said to them, Have ye seen what was done? And they said to the governor, There has been an eclipse of the sun, as is usual.

Now his acquaintance and the women who had followed him out of Galilee, stood afar off beholding these things. And behold, a certain man, Joseph by name, a counsellor, of Arimathea a city of the Jews, a good and just man, who did not consent to their counsels nor deeds, and who himself expected the kingdom of God, went away to Pilate and begged the body of Jesus. And taking him down from the cross, he wrapped him in a clean linen cloth, and placed him in his own new tomb wherein no one had been laid.

CHAPTER XII.

Now the Jews having heard that Joseph had begged the body of Jesus, sought for him and the twelve men who had said that he was not born of fornication, and for Nicodemus, and for many others who had stood before Pilate and made known his good works. But they were all hidden, and Nicodemus alone appeared to them, because he was a chief man of the Jews, and he said to them, How did ye come into the synagogue? The Jews say unto him, And how didst thou come into the synagogue, for thou dost consent with him? His portion be with thee in the world to come! Nicodemus said, Amen, Amen, Amen! Likewise also Joseph, coming forth, saith to them, Why are ye aggrieved against me because I begged the body of Jesus? Behold, I have placed him in my own new tomb, wrapping him in a clean linen cloth; and I have rolled a stone to the door of the cave. And ye have not acted well towards the Just One, because ye have not laid it to heart that ye crucified him and pierced him with a spear. The Jews therefore, seizing Joseph commanded him to be guarded because of the sabbath day, and they said unto him, Know that the time doth not demand anything to be done with thee because the sabbath beginneth to dawn. But know that thou art not worthy of burial, but we will give thy flesh to the fowls of heaven and the beasts of earth.

Joseph saith unto them, That is the speech of haughty Goliath, who reproached the living God (speaking) against holy David. But God hath said, Vengeance is mine, I will repay, saith the Lord. And Pilate, being convinced in heart, took water and washed his hands before the sun, saying, I am innocent of the blood of this just man: ye will see. And ye answered Pilate and said, His blood be upon us and upon our children. And now I fear lest the wrath of God should come upon you and upon your children as ye have said. But when the Jews heard this they were embittered in their heart, and took Joseph and shut him in a house where there was no window, and put keepers at the doors, and sealed up the door where Joseph was shut in.

Now on the Sabbath in the morning they took counsel with the priests and Levites that all should be assembled after the sabbath day. And, rising at daylight, all the multitude took counsel in the synagogue, by what death they should kill him. And while the congregation was sitting, they commanded him to be brought with much insult; and on opening the door they found him not. Therefore all the people were afraid, and they wondered with exceeding astonishment, because they found the seals sealed, and because Caiaphas had the keys. And they dared no more to lay a hand on those who had spoken for Jesus before Pilate.

CHAPTER XIII.

Now while they sat in the synagogue and disputed about Joseph, some of the keepers came whom they had asked from Pilate to guard the sepulchre of Jesus, lest his disciples should come and steal him away. And they made known and told the rulers of the synagogue, and the priests and the Levites, what was done; how there had been a great earthquake, and, We saw how the angel of the Lord descended from heaven, and rolled away the stone from the door of the sepulchre, and sat upon it; and his appearance was as lightning, and his raiment like snow: and for fear we became as dead men. And we heard the voice of the angel talking to the women who had come to the sepulchre, and saying, Fear not: for I know that ye seek Jesus who was crucified: he is not here, he is risen, as he said: come and see the place where the Lord was laid. And go forth quickly, and tell his disciples that he is risen from the dead, and will go before you into Galilee, as he told you.

The Jews say, With what women did he talk? The soldiers answer, We know not what women they were. The Jews say, At what hour was it? The keepers answer, At midnight. The Jews say, And why did ye not take them? The keepers answer, We became as dead men through fear of the angel, not hoping now to see the light of day; and how could we take them? The Jews say, As the Lord God liveth, we do not believe you. And the keepers said to the Jews, Ye have seen so great signs in that man and have not believed, and how can ye believe us that the Lord liveth? Ye have well sworn; because the Lord Jesus Christ doth live. The keepers say again to the Jews, We have heard that ye shut up in prison and sealed it with your rings, Joseph, who begged the body of Jesus, and when ye opened it ye found him not. Therefore give us Joseph, and we will give you Jesus Christ. The Jews said, Joseph is gone to Arimathea, his own city. The keepers say to the Jews, And Jesus, as we have heard from the angel, is in Galilee.

Now when they heard these sayings the Jews feared greatly, and said, Lest this saying should be heard, and all men should believe in Jesus. And the Jews took counsel together, and took money enough and gave it to the soldiers, saying, Say ye, While we slept his disciples came and stole him. And if this should be heard by the governor, we will assure him and make you safe. And the soldiers, receiving it, said as they were admonished by the Jews, and their saying was sent abroad among all men.

CHAPTER XIV.

Now a certain priest named Phinehas, and Addas a teacher, and Egeas a Levite, came down from Galilee unto Jerusalem, and reported unto the rulers of the synagogue, and priests, and Levites, how they had seen Jesus sitting, and his disciples with him, on the mount of Olivet, which is called Mambre or Malech,[1] and he was saying to his disciples, Go into all

[1] Some copies call this Amalech. The placing of the Mount of Olives in Galilee is a topographical blunder, and confounding it with Mamre is another. See p. 252, note.

the world and preach the Gospel of the Kingdom of God to every creature. He that shall believe and be baptised, shall be saved; but he that shall not believe, shall be condemned. Now these signs shall follow them that shall believe: in my name they shall cast out demons, they shall speak with new tongues, they shall take up serpents, and if they drink any deadly thing, it shall not hurt them; they shall lay hands upon the sick, and they shall recover. While Jesus spake these things to his disciples we saw him taken up into heaven.

The priests, and Levites, and elders said unto them, Give glory to the God of Israel, and give acknowledgement to him, if ye have seen and heard these things which ye tell. They who had declared this said, As the Lord God of our fathers liveth, the God of Abraham, and the God of Isaac, and the God of Jacob, we saw and heard. The Jews say unto them, Have ye come for this cause, to tell us, or have ye come to offer prayer to God? They said, We are come to offer prayer to God. The elders, and chief priests, and Levites say unto them, And if ye are come to offer prayer to God, why have ye talked of this madness before all the people? Phinehas the priest, and Addas the teacher, and Egeas the Levite, say unto the rulers of the synagogue, and the priests, and the Levites, If the things which we have spoken, which we have seen and heard, are sin, behold, we are in your presence: do unto us according to that which is good in your eyes. And taking the law they made them swear to tell no one those things any more. And they gave them to eat and drink, and sent them out of the city, giving them money, and three men with them to conduct them as far as Galilee.

Then when those men went up into Galilee, the Jews counselled together, and the rulers of the synagogue shut themselves up, and fell into a great fury, saying, Why hath this sign happened in Israel? But Annas and Caiaphas said, Why are your souls sad? Ought we to believe the soldiers that the angel of the Lord descended from heaven, and rolled away the stone from the door of the sepulchre? Nay, but that his disciples gave much gold to those who kept the sepulchre, and took away Jesus, and taught them to say thus, Say that the angel of the Lord descended from heaven and rolled away the stone from the door of the sepulchre. Know ye not that it is unlawful for Jews to believe strangers in anything, knowing that the same who received money enough from us have said as we taught them.

CHAPTER XV.

THEN Nicodemus arose and stood in the midst of the council, and said, Ye have said rightly. Are not they who came down from Galilee men who fear God, men of peace, and hating a lie? And they said with an oath, We saw Jesus sitting on mount Mambre with his disciples, and he taught them in our hearing: and they saw him taken up into heaven. Now no one has asked them how he was taken up into heaven. And in like manner the scripture of the holy book teacheth us that holy Elijah also was taken up into heaven: and Elisha cried with a loud voice, and Elijah cast his mantle of sheepskin upon Elisha; and Elisha again cast the mantle upon the Jordan, and passed over and came to Jericho. And the sons of the prophets met him, and said to Elisha, Where is thy lord Elijah? and he said, He is taken up into heaven. And they said to Elisha, Hath a spirit seized him and cast him on one of the mountains? But let us rather take our young men with us and seek for him. And they prevailed on Elisha, and he went with them; and they sought for him three days and three nights, and found him not, because he was taken up. And now, O men, hear me, and let us send into all Israel, and see lest Jesus hath been taken up somewhither and cast on one of the mountains. And that saying pleased them all: and they sent among all the mountains of Israel to seek for Jesus, and found him not; but they found Joseph of Arimathea, and no one dared lay hold upon him.

And they reported unto the elders, and priests, and Levites, saying, We have gone about all the mountains of Israel, and have not found Jesus; but we have found Joseph in Arimathea. Now when they heard about Joseph they rejoiced, and gave glory to the God of Israel. And the rulers of the synagogue and priests and Levites took counsel in what way they should send to Joseph; and they took paper and wrote to Joseph:—

Peace be to thee and to all that is thine. We know that we have sinned against God and against hee: and thou hast supplicated the God of Israel, and he hath delivered thee out of our hands. And now deign to come to thy fathers and thy sons, for we are greatly distressed. We, who opened the door and found thee not, have all sought for thee. We know that we have taken evil counsel against thee, but the Lord hath supplanted our counsel against thee. Father Joseph, thou art worthy to be honored by all the people.

And they chose out of all Israel seven men who were friends of Joseph, whom Joseph also knew as friends; and the rulers of the synagogue and priests, and Levites said to them, See ye: if he receiveth the letter and readeth it, for certain he will come to us with you; but if he doth not read it, know that he is ill-disposed towards us, and when ye have saluted him in peace return to us. And they blessed them and sent them away. And they came to Arimathea to Joseph, and worshipped him with their face to the ground, and said, Peace be to thee, and to all thine. And Joseph said, Peace be to you, and to all the people of Israel. And they gave him the letter; and Joseph took it and read it, and he embraced the letter, and blessed God, and said, Blessed be the Lord God who hath delivered Israel, that it might not shed innocent blood: and blessed be God who hath sent his angel and sheltered me under his wings. And he kissed them, and set a table for them, and they ate and drank, and slept there.

And when they arose in the morning, Joseph saddled his ass and went with them, and they entered the holy city of Jerusalem. And all the people met him, crying out, and saying, Peace be on thy coming in, father Joseph. In answer to them, he said, The Lord's peace be on all the people. And they all kissed him; and they prayed with Joseph, and were afraid when they saw him. And Nicodemus received him into his house, and made a great feast, and invited Annas and Caiaphas and the elders and chief priests and Levites to his house; and making merry and eating and drinking with Joseph they blessed God, and went away every one to his own home. But Joseph abode in the house of Nicodemus.

Now on the next day, which was the preparation,

the priests and rulers of the synagogue and Levites arose early and came to the house of Nicodemus. And Nicodemus met them, and said to them, Peace be to you. And they said to him, Peace to thee and to Joseph, and to thy house, and the house of Joseph. And Nicodemus led them into his house. And a council sat; and Joseph sat between Annas and Caiaphas, and no one dared speak a word. And Joseph said to them, Why have ye invited me? But they signified with their eyes to Nicodemus that he should speak with Joseph. And Nicodemus opened his mouth and said, Father Joseph, thou knowest that our venerable teachers, priests, and Levites, seek to hear a word from thee; and Joseph said, Ask on. And Annas and Caiaphas took the law and caused Joseph to swear, saying, Give glory to the God of Israel, and give to him acknowledgement, so as not to hide from us any word. And they said to him, We have been greatly grieved because thou didst beg the body of Jesus, and didst wrap it in a clean linen cloth, and didst lay him in the sepulchre. Therefore we shut thee up in a house where there was no window, and we put a lock and a seal on the door, and on the first day of the week we opened the doors and found thee not. Therefore were we greatly grieved, and astonishment came over all the people of God; and therefore art thou invited, and now tell us what was done.

Then said Joseph, On the day of preparation, about the tenth hour, ye shut me in, and I remained there the whole of the sabbath. And when midnight came, while I stood and prayed, the house wherein ye shut me was suspended by the four corners, and there was a flashing of light in mine eyes, and I fell trembling upon the ground. Then one lifted me up from the place where I had fallen, and poured abundance of water upon me from my head to my feet, and put about my nostrils the fragrance of wonderful ointment, and rubbed my face with the water, as if washing me, and kissed me, and said to me, Joseph, fear not, but open thine eyes, and see who it is that speaketh to thee. And looking, I saw Jesus, and being afraid, I thought it was an apparition. And with prayer and other utterances I spake to him, and he talked with me. And I said to him, Art thou Rabbi Elijah? And he said to me, I am not Elijah. And I said to him, Who art thou, Lord? And he said to me, I am Jesus, whose body thou didst beg from Pilate, and didst wrap in a clean linen cloth, and didst put a napkin upon my face, and didst lay me in thine own new sepulchre, and didst roll a stone to the mouth of the sepulchre. Then I said to him that spake to me, Show me, Lord, where I laid thee. And he led me and showed me the place where I laid him, and the linen cloth which I had put upon him, and the napkin which I had wrapped about his face; and I knew that it was Jesus. And he took hold of me with his hand, and put me in the midst of my house, the doors being shut, and he put me in my bed, and said to me, Peace be to thee! And he kissed me and said to me, For forty days go not from thine house; for behold, I go into Galilee to my brethren.

CHAPTER XVI.

Now when the rulers of the synagogue, and the priests, and Levites, heard these words from Joseph, they became as dead men, and fell upon the ground, and fasted until the ninth hour. And Joseph and Nicodemus besought them, saying, Arise, and stand upon your feet, and taste bread, and refresh your souls, for to-morrow is the sabbath of the Lord. And they arose and besought the Lord, and ate and drank, and went away, every man to his own house.

Now on the sabbath the teachers and doctors sat questioning together and saying, What is this wrath which is come upon us? for we know his father and mother. Levi the teacher said, I know his parents feared God, and never departed from prayer, and gave tithes three times in the year. And when Jesus was born his parents presented him in this place, and offered sacrifices and burnt offerings to God. For also the old man Simeon, the teacher, took him in his arms, and said, Now, Lord, lettest thou thy servant depart in peace, according to thy word; for mine eyes have seen thy salvation, which thou hast prepared before the face of all peoples, to be a light to lighten the Gentiles, and to be the glory of thy people Israel. And he blessed Mary, his mother, and said, I declare unto thee concerning this child. And Mary said, Good, my lord. And Simeon answered, Good. And he said again, Behold, he is set for the fall and rising again of many in Israel, and for a sign which shall be spoken against; and a sword shall pierce through thine own soul, that the thoughts of many hearts may be revealed.[1]

And the Jews said to Levi, and how knowest thou these things? Levi saith, Know ye not that I learned the law from him? They of the council say unto him, We would see thy father. And they sought out his father, and obtained information, for he said, Why have ye not believed my son? Simeon the blessed and just taught him the law. The council said to Rabbi Levi, The saying which thou hast spoken is true. And the chief priests, and rulers of the synagogue, and the Levites, said among themselves, Come, let us send into Galilee to the three men who came hither, and told us of his teaching and assumption, and let them tell us how they

[1] Luke ii. 28-32, 34, 35. From Lat. Vulgate.

saw him taken up into heaven. And that saying pleased them all. Then they sent three men into Galilee, and said, Go and say to Rabbi Addas, and Rabbi Phinehas, and Rabbi Egeas, Peace be to you and yours! Many inquiries have been made in the council concerning Jesus, therefore we are directed to invite you to the holy place, to Jerusalem.

The men departed into Galilee and found them sitting and meditating upon the law. And they greeted them in peace. And they said, Why are ye come? The messengers answered, The council calleth you to the holy city of Jerusalem. And when they heard that they were required by the council, they prayed to God, and sat down with the men and ate and drank with them. And rising in the morning they departed for Jerusalem in peace.

And on the morrow the council sat, and asked them saying, Did ye clearly see Jesus sitting on Mount Mambre, teaching his disciples, and taken up into heaven?

First Addas the teacher said, Truly I saw him sitting on Mount Mambre teaching his disciples; and a shining cloud overshadowed him and his disciples, and he ascended into heaven; and his disciples were praying with their faces to the ground. And then calling Phinehas the priest, they asked him also, saying, How didst thou see Jesus taken up? And he said the same as the other. And, again, on their calling and asking the third Rabbi, Egeas, he said the same as the first and second. And they who were in the council said, It is contained in the law of Moses that by the mouth of two or three every word is established. The teacher Abudem, one of the doctors, saith, It is written in the law, that Enoch walked with God, and he was translated, because God took him. Jairus, a teacher, said, And we have heard of the death of holy Moses, and have not seen it; for it is written in the law of the Lord, And Moses died according to the mouth of the Lord, and no man knoweth his sepulchre unto the present day. Rabbi Levi said, What is that which Rabbi Simeon said, Behold he is set for the fall and rising again of many in Israel, and for a sign which shall be spoken against? Rabbi Isaac said, It is written in the law, Behold I send my Angel, who shall go before thy face to keep thee in every good way; for I have brought in his new name.[1]

Then Annas and Caiaphas said, Ye have rightly said, that these things are written in the law of Moses, that no one saw the death of Enoch, and no one hath named the burial-place of holy Moses. But Jesus gave answer to Pilate, and we saw him scourged, and his face spit upon, and the soldiers put a crown of thorns upon him, and he received sentence from Pilate, and he was lately crucified, and they

[1] Mat. iii. 1; Is. lxii. 2.

gave him gall and vinegar to drink, and two robbers were crucified with him, and Longinus, a soldier, pierced his side with a spear; and our dear father Joseph asked for his body; and he rose again; and as the three teachers say, they saw him taken up into heaven. And Rabbi Levi hath testified what was spoken by the old man Simeon, that he was set for the fall and rising again of many in Israel, and for a sign which shall be contradicted.

Then Didas, the teacher, said to all the congregation, If all things which these men have testified concerning Jesus have come to pass, they are from God, and let it not be marvellous in our eyes. The chiefs of the synagogue, and the priests, and Levites said among themselves, It is contained in our law, His name shall be blessed for ever; His place continueth before the sun, and his seat before the moon; and all the tribes of the earth shall be blessed in him; and all nations shall serve him, and kings shall come from afar adoring and magnifying him.[1]

[1] Ps. lxxii. 11, 17.

THE LATIN GOSPEL OF NICODEMUS,

Part II.,

OR, DESCENT OF CHRIST TO THE UNDERWORLD.

CHAPTER I. (XVII.)

AND Joseph arose and said to Annas and Caiaphas, Truly and well do ye wonder that ye have heard how Jesus hath been seen to ascend into heaven alive from the dead. But it is more to be wondered at that he rose not alone from the dead, but that he raised alive from their tombs many other dead men, and they have been seen by many in Jerusalem. And now hear me, for we all know the blessed Simeon, the great priest, who in the temple took the infant Jesus in his hands. And the same Simeon had two sons, both of one mother, and we were all present at their death and burial. Go, therefore, and see their tombs, for they are open, because they have arisen: and, behold, they are in the city of Arimathea living together in prayer. And indeed they are heard crying out, but speaking with no one, but are speechless as dead men.[1] But come, let us go to them, and let us bring them to us with all honour and gentleness. And if we adjure them, perhaps they will speak to us of the mystery of their resurrection.

When they heard this they all rejoiced. And Annas and Caiaphas, Nicodemus and Joseph and Gamaliel went and found them not in their sepulchre; but on going into the city of Arimathea there they found them on bended knees and occupied in prayer. And kissing them, with all veneration, and in the fear of God, they brought them to Jerusalem to the synagogue. And when the doors were shut, they took the law of the Lord and put it in their hands, adjuring them by the God Adonai and the God of Israel, who spake by the law and the prophets to our fathers, saying, If ye believe that it is Jesus who raised you from the dead, tell us how ye rose from the dead.

When Karinus and Leucius heard this adjuration, they trembled in body and groaned, being troubled in heart. And looking together to heaven they made the sign of the cross on their tongues with their fingers, and immediately they spake together, saying, Give us separate sheets of paper, and let us write what we have seen and heard. And they

[1] The writer seems to mean that they neither heard what was said to them, nor said anything to men.

gave them unto them. And sitting down they both wrote, saying:

CHAPTER II. (XVIII.)

LORD JESUS CHRIST, the resurrection and life of the dead, permit us to speak mysteries by the death of thy cross, because we are adjured by thee. For thou hast commanded thy servants to relate to no one the secrets of thy Divine Majesty, which thou hast accomplished in the underworld. Now when we had been laid with all our fathers in the pit, in the gloom of darkness, there suddenly appeared the golden glow of the sun and a purple royal light shining upon us. And immediately the father of all the human race, with all the patriarchs and prophets, exulted, saying, This light is the author of eternal light, which hath promised to send us the co-eternal light. And Isaiah cried out, and said, This is the light of the Father, the Son of God, as I foretold when I was living upon earth: The land of Zebulun and the land of Naphtali beyond Jordan, in Galilee of the Gentiles, the people which sat in darkness saw a great light; and they who are in the region of the shadow of death, light was shining among them.[1] And now it is come and hath illumined us who sit in death.

[1] Is. ix. 2.

And while we all exulted in the light which shone upon us, our father Simeon came to us, and he said to us, joyfully, Glorify the Lord Jesus Christ, the Son of God; for when he was born an infant I took him in my hands in the temple, and, moved by the Holy Spirit, I said, confessing him, For now mine eyes have seen thy salvation, which thou hast prepared in the sight of all people, a light to lighten the Gentiles, and the glory of thy people Israel.[1] On hearing this, the whole multitude of the saints rejoiced the more.

And after this there came one like a dweller in the wilderness, and was asked by all, Who art thou? To whom, in reply, he said, I am John, the voice and prophet of the Highest, preceding the presence of his coming, to prepare His ways, to give knowledge of salvation to His people for remission of their sins. And when I saw him coming to me, I was impelled by the Holy Spirit, and said, Behold, the Lamb of God, behold, it is He who taketh away the sins of the world. And I baptised Him in the river Jordan, and I saw the Holy Spirit descending upon Him in the form of a dove, and I heard a voice from heaven, saying, This is my beloved Son in whom I am well pleased. And now I have come before His face, and descended to announce to you that the dayspring itself, the Son of God coming from on high, is about

[1] Luke ii. 30-32.

to visit us as we sit in darkness and the shadow of death.

CHAPTER III. (XIX.)

AND when father Adam, the first-formed, heard this, that Jesus was baptised in the Jordan, he cried to his son Seth, Tell unto thy sons, the patriarchs and prophets, all that thou didst hear from Michael the Archangel, when I sent thee to the gates of Paradise to pray God to send thee his angel to give thee the oil of the tree of mercy, to anoint my body when I was sick. Then Seth drew nigh to the holy patriarchs and prophets, and said, When I Seth was praying to the Lord at the gates of Paradise, behold, Michael, the angel of the Lord, appeared unto me, saying, I am sent to thee by the Lord; I am appointed over the human body. I say unto thee, Seth, do not labour with tears by prayer and supplication for the oil of the tree of mercy to anoint thy father Adam for the pain of his body, for thou canst in no wise receive of it, save in the last days and times, nor until 5500 years have been accomplished : then shall come upon earth the most beloved Son of God to raise the body of Adam and the bodies of the dead, and at His coming He shall be baptised in the Jordan. But when He shall have gone forth from the water of Jordan, then with the oil of His mercy shall He anoint all who believe in Him, and that oil of mercy shall be for the generation of those who are to be born of water and the Holy Spirit unto life eternal. Then coming down into the earth,[1] the most loving Son of God, Jesus Christ, shall lead our father Adam into Paradise to the tree of mercy.

When they heard all these things from Seth, all the patriarchs and prophets rejoiced with great joy.

CHAPTER IV. (XX.)

AND when all the saints were rejoicing, behold Satan, the prince and leader of death, said to Hades,[2] Prepare thyself to receive Jesus, who boasteth that He is the Son of God, and is a man who feareth death, and saith, My soul is sorrowful unto death. And He hath opposed me in very many things and done me mischief, and many whom I made blind, lame, deaf, leprous, and demoniacs, He hath healed with a word; and those whom I brought dead unto thee he hath taken from thee.

Hades answered and said to Satan, the prince, Who is he that is so powerful, while he is a man that feareth death? For all the powerful of the earth are held subject to my power, and as subject

---

[1] That is, literally so; the underworld being located like purgatory, within this globe.
[2] The Latin has *ad inferum*; when Inferus is personified I render it Hades; but when plural 'Inferi' I translate it Underworld.

thou hast by thy power brought them down. If thou then art powerful, what is that man Jesus, who feareth death and yet resisteth thy power? If he is so powerful in his humanity, I tell thee truly, he is omnipotent in his divinity, and no one can withstand his power, and while he saith that he feareth death, he is intending to seize thee, and it will be woe unto thee through eternal ages.

But Satan the prince of Tartarus said, Why hast thou hesitated and feared to receive that Jesus, my enemy and thine? For I have tempted him, and my ancient Jewish people I have stirred up with jealousy and anger against him; I have sharpened a lance to wound him, I have mingled gall and vinegar to be given him to drink, and I have prepared the wood for his crucifixion, and nails to fasten him, and his death is at hand, that I may lead him to thee subject to thee and to me.

Hades answered and said, Thou hast told me that it is he who took the dead from me. For there are many who are detained by me here, who while they lived on earth took the dead from me, not by their own power, but by divine prayers; and their omnipotent God took them from me. Who is that Jesus, who by his word drew from me the dead, without prayers? Perhaps it is he who made alive by the word of his power Lazarus, that had been four days in corruption and decay, whom I held dead.

Satan the prince of death answered and said, It is that same Jesus. Now when Hades heard this, he said to him, I conjure thee by my powers and thine, not to bring him to me. For when I heard the command of his word, I was greatly terrified with dread and trembled, and all my agents were thrown into confusion with me. Neither could we hold Lazarus, but shaking himself off, like an eagle with all agility and speed, he leaped up and left us, and the very earth which held the dead body of Lazarus straightway gave him back alive. So now I know that the man who could do this is God, mighty in dominion, powerful in his humanity, and Saviour of the human race; and if thou shalt bring him to me, he will release and conduct to the life of his divinity for ever, all who are here shut up in the severity of prison, and bound in the firm bonds of their sins.

CHAPTER V. (XXI.)

AND while Satan the prince, and Hades were talking thus together, there was suddenly a sound as of thunder and a crying of spirits: Lift up your gates, ye princes, and be ye lift up, ye everlasting doors, and the King of Glory shall come in.[1] When Hades heard this, he said to Satan the prince,

[1] Ps. xxiv. 7.

Depart from me and go forth out of my abode; if thou art a powerful warrior, fight against the King of Glory. But what hast thou to do with him? And Hades cast forth Satan out of his abode. And Hades said to his impious agents, Shut the cruel brazen gates, and place iron bars against them, and strongly resist, lest we be led captive who hold captivity.

Now when all the multitude of saints heard this, they said with a voice of rebuke to Hades, Open thy gates that the King of Glory may come in. And David cried, saying, When I was alive on earth, did I not foretell to you, Let the mercies of the Lord be confessed unto him, and his wonderful works to the children of men, because He hath broken the brazen gates and crushed the iron bars:[1] He hath taken them from the way of their iniquity.

And after this, Isaiah likewise said, When I was alive on earth, did I not foretell to you, The dead shall arise, and they shall arise who are in the tombs, and they shall exult who are in the earth, for the dew which is from the Lord is health to them. And again, I said, O death, where is thy sting? O Hades, where is thy victory?[2]

Now all the saints who heard these things from Isaiah said to Hades, Open thy gates; conquered now, thou wilt be feeble and powerless. And there was

[1] Ps. cvii. 16.   [2] Is. xxvi. 19; Hos. xiii. 14.

a great voice like thunder, saying, O ye princes, lift up your gates, and be ye lifted up ye gates of Hades, and the King of Glory shall come in. Hades, seeing that they cried this twice, said, as if he knew not, Who is the King of Glory? David answered and said to Hades, I understand the words of this cry, for I prophesied the same by his Spirit; and now, what I said above I say to thee, The Lord strong and mighty, the Lord mighty in battle, He is the King of Glory.[1] And the Lord himself hath looked down from heaven upon earth to hear the groaning of the prisoners, and to loose the children of the slain.[2] And now most vile and most polluted Hades, Open thy gates that the King of Glory may come in. When David said this to Hades, the Lord of Majesty came in the form of man, and illumined the eternal darkness, and broke the indissoluble chains, and the help of unconquered excellence visited us who sat in the deep darkness of offences, and in the death-shadow of sins.

CHAPTER VI. (XXII.)

On seeing these things, Hades, and Death, and their wicked agents, with their cruel ministers, trembled at the brightness of so great a light, perceived in their own realms, while they suddenly beheld Christ in

[1] Ps. xxiv. 7, 8.   [2] Ps. lxxix. 11.

their abode, and they cried out, saying, We are conquered by thee. Who art thou that orderest our confusion before the Lord? Who art thou that without the ruin of corruption, by unfailing evidence of majesty, in thy fury condemnest our power? Who art thou, so great and small, humble and high, soldier and commander, admirable warrior in the form of a servant, and king of glory, dead and alive, whom when slain the cross upheld? Thou who didst lie dead in the sepulchre, hast come down alive unto us; and at thy death every creature trembled, and all the stars were shaken; and now thou art become free among the dead, and dost disturb our legions. Who art thou that dost loose the captives that are held bound in original sin, and recallest them to their primeval liberty? Who art thou that sheddest divine and splendid and lustrous light upon them that are blinded by the darkness of sin?

Likewise also all the legions of demons, terrified with similar fear, because of their fearful overthrow, with one voice cried out, and said, Whence art thou, O Jesus, so mighty a man, and splendid in majesty, so illustrious without spot, and pure from fault? For that earthly world, which hath ever been subject unto us till now, which paid tribute to our use, never sent us such a dead man, and never assigned such gifts to the underworld. Who then art thou that hast entered our borders so fearlessly, and not only dost not fear our punishments, but dost aim to remove all from our bonds? Perhaps thou art that Jesus, of whom Satan, our prince, said, that by thy death on the cross thou wouldst receive power over the whole world.

Then the King of Glory, in his majesty, spurning Death, and seizing Satan the prince, delivered him to the power of Hades, and drew Adam into his glory.

CHAPTER VII. (XXIII.)

Then Hades, receiving Satan the prince, with strong rebuke said to him, O prince of perdition, and leader of destruction, Beelzebub, the mockery of angels, and the contempt of the just! Why hast thou determined to do this? Hast thou resolved to crucify the King of Glory, in whose removal by death thou didst promise us so great spoils? Like a fool thou knewest not what thou didst. For behold, that Jesus, by the splendor of his divinity, scattereth all the darkness of death, and hath broken up the lowest strongholds of our prisons, and cast out the captives, and loosed them that were bound. And all who used to groan under our torments, mock at us, and by their prayers our domains are overcome, and our realms are conquered, and no race of men now feareth us. Moreover, the dead who were never haughty towards us, nor could ever be joyful as captives, boldly threaten us. O prince Satan, father of all the impious, wicked, and apostate, why hast thou determined to do thus? They who from the beginning until now despaired of safety and life, their wonted howling is now no longer heard, neither doth any of them utter a groan, nor is a trace of tears found upon the face of any one of them. O prince Satan, possessor of the keys of the underworld, those thy riches which thou hadst gained by the tree of prevarication and the loss of paradise, thou hast now lost by the tree of the cross, and all thy joy is perished. When thou didst hang up that Christ Jesus the King of Glory, thou didst act against thyself and against me. Henceforth thou wilt know what eternal torments and infinite punishments thou shalt suffer in my everlasting prison. O prince Satan, the cause of death and source of all pride, thou oughtest first to have sought out the guilt of that Jesus. Why, when thou knewest no fault in him, didst thou dare to crucify him unjustly, without cause, and bring the innocent and just to our region, and lose the guilty, wicked, and unrighteous of all the world?

And while Hades was saying these things to Satan the prince, then the King of Glory said to Hades, Satan the prince shall be under thy power, for endless ages, in the place of Adam and his sons, my righteous ones.

CHAPTER VIII. (XXIV.)

And the Lord stretched out his hand and said, Come unto me, all my saints who have my image and likeness. Ye who have been condemned by the tree, and the devil, and death, now see the devil and death condemned by the tree. Immediately all the saints were assembled together under the hand of the Lord. And the Lord took hold of the right hand of Adam and said to him, Peace be unto thee with all thy children, my just ones. And Adam, falling down at the knees of the Lord, with tearful entreaty besought him with a loud voice and said, I will exalt thee, O Lord, because thou hast received me, and hast not suffered mine enemies to rejoice over me. O Lord God, I have cried unto thee, and thou, O Lord, hast healed me; thou hast brought out my soul from the underworld, thou hast saved me from them that go down into the pit. Praise ye the Lord, all his saints, and confess to the remembrance of his holiness; because wrath is in his indignation, and life in his good pleasure. In like manner also all the saints of God, falling on their knees before the feet of the Lord, with one voice said, Thou hast come, O Redeemer of the world: As thou hast predicted by the law and thy prophets, thou hast fulfilled in deed. Thou hast redeemed the living by thy cross, and by the death of the cross thou hast come down to us, to deliver us by thy majesty from the underworld and death. O Lord, as thou hast set the title of thy glory in heaven, and hast raised up thy cross on earth as the title of redemption, so Lord, set on Hades the sign of the victory of thy cross, that death may reign no more.

And the Lord stretched out his hand and made the sign of the cross over Adam and over all his saints, and taking hold of the right hand of Adam He went up from the underworld, and all the saints followed him. Then holy David cried aloud, saying, Sing unto the Lord a new song; for He hath done marvellous things. His right hand and his holy arm hath brought him salvation. The Lord hath made known his salvation; He hath revealed his justice in the sight of the nations.[1] And all the multitude of the saints answered and said, This is glory unto all his saints. Amen. Alleluia.[2]

And after this Habakkuk, the prophet, cried and said, Thou wentest forth for the salvation of thy people, to deliver thy chosen. And all the saints answered and said, Blessed is he that cometh in the name of the Lord; God is the Lord, and he hath showed light unto us. Amen. Alleluia.[3]

---

[1] Ps. xcviii. 1. 2.   [2] Ps. cxlix. 9; Rev. xix. 4.
[3] Ps. cxviii. 26, 27. For the quotation from Habakkuk the Vulgate

In like manner after this the prophet Micah cried and said, Who is God like thee, O Lord, taking away iniquities and passing over sins? And now thou restrainest thy wrath for a testimony, for thou takest pleasure in mercy; and thou turnest away, and hast compassion on us, and forgivest all our iniquities, and hast sunk all our sins in the multitude of death, as thou swarest unto our fathers in ancient days.[1] And all the saints answered and said, This is our God for ever and ever, and He shall rule us for evermore.[2] Amen. Alleluia. So also all the prophets, rehearsing sacred utterances from their praises, and all the saints, crying, Amen, Alleluia, followed the Lord.

CHAPTER IX. (XXV.)

Now the Lord held Adam by the hand, and gave him over to Michael the Archangel. And all the saints followed Michael the Archangel, and he introduced them all to the glorious grace of Paradise. And there met them two men, very ancient of days. And the saints asked them, Who are ye that have not yet been dead with us in the underworld, and

---

has *Egressus es in salutem populi tui, in salutem cum Christo tuo*, 3, 13. "Thou went forth the salvation of thy people: salvation with thy Christ," Douay Version. "Thou wentest forth for the salvation of thy people, to save thine anointed," Septuagint.

[1] Mic. vii. 18–20.   [2] Ps. xlviii. 14.

have been stationed in Paradise in the body? One of them answered and said unto them, I am Enoch, who was translated hither by the word of the Lord; and he that is with me is Elijah the Tishbite, who was taken up in a fiery chariot. Here and hitherto we have not tasted death, but are reserved to the coming of Antichrist, and we shall fight with him by divine signs and prodigies; and when we have been slain by him in Jerusalem, after three days and a-half, we are again to be taken up alive, in the clouds.[1]

CHAPTER X. (XXVI.)

AND while these things were talked of with the saints, Enoch and Elijah, behold, there came up another, a very wretched man, bearing on his shoulders the sign of the cross. When they saw him all the saints said unto him, Who art thou? for thy appearance is that of a robber. And what is the sign which thou bearest on thy shoulders? He answered and said to them, Ye have said truly, for I was a robber, and did all evil upon earth; and the Jews crucified me along with Jesus, and I saw the miracles which were done to the creatures by the cross of Jesus that was crucified, and I believed Him to be the creator of all creatures, and the omnipotent

[1] Rev. xi. 9, 12.

king; and I entreated Him, saying, Lord, remember me when thou comest into thy kingdom. And He straightway received my prayer, and said unto me, Verily I say unto thee, This day thou shalt be with me in Paradise.[1] And He gave me this sign of the cross, saying, Go to Paradise, bearing this; and if the angel guardian of Paradise suffer thee not to enter, show him the sign of the cross, and say to him, Jesus Christ, the Son of God, who now is crucified, hath sent me. When I had done this I said all these things to the angel guardian of Paradise, who, when he heard these things from me, straightway opened the gate and took me in, and placed me on the right side of Paradise, saying, Behold, wait a little, and Adam, the father of all the human race, shall come in with all his sons that are holy and just, after the triumph and glory of the ascension of the crucified Lord Christ.

When they heard all these words of the robber, all the holy patriarchs and prophets with one voice said, Blessed art thou, the Lord Almighty, the Father of eternal good, and Father of mercies, who hast given such grace to thy sinful ones,[2] and hast restored them to the grace of Paradise, and to thy fat pastures, for this is most certain spiritual life. Amen, Amen.

[1] Luke xxiii. 42, 43.
[2] The Latin *peccatoribus* looks like an error for *pecoribus*, "sheep," which is in harmony with the rest of the sentence.

CHAPTER XI. (XXVII.)

THESE are the divine and sacred mysteries which we saw and heard—I Karinus, and Leucius. We are not permitted further to record the other mysteries of God, inasmuch as Michael the Archangel protested, and said unto us, When ye go with your brethren into Jerusalem, ye shall cry aloud in your prayers, and glorify the resurrection of the Lord Jesus Christ, who raised you from the dead with himself. And ye shall speak with no man, and shall abide as if dumb, until the hour cometh when the Lord shall himself permit you to relate the mysteries of his divinity. And Michael the Archangel commanded us to walk over Jordan into a fat and fruitful place, where there are many who arose with us in witness of the resurrection of Christ the Lord. For we, who arose from the dead, were only permitted to be three days in Jerusalem to celebrate the passover of the Lord with our kindred who were living, in witness of the resurrection of Christ the Lord; and we were baptised in the holy river Jordan, and each received white robes. And after three days, when the passover of the Lord had been celebrated, all who arose with us were carried away in clouds, and were taken beyond Jordan, and were seen no more by any. But it was said unto us that we should continue in prayer in the city of Arimathea.

These are the great things which the Lord commanded us to relate to you. Give praise and confession to him, and repent, that he may have mercy on you. Peace be unto you from Jesus Christ himself, the Lord and the Saviour of us all. Amen.

And after they had finished writing all on separate sheets of paper, they arose. What Karinus wrote he gave into the hands of Annas and Caiaphas and Gamaliel; and in like manner what Leucius wrote, he gave into the hands of Nicodemus and Joseph. And being suddenly transfigured they appeared all in white, and were seen no more. And their writings were found to be alike, neither more nor less by a single letter.

When all the synagogue of the Jews heard all these wonderful sayings of Karinus and Leucius, they said to one another, Truly all these things were done by the Lord, and blessed be the Lord for ever and ever. Amen. And they all went out with great seriousness, smiting their breasts with fear and trembling, and departed every one to his own home.

Immediately Joseph and Nicodemus reported to the governor all those things which were spoken by the Jews in their synagogue. And Pilate himself wrote all that was said and done by the Jews concerning Jesus and put all the words in the public documents of his judgment hall.

CHAPTER XII. (XXVIII.)

AFTER these things Pilate went into the temple of the Jews and assembled all the chief priests, and grammarians, and scribes, and teachers of the law; and he went with them into the sanctuary of the temple, and commanded that all the doors should be shut, and said to them, We have heard that ye have in this temple a certain great volume; therefore I pray you that it may brought before us. And when the same volume was brought by four ministers, adorned with gold and precious jewels, Pilate said to them all, I adjure you by the God of your fathers, who commanded you to build this temple in the place of his sanctuary, not to withold the truth from me. Ye know all that is written in this volume; but now say whether ye have found in the Scriptures that Jesus, whom ye crucified, that he was the Son of God, who should come for the salvation of the human race, and in how many years of time he ought to have come. Manifest unto me whether ye crucified him ignorantly or knowingly.

When they were thus adjured, Annas and Caiaphas commanded that all the others who were with them should go out of the sanctuary, and they closed all the doors of the temple and the sanctuary, and said to Pilate, We have been adjured by thee, O good judge, by the building of this temple, to make truth and reason plain unto thee. After we had crucified Jesus, not knowing him to be the Son of God, thinking he wrought these miracles by some incantation, we held a large assembly in this temple, and when we consulted together concerning the miraculous signs which Jesus had wrought, we found many witnesses of our own nation, who said that they had seen Jesus alive after the suffering of death, and that he entered the height of heaven. And we have seen two witnesses whom Jesus raised from the dead, who made known unto us many miracles which Jesus did among the dead, which we have in our hands in writing. And our custom is, every year to open this holy volume before our assembly and seek the witness of God. And we have found, in the first book of the Seventy, where Michael, the archangel, talked with the third son of the first man Adam, about the 5500 years,[1] after which should come from heaven, Christ, the most beloved Son of God: and, moreover, we have supposed that perhaps he was the God of Israel who said to Moses, Make thee the ark of the covenant, two cubits and a half in length, one cubit and a half in breadth, and a cubit and a half in height. By these five cubits and a half we under-

[1] See Chapter iii. (xix.)

stood and knew the frame of the ark of the old covenant, that in five thousand five hundred years Jesus Christ should come in the ark of the body, and we find that he is the God of Israel, the Son of God. For after his passion we, the chief priests, wondering at the signs which came to pass because of him, opened this volume, seeking out all the generations unto the generation of Joseph, and reckoning that Mary, the mother of Christ, was of the seed of David: and we found that from the time in which God made heaven and earth and the first man, there were 2212 years to the Flood; and from the Flood to the building of the tower 531 years; and from the building of the tower to Abraham 606 years; and from Abraham to the coming of the children of Israel out of Egypt 470 years; from the departure of the children of Israel out of Egypt to the building of the temple 511 years; and from the building of the temple to the destruction of the same temple 464 years; thus far we found in the volume of Ezra: and reckoning from the burning of the temple to the coming of Christ and his nativity we find there are 636 years. These together are 5500 years,[1] as we find written in the volume that Michael, the archangel, foretold to Seth, the third son of Adam, that Christ, the Son of God, would come in 5500 years. Hitherto we

---

[1] The sum of the foregoing numbers is 5430, and not 5500 as stated in the text. Other copies give even a lower sum.

have told no one, that there might be no dissension in our synagogues; and now, thou, O good judge, hast adjured us by this holy volume of the testimonies of God, and we make it plain to thee. And we adjure thee, by thy life and salvation, not to make known these words to any in Jerusalem.

CHAPTER XIII. (XXIX.)

When Pilate heard these words of Annas and Caiaphas he inserted them all in the Acts of the Lord the Saviour, in the public documents of his judgment hall, and wrote a letter to Claudius, the king of the city of Rome, saying,

Pontius Pilate to Claudius, his king, greeting.

It hath lately happened, as I have myself proved, that the Jews, through envy, punished themselves and their posterity by a cruel condemnation. For when their fathers had a promise that their God would send his Holy One from heaven who should be deservedly called their king, and promised that he would send him to earth by means of a virgin; when, therefore, while I was governor, He had come into Judea, and they had seen that he gave sight to the blind, that he cleansed lepers, that he healed the paralysed, that he expelled demons from men, raised the dead, commanded the winds, walked with dry feet upon the waves of the sea, and wrought many other miraculous signs; and when all the people of the Jews said he was the Son of God, the chief priests were moved with envy against him, and took him and delivered him to me, and perversely lying unto me said that he was a magician and did contrary to their law.

Now I believed it was so, and when he had been scourged, I surrendered him to their will. And they crucified him, and set a watch over him after he was buried. But while my soldiers were guarding him he rose again on the third day. To such a degree did the iniquity of the Jews rage that they gave money to my soldiers, saying, Say that his disciples stole his body. But when they had taken the money they could not keep silence as to what had been done, for they testified that they had seen that he had risen, and that they had received money from the Jews.

I have put these things down, that no one may falsely speak otherwise, and lest thou shouldst think the falsehoods of the Jews are to be believed.

THE GOSPEL OF NICODEMUS, PART II.

OR, THE DESCENT OF CHRIST TO THE UNDERWORLD.

(From the Latin Text. B.)

CHAPTER I. (XVII.)

THEN Rabbi Addas, and Rabbi Phinehas, and Rabbi Egeas, three men who had come from Galilee testifying that they had seen Jesus taken up into heaven, arose in the midst of the multitude of the chiefs of the Jews, and said before the priests and Levites who were called to the Lord's council, As we came out of Galilee unto Jordan there met us a very great multitude of men, Abbats[1] who had been long dead. Among whom we saw Karinus and Leucius together present along with them. And as they came unto us and kissed us, for they had been our dear friends, we asked them, Tell us, friends and brethren, What is this soul and flesh? And who are these with whom ye are walking? And how do ye continue in the body who have been long time dead?

[1] *i.e.* fathers.

They answered and said, We arose with Christ from the underworld, and He raised us from the dead. And hereby ye may know that the gates of death and darkness are destroyed, and the souls of the saints are taken thence and have ascended into heaven with Christ the Lord. For it hath been commanded us by the Lord himself that for a certain time we should walk about the banks of the Jordan and the mountains; yet not appearing unto all, nor speaking with all, but only those whom it hath pleased him. And now we could neither have appeared nor spoken unto you unless it had been permitted us by the Holy Spirit.

Now when all the multitude that was present in the council heard this, being filled with fear and trembling, they wondered if those things had been really done which the Galileans declared. Then Caiaphas and Annas said to the council, All that these have declared, both before and after, must now be cleared up. If it is found true that Karinus and Leucius continue alive in the body, and if we can behold them with our eyes, then all is true which they have declared; and they who find them will certify us concerning everything. But if not, ye may know that all is false.

Then the council forthwith arose, and it seemed good to them to choose fit men who feared God and who knew when they died, and where they were buried, and who should enquire diligently and see whether it was as they had heard. There proceeded thither therefore fifteen men, who were all along present at their deaths, and had stood at their feet when they were buried, and had seen their sepulchres. And they came and found their sepulchres open, and very many more, and found no trace of their bones or dust. And they returned in all haste and told what they had seen.

Then their whole assembly was troubled with great sorrow, and they said to one another, What shall we do? Annas and Caiaphas said, Let us send to where we have heard they are, and let us send to them some of our more honourable men, to beg and entreat them: perhaps they will deign to come to us. Then they sent unto them Nicodemus and Joseph, and the three men, Rabbis of Galilee, who had seen them, to beg them to deign to come to them. These, going forth, walked about all the region of the Jordan and the mountains, and not finding them, turned back.

And behold there suddenly appeared descending from mount Amalek,[1] a very great multitude, about twelve thousand men, who had risen with the Lord. Although they recognised very many that were there, they could not say anything to them because of fear and the angelic vision, and stood afar off gazing at them, and hearing them, as they marched along,

[1] Elsewhere called Olivet. See page 252, note.

singing and saying, The Lord hath risen from the dead, as He had said: Let us all rejoice and be glad, for He reigneth for ever. Then they that had been sent were astonished, and through fear fell to the ground, and they received an answer from them, that they should seek for Karinus and Leucius at their own houses.

And they arose and came to their homes, and found them occupied in prayer. And when they went in unto them they fell with their faces to the ground, saluting them; and standing up they said, Friends of God, the whole multitude of the Jews hath sent us to you, hearing that ye have risen from the dead, asking and beseeching you to come to them, that we may all know the wonders of God which have been wrought about us in our times. And straightway arising, at a sign from God, they came with them and entered their synagogue. Then the multitude of the Jews, with their priests, placed in their hands the books of the law, and adjured them, by the God Heloi and the God Adonai, and by the law and the prophets, saying, Tell us how ye arose from the dead, and what are these wonders which have been wrought in our times, such as we have never heard to have been done at any time; because through fear all our bones are astonished and dried up, and the earth trembleth under our feet; for all our hearts have conspired to shed the just and holy blood.

Then Karinus and Leucius made signs to them with their hands, that they should give them a sheet of paper and ink. Now they did this because the Holy Spirit suffered them not to speak with them. And giving them each a sheet they put them apart from one another, into separate cells. And when they had made the sign of the cross of Christ with their fingers, they began to write on separate papers; and when they finished, as if with one mouth they cried out, Amen, from their separate cells. And they rose up, and Karinus gave his paper to Annas, and Leucius to Caiaphas, and when they had saluted one another, they went out, and returned to their sepulchres.

Then Annas and Caiaphas opened the sheet of paper, and each of them began to read in secret. But all the people took it amiss, and all cried out thus, Read these writings openly unto us; and after they have been read we will preserve them, lest, perchance, this truth of God should be turned into falsehood through their blindness by the unclean and deceitful. Then Annas and Caiaphas, being filled with trembling, delivered the sheet of paper to Rabbi Addas and Rabbi Phinehas, and Rabbi Egias, who had come from Galilee, and announced that Jesus was taken up into heaven. And all the multitude of the Jews entrusted to them to read the writing. And they read the paper, which contained these things:—

CHAPTER II. (XVIII.)

I AM Karinus. Lord Jesus Christ, the Son of the living God, suffer me to speak thy marvels which thou hast wrought in the underworld. When, therefore, we were confined in darkness, and the shadow of death, in the underworld, suddenly there shone upon us a great light, and Hades and the gates of death trembled. And the voice of the Son of the Father most High was heard, as the sound of loud thunder, and crying out mightily, it thus exclaimed, O ye princes, throw back your gates, lift up the eternal gates; the King of Glory, Christ the Lord, approacheth to enter.

Then came Satan, the leader of death, fleeing in terror, saying to his servants and the shades below, O my servants and all ye shades below, run together, shut your gates, put against them iron bars, and fight bravely and resist, lest we who hold should be held captive in chains. Then all his impious agents were troubled, and began to shut the gates of death, with all diligence, little by little to fasten the locks and iron bars, to grasp all their ornaments[1] with firmly closed hands, and to utter the howlings of a dreadful and most horrible voice.

---

[1] *Ornamenta*—another and more probable reading is *armamenta*, weapons.

CHAPTER III. (XIX.)

Then said Satan unto Hades, Prepare thyself to receive him that I shall bring down to thee. Thereupon Hades thus addressed Satan, That sound came only from the cry of the Son of the Father most High, for earth and all the places of hell beneath it so trembled. Wherefore, I think that I and all my bonds now lie exposed. But I conjure thee, Satan, chief of all evil, by thy powers and mine, bring him not to me, lest, while we would take him captive, we should be taken captive by him. For if, at the sound of his voice alone, all my power is thus destroyed, what thinkest thou he will do when his presence approacheth?

To whom Satan, the leader of death, thus answered, Why dost thou cry out? fear not, my ancient friend most vile; for I have stirred up the people of the Jews against him, I have bidden him to be buffeted, and I have accomplished against him his betrayal by his disciple; and he is a man who much feareth death, and through fear hath said, My soul is sorrowful even unto death; and I have brought him to this, that he now hangeth lifted up on the cross.

Then said Hades to him, If it is he who by the mere word of his command caused Lazarus to fly like an eagle out of my bosom when he had been dead already four days, he is not a man in humanity, but is God in Majesty. I beseech thee not to bring him to me. To whom Satan said, Prepare thyself, notwithstanding; fear not: since he now hangeth upon the cross, I cannot do otherwise. Then Hades thus exclaimed to Satan, If, therefore, thou canst not do otherwise, behold thy ruin approacheth. I, indeed, shall remain cast down and without honour; but thou wilt be under my dominion tormented.

CHAPTER IV. (XX.)

Now the saints of God heard the contention between Satan and Hades; but although they were as yet without recollection of one another, nevertheless, they had knowledge. But our holy father Adam thus thoroughly answered Satan, Leader of death, why dost thou fear and tremble? Behold the Lord cometh, who will now destroy all thy devices, and thou shalt be taken by him and bound for ever.

Then all the saints, hearing the voice of our father Adam, with what constancy he thoroughly answered Satan, were confirmed in their joy; and all of them running to father Adam, were crowded together about him. Then our father Adam, regarding narrowly all that multitude, wondered if they had all been descended from him in the world. And embracing those who stood with him all around, shedding most bitter tears, he called to his son Seth, saying, O son Seth, tell the holy patriarchs and prophets what the guardian of Paradise said to thee, when I sent thee to bring to me of the oil of mercy to anoint my body when I was weak.

Then he answered, When thou sentest me to the gates of Paradise, I prayed and besought the Lord, with tears, and called to the guardian of Paradise that he would give me thereof. Then came forth Michael the archangel and said to me, Seth, Wherefore dost thou lament? Know beforehand that thy father Adam shall not receive of this oil of mercy now, but after many generations of the world. For the most kind Son of God will come into the world from heaven, and will be baptised by John in the river Jordan; and then shall thy father Adam, with all who believe in him, receive of this oil[1] of mercy; and the kingdom of those that believe in Him shall abide for ever.

CHAPTER V. (XXI.)

THEN all the saints when they heard this rejoiced again with joy. One of those who stood around, Isaiah by name, crying aloud exclaimed, Father

[1] Tischendorf has *de hoc deo*, 'of this God;' an evident misprint for *de hoc oleo*.

Adam, and all who stand around, hear my words. When I was on earth, and the Holy Spirit taught me, I sang of this light in prophecy, that The people which sat in darkness hath seen a great light, and to those who dwell in the region of the shadow of death, light is sprung up. At his voice, father Adam and all of them turned and asked him, Who art thou, for what thou sayest is true? And he answered and said, My name is Isaiah.

Then appeared another near him, like a dweller in the wilderness. And they asked him and said, Who art thou, who wearest such things on thy body? And he answered confidently, I am John the Baptist, the voice and prophet of the most High. I went before the face of the same Lord, to turn desert and rough places into plain paths. With my finger I pointed out and made known the Lamb of the Lord, and the Son of God, to the men of Jerusalem. I baptised him in the river Jordan. I heard the voice of the Father sounding out of heaven above him, and declaring, This is my beloved Son in whom I am well pleased. I received from him the reply that he should go down to the underworld.

Then father Adam, hearing this, cried with a loud voice, exclaiming, Alleluia, which is interpreted, The Lord cometh, assuredly.[1]

---

[1] The writer clearly did not understand Hebrew.

CHAPTER VI. (XXII.)

THEN another who stood by, distinguished as though by some royal ensign, David by name, cried out thus, and said, When I was on earth I made a revelation, concerning the mercy of God and his visitation, to the people, prophesying joys to come, saying, Through all ages, let the mercies of the Lord be confessed, and his wonderful works to the children of men, for he hath broken the gates of brass, and burst asunder the iron bars. Then the holy patriarchs and prophets began to call to mind in turn, and every one to say something from his prophecies. Then holy Jeremiah, examining his prophecies, said to the patriarchs and prophets, When I was on earth I prophesied of the Son of God, that he appeared on earth and conversed with men.

Then all the saints, rejoicing in the light of the Lord, and in the sight of father Adam, and in the answer of all the patriarchs and prophets, cried, saying, Alleluia, blessed is he that cometh in the name of the Lord; so that at their cry Satan trembled and sought a way of escape. And he could not, for Hades and his officers held him bound in the underworld and securely guarded on all sides; and said to him, Why dost thou tremble? We by no means suffer thee to go hence. But receive this, as thou deservest, from him that thou daily wast fighting against: but whether or not, know, that bound by him thou wilt be in custody under me.

CHAPTER VII. (XXIII.)

AND a second time the voice of the Son of the Father most High came as a voice of great thunder, saying, O ye princes, lift up your gates, and be ye lifted up ye eternal doors, and the King of Glory shall come in. Then Satan and Hades cried and said, Who is that King of Glory? And the voice of the Lord answered them, The Lord strong and mighty, the Lord mighty in battle.

After this voice there came a man whose aspect was as that of a robber, bearing a cross on his shoulder, crying outside, saying, Open for me that I may come in. And Satan opening the door for him a little way, brought him inside into the abode, and closed the door again after him. And all the saints saw that he was very bright, and said to him forthwith, Thy aspect is that of a robber. Tell us, what is that thou bearest on thy back? He answered humbly, and said, In truth I was altogether a robber, and the Jews hung me on a cross along with my Lord Jesus Christ, the Son of the Father most high.

I am come as first sent, but He Himself cometh after me immediately.

Then holy David, burning with anger against Satan, cried aloud, O thou most polluted one, open thy gates that the King of Glory may come in. In like manner also all the saints of God arose against Satan and wished to take him and rend him in pieces. And again the cry was uttered within, O princes, lift up your gates, and be ye lifted up, ye eternal doors, and the King of Glory shall come in. Hades and Satan asked again at that distinct utterance, saying, Who is this King of Glory? And it was said unto them by that marvellous voice, The Lord of Hosts, He is the King of Glory.

CHAPTER VIII. (XXIV.)

AND behold Hades suddenly trembled, and the gates and locks of death were demolished, and the iron bars were broken, and they fell to the ground, and all things were laid open. And Satan remained in the midst, and stood confused and dejected, fastened with a fetter on his feet. And lo, the Lord Jesus Christ, coming in the glory of celestial light, gentle, great, and humble, and bearing a chain in his hands, bound Satan by the neck, and again tying his hands behind him, threw him on his back into Tartarus, and set his holy foot upon his throat, saying, Through all ages thou hast wrought many evils, thou hast not rested in any wise; I deliver thee this day unto everlasting fire. And having quickly called Hades, he commanded him, saying, Take this most base and wicked one, and hold him in thy custody until the day when I shall command thee. And when he had received him he sank down with him beneath the feet of the Lord, into the depth of the Abyss.[1]

CHAPTER IX. (XXV.)

THEN the Lord Jesus, the Saviour of all, who is kind and most gentle, saluted Adam graciously, and said unto him, Peace be unto thee, Adam, together with thy children through immeasurable ages of ages. Amen. Then father Adam fell down at the feet of the Lord, and arose again and kissed his hands, and wept violently, saying, Behold the hands which formed me. And he testified unto all; and said to the Lord, Thou art come, O King of Glory, delivering men and gathering them to thine eternal kingdom. Then also our mother Eve in like manner fell down at the feet of the Lord, and arose again and kissed his hands, and weeping violently said, Behold the hands which fashioned me. And she testified unto all.

[1] Rev. xx. 1-3.

Then all the saints worshipped him and cried, saying, Blessed is he that cometh in the name of the Lord; God the Lord hath given us light. Amen, through all ages. Alleluia, for evermore; praise, honour, might, and glory, because thou hast come from on high to visit us. And singing Alleluia all together, and rejoicing together in glory, they ran together under the hands of the Lord. Then the Saviour, making inquiry concerning all of them, smote Hades; and immediately he cast down some into Tartarus, and took others with him to the world above.

CHAPTER X. (XXVI.)

THEN all the saints of God besought the Lord to leave in the underworld the symbol of victory (that of the holy cross), that his most wicked ministers might not prevail to detain any under accusation whom the Lord had absolved. And so it came to pass, and the Lord set his cross in the midst of Hades, and it is the symbol of victory, and will remain so for ever.

Then we all went out thence with the Lord, and left Satan and Hades in Tartarus. And command was given to us and to many others, that we should rise with the body, to bear witness in the world unto the resurrection of our Lord Jesus Christ, and of the things which were done in the underworld.

These, dearest brethren, are the things which we have seen, and, being adjured, testify unto you, He also attesting who died for us and rose again: for as it is written, so hath it come to pass in all things.

CHAPTER XI. (XXVII.)

Now when the paper was finished and read, all who heard fell upon their faces, weeping bitterly, and violently smiting their breasts, crying and saying with one accord, Woe unto us: Wherefore hath this befallen us unhappy ones? Pilate fled, Annas and Caiaphas fled, the priests and Levites fled, and also the people of the Jews, lamenting and saying, Woe unto us unhappy ones: we have shed holy blood upon earth.

Therefore for three days and three nights they tasted neither bread nor water, neither did any of them return into the synagogue. But on the third day, when the council assembled again, the other paper (that of Leucius) was read; and it was found to be neither more nor less by a single letter than what the writing of Karinus contained. Then the assembly was troubled, and they all lamented forty days and forty nights, looking for destruction from God, and the vengeance of God. But the kind and most high merciful One did not at once destroy them, liberally vouchsafing to them space for repentance. But they were not found worthy to be converted unto the Lord.

These are the testimonies of Karinus and Leucius, dearest brethren, concerning Christ the Son of God, and his holy deeds in the underworld: to Him let us all give praise and glory through immeasurable ages of ages. Amen.

LETTER OF PILATE TO TIBERIUS.[1]

At that time in this territory there was a certain man whom his disciples called God, and who performed various miracles, whom many men have seen, and who ascended alive into heaven, and his disciples now do great things in his name, and testify that he is God, and a teacher of the way of salvation in truth.

[1] This letter is from the semi-fabulous "History of Christ," in Persian, written by Jerome Xavier, a Jesuit. It was published with a Latin version by L. de Dieu, at Leyden, in 1639. I translate from de Dieu's Latin, p. 533. Its source is unknown, but it is probably a fiction of Xavier's.

LETTERS OF HEROD AND PILATE.

IN 1854 or 1855 I published an English version of these letters in a newspaper. Of that translation I have no copy, and I have therefore made another. Dr. Wright has included them in his "Contributions to the Apocryphal Literature of the New Testament from Syriac MSS.," and I have made use of both his text and his translation. The letters occur in a Syriac MS., of the sixth or seventh century, in the British Museum. Dr. Tischendorf states in his Apocalypses Apocryphæ (Prolegg. p. 56) that he has a copy of the same in Greek from a Paris MS. of which he says "scriptura satis differt, non item argumentum." Of course the two letters are forgeries; produced perhaps about A.D. 400.

The letters are followed by a few extracts which seem to have been added by some copyist, although they are followed by the subscription to Pilate's letter. I suppose that by Justinus, we are to understand Justus of Tiberias of whom Josephus speaks as a historian of his time. I cannot venture an opinion favorable to the genuineness of this extract, because Photius says Justus did not mention Christ.

By Theodorus, I understand the emperor Tiberius. The question and answer agree in sense with what is read in the "Anaphora," or Response of Pilate. It is probably from one of the spurious documents, of which this volume contains sufficient examples.

Josephus is of course the Jewish historian.

LETTER OF HEROD TO PILATE THE GOVERNOR.

Herod to Pontius Pilate the Governor of Jerusalem: Peace.

I am in great anxiety. I write these things unto thee, that when thou hast heard them thou mayest be grieved for me. For as my daughter Herodias, who is dear to me, was playing upon a pool of water which had ice upon it, it broke under her, and all her body went down, and her head was cut off and remained on the surface of the ice. And behold, her mother is holding her head upon her knees in her lap, and my whole house is in great sorrow. For I, when I heard of the man Jesus, wished to come to thee, that I might see him alone, and hear his word, whether it was like that of the sons of men.

And it is certain that because of the many evil things which were done by me to John the Baptist, and because I mocked the Christ, behold I receive the reward of righteousness,[1] for I have shed much blood of others' children upon the earth.[2] Therefore the judgments of God are righteous; for every man receives according to his thought. But since thou wast worthy to see that God-man, therefore it becometh you to pray for me.

My son Azbonius also is in the agony of the hour of death.

And I too am in affliction and great trial, because I have the dropsy; and am in great distress, because I persecuted the introducer of baptism by water, which was John. Therefore, my brother, the judgments of God are righteous.

And my wife, again, through all her grief for her daughter, is become blind in her left eye, because we desired to blind the Eye of righteousness. There is no peace to the doers of evil, saith the Lord.[3] For already great affliction cometh upon the priests and upon the writers of the law; because they delivered unto thee the Just One. For this is the consummation of the world, that they consented that the

---

[1] 2 Peter ii. 13.
[2] Matt. ii. 16. It is scarcely necessary to say that it was not the Herod of the epistle who caused the massacre of the children at Bethlehem.
[3] Is. xlviii. 22; lvii. 21.

Gentiles should become heirs. For the children of light shall be cast out,[1] for they have not observed the things which were preached concerning the Lord, and concerning his Son. Therefore gird up thy loins,[2] and receive righteousness, thou with thy wife remembering Jesus night and day; and the kingdom shall belong to you Gentiles, for we the (chosen) people have mocked the Righteous One.

Now if there is place for our request, O Pilate, because we were at one time in power, bury my household carefully; for it is right that we should be buried by thee, rather than by the priests, whom, after a little time, as the Scriptures say, at the coming of Jesus Christ, vengeance shall overtake.

Fare thee well, with Procla thy wife.

I send thee the earrings of my daughter and my own ring, that they may be unto thee a memorial of my decease. For already do worms begin to issue from my body,[3] and lo, I am receiving temporal judgment, and I am afraid of the judgment to come. For in both we stand before the works of the living God; but this judgment, which is temporal, is for a time, while that to come is judgment for ever.

End of the Letter to Pilate the Governor.

---

[1] Luke xvi. 8. [2] 1 Peter i. 13.
[3] A palpable anachronism. Acts xii. 23.

LETTER OF PILATE TO HEROD.

Pilate to Herod the Tetrarch : Peace.

Know and see, that in the day when thou didst deliver Jesus unto me, I took pity on myself, and testified by washing my hands, (that I was innocent) concerning him who rose from the grave after three days, and had performed thy pleasure in him, for thou didst desire me to be associated with thee in his crucifixion. But I now learn from the executioners and from the soldiers who watched his sepulchre, that he rose from the dead. And I have especially confirmed what was told me, that he appeared bodily in Galilee, in the same form, and with the same voice, and with the same doctrine, and with the same disciples, not having changed[1] in anything, but preaching with boldness his resurrection, and an everlasting kingdom.

And behold, heaven and earth rejoice ; and behold, Procla my wife is believing in the visions which appeared unto her, when thou sentest that I should deliver Jesus to the people of Israel, because of the ill-will they had.

Now when Procla, my wife,[2] heard that Jesus was

---

[1] Literally 'renewed anything.'
[2] Literally 'his wife:' a manifest error.

risen, and had appeared in Galilee, she took with her Longinus the centurion and twelve soldiers, the same that had watched at the sepulchre, and went to greet the face of Christ, as if to a great spectacle, and saw Him with his disciples.

Now while they were standing, and wondering, and gazing at Him, He looked at them, and said to them, What is it? Do ye believe in me? Procla, know that in the covenant which God gave to the fathers, it is said that every body which had perished should live by means of my death, which ye have seen. And now, ye see that I live, whom ye crucified. And I suffered many things, till that I was laid in the sepulchre. But now, hear me, and believe in my Father—God who is in me. For I loosed the cords of death, and brake the gates of Sheol; and my coming shall be hereafter.

And when Procla my wife and the Romans heard these things, they came and told me, weeping; for they also were against Him, when they devised the evils which they had done unto Him. So that, I also was on the couch of my bed in affliction, and put on a garment of mourning, and took unto me fifty Romans with my wife and went into Galilee.

And when I was going in the way I testified these things; that Herod did these things by me, that he took counsel with me, and constrained me to arm my hands against Him, and to judge Him that judgeth all, and to scourge the Just One, Lord of the just. And when we drew nigh to Him, O Herod, a great voice was heard from heaven, and dreadful thunder, and the earth trembled, and gave forth a sweet smell, like unto which was never perceived even in the temple of Jerusalem. Now while I stood in the way, our Lord saw me as He stood and talked with his disciples. But I prayed in my heart, for I knew that it was He whom ye delivered unto me, that He was Lord of created things and Creator of all. But we, when we saw Him, all of us fell upon our faces before his feet. And I said with a loud voice, I have sinned, O Lord, in that I sat and judged Thee, who avengest all in truth. And lo, I know that thou art God, the Son of God, and I beheld thy humanity and not thy divinity. But Herod, with the children of Israel, constrained me to do evil unto thee. Have pity, therefore, upon me, O God of Israel!

And my wife, in great anguish, said, God of heaven and of earth, God of Israel, reward me not according to the deeds of Pontius Pilate, nor according to the will of the children of Israel, nor according to the thought of the sons of the priests; but remember my husband in thy glory!

Now our Lord drew near and raised up me and my wife, and the Romans; and I looked at Him and saw there were on Him the scars of his cross. And

He said, That which all the righteous fathers hoped to receive, and saw not,—in thy time the Lord of Time, the Son of Man, the Son of the most High, who is for ever, arose from the dead, and is glorified on high by all that he created, and established for ever and ever.

1. Justinus, one of the writers that were in the days of Augustus and Tiberius and Gaius, wrote in his third discourse: Now Mary the Galilæan, who bare the Christ that was crucified in Jerusalem, had not been with a husband. And Joseph did not abandon her; but Joseph continued in sanctity without a wife, he and his five sons by a former wife; and Mary continued without a husband.

2. Theodorus wrote to Pilate the governor: Who was the man, against whom there was a complaint before thee, that he was crucified by the men of Palestine? If the many demanded this righteously, why didst thou not consent to their righteousness? And if they demanded this unrighteously, how didst thou transgress the law and command what was far from righteousness?

Pilate sent to him:—Because he wrought signs I did not wish to crucify him: and since his accusers said, He calleth himself a king, I crucified him.

3. Josephus saith: Agrippa, the king, was clothed in a robe woven with silver, and saw the spectacles in the theatre of Cæsarea. When the people saw

that his raiment flashed, they said to him, Hitherto we feared thee as a man: henceforth thou art exalted above the nature of mortals. And he saw an angel standing over him, and he smote him as unto death.[1]

End of the Letter of Pilate to Herod.

[1] This extract from Josephus (Ant. 19, 8) is abridged from the account of Eusebius (Hist. Eccles. 2, 10). The figures 1, 2, 3, indicate the extracts which have been appended to the epistle.

THE EPISTLE OF PONTIUS PILATE.

Which he wrote to the Roman Emperor, concerning our Lord Jesus Christ.

Pontius Pilate to Tiberius Cæsar the emperor: Greeting.

Upon Jesus Christ, whom I fully made known to thee in my last, a bitter punishment hath at length been inflicted by the will of the people, although I was unwilling and apprehensive. In good truth, no age ever had or will have a man so good and strict. But the people made a wonderful effort, and all their scribes, chiefs, and elders agreed to crucify this ambassador of truth, their own prophets, like the Sibyls with us, advising the contrary; and when he was hanged supernatural signs appeared, and in the judgment of philosophers menaced the whole world with ruin. His disciples flourish, not belying their master by their behaviour and continence of life; nay, in his name they are most beneficent.[1] Had I not feared a sedition might

---

[1] *Cf.* Joseph. Ant. xviii. 3, 3.

arise among the people, who were almost furious, perhaps this man would have yet been living with us. Although, being rather compelled by fidelity to thy dignity, than led by my own inclination, I did not strive with all my might to prevent the sale and suffering of righteous blood, guiltless of every accusation, unjustly, indeed, through the maliciousness of men, and yet, as the Scriptures interpret, to their own destruction.

Farewell. The 5th of the Calends of April.

THE REPORT OF PILATE THE GOVERNOR,

Concerning our Lord Jesus Christ; which was sent to Augustus Cæsar, in Rome.

IN those days, when our Lord Jesus Christ was crucified under Pontius Pilate the governor of Palestine and Phœnicia, the things here recorded came to pass in Jerusalem, and were done by the Jews against the Lord. Pilate therefore sent the same to Cæsar in Rome, along with his private report, writing thus:—

To the most potent, august, divine, and awful Augustus Cæsar, Pilate, the administrator of the Eastern Province.

I have received information, most excellent one, in consequence of which I am seized with fear and trembling. For in this province which I administer, one of whose cities is called Jerusalem, the whole multitude of Jews delivered unto me a certain man called Jesus, and brought many accusations against him, which they were unable to establish by consistent evidence. But they charged him with one heresy in particular, namely, That Jesus said the Sabbath was not a rest, nor to be observed by them. For he performed many cures on that day, and made the blind see, and the lame walk, raised the dead, cleansed lepers, healed the paralytic who were wholly unable to move their body or brace their nerves, but could only speak and discourse, and he gave them power to walk and run, removing their infirmity by his word alone. There is another very mighty deed which is strange to the gods we have: he raised up a man who had been four days dead, summoning him by his word alone, when the dead man had begun to decay, and his body was corrupted by the worms which had been bred, and had the stench of a dog; but, seeing him lying in the tomb he commanded him to run, nor did the dead man at all delay, but as a bridegroom out of his chamber, so did he go forth from his tomb, filled with abundant perfume. Moreover, even such as were strangers, and clearly demoniacs, who had their dwelling in deserts, and devoured their own flesh, and wandered about like cattle and creeping things, he turned into inhabiters of cities, and by a word rendered them rational, and prepared them to become wise and powerful, and illustrious, taking their food with all the enemies of the unclean spirits which were destructive in them, and which he cast into the depth of the sea.

And, again, there was another who had a withered hand, and not only the hand but rather the half of the body of the man was like a stone, and he had neither the shape of a man nor the symmetry of a body: even him He healed with a word and rendered whole. And a woman also, who had an issue of blood for a long time, and whose veins and arteries were exhausted, and who did not bear a human body, being like one dead, and daily speechless, so that all the physicians of the district were unable to cure her, for there remained unto her not a hope of life; but as Jesus passed by she mysteriously received strength by his shadow falling on her, from behind she touched the hem of his garment, and immediately, in that very hour, strength filled her exhausted limbs, and as if she had never suffered anything, she began to run along towards Capernaum, her own city, so that she reached it in a six days' journey.

And I have made known these things which I have recently been informed of, and which Jesus did on the Sabbath. And he did other miracles greater than these, so that I have observed greater works of wonder done by him than by the gods whom we worship.

But Herod and Archelaus and Philip, Annas and Caiaphas, with all the people, delivered him to me, making a great tumult against me in order that I might try him. Therefore, I commanded him to be crucified, when I had first scourged him, though I found no cause in him for evil accusations or dealings.

Now when he was crucified, there was darkness over all the world, and the sun was obscured for half a day, and the stars appeared, but no lustre was seen in them; and the moon lost its brightness, as though tinged with blood; and the world of the departed was swallowed up; so that the very sanctuary of the temple, as they call it, did not appear to the Jews themselves at their fall, but they perceived a chasm in the earth, and the rolling of successive thunders. And amid this terror the dead appeared rising again, as the Jews themselves bore witness, and said that it was Abraham, and Isaac, and Jacob, and the twelve patriarchs, and Moses, and Job, who had died before, as they say, some three thousand five hundred years. And there were very many whom I myself saw appearing in the body, and they made lamentation over the Jews, because of the transgression which was committed by them, and because of the destruction of the Jews and of their law.

And the terror of the earthquake continued from the sixth hour of the preparation until the ninth hour; and when it was evening on the first day of the week, there came a sound from heaven, and the heaven became seven times more luminous than on all other days. And at the third hour of the night the sun appeared more luminous than it had ever shone, lighting up the whole hemisphere. And as lightning-flashes suddenly come forth in a storm, so there were seen men, lofty in stature, and surpassing in glory, a countless host, crying out, and their voice was heard as that of exceedingly loud thunder, Jesus that was crucified is risen again: come up from Hades ye that were enslaved in the subterraneous recesses of Hades. And the chasm in the earth was as if it had no bottom; but it was so that the very foundations of the earth appeared, with those that shouted in heaven, and walked in the body among the dead that were raised. And He that raised up all the dead and bound Hades said, Say to my disciples, He goeth before you into Galilee, there shall ye see Him.

And all that night the light ceased not shining. And many of the Jews died in the chasm of the earth, being swallowed up, so that on the morrow most of those who had been against Jesus, were not to be found. Others saw the apparition of men rising again whom none of us had ever seen. One synagogue of the Jews was alone left in Jerusalem itself, for they all disappeared in that ruin.

Therefore being astounded by that terror, and being possessed with the most dreadful trembling, I have written what I saw at that time and sent it to thine excellency; and I have inserted what was done against Jesus by the Jews, and sent it to thy divinity, my lord.

THE REPORT OF PONTIUS PILATE,

GOVERNOR OF JUDEA;

Which was sent to Tiberius Cæsar in Rome.

To the most potent, august, dreadful, and divine Augustus, Pontius Pilate, administrator of the Eastern Province.

I have undertaken to communicate to thy goodness by this my writing, though possessed with much fear and trembling, most excellent king, the present state of affairs, as the result hath shown. For as I administered this province my lord, according to the command of thy serenity, which is one of the eastern cities called Jerusalem, wherein the temple of the nation of the Jews is erected, all the multitude of the Jews, being assembled, delivered up to me a certain man called Jesus, bringing many and endless accusations against him; but they could not convict him in anything. But they had one heresy against him, that he said the sabbath was not their proper rest.

Now that man wrought many cures and good works: he caused the blind to see, he cleansed lepers, he raised the dead, he healed paralytics, who could not move at all, but had only voice, and all their bones in their places; and he gave them strength to walk and run, enjoining it by his word alone. And he did another yet more mighty work, which had been strange even among our gods, he raised from the dead one Lazarus, who had been dead four days, commanding by a word alone that the dead man should be raised, when his body was already corrupted by worms which bred in his wounds. And he commanded the fetid body, which lay in the grave, to run, and as a bridegroom from his chamber so he went forth from his grave, full of sweet perfume. And some that were grievously afflicted by demons, and had their dwellings in desert places, and devoured the flesh of their own limbs, and went up and down among creeping things and wild beasts, he caused to dwell in cities in their own houses, and by a word made them reasonable, and caused to become wise and honourable those that were vexed by unclean spirits, and the demons that were in them he sent out into a herd of swine into the sea and drowned them. Again, another who had a withered hand, and lived in suffering, and had not even the half of his body sound, he made whole by a word alone. And a woman who had an issue of blood for a long time, so that because of the discharge all the joints of her bones were seen and shone through like glass, for all the physicians had dismissed her without hope, and had not cleansed her, for there was in her no hope of health at all; but once, as Jesus was passing by she touched from behind the hem of his garments, and in that very hour the strength of her body was restored, and she was made whole, as if she had no affliction, and began to run fast towards her own city of Paneas. And these things happened thus: but the Jews reported that Jesus did these things on the sabbath. And I saw that greater marvels had been wrought by him than by the gods whom we worship. Him then Herod and Archelaus and Philip, and Annas and Caiaphas, with all the people, delivered up to me, to put him on his trial. And because many raised a tumult against me, I commanded that he should be crucified.

Now when he was crucified darkness came over all the world; the sun was altogether hidden, and the sky appeared dark while it was yet day, so that the stars were seen, though still they had their lustre obscured, wherefore, I suppose your excellency is not unaware that in all the world they lighted their lamps from the sixth hour until evening. And the moon, which was like blood, did not shine all night long, although it was at the full, and the stars and Orion made lamentation over the Jews, because of the transgression committed by them.

And on the first day of the week, about the third hour of the night, the sun appeared as it never shone before, and the whole heaven became bright. And as lightnings come in a storm, so certain men of lofty stature, in beautiful array, and of indescribable glory, appeared in the air, and a countless host of angels, crying out and saying, Glory to God in the highest, and on earth peace, good will among men: Come up from Hades, ye who are in bondage in the depths of Hades. And at their voice all the mountains and hills were moved, and the rocks were rent, and great chasms were made in the earth, so that the very places of the abyss were visible.

And amid the terror dead men were seen rising again, so that the Jews who saw it said, We beheld Abraham, and Isaac, and Jacob, and the twelve patriarchs, who died some two thousand five hundred years before, and we beheld Noah clearly in the body. And all the multitude walked about and sang hymns to God with a loud voice, saying, The Lord our God, who hath risen from the dead, hath made alive all the dead, and Hades he hath spoiled and slain.

Therefore, my lord king, all that night the light ceased not. But many of the Jews died, and were sunk and swallowed up in the chasms that night, so that not even their bodies were to be seen. Now I mean, that those of the Jews suffered who spake against Jesus. And but one synagogue remained in

Jerusalem, for all the synagogues which had been against Jesus were overwhelmed.

Through that terror, therefore, being amazed and being seized with great trembling, in that very hour, I ordered what had been done by them all to be written, and I have sent it to thy mightiness.

THE TRIAL AND CONDEMNATION OF PILATE.[1]

Now when the letters came to the city of the Romans, and were read to Cæsar with no few standing there, they were all terrified, because, through the transgression of Pilate, the darkness and the earthquake had happened to all the world. And Cæsar, being filled with anger, sent soldiers and commanded that Pilate should be brought as a prisoner.

And when he was brought to the city of the Romans, and Cæsar heard that he was come, he sat in the temple of the gods, above all the senate, and with all the army, and with all the multitude of his power, and commanded that Pilate should stand in the entrance. And Cæsar said to him, Most impious one, when thou sawest so great signs done by that man, why didst thou dare to do thus? By daring to do an evil deed thou hast ruined all the world.

---

[1] Commonly called "the Paradosis of Pilate." It may be regarded as an historical continuation of the preceding, which it usually follows in the MSS. without any title.

And Pilate said, King and Autocrat, I am not guilty of these things, but it is the multitude of the Jews who are precipitate and guilty. And Cæsar said, And who are they? Pilate saith, Herod, Archelaus, Philip, Annas and Caiaphas, and all the multitude of the Jews. Cæsar saith, For what cause didst thou execute their purpose? And Pilate said, Their nation is seditious and insubordinate, and not submissive to thy power. And Cæsar said, When they delivered him to thee thou oughtest to have made him secure and sent him to me, and not consented to them to crucify such a man, who was just and wrought such great and good miracles, as thou saidst in thy report.[1] For by such miracles Jesus was manifested to be the Christ, the King of the Jews.

And when Cæsar said this and himself named the name of Christ, all the multitude of the gods fell down together, and became like dust where Cæsar sat with the senate. And all the people that stood near Cæsar were filled with trembling because of the utterance of the word and the fall of their gods, and being seized with fear they all went away, every man to his house, wondering at what had happened. And Cæsar commanded Pilate to be safely kept, that he might know the truth about Jesus.

And on the morrow when Cæsar sat in the capitol with all the senate, he undertook to question Pilate

[1] Gr. $\tau\hat{\eta}s$ $\sigma\hat{\eta}s$ $\dot{a}\nu a\phi o\rho\hat{a}s$

again. And Cæsar said, Say the truth, most impious one, for through thy impious deed which thou didst commit against Jesus, even here the doing of thy evil works was manifested, in that the gods were brought to ruin. Say then, who is he that was crucified, for his name hath destroyed all the gods? Pilate said, And verily his records are true; for even I myself was convinced by his works that he was greater than all the gods whom we venerate. And Cæsar said, For what cause then didst thou perpetrate against him such daring and doing, not being ignorant of him, or assuredly designing some mischief to my government? And Pilate said, I did it because of the transgression and sedition of the lawless and ungodly Jews.[1]

And Cæsar was filled with anger, and held a council with all his senate and officers, and ordered a decree to be written against the Jews, thus:—

> To Licianus who holdeth the first place in the East Country: Greeting.

I have been informed of the audacity perpetrated very recently by the Jews inhabiting Jerusalem and the cities round about, and their lawless doing, how they compelled Pilate to crucify a certain god called Jesus, through which great transgression of theirs the world was darkened and drawn into ruin. Determine therefore, with a body of soldiers, to go to

[1] See Letter of Pilate to Herod, Add. 2. p. 396.

them there at once and proclaim their subjection to bondage by this decree. By obeying and proceeding against them, and scattering them abroad in all nations, enslave them, and by driving their nation from all Judea as soon as possible show, wherever this hath not yet appeared, that they are full of evil.

And when this decree came into the East Country, Licianus obeyed, through fear of the decree, and laid waste all the nation of the Jews, and caused those that were left in Judea to go into slavery with them that were scattered among the Gentiles, that it might be known by Cæsar that these things had been done by Licianus against the Jews in the east country, and to please him.

And again Cæsar resolved to have Pilate questioned, and commanded a captain, Albius by name, to cut off Pilate's head, saying, As he laid hands upon the just man, that is called Christ, he also shall fall in like manner, and find no deliverance.

And when Pilate came to the place he prayed in silence, saying, O Lord, destroy not me with the wicked Hebrews, for I should not have laid hands upon thee, but for the nation of lawless Jews, because they provoked sedition against me: but thou knowest that I did it in ignorance. Destroy me not, therefore, for this my sin, nor be mindful of the evil that is in me, O Lord, and in thy servant Procla who standeth with me in this the hour of my death, whom thou taughtest to prophesy that thou must be nailed to the cross. Do not punish her too in my sin, but forgive us, and number us in the portion of thy just ones. And behold, when Pilate had finished his prayer, there came a voice from heaven, saying, All generations and the families of the Gentiles shall call thee blessed, because under thee were fulfilled all these things that were spoken by the prophets concerning me; and thou thyself must appear as my witness at my second coming, when I shall judge the twelve tribes of Israel, and them that have not confessed my name. And the Prefect cut off the head of Pilate, and behold an angel of the Lord received it. And when his wife Procla saw the angel coming and receiving his head, she also, being filled with joy, forthwith gave up the ghost, and was buried with her husband.[1]

[1] The Synaxaria of the Greeks, under Oct. 28th, intimate the commemoration of Procla, the wife of Pilate. The Æthiopic calendar inserts 'Pilate and his wife Procla' under June 25th. The reason for putting these names among the saints is, that Pilate by washing his hands attested the innocence of Jesus, while Procla sought to dissuade her husband from complying with the Jews. The above story makes of Pilate almost a martyr; and Tertullian makes him almost a saint in Apol. c. Gentes. cap. 21.

THE DEATH OF PILATE,

WHO CONDEMNED JESUS.

Now whereas Tiberius Cæsar emperor of the Romans was suffering from a grievous sickness, and heard that there was at Jerusalem a certain physician, Jesus by name, who healed all diseases by his word alone; not knowing that the Jews and Pilate had put him to death, he thus bade one of his attendants, Volusianus by name, saying, Go as quickly as thou canst across the sea, and tell Pilate, my servant and friend, to send me this physician to restore me to my original health. And Volusianus, having heard the order of the emperor, immediately departed, and came to Pilate, as it was commanded him. And he told the same Pilate what had been committed to him by Tiberius Cæsar, saying, Tiberius Cæsar, emperor of the Romans, thy lord, having heard that in this city there is a physician who healeth diseases by his word alone, earnestly entreateth thee to send him to him to heal his disease. And Pilate was greatly terrified on hearing this, knowing that through envy he had caused him to be slain. Pilate answered the messenger, saying thus, This man was a malefactor, and a man who drew after himself all the people; so, after counsel taken of the wise men of the city, I caused him to be crucified. And as the messenger returned to his lodgings he met a certain woman named Veronica, who had been acquainted with Jesus, and he said, O woman, there was a certain physician in this city, who healed the sick by his word alone, why have the Jews slain him? And she began to weep, saying, Ah, me, my lord, it was my God and my Lord whom Pilate through envy delivered up, condemned, and commanded to be crucified. Then he, grieving greatly, said, I am exceedingly sorry that I cannot fulfil that for which my lord hath sent me.

Veronica said to him, When my Lord went about preaching, and I was very unwillingly deprived of his presence, I desired to have his picture painted for me, that while I was deprived of his presence, at least the figure of his likeness might give me consolation. And when I was taking the canvas to the painter to be painted, my Lord met me and asked whither I was going. And when I had made known to him the cause of my journey, He asked me for the canvas, and gave it back to me printed with the likeness of his venerable face. Therefore, if thy lord will devoutly look upon the sight of this, he will straightway enjoy the benefit of health.

DEATH OF PILATE.

Is a likeness of this kind to be procured with gold or silver? he asked. No, said she, but with a pious sentiment of devotion. Therefore, I will go with thee, and carry the likeness to Cæsar to look upon, and will return.

So Volusianus came with Veronica to Rome, and said to Tiberius the emperor, Jesus, whom thou hast long desired, Pilate and the Jews have surrendered to an unjust death, and through envy fastened to the wood of the cross. Therefore, a certain matron hath come with me bringing the likeness of the same Jesus, and if thou wilt devoutly gaze upon it, thou wilt presently obtain the benefit of thy health. So Cæsar caused the way to be spread with cloths of silk, and ordered the portrait to be presented to him; and as soon as he had looked upon it he regained his original health.

Then Pontius Pilate was apprehended by command of Cæsar, and brought to Rome. Cæsar, hearing that Pilate had come to Rome, was filled with exceeding wrath against him, and caused him to be brought to him. Now Pilate brought with him the seamless coat of Jesus, and wore it when before the emperor. As soon as the emperor saw him, he laid aside all his wrath, and forthwith rose to him, and was unable to speak harshly to him in anything: and he who in his absence seemed so terrible and fierce, now in his presence is found comparatively gentle.

And when he had dismissed him, he soon became terribly inflamed against him, declaring himself wretched, because he had not expressed to him the anger of his bosom. And immediately he had him recalled, swearing and protesting that he was a child of death, and unfitted to live upon earth. And when he saw him, he instantly greeted him, and laid aside all the fury of his mind.

All were astonished, and he was astonished himself, that he was so enraged against Pilate while absent, and could say nothing to him sharply while he was present. At length, by Divine suggestion, or perhaps by the persuasion of some Christian, he had him stripped of the coat, and soon resumed against him his original fury of mind. And when the emperor was wondering very much about this, they told him it had been the coat of the Lord Jesus. Then the emperor commanded him to be kept in prison till he should take counsel with the wise men what ought to be done with him. And after a few days sentence was given against Pilate, that he should be condemned to the most ignominious death. When Pilate heard this, he slew himself with his own dagger, and by such a death put an end to his life.

When Pilate's death was made known, Cæsar said,

DEATH OF PILATE.

Truly he has died a most ignominious death, whose own hand has not spared him. He was therefore fastened to a great block of stone and sunk in the river Tiber. But wicked and unclean spirits, rejoicing in his wicked and unclean body, all moved about in the water, and caused in the air dreadful lightning and tempests, thunder and hail, so that all were seized with horrible fear. On which account the Romans dragged him out of the river Tiber, bore him away in derision to Vienne, and sunk him in the river Rhone. For Vienne means as it were, Way of Gehenna, because it was then a place of cursing. And evil spirits were there and did the same things.[1]

Those men, therefore, not enduring to be so harassed by demons, removed the vessel of cursing from them and sent it to be buried in the territory of Losania. But when they were troubled exceedingly by the aforesaid vexations, they put it away from them and sunk it in a certain pool surrounded by mountains, where even yet, according to the account of some, sundry diabolical contrivances are said to issue forth.[2]

[1] Various legends connecting Pilate with the neighbourhood of Vienne are still current on the banks of the Rhone, but I do not think it needful to repeat them here. The explanation of Vienne in the text is simply ridiculous.

[2] By Losania we must understand the Swiss canton of Lucerne, at some distance to the South of which is a mountain bearing the name of Pilate, and a small lake also called after him. The people of the country have plenty of legends relating to poor Pilate, who, it seems, could rest neither alive nor dead. I fancy that the story I have here translated is a mediæval Latin concoction of elements of various dates. The Latin name of Lucerne is properly Luceria.

THE STORY OF JOSEPH.

The Story of Joseph of Arimathea, who begged the body of the Lord: in which he also introduces the Case of the two Robbers.

CHAPTER I.

I Joseph of Arimathea begged from Pilate the body of the Lord Jesus for burial, and for the same cause was bound with fetters by the murderous and God-opposing Jews, who also, by setting aside the law, became to Moses himself ministers of tribulation, and after provoking the lawgiver, and not acknowledging God, crucified Him, and made Him manifest to them that knew God.

In those days in which they condemned the Son of God to be crucified, seven days before the passion of Christ, two robbers, who had been condemned, were sent from Jericho[1] to Pilate, the governor, and their case was this:—

The first, whose name was Gestas, slew wayfarers

[1] Luke x. 30.

with the sword, some he stripped, women he hung by their heels with their head downward, and cut off their breasts, and he drank the blood from the limbs of infants; he never acknowledged God, nor obeyed the laws, but practised such deeds of violence from the beginning.

Now the case of the other was this: He was called Demas, was a Galilean by origin, and kept an inn. He practised extortion upon the rich, but did good to the poor. The thief was like Tobit, for he buried the poor when they were dead.[1] He endeavoured to plunder the multitude of the Jews, taking away the very law at Jerusalem, and stripping the daughter of Caiaphas, who was a priestess of the sanctuary, taking away the mystical deposit of Solomon, which was laid up in the place. Such were his actions.

And Jesus also was apprehended on the third day before the passover, when it was evening. And no passover was held by Caiaphas and the multitude of the Jews, but they were in great heaviness because of the spoil which the robber had caused in the sanctuary. And they called Judas Iscariot and spake to him, for he was (son) of the brother of Caiaphas, the priest. Now he was not a disciple in the presence of Jesus, but all the multitude of the Jews urged him with guile to follow Jesus; not that he might be obedient to the miracles which were done

[1] Tobit i. 17. A questionable compliment to Tobit!

by him, nor that he should confess him, but that he should deliver him to them, desiring to obtain a false report of him; and for an honourable deed like this they gave him gifts, daily a didrachma of gold. And he consorted with Jesus for two years, as one of the disciples, called John, saith.

And on the third day, before Jesus was taken, Judas saith to the Jews, Come and let us hold a council, for the robber did not steal the law, but Jesus himself, and I convict him. And while such words were being spoken, there came in to us Nicodemus, who kept the keys of the sanctuary, and he said to all, Do not perpetrate such a deed. For Nicodemus was truthful beyond all the multitude of the Jews. And the daughter of Caiaphas, Sarah by name, cried aloud and said, He said before all against this holy place, I am able to destroy this temple and to raise it up in three days. The Jews said unto her, Thou hast credit with us all. For they regarded her as a prophetess. And when the council had been held Jesus was taken.

CHAPTER II.

AND on the morrow, being the fourth day, they brought him at the ninth hour into the court of Caiaphas. And Annas and Caiaphas said to him, Tell us for what cause thou hast stolen our law, and forbidden the precepts of Moses and the prophets? And Jesus answered nothing. And again a second time, the multitude also being present, they said unto him, Wherefore dost thou wish at one stroke to destroy the sanctuary which Solomon erected in forty-six years? And Jesus answered nothing to this. For the sanctuary of the synagogue had been plundered by the robber.

And at the close of the evening of the fourth day, all the multitude sought for the daughter of Caiaphas to burn her with fire, because of the loss of the law, for they could not keep the passover. And she said to them, Wait my children, and let us destroy this Jesus, and the law will be found, and the holy feast which is ordained will be kept. And Annas and Caiaphas secretly gave much gold to Judas Iscariot, saying, Say as thou saidst to us before: I know that the law was stolen by Jesus; that the accusation may be turned against him, and not against this innocent maiden. And Judas assented to these things and said to them, Let not all the multitude know that I have been taught by you to do this against Jesus. But dismiss Jesus, and I will persuade the multitude that these things are so. And they craftily dismissed Jesus.

And Judas went into the sanctuary when the fifth day began to dawn, and said to all the people, What will ye give me, that I may deliver to you the destroyer of the law and the plunderer of the prophets? The Jews said unto him, If thou deliver him to us we will give thee thirty silverlings of gold. Now the people knew not that Judas spake concerning Jesus; for many confessed him to be the Son of God. And Judas took the thirty silverlings of gold.

And he went out at the fourth hour, and at the fifth he found Jesus walking in the street. And when evening was coming on, Judas saith to the Jews, Give me the help of soldiers with swords and staves, and I will deliver him to you. Therefore they gave him assistants to take him. And as they went Judas saith to them, Lay hold on him whom I shall kiss; for he hath stolen the law and the prophets. So he went up to Jesus and kissed him, saying, Hail, Rabbi! And it was the fifth evening, and they laid hold on him and delivered him to Caiaphas and the chief priests; and Judas said, This is he who stole the law and the prophets. And the Jews gave Jesus an unjust trial, saying, Why hast thou done this? And he answered nothing.

And Nicodemus and I, Joseph, seeing the sitting of the pestilent[1] departed from them, not wishing to perish with the council of the ungodly.

[1] Ps. i. 1.

CHAPTER III.

When, therefore, they had perpetrated many other shocking things that night against Jesus, they gave him over to Pilate the governor, when the preparation began to dawn, to have him crucified, and for this cause they all came together. So after examination had been made, Pilate the governor commanded him to be nailed to the cross with two robbers. And they were nailed up together with Jesus; Gestas on the left hand and Demas on the right.

And he that was on the left hand began to cry out, saying unto Jesus, See how much evil I have done in the earth; and if I had known that thou art the king, I should have destroyed thee also. But why callest thou thyself the Son of God, and canst not help thyself in thy necessity? or how canst thou afford help to another when he prayeth? If thou art the Christ, come down from the cross, that I may believe thee. But now I see thee perishing with me, not like a man, but like a wild beast. And he began to say many other things against Jesus, blaspheming, and gnashing his teeth at him. For the robber was caught in the snare of the devil.[1]

But the robber on the right hand, whose name

[1] 1 Tim. iii. 7.

was Demas, seeing the divine grace of Jesus, cried out thus: I know thee, Jesus Christ, that thou art the Son of God. I see that thou art Christ, worshipped by countless myriads of angels. Forgive me my sins which I have committed; at my trial cause not the stars or the moon to come against me, when thou shalt judge all the world, because by night I wrought my evil counsels; move not the sun, which is now darkened because of thee, to utter the evils of my heart: for I can offer thee no gift for the remission of my sins. Death is already overtaking me for my sins; but forgiveness is thine; deliver me, O Lord of all, from thy fearful judgment; give not power to the enemy to devour me, and to become the inheritor of my soul, as of him that hangeth at thy left hand: for I perceive how the devil joyfully receiveth his soul, and his flesh becometh invisible. Ordain not that I should depart into the portion of the Jews; for I see that Moses and the patriarchs are in great lamentation, and the devil rejoicing over them. Therefore, Lord, before my spirit departeth command that my sins may be blotted out, and remember me, a sinner, in thy kingdom when upon the great throne of the Most High, thou shalt judge the twelve tribes of Israel,[1] for thou hast prepared much chastisement for thy world through its own fault.

[1] Matt. xix. 28; Luke xxii. 30.

And when the robber had said these things, Jesus saith unto him, Verily, verily, I say unto thee, Demas, that this day thou shalt be with me in Paradise. And the children of the kingdom, the children of Abraham, and Isaac, and Jacob, and Moses, shall be cast out into outer darkness; there shall be weeping and gnashing of teeth.[1] And thou alone shalt dwell in Paradise until my second coming, when I shall judge those who have not confessed my name. And he said to the robber, Go and tell the Cherubim and the powers, who wave the flaming sword, who have guarded Paradise since Adam the first formed was in Paradise, and transgressed, and kept not my commandments, and I cast him out from thence: and none of the former shall see Paradise until I am about to come the second time to judge the living and the dead,—writing thus,—

Jesus Christ the Son of God, who descended from the heights of heaven, who came forth from the bosom of the invisible Father inseparably, and came down into the world to become incarnate and to be nailed to the cross, that I might save Adam whom I formed,—to my archangelic powers, the door-keepers of Paradise, the servants of my father: I will and command that the man who is crucified with me should enter, that he should receive remission of sins for my sake, and that arrayed in an incorruptible body he should enter

[1] Luke xxiii. 43; Matt. viii. 11, 12.

into Paradise, and should dwell there, where no one yet has been able to dwell.[1]

And behold, when these things had been said, Jesus gave up the ghost, on the day of the preparation, at the ninth hour. And darkness was upon all the earth, and there was a great earthquake, and the sanctuary fell, and the pinnacle of the temple.

CHAPTER IV.

Now I Joseph begged the body of Jesus and laid it in a new sepulchre, where no one had been placed. And the body of the robber on the right hand was not found; but of him upon the left hand, as the shape of a dragon, such was his body.

And when I had begged the body of Jesus to bury it, the Jews, being carried away with angry jealousy, confined me in prison, where force was used to them that did evil. And this was done to me when it was evening, on the sabbath, wherein our nation transgressed. And, behold, this nation of ours suffered dreadful tribulations on the sabbath.

And when it was evening, on the first day of the week, at the fifth hour of the night, Jesus cometh to me in prison, with the robber that was crucified with him on the right hand, whom he had sent into

[1] See the answer to this epistle in the next chapter.

STORY OF JOSEPH.

Paradise. And there was much light in the dwelling; and the house was suspended by the four corners, and the place was free, and I went out. I recognised Jesus first, therefore, and then the robber, who was bringing letters to Jesus. And as we journeyed into Galilee there shone a great light, such as nature never produced, and great was the fragrance of the robber, which came from Paradise.

And while Jesus was sitting in a certain place he read thus:—

The Cherubim and the six-winged ones that are commanded by thy Divinity to keep the garden of Paradise, by the hands of the robber who was crucified with Thee by thine arrangement we declare this.

Seeing the mark of the nails on the robber that was crucified with thee, and in the letters the splendour of thy divinity, the fire was extinguished indeed, being unable to endure the brightness of the symbol, and we being in great fear were filled with dismay; for we had heard that the Maker of heaven and earth and all creation had journeyed from on high into the lower parts of the earth for the sake of Adam the first-formed. For when we saw the undefiled cross flashing upon the robber, with a light sevenfold greater than that of the glittering sun, trembling came upon us who shared the agitation of those in the underworld, and with a loud voice the ministers of Hades said with us, Holy, holy, holy is He who was in the beginning in the highest! And the powers shouted aloud, Lord, thou art manifest in heaven and upon earth, sending joy to the world; and greater than such a gift, delivering thine own handywork from death by the invisible counsel of of ages.

CHAPTER V.

Having seen these things, as I went into Galilee with Jesus and the robber, Jesus was transfigured, and was not as formerly before he was crucified, but was altogether light, and angels continually ministered unto him; and Jesus talked with them. And I passed three days with him; and no one of his disciples was with him save only the robber.

And when the feast of unleavened bread arrived, his disciple John came, and we no longer saw the robber, whatever became of him.[1] And John asked Jesus, Who is he that thou hast not caused me to be seen by him? And Jesus answered him nothing. And falling before him, he said, Lord, I know that thou hast loved me from the beginning; and wherefore dost thou not reveal this man to me? Jesus saith to him, Why dost thou seek after hidden things? Art

---

[1] It would appear from the subsequent revelations of the robber and his honours, that he was gone back to Paradise.

thou still foolish? Dost thou not perceive the fragrance of Paradise which has filled the place? Dost thou not know who he was? The robber upon the cross became an heir of Paradise. Verily, verily, I say unto thee that it is for him alone until the great day shall come. And John said, Make me worthy to see him.

And while John was yet speaking the robber suddenly appeared, and John being terrified fell to the ground. And the appearance of the robber was not in the same fashion as before John came, but was like a king in great power, arrayed with the cross. And the voice of many multitudes exclaimed, Thou art come into the place of Paradise which hath been prepared for thee: We have been appointed by Him that sent thee to minister unto thee until the great day. And when this voice came, both the robber and I, Joseph, disappeared, and I was found in my house; and I saw Jesus no more.

And I, who beheld these things, have written them that all may believe in Jesus Christ our Lord, who was crucified, and may no longer minister in the law of Moses, but may believe in the signs and wonders that were done by him, and that, believing, we may inherit eternal life, and be found in the kingdom of heaven; for unto Him glory, power, praise, and majesty is due for ever and ever. Amen.

THE REVENGING OF THE SAVIOUR.

IN the days of Tiberius Cæsar the emperor, when Herod was tetrarch, Christ was delivered by the Jews under Pontius Pilate, and revealed by Tiberius.

In those days Titus was ruler under Tiberius in the region of Equitania in the city of Libia which is called Burgidalla.[2] For Titus had a wound in his right nostril because of a cancer, and his face was laid open as far as his eye. There went forth a certain man from Judæa, Nathan, the son of Nahum,

---

[1] The antiquity of this document is considerable, as it exists in an Anglo-Saxon translation. The Latin original is exceedingly barbarous in style, and probably much corrupted. The incidents, characters, and localities are introduced in utter disregard of history, geography, and reason. It would be a waste of time to point out all the absurdities of this narration.

[2] It might seem that Equitania, Libia, and Burgidalla, represent the more recent names Aquitaine, Albi, and Bourdeaux. But this opinion is opposed to the circumstance that a ship sailing to Rome was driven thither by a "north-wind." By Equitania I understand the African province of Zeugitana; for Libia I suggest Clypea; and Burgidalla I would reject as an interpolation by some scribe who thought Zeugitana meant Aquitaine. The last of these suggestions is at least favoured by the various reading which omits Burgidalla altogether. With regard to Clypea or Aspis, it was a few miles south-east of the Hermæan promontory, or Cape Bon, and some distance east of Utica and Carthage; the old town still exists under the name of Calibia or Kelibia. For an account of it, it may suffice to refer to Davis's "Carthage and her Remains," chapter xvi. I think we may expect any amount of blundering in a document which rests on a basis so unstable.

by name; for he was an Ishmaelite, who went from land to land, and from sea to sea, and in all the borders of the earth. Now Nathan was sent from Judæa to Tiberius the emperor, to carry their treaty to the city of Rome. Now Tiberius was sick, and full of ulcers and fevers, and had nine sorts of leprosy. And Nathan wished to proceed to the city of Rome. But the north wind blew and hindered his voyage and carried him to the port of the city of Libia. And Titus seeing the ship coming knew that it was from Judæa; and they all wondered and said that they had never seen any bark come this way from thence. But Titus bade the captain of the vessel come to him, and asked who he was. And he said, I am Nathan, the son of Nahum, of the race of the Ishmaelites, and I am subject to Pontius Pilate in Judæa. And I am sent to go to Tiberius the Roman emperor to carry a treaty from Judæa. And a mighty wind came down upon the sea and brought me to a land which I know not.

And Titus said, If ever thou canst find any thing, whether of drugs or of herbs, which can heal the wound which I have in my face, as thou seest, so that I may become well and receive my former health, I will bestow upon thee many benefits. And Nathan said unto him, My lord, I am not aware, nor do I know of such things as thou sayest to me. But if thou hadst been in time past in Jerusalem, thou wouldst have found there a chosen prophet whose name was Emmanuel: for he shall save his people from their sins. He made wine of water in Cana of Galilee as his first sign, and cleansed the lepers by his word, enlightened the eyes of one born blind, healed the paralytic, put demons to flight, and raised three who were dead; he delivered a woman taken in adultery and condemned by the Jews to be stoned; another woman named Veronica who had an issue of blood twelve years and came behind him and touched the hem of his garment, even her he healed; and with five loaves and two fishes he fed five thousand men, leaving out children and women, and there remained of the fragments twelve baskets; all these things and many more were done before he suffered. We saw him after his resurrection, in the flesh as he was before.

Titus said to him, How did he rise from the dead, when he was dead? And Nathan answered and said, He was manifestly dead, and hung upon the cross, and taken down again from the cross, and for three days lay in a sepulchre: then he arose from the dead and descended into Hades, and delivered the patriarchs and prophets and all the human race: then he appeared unto his disciples and ate with them: then they saw him ascending into heaven. And so all that I tell thee is the truth. I saw it with my own eyes and also all the house of Israel.

And Titus said these words,[1] Woe unto thee, emperor Tiberius, thou art full of ulcers and enveloped in leprosy, because such an offence hath been committed in thy realm; that hast made such laws[2] in Judæa, in the land of the nativity of our Lord Jesus Christ that they seized the king and slew the governor of the people, and did not cause him to come to us to cure thee of thy leprosy, and to cleanse me from my infirmity. Wherefore if they had been in my presence, with mine own hands I would have slain the bodies of those Jews, and hung them upon green wood, because they destroyed my Lord, and my eyes were not thought worthy to see his face.

And when he had said this, immediately the wound fell from the face of Titus, and his flesh and face were restored to health. And all the sick who were there were made whole in that hour. And Titus cried out with all of them with a loud voice, saying, My King and my God, because I have never seen thee and thou hast made me whole, command me to go with the ship upon the water to the land of thy nativity, that I may execute vengeance upon thy enemies: and help me, Lord, to blot them out and to avenge thy death. Do thou, Lord, deliver

---

[1] Literally "in his words."
[2] I would read *reges* for *leges*, because of the following *qui*. In fact we read of the 'reges Judæorum' a little further on. I would also read 'ut te *mundaret* a lepra et me *curaret* ab infirmitate mea,' because leprosy is said to be *cleansed*, and infirmity to be *cured*.

them into my hand. And when he had said this, he gave order for himself to be baptised. And he called Nathan to him, and said to him, How didst thou see those baptised who believe in Christ? Come to me and baptise me in the name of the Father, and of the Son, and of the Holy Spirit, Amen. For I also firmly believe in the Lord Jesus Christ with all my heart and with all my soul; for there is no other in the universe who hath created me and healed me of my wounds.

And when he had said this, he sent messengers with all speed to Vespasian, to come with the most valiant men prepared as for war

Then Vespasian took with him five thousand armed men, and they hastened to Titus. And when they had come to the city of Libia, he said to Titus, Why is it that thou hast caused me to come hither? And he answered, Thou shouldst know that Jesus came into this world, and was born in Judæa in a place which is called Bethlehem, and was delivered by the Jews, and scourged, and crucified on mount Calvary, and on the third day he arose from the dead; and his disciples saw him in the same flesh in which he was born; and he manifested himself to his disciples, and they believed on him. And we indeed wish to become his disciples. Now let us go and blot out his enemies from the earth, and now let them know that there is none like the Lord our God on the face of the earth.

Now when they had taken counsel they departed from the city of Libia, which is called Burgidalla,[1] and they went into a ship and proceeded to Jerusalem, and surrounded the kingdom of the Jews, and began to send them to destruction. When the kings of the Jews had heard of their deeds, and the ruin of the land, fear fell upon them, and they were greatly troubled. Then Archelaus was troubled in his words, and said to his son, Son, take my kingdom and judge it, and take counsel with the other kings who are in the land of Judæa, that ye may be able to escape from our enemies. And when he had said this, he drew his sword and fell upon it, and he directed his very sharp sword and thrust it into his breast and he died. Now his son joined himself with the other kings who were under him, and they took counsel among themselves, and went into Jerusalem with their chief men who were in their counsel, and abode there seven years. And Titus and Vespasian took counsel in order to surround their city. And they did so. Now when seven years were accomplished, the famine became very grievous, and for lack of bread they began to eat earth.

Then all who were the soldiers of the four kings took counsel among themselves, and said, We are going to die, what will God do with us? or what

[1] The mention of Burgidalla is also omitted here by the Cottonian Anglo-Saxon MS.

doth our life profit us, inasmuch as the Romans have come to take our place and nation? It is better that we should kill ourselves, than for the Romans to say they slew us and gained a victory over us. And they drew their swords and smote themselves, and there died of them the number of 12,000 men.

Then there arose a great stench in that city from the bodies of those dead men; and their kings feared with a great fear even unto death, and were not able to endure the stench of them, nor to bury them, nor to cast them out of the city. And they said among themselves, What shall we do? We, indeed, delivered Christ unto death, and now we are delivered unto death. Let us bow down our heads, and give up the keys of the city to the Romans, for God hath already delivered us unto death. And they straightway went up on the walls of the city, and all cried with a loud voice, saying, Titus and Vespasian, receive the keys of the city which were given to you by Messiah who is called Christ.

Then they delivered themselves into the hands of Titus and Vespasian, and said, Judge us, for we ought to die, because we judged Christ, and he was given up without cause. And Titus and Vespasian took them, and part they stoned, and part they hung upon a tree with their feet up and their heads downwards, and smote them with lances. Some they gave up to be sold, and some they divided among themselves, and they made four parts of them, as they had done with the garments of the Lord. And they said, They sold Christ for thirty pieces of silver, and let us sell thirty of them for one denarius. And they did so. And when they had done this, they took possession of all the lands of Judæa and Jerusalem.

Then they made inquiry for the likeness or portrait of Christ, how they might find it. And they found a woman named Veronica who had it. Then they took Pilate and sent him to prison to be kept by four quarternions of soldiers at the door of the prison. Then they straightway sent their messengers to Tiberius, the emperor of the city of Rome, that he would send Velosianus to them. And he said to him, Take all that is necessary for thee at sea, and go down to Judæa, and ask for one of the disciples of him that was called Christ and Lord; that he may come to me, and in the name of his God heal me of the leprosy and the infirmities with which I am daily oppressed, and of my wounds, for I lie sick. And send against the kings of the Jews who are subject to my empire thy forces and terrible torments, and condemn them to death, because they slew Jesus Christ our Lord. And if thou shalt find there any man who can deliver me from this my infirmity, I will believe in Christ the Son of God and be baptized in his name. And Velosianus said, My lord emperor, If I find any man who can help and deliver us, what reward shall I promise him? And Tiberius said unto him, The half of my kingdom without fail, that it may be in his hand.

Then Velosianus straightway went and entered a ship and hoisted sail for the voyage, and went sailing over the sea. And he sailed one year and seven days, in which time he came to Jerusalem. And he immediately commanded some of the Jews to come to his mightiness,[1] and began to inquire diligently what were the deeds of Christ. Then Joseph of the city of Arimathea, and Nicodemus both came together. And Nicodemus said, I saw him, and know truly that he is the Saviour of the world. And Joseph said to him, And I took him down from the cross and placed him in a new sepulchre which was cut out of a rock. And the Jews shut me up on the day of preparation at evening, and while I stood in prayer on the Sabbath day, the house was suspended by the four corners, and I saw the Lord Jesus Christ as a flash of light, and for fear I fell to the earth. And he said to me, Look on me, for I am Jesus whose body thou didst bury in thy tomb. And I said to him, Show me the sepulchre where I placed thee. And Jesus, taking my hand with his right hand, led me to the place where I had buried him.

[1] The Latin is *ad ejus potentiam*, 'to his potency,' *i.e.*, to himself as having power: the use of abstract for concrete in speaking of dignities is of most common occurrence

Now there came also a woman, named Veronica, and said to him, I touched the hem of his garment in the crowd, for I had an issue of blood twelve years, and straightway he healed me.

Then said Velosianus to Pilate, Pilate, thou impious and cruel one, wherefore didst thou slay the Son of God? And Pilate answered, His own nation and the chief priests, Annas and Caiaphas, delivered him unto me. Velosianus said, Thou impious and cruel one, thou art worthy of death, and of a cruel punishment. And he sent him back to prison.

And Velosianus at length inquired after the likeness or portrait of the Lord; and all who were there said unto him, It is a woman named Veronica who has the Lord's portrait in her house. And he immediately commanded her to be brought before his mightiness. And he said to her, Hast thou the Lord's portrait in thy house? But she denied it. Then Velosianus commanded her to be put to torture until she produced the Lord's portrait; and being compelled she said, I have it in a clean linen cloth, my lord, and I daily adore it.[1] Velosianus said, Show it to me. Then she showed the Lord's portrait. When Velosianus saw it, he threw himself upon the ground; and with a ready heart and a right faith he took it

---

[1] The writers of legends universally appear to ignore the moral obligation of truthfulness; but surely a man may write fiction without canonizing what are vulgarly called *lies.*

and wrapped it in a cloth of gold, and placed it in a shrine and sealed it with his ring. And he sware by an oath and said, As the Lord God liveth, and by the safety of Cæsar, man shall see it no more upon the face of the earth, until I see the face of my lord Tiberius.

And when he had said this, the chief men, who were the principal men of Judæa, took Pilate and led him to the sea-port. But [Velosianus] took the Lord's portrait with all his own disciples and followers, and the same day they entered the ship. Then the woman Veronica forsook all she possessed for the love of Christ, and followed Velosianus. And Velosianus said to her, Woman, what dost thou wish, or what dost thou seek? And she answered, I seek the portrait of our Lord Jesus Christ, who enlightened me, not for my merits, but of his holy pity.[1] . . . Restore to me the portrait of my Lord Jesus Christ, for I am dying of this good desire. But if thou dost not restore it to me, I will not leave it until I see where thou dost place it; for most unhappy I will serve him all the days of my life. For I believe that he, my Redeemer, liveth for ever.

Then Velosianus commanded the woman Veronica to be conveyed with him into the ship. And when the sails were hoisted they began to proceed on their

[1] At this point the copies are so corrupt that Tischendorf omits a few lines as unintelligible; but he gives the various readings in his notes. The omission is of trifling moment.

REVENGING OF THE SAVIOUR. 443

voyage in the name of the Lord, and sailed over the sea. But Titus with Vespasian came into Judæa, taking vengeance upon all the nations of their land. At the end of a year Velosianus arrived at the city of Rome, left his ship in the river, which is called Tiberis or Tiber, and entered the city, which is called Rome. And he sent his messenger to his lord Tiberius the emperor at the Lateran concerning his happy arrival.

Then Tiberius the emperor, having heard the messenger of Velosianus, rejoiced greatly, and commanded that he should come into his presence. And when he had come he called him, saying, Velosianus, how hast thou come, and what hast thou seen concerning Christ the Lord and his disciples in the region of Judæa? Show me, I pray thee, one that will heal me of my infirmity, that I may be forthwith cleansed from this leprosy which I have upon my body, and I will deliver all my realm into the power of thee and of him.

And Velosianus said, My lord emperor, I found thy servants Titus and Vespasian in Judæa fearing the Lord, and they are cleansed from all their ulcers and sufferings. And I found all the kings and governors of Judæa hanged by Titus; Annas and Caiaphas are stoned, and Archelaus has stabbed himself; but Pilate I left at Damascus,[1] bound and

---

[1] This hardly agrees with the statement above that Pilate was taken to a sea-port.

put in prison under safe keeping. Moreover, I have received information concerning Jesus whom the Jews most wickedly rushed upon with swords and staves and weapons, and crucified him, when he should have come to us to deliver us and to enlighten us, and they hung him on a tree. And Joseph came from Arimathea, and Nicodemus with him, bringing a mixture of myrrh and aloes, about a hundred pounds, to anoint the body of Christ; and they took him down from the cross and laid him in a new sepulchre. But on the third day he most assuredly arose from the dead, and showed himself to his disciples in the same flesh in which he was born. At length, after forty days, they saw him ascending into heaven. And many other signs Jesus wrought, before and after his passion. First, he made wine of water, he raised the dead, he cleansed lepers, he gave sight to the blind, he healed the paralytic, he put to flight demons, and made the deaf hear and the dumb speak. He raised Lazarus from the grave after four days; and he made whole the woman Veronica, who had suffered an issue of blood twelve years, and touched the hem of his garment. Then it pleased the Lord in heaven, that the Son of God, who, being sent into this world as the first-formed, died on earth, should send his angel, and he commanded Titus and Vespasian, whom I knew, in the place where thy throne is. And it pleased Almighty

God that they went into Judæa and Jerusalem, and took thy subjects, and pronounced on them the same judgement as they did when thy subjects took Jesus and bound him. And Vespasian afterwards said, What shall we do with those who will remain? Titus answered, They hung our Lord on a green tree and pierced him with a lance; and let us hang them on a dry tree, and run their bodies through with a lance. And they did so. And Vespasian said, What of those who remain? Titus answered, They took the coat of our Lord Jesus Christ and made four parts of it; now let us take them and divide them into four parts, one for thee, one for me, another for thy men, and a fourth part for my servants. And they did so.

And Vespasian said, What shall we do with those that remain? Titus answered him, The Jews sold our Lord for thirty pieces of silver, but let us sell thirty of them for one piece of silver. And they did so.

And they took Pilate and delivered him to me, and I put him in prison, in Damascus, to be kept by four quarternions of soldiers. Then they made inquiry with great diligence to seek out the Lord's portrait; and they found a woman named Veronica, who had the Lord's portrait. Then Tiberius the emperor said to Velosianus, How dost thou possess it? He answered, I have it in a pure cloth of gold, wrapped in a mantle. And Tiberius the emperor said, Bring it to me, and spread it before my face, that falling to the ground and bending my knees I may adore it on the earth. Then Velosianus spread out his mantle, with the cloth of gold wherein the portrait of the Lord was depicted; and Tiberius the emperor saw it. And immediately he adored the image of the Lord, with a pure heart, and his flesh was made clean as the flesh of a little child. And all the blind, leprous, lame, dumb, deaf, and others suffering from various infirmities who were there, were healed and cured and cleansed.

Now Tiberius the emperor, with head bowed, and bending his knees, considering that saying—Blessed is the womb which bare thee and the breasts which thou hast sucked—groaned unto the Lord, with tears, saying, God of heaven and earth, suffer me not to sin, but confirm my soul and body, and place me in thy kingdom, for I ever trust in thy name. Deliver me from all evils, as thou deliveredst the three children[1] from the furnace of burning fire.

Then said Tiberius the emperor to Velosianus, Velosianus, hast thou seen any man of those who saw Christ? Velosianus answered, I have seen such. He said, Hast thou asked how they baptise them that believed in Christ? Velosianus said, My lord, we have here one of the disciples of Christ himself.

---

[1] Daniel and his two friends. Dan. iii. 19-27.

Then he commanded Nathan to be called to come to him. Therefore, Nathan came and baptised him in the name of the Father, and of the Son, and of the Holy Spirit, Amen.

Immediately, Tiberius the emperor being made whole of all his infirmities, ascended his throne and said, Blessed art thou, Lord God Almighty, and worthy of praise, who hast delivered me from the snare of death, and purified me from all my iniquities, for I have sinned much before thee, O Lord my God, and I am not worthy to see thy face. And then Tiberius the emperor was fully and with a firm faith instructed in all the articles of belief.

May God Almighty, who is King of Kings and Lord of Lords, protect us in his faith, and defend and deliver us from all peril and evil, and deign to lead us on to life eternal, when our temporal life shall cease. He is blessed for ever and ever, Amen.

APPENDIX.

THE SYRIAC GOSPEL OF THE BOYHOOD OF OUR LORD JESUS.

It will be seen that the following document resembles very closely the first Greek text of the Gospel of Thomas, but it differs in isolated words, contains additional sentences, and omits extensive portions. Dr. William Wright edited this Syriac from a MS. of the sixth century in the British Museum. I have not exactly followed his translation, because it has been made closely literal for critical purposes. Readers who wish for a more minute rendering than the following must consult Dr. Wright's valuable work[1] of which I have made free use with his full concurrence. I believe this to be the most ancient extant form of the so-called Gospel of Thomas; I have therefore thought it would be interesting to the student who wishes to see the different forms of these documents. The quotations from St. Luke ii. 41-52, in chap. xv., are not made from either the Peshito, Curetonian, or Heraclean Syriac; although the translator may have known the first and second of these.

[1] Contributions to the Apocryphal Literature of the New Testament, collected from Syriac MSS. in the British Museum, and edited with an English translation and notes by W. Wright, LL.D., &c:—8vo. *London*, 1865.

APPENDIX.

THE BOYHOOD OF OUR LORD JESUS.

CHAPTER I.

Now the boy Jesus Christ when he was five years old was playing at the ford of streams of water, and he collected and confined the waters, and directed them in channels, and caused them to enter pools, and made them become clear and bright. And he took soft clay out of the moisture, and formed twelve birds. For it was the Sabbath, and there were many boys with him. Now a man of the Jews saw him with the boys when he made these, and told Joseph his father, and provoked him against Jesus, and said to him, On the Sabbath he hath moulded clay and made birds, which is not lawful on the Sabbath. And Joseph went and rebuked him, and said to him, Why dost thou make these on the Sabbath? Then Jesus clapped his hands and made the birds fly away before those that spake,[1] and he said, Go fly away, and remember me ye who live! and the birds went away twittering. Now when the Pharisee saw it he was greatly astonished, and went and told his friends.

CHAPTER II.

Now the son of Annas the scribe also was with Jesus. And he took a stick from a willow tree and

[1] Dr. Wright renders 'Before the things which he said;' very reasonably conjecturing that the Syriac text is corrupt.

destroyed and broke down the pool, and let out the waters which Jesus had collected, and made their pools dry. And when Jesus saw what he did, he said to him, Without root shall thy shoot be, and thy fruits shall dry up like a bough of the wood which is broken by the wind, and is no more. And the boy immediately withered away.

CHAPTER III.

AND again, Jesus was going with his father, and a certain boy who was running struck him with his shoulder. Jesus saith unto him, Thou shalt not go thy way. And immediately he fell down and died. And all that saw him cried and said, Whence was this boy born, that all his words become deeds? And the kindred of him that was dead drew nigh to Joseph, and said to him, This boy is thine; thou canst not dwell with us in this village; but teach him to bless.[1]

CHAPTER IV.

Now he came near to the boy and taught him, and said, Why dost thou these things? and wherefore speakest thou these things? and they consider and hate thee. Jesus said, If the words of my Father were not wise he would not know how to instruct children. And again he said, If they were the children of the bridechamber they would not receive

[1] *i.e*, except thou teach him to bless.

curses: these will not see torment. And straightway they became blind who accused him. But Joseph was angry and took hold of his ear and pulled it. Then Jesus answered, and said to him, It is enough for thee to command me and control me,[1] for thou hast acted without knowledge.

CHAPTER V.

Now a certain teacher whose name was Zacchæus heard him talking with his father, and said, O thou naughty boy! And he said to Joseph his father, How long wilt thou be unwilling to send this boy to learn to love children of his own age, and to honour old age? Joseph answered and said, And who is able to instruct a boy like this? Does he suppose that he is deserving of a small cross? Joseph[2] answered and said to the teacher, These words which thou hast spoken, and these names, I am a stranger to them. For I am apart from you, and I dwell within you.[3] Honour in the flesh I have not. Thou art in the law and in the law abidest; for when thou wast born I was; but thou supposest thou art my father. Thou shalt learn from me instruction which no other man knoweth, nor is able to learn, and the cross which thou didst speak of, he shall bear whose it is. For when I am greatly exalted I will lay aside what-

---

[1] Literally, find me. [2] So the Syriac, but Jesus is necessarily meant. [3] Or, among you.

ever is mingled in your nature; for thou knowest not whence thou art; for I alone know truly when ye were born, and how long time ye have to remain here.

CHAPTER VI.

Now when they heard they were astonished, and cried out and said, O sight and sound of wonder! We never heard that man spake such words as these, neither priests, nor scribes, nor Pharisees. Whence was this one born that is but a child of five years, and speaks these words? Man hath never seen such a one as He. Jesus answered and said to them, Ye marvel at what I said to you, That I know when ye were born. And again, I have something more to say to you. Now when they heard they were silent and could not speak. And Zacchæus the teacher said to Joseph, I will teach him what he ought to learn. And he took him into the school. But when He came in He was silent. But Zacchæus the scribe began to say to him from Aleph; and repeated to him all the alphabet many times; and told him to answer and say after him. But he was silent. Then the scribe was angry, and struck him with his hand upon his head. And Jesus said, A blacksmith's anvil when it is beaten receives correction, and it does not feel. But I am able to say the things which are spoken by you with knowledge and understanding. The scribe answered and said, He is something great; either he is God, or an angel, or—what to say I know not.

CHAPTER VII.

THEN the boy Jesus laughed, and said, Let those bear fruit in whom is no fruit, and let the blind see the living fruit of the Judge.[1]

CHAPTER VIII.

And again, once on the sabbath day Jesus was playing on the housetop, and one of the boys fell down and died. And when the others saw this they fled, and Jesus was left alone. And the kindred of him that was dead took hold of him, and said, Thou didst cast the boy down. And Jesus said, I did not cast him down. And they reviled him. Then he came down beside the dead, and said to him, Zeno,—for this was his name,—did I cast thee down? Now he forthwith leaped up and stood[2] and said, No, my Lord. And all of them marvelled; the kindred also of the boy praised God for these wonders.

CHAPTER IX.

Now again, once after Jesus was seven years old

---

[1] This passage partly corresponds with what may be found above pp. 135 and 161. It is also analogous to a few words extracted by Tischendorf from a Latin MS., of the fifth or sixth century: "fructuosa; vident cœci fructuosa judicii." (Tischend. Evangelia Apocr. Prolegg. p. xlvii.) In plain words the sense of the Syriac *may* be, "Let the fruitless be fruitful, and the blind see the living fruit of judgment."

[2] Cf. Acts iii. 8.

his mother sent him to draw water. And in the press of a great crowd, his pitcher struck (something) and was broken. But Jesus spread out the cloak which he wore, and gathered up and brought the water. Now his mother Mary was astonished at all she saw.

CHAPTER X.

And again, once Jesus was playing, and he sowed one bushel of wheat, and reaped a hundred quarters, and gave them to the people of the village.

CHAPTER XI.

Jesus was eight years old; and Joseph was a carpenter, and made nothing else but ploughs and yokes. And a man ordered of him a couch of six cubits. And there was not the proper measure in one piece of one side, but it was shorter than its fellow. And the boy Jesus took the measure of the wood, and pulled and stretched it, and made it equal to its fellow. And he said to Joseph his father, Do all that thou wishest.

CHAPTER XII.

Now Joseph, when he saw that he was clever, wished to teach him letters, and brought him to the house of a scribe. And the scribe said to him, Say Aleph; and Jesus said it. And the scribe went on that he should say Beth. And Jesus said to him, Tell me first what Aleph is, and then I will tell thee about Beth. And the scribe took and smote him; and forthwith he fell down and died. And Jesus went to his kindred. And Joseph called Mary his mother, and commanded her that she should not let him go out of the house, lest those should die who smote him.

CHAPTER XIII.

Now a certain scribe said to Joseph, Hand him over to me, and I will teach him. But Jesus entered the house of the scribe, and took a volume and read, not what was written, but great marvels.

CHAPTER XIV.

AND again, Joseph sent his son James to gather wood, and Jesus went with him. But while they gathered wood, a certain viper bit James in his hand. And when Jesus came near him, he did nothing else to him but stretch out his hand to him and blow upon the bite, and it was cured.

CHAPTER XV.

AND when Jesus was twelve years old they went to Jerusalem, as it was the custom with Joseph and Mary to go to their festival. And when they had observed the passover, they came back to their house. And when they set out to come back, Jesus tarried in Jerusalem. And neither Joseph nor Mary his mother knew, but supposed he was with their company. And when they came to the resting-place for that day, they sought him among their kindred, and among their acquaintance. And when they found not Jesus they came back to Jerusalem and sought for him. And after three days they found him sitting among the doctors, both hearing them and questioning them. And all who heard him were astonished, because he silenced these doctors; for he expounded unto them the parables of the prophets, and the mysteries and hard sayings which are in the law. And his mother said to him, My son, why hast thou done these things to us who have been distressed and troubled, and seeking for thee? Jesus answered and said, Why did ye seek me? Know ye not that it behoveth me to be in the house of my Father? The scribes and Pharisees answered and said to Mary, Art thou the mother of this boy? The Lord hath blessed thee; for glory and wisdom like this we have not seen in boys, nor have we heard that any man has mentioned. And he arose and went with his mother, and was subject to them. But his mother retained all these words. Now Jesus increased and advanced in wisdom and in grace with God, and with men. Amen.

HERE ENDETH THE BOYHOOD OF OUR LORD JESUS.

www.ingramcontent.com/pod-product-compliance
Lightning Source LLC
Chambersburg PA
CBHW052109010526
44111CB00036B/1598